In September 1918 Second Army was the weakest of the British Armies on the Western Front; many of its formations had been rebuilt through young conscripts and men reclassified as fit for the frontline. It was, however, commanded by General Herbert Plumer ('Plumer of Messines'), considered by some historians to be perhaps the most successful of the British generals. During the final months of the First World War, Second Army fought and won two major battles. In coalition with Belgian and French forces in the Groupe d'Armées des Flandres, Second Army became the spearhead of a successful war of liberation which drove the German occupying forces out of Flanders. Its victories assisted Allied forces to clear the Channel coast, and led to the liberation of occupied Belgium. The story is presented from the perspective of Second Army and is based largely on original research – primarily the war diaries of the Army's formations – together with selected contemporary writing, unit histories and current academic analysis of the latter part of the war. This volume describes events on the Western Front in 1918 which have received little or no attention in the available literature on the war. It tells of a war of movement… a war of liberation… a war where men fought and died for control of cottages and farms, villages and towns. The liberation offensive in Belgium began on 28 September with the final breakthrough to eliminate the iconic salient around Ypres – it ended on 11 November with the British Commander-in-Chief Douglas Haig threatening to resign his post unless Second Army was restored to his command. The background to these and other events are addressed in this comprehensive military history of the campaign. From the initial planning and preparations, strategy, tactics and subsequent fighting – all examined through exhaustive British war diary research. As a result, novel and challenging conclusions emerge.

Dennis Williams B Ed, M Ed, MA, M Phil, professional background in teaching, education management, and children's services; after leaving local government he undertook a range of consultancy, interim management and administrative roles. He has pursued his interest in military history through his research and writing, and in his second-hand book business. Dennis also works in support of his wife Sue's vintage and design business and as an independent chair for NHS Continuing Healthcare services. Having resided in Yorkshire for many years, Dennis and Sue – and the family whippet – now live in East Sussex. In 2003 Dennis was awarded the MA in Military History at the University of Leeds. He undertook subsequent research through the University of Birmingham, receiving an M Phil award in 2016 for his work on British Second Army in Flanders. Dennis also contributed a chapter for a recent book on the British Army in the Hundred Days,[1] has written a 19th century Europe wargames rulebook,[2] and is a book reviewer for the Western Front Association. *Pouring With Rain Troops Fed Up* is his first book.

1 D. Williams, 'War of Liberation: British Second Army and Coalition Warfare in Flanders in the Hundred Days', in G. D. Sheffield and P. Gray, ed., *Changing War: The British Army, the Hundred Days Campaign and the Birth of the Royal Air Force, 1918* (London: Bloomsbury Academic, Birmingham War Studies, 2013).

2 D. Williams, *There Are Your Guns: Warfare in the Age of Steam 1816-1897* (Leigh-on-Sea: Partizan Press, 2007).

"POURING WITH RAIN – TROOPS FED UP"

British Second Army and the liberation offensive in Flanders 1918

Dennis Williams

Helion & Company Limited

Helion & Company Limited
26 Willow Road
Solihull
West Midlands
B91 1UE
England
Tel. 0121 705 3393
Fax 0121 711 4075
Email: info@helion.co.uk
Website: www.helion.co.uk
Twitter: @helionbooks
Visit our blog http://blog.helion.co.uk/

Published by Helion & Company 2018
Designed and typeset by Mach 3 Solutions Ltd (www.mach3solutions.co.uk)
Cover designed by Paul Hewitt, Battlefield Design (www.battlefield-design.co.uk)
Printed by Short Run Press Limited, Exeter, Devon

ISBN 978-1-911096-55-9

British Library Cataloguing-in-Publication Data.
A catalogue record for this book is available from the British Library.

Jerry's bid for Paris failed, as we fought rearguard action
Were cut off for three days, no food, but got great satisfaction
For he advanced too far, was caught in trap and enfiladed
Whilst we survivors found fresh troops behind, dug in and barricaded.
They were all ready and prepared to take the offensive
As we passed through and out we saw our guns so comprehensive.
Firing, roaring, spitting shells just like a hurricane
And then we knew, we had the men, the guns we'd sought in vain...

We were soon on the move again, this time we were excited
For we were chasing him over hill and dale, the Aisne and into Belgium ...

Corporal Henry Barratt Reynolds
Nr. 11/234
Age 78
1971

Ode to the 11th Battalion, East Yorkshire Regiment 1914-1918
92 Brigade, 31st Division, XV Corps, British Second Army
(Culled from the 11/East Yorkshire Regiment War Diary)

Contents

List of Maps

Acknowledgements

I owe a debt of appreciation to the staff of the museums and archive sources I have visited, and to the other contacts I have made during my research, for their help, consideration and patience. It is my hope they know who they are given the passage of time since I commenced this project. I also acknowledge my association with members of the former Centre for First World War Studies at the University of Birmingham, notably the research group supervised by Dr John Bourne.

I am also grateful to the staff and students of the University of Leeds MA in Military History course (2001-03) where this all began; to Professor Peter Simkins for his inspiration, and for making the initial suggestion of Second Army in 1918 as a topic deserving of new research; and to Patricia Skeet who translated a number of French language primary documents. Helion Books – Duncan and Michael et al – have been a source of encouragement and support throughout the process of making this book a reality. On seeing the excellent maps drawn by Gerry Anderson, I believed for the first time that the story of Second Army would reach the printed page.

Finally, this book would not have been possible without the ongoing support of my family, who helped to create the necessary time and space when I could see none.

Terminology & Abbreviations

I have sought to apply the following conventions regarding terms, acronyms and abbreviations used in the text and accompanying notes; I may slip from this convention on occasion, for example when making a first reference in a chapter (despite having made a previous reference earlier in the study); or to give a better flow to the text.

a) For numbering the different units of the British Army I have in general applied the convention of alternating at each level between ordinal and integer numbers, with roman numerals for corps, full spelling for armies, i.e. 1st Battalion, 2 Brigade, 3rd Division, IV Corps, and Fifth Army.

b) For the names of battalions I normally use the full name for the first reference in the study, including any particular title or nickname:

   For example, 7th Battalion, Seaforth Highlanders; 12th (Norfolk Yeomanry) Battalion, The Norfolk Regiment; 12th (Miners) Battalion, The King's Own Yorkshire Light Infantry.

   For subsequent references, I have used the Battalion's number and description, incorporating any popular abbreviation:

   For example, 7/Seaforth Highlanders; 12/Norfolks; 12/KOYLI.

c) Within notes and references, I have retained all the titles and terms from the original source; together with the original spellings and abbreviations (where appropriate, I have provided descriptions or explanations).

d) Where a term or title has a commonly used abbreviation or acronym then, for the first reference, the full wording is used with the abbreviation given in brackets; the abbreviation may then be used for future references, with an allowance made for the flow of the text, for example, Commander, Royal Engineers (CRE).

e) For dates and times I have used integer dates and the 24 hour clock, for example 18 July 1918 at 2215 hours.

f) The spelling of place names is that used by the source, whether memoir, diary, Official History, or secondary text; where a difference occurs I have usually opted for the spelling used in the Official History and noted the discrepancy. In some cases, alternative spellings may be used by different sources, for example River Scheldt, River Schelde.

It should be noted that many locations in Flanders have alternative French and Dutch names, which can cause some confusion; for example River L'Escaut, River Scheldt. I have generally opted for the name used within the particular source or reference.

Common Abbreviations – used in the text and in references

AA	Anti-Aircraft
AADC	Anti-Aircraft Defence Commander
AA and QMG	Assistant Adjutant and Quartermaster General
AASC	Anti-Aircraft Searchlight Company
AASS	Anti-Aircraft Searchlight Section
ACC	Army Cyclist Corps
ACME	Assistant Chief Mechanical Engineer
ADC	Aide de Camp
ADGT	Assistant Director-General of Transportation
ADL	Assistant Director of Labour
ADMS	Assistant Director Medical Services
ADOS	Assistant Director Ordnance Services
ADS	Advanced Dressing Station
AD Signals	Assistant Director Signals
ADTn	Assistant Director Transportation
ADVS	Assistant Director Veterinary Services
AEF	American Expeditionary Force
AMO	Assistant Medical Officer
APM	Assistant Provost Marshal
Arty	Artillery
ASC	Army Service Corps
AVC	Army Veterinary Corps
Bde	Brigade
BEF	British Expeditionary Force
BGGS	Brigadier General General Staff
BGRA	Brigadier General Royal Artillery
Battn	Battalion
Bn	Battalion
Cdr	Commander
CE	Chief Engineer
CGS	Chief of the General Staff
CHA	Commander Heavy Artillery
CIGS	Chief of the Imperial General Staff
CinC	Commander in Chief
CMG	Commander of the Order of St Michael and St George
CO	Commanding Officer
Coy	Company

CRA	Commander, Royal Artillery
CRE	Commander, Royal Engineers
DA and QMG	Deputy Adjutant and Quartermaster General
DAPM	Deputy Assistant Provost Marshal
DDMS	Deputy Director Medical Services
DDOS	Deputy Director Ordnance Services
DDR	Deputy Director Remounts
DDS	Deputy Director Signals
DDST	Deputy Director Supply and Transport
DDVS	Deputy Director Veterinary Services
DHQ (Div Hd Qrs)	Divisional Headquarters
Div	Division
DLI	Durham Light Infantry
DMS	Director of Medical Services
DR	Director of Remounts
DR	Dispatch Rider
DSO	Distinguished Service Order
EA	Enemy aircraft
ELR	East Lancashire Regiment
EYR	East Yorkshire Regiment
FA	Field Artillery
FOO	Forward Observation Officer (Artillery)
GAF	*Groupe d'Armées des Flandres* (Army Group, Flanders)
GB	Garrison Battalion
GGB	Garrison Guard Battalion
GHQ	General Headquarters
GOC	General Officer Commanding
GQG	Grand Quartier Général (French High Command)
GSO	General Staff Officer (three grades)
GSO1	General Staff Officer (Lieutenant Colonel)
GSO2	General Staff Officer (Major)
GSO3	General Staff Officer (Captain)
HA	Heavy artillery
HE	High explosive (shell)
HQ	Headquarters
Hrs	Highlanders
IB	Infantry Brigade
Inf Bde	Infantry Brigade
KOSB	King's Own Scottish Borderers
KOYLI	King's Own Yorkshire Light Infantry
KRRC	King's Royal Rifle Corps
LG	Lewis gun
Lieut	Lieutenant
Lt	Lieutenant
Lt-Col	Lieutenant Colonel

LTM	Light Trench Mortar
LTMB	Light Trench Mortar Battery
MG	Machine gun
MGC	Machine Gun Corps
MGGS	Major General General Staff
MGRA	Major-General Royal Artillery
MT	Mechanical Transport
NCO	Non-Commissioned Officer
OC	Officer Commanding (followed by a unit or section)
OHL	Oberste Heeresleitung (German High Command)
OR	Other ranks (i.e. NCOs and private soldiers)
PA	Personal ammunition
PM	Provost Marshal
QF	Quick firing
QM	Quartermaster
RA	Royal Artillery
RAF	Royal Air Force
RAMC	Royal Army Medical Corps
RAP	Regimental Aid Post
RE	Royal Engineers
RFA	Royal Field Artillery
RGA	Royal Garrison Artillery
RHA	Royal Horse Artillery
RWS	Royal West Sussex (Queen's) Regiment
SAA	Small Arms Ammunition (i.e. for infantry weapons)
SMLE	Short Magazine Lee Enfield (the rifle of the British infantryman)
SMO	Senior Medical Officer
TM	Trench mortar
TMB	Trench Mortar Battery
Y&L	York and Lancaster Regiment

Introduction

> Somewhere within the pages of many of the personal photograph albums kept by German officers would be found an aerial photograph of Ypres... These photographs give us a sense of the feeling that must have weighed on any German commander who had been posted to that front for any length of time: so tantalisingly near and yet so frustratingly far.[1]

War of Liberation is not a description usually associated with the First World War. Yet in the autumn of 1918 British and Empire troops, together with their French and American allies, finally broke free of the four year stranglehold held by the trench lines on the Western Front. A series of victorious battles during the final 'Hundred Days' (as the campaign has become known) of the war released northern France from four years of enemy occupation. At the same time to the north in Belgium, a coalition of British, French and Belgian forces fought together to liberate the Belgian people from four years of life under the occupying power of Imperial Germany.

Writing in his diary on the final day of the war, Brigadier-General J. L. Jack, commander of 28 Brigade (9th (Scottish) Division) during the Liberation Offensive in Flanders, recalled with satisfaction '...the stupendous victories of the last few months: our enemies all beaten to their knees'.[2]

There is little public knowledge in Britain of this campaign; its story is buried even deeper than the forgotten history of the British Expeditionary Force (BEF) and its successful series of victories during the final months of the war.[3] The scale of this remarkable achievement by the British Army has been aptly summed up in the following terms:

> The campaign of the 'Hundred Days', 8 August to 11 November 1918, was, in terms of sheer scale, the greatest in British military history. It was also, arguably, the campaign in

1 B. Stichelbaut and P. Chielens, *The Great War Seen From the Air: In Flanders Fields 1914-1918* (Brussels: Mercatorfonds, 2013), p. 12.

2 J. Terraine, ed., *General Jack's Diary: War on the Western Front 1914-1918 – The Trench Diary of Brigadier-General J. L. Jack, D.S.O.* (London: Cassell & Co., 2000; first published, London, Eyre & Spottiswoode, 1964), p. 297.

3 This amnesia can be addressed via G. Sheffield, *Forgotten Victory – The First World War: Myths and Realities*, (London: Headline Book Publishing, 2001); or for an earlier overview, J. Terraine, *To Win A War: 1918, The Year of Victory* (London: Cassell, 2008; first published, London: Sidgwick & Jackson, 1978).

which ground forces under British command exercised the most influence on the history of the world in the twentieth century.[4]

In 1964 the renowned historian John Terraine, edited the diaries of the commander of 28 Brigade during the 1918 Flanders' offensive. Terraine referred to the public amnesia regarding the British Army's successes during the Hundred Days and their vital contribution to ending the war. He pointed out that these 'stupendous victories' of the British armies 'which did so much to hasten the Armistice, form, oddly enough, a little-known chapter of British military history.[5]

Within this 'little-known chapter' there lies buried the lost story of the achievements of the British Second Army. During the final months of the war this formation fought as part of a combined army group also containing forces from Belgium and France. The army was commanded by General Herbert Plumer, arguably one of Britain's finest military leaders during the war.

With the exception of the *Official History of the War*,[6] there has been no detailed record of British Second Army's operations during this period. Division and battalion histories, as their titles make clear, have recorded the activities of the particular named formation rather than presenting the overall picture. Many military historians and others writing subsequently on the war and in particular on its final year, describe the victories of 1918 and the achievements of the BEF and its commanders. Yet they make little or no reference to Second Army and the battles in Flanders during the final months. By way of illustration I suggest the reader may wish to check out the index at the backs of these books – where you will find no listing of *Courtrai* and the references to *Ypres* and *Plumer* are usually confined to the defensive battles fought by the British armies in the spring of 1918.[7]

The country of Belgium and its fate had been central to the initial decision of the British Government in 1914 to enter the war. The German invasion of neutral Belgium had been the catalyst, not least in terms of the public mood, for Britain's declaration of war – and the early reports of German atrocities had boosted support for Britain's army and the commitment of the nation to the defeat of Germany.

Irrespective of the range of views on the rights and wrongs of the First World War, its causes and conduct, what we find in Belgium in the final months of the war is a small British Army

4 J. P. Harris with N. Barr, *Amiens to the Armistice: The BEF in the Hundred Days Campaign, 8 August-11 November 1918* (London: Brassey's, 1998).

5 Terraine, ed., *General Jack's Diary*, p. 297.

6 For the purposes of this book the key volumes are, J. Edmonds, *Military Operations France and Belgium 1918 Vol. IV, 8th August-26 September (Official History)* (London: HMSO, 1947); J. Edmonds with R. Maxwell-Hyslop, *Military Operations France and Belgium 1918 Vol. V 26 September-11th November (Official History)*, (HMSO, 1947).

7 Examples include P. Hart, *1918*, (London: Weidenfeld & Nicolson, 2008); M. Brown, *1918 Year of Victory*, (London: Sidgwick & Jackson, 1998); M. M. Evans, *1918, The Year of Victories*, (London: Arcturus, 2002), W. Groom, *A Storm in Flanders: The Ypres Salient 1914-1918: Tragedy and Triumph on the Western Front*, (London: Cassell, 2003); J. H. Johnson, *1918: The Unexpected Victory*, (London: Cassell & Co, 1997); J. Toland, *No Man's Land: The Story of 1918*, (London: Eyre Methuen, 1980); N. Lloyd, *Hundred Days: The End of the Great War* (London: Viking, 2013). The one notable exception is Harris with Barr, *Amiens to the Armistice*, though the detail concentrates primarily upon the other theatres of the Western Front.

fighting alongside the country’s own soldiers, to free it from four years’ occupation by a foreign power. Belgium had not been party to the build up to war; it had sought to be neutral and been attacked despite this.[8] As a consequence the fighting in Flanders in the autumn of 1918 took the form of a war of liberation. The key part played by British Second Army in returning Belgium back to its king and people should in retrospect be seen as an important conclusion – the endgame, even – to Britain’s role in the war.

With the 100 years’ anniversary of the First World War, there are as might be expected an increasing number of history reprints and new titles. Many cover similar ground while others stand out in terms of their quality and subject matter. Missing from the range of research and writing undertaken on the final three months of the First World War is a description of – and in some cases even recognition of – British Second Army fighting two major battles plus a host of supporting operations, and advancing 53 miles across Belgium before the Armistice on 11 November 1918.[9]

> … The [British Second] Army swept forward with a magnificent dash and elation that carried the very spirit of victory over the arena of the long conflict – over the mortal resting-place of those who died that this day might come.[10]

A series of victories in battle by a British Army, commanded by one of the most respected and successful British generals of the war,[11] has become forgotten over time. Britain’s contribution to an important and unique coalition force on the Western Front – and its crucial role in the liberation of Belgium – has been consistently overlooked.

This oversight can be considered as surprising given the regular references since the war to the Ypres Salient in Flanders. ‘Ypres’ – or ‘Wipers’ in the parlance of the British soldier – is a name with a wider resonance within the public knowledge of the First World War; a consequence of the sacrifice made by British troops in its defence. Much of this attention focuses upon the battles of *Third Ypres*[12] (more commonly summarised as ‘Passchendaele’) and to a lesser extent the battles of *First Ypres 1914* and *Second Ypres 1915*.[13] Map 14 shows the area of concentration of the fighting around Ypres and the Salient during the course of the war; it was over these well-trodden battlefields that Second Army would finally defeat its German enemy during the Battle of Ypres 1918.

8 For a recent summary see M. MacMillan, *The War That Ended Peace: How Europe Abandoned Peace for the First World War* (London: Profile Books Ltd., 2013), pp. 584-592.
9 J. Edmonds with R. Maxwell-Hyslop, *Official History Vol. V.*
10 B. Brice, *The Battle Book of Ypres: A Reference to Military Operations in the Ypres Salient 1914-18* (Stevenage: Spa Books in association with Tom Donovan Military Books, 1987; first published 1927), p. 49; a book that celebrates the achievements in battle of British troops fighting in the Ypres Salient.
11 See the chapter on Plumer’s record in J. Terraine, *The Western Front 1914-1918* (Hutchinson, 1964) (Pen &Sword, 2003); also P. Simkins, ‘Herbert Plumer’, in Beckett, I. F. W. and Corvi, S. J. ed., *Haig’s Generals* (Barnsley: Pen & Sword Military, 2006).
12 There were nine phases of what would be better described as the Third Ypres campaign: Pilkem Ridge, Capture of Westhoek, Battle of Langemarck, Battle of Menin Road, Battle of Polygon Wood, Battle of Broodseinde, Battle of Poelcappelle, First Battle of Passchendaele, Second Battle of Passchendaele.
13 There were four battles making up Second Ypres 1915: Gravenstafel Ridge (22-23 April), St. Julien (24 April-4 May), Frezenberg Ridge (8-13 May), Bellewaarde Ridge (24-25 May).

The *Battles of the Lys* in April 1918, the resistance to the Germans' *Georgette* offensive, are sometimes confusingly termed the *Fourth Battle of Ypres*. The official *Battle of Fourth Ypres* in September-October 1918 – the opening attack of the liberation offensive in Flanders – is confusingly also referred to as the *Fifth Battle of Ypres*. This final battle, in which Second Army successfully broke through the German lines and cleared the salient, has received minimal attention. The subsequent campaign to liberate occupied Belgium (a phrase more commonly associated with the advances made by British forces and their allies during the closing stages of the Second World War) has equally been largely overlooked.

One likely reason for this amnesia is that for most of the campaign, Second Army operated under foreign command and independently of the other British forces. In addition its initial purpose was officially restricted to the role of flank guard for the Belgian Army and its French support. Such circumstances have not brought Plumer's army into prominence within the assessments of the final period of the war; it has become a 'forgotten army' from a campaign which has itself received limited coverage within modern histories of the war.

Most surprising of all is that the commander of the forgotten army was General Herbert Plumer, considered to be one of the most successful British generals during the war.[14] However he left no private papers – these were destroyed at his instruction before he died – which will have been a further reason why there has been less attention paid to his role during the final year of the war. There is much more material available regarding other British Army and Corps commanders who were prominent during this period.

Plumer's emphasis on the planned, set-piece attack has been described as the fore-runner to the methods that Montgomery applied in the Second World War – most famously, when winning victory at El Alamein in 1942.[15] David Reynolds has pointed out the difference between modern memories of these two wars:

> Alamein featured concentrated firepower, in a battle plan that had distinct echoes of Haig's victories of 1918. The irony is that Haig's sixty-division army was the biggest that the British Army ever put into the field, yet its achievements were largely forgotten by the 1940s and remain so today...[16]

Reynolds proceeds to explain why, in his opinion, the public remember The Battle of El Alamein and Bernard Montgomery, and know nothing of the final battles of the First World War; he links this to the different perceptions of the two wars:

> Alamein was an unequivocal victory occurring at the midpoint of the conflict, whereas Haig's 'Hundred Days' of surging advance came near the end of the Great War and were obscured by the breathtaking internal collapse of the Kaiser's Germany.[17]

14 Simkins, 'Herbert Plumer'.
15 J. Latimer, *Alamein* (London: John Murray, 2002), p. 96; N. Hamilton, *Monty: The Making of a General 1887-1942* (London: Coronet, 1984), pp. 117-18. This comparison is referred to again in chapter one.
16 D. Reynolds, *The Long Shadow: The Great War and the Twentieth Century* (London: Simon & Schuster, 2013), p. 270.
17 Reynolds, *The Long Shadow*, p. 271.

In recent years there has grown an increasing adherence to the *Minute's Silence* at 11.00 am on 11th November. (The eleventh hour on the eleventh day of the eleventh month). All but forgotten, this symbol of remembrance linked to the commencement of the 1918 Armistice has now become a nationally recognised act. Schools, workplaces, offices, supermarkets, public institutions and events, cease their business to reflect upon war and those who have lost their lives as a consequence of it. Not all who respect the silence will know that the chosen timing is from the conclusion to the First World War (many probably think it relates to the 1939 –1945 war). The timing was also, as well as remembering the soldiers and others who gave their lives, originally designed to celebrate the victory of Britain and the British Army in that war.

Despite the failures of the peace that followed, it *was* important for the Allies to win the war.[18] This book does not have the space to address the wider debate on this issue. Suffice it to say that fundamentally, the final catalyst for Great Britain to enter the war was in defence of a principle: the right of the neutral country of Belgium to its independence and to be free of invasion by another. The wider context was to fight for a Europe free from the hegemony of one country. After four bruising years of conflict, there was still a final price to pay for these achievements however: 'As far as the British were concerned, they not only suffered more casualties in 1918 than in any other year of the war, but also, remarkably, than in the whole of the second war'.[19] The year 1918 is therefore worthy of remembrance both for success and sacrifice.

Over time the British people have developed selective perception and memory relating to the First World War. The why and how the First World War ('a no man's land in the historical landscape'[20]) has come to be remembered primarily in Britain for its savage loss of life – while in pursuit of a futile cause – has been an increasing source for comment . Dan Todman has described how a variety of myths and half-truths have come to represent what Britons today can recall of the Great War.[21] Todman, in common with many other writers who have reviewed Britain's ongoing relationship with the First World War,[22] identifies the 1960s as a crucial period in shaping current perceptions. He writes '...It has become a matter of orthodoxy that the 1960s were the key moment for the formation of the modern myth of the war...'. Whilst acknowledging that the war has been the subject of controversy and debate in Britain 'from the day it broke out', he concludes that 'By the 1970s, however, many [different and earlier] views had died out or been hushed, as a set of myths which depicted the First World War in purely negative terms achieved universal dominance'.[23] Although referring specifically to the Battle of the Somme, William Philpott has set out a strident case for the positive recall of the First World War: 'It is wrong and morally reprehensible to dismiss this human phenomenon on the grandest scale as a futile engagement in a futile conflict, as so many do'.[24]

18 These arguments are addressed in, for example, Sheffield, *Forgotten Victory*.
19 M. Brown, *1918: Year of Victory* (London: Sidgwick & Jackson, 1998).
20 B. Bond, ed., *The First World War and British Military History* (Oxford University Press, 1991), p. 1.
21 D. Todman *The Great War: Myth and Memory* (London: Hambledon, 2005).
22 For other examples see Sheffield, *Forgotten Victory*; the Introduction to Bond, ed., *The First World War*; the Introduction to G. Braybon, ed., *Evidence, History and the Great War: Historians and the Impact of 1914-18* (Oxford: Berghan Books, 2003).
23 Todman, *The Great War*, pp. 221-222.
24 W. J. Philpott, *Bloody Victory: The Sacrifice on the Somme* (London: Little, Brown, 2009), p. 6.

In his 2013 book, *The Long Shadow: The Great War and the Twentieth Century*,[25] David Reynolds draws comparisons between our respective memories of the First and Second World Wars; and how our memory of the former has been shaped by the impact of the later conflict. Pointing out how Britain, as one of the victors of the Second World War, is viewed as having triumphed over the accepted 'evil' of Germany and Japan, he writes:

> Victory was therefore sanctified by morality – further sharpening the contrast with the equivocal ending and moral ambiguity of the Great War… The British were unique in treating the First World War as an almost totally negative experience by which to accentuate the positives of the Second.[26]

This contrast has led to the heavy loss of life in the First World War becoming its overwhelming legacy – viewed through the prism of the Second World War which is remembered primarily as a 'good fight' to defeat unambiguous evil.[27] Hence the military achievements of 1914-1918, and the successful prosecution of the war by the British Army in the second half of 1918, have been eclipsed in our memories of the conflict.

Reynolds also shows how,

> …from the 1960s the British rediscovered the Great War with a vengeance. More exactly they reconstructed it, in forms that accorded with contemporary social attitudes and with perceptions of how 1914-18 and 1939-45 fitted into the trajectory of modern British History.[28]

The invasion of Belgium by Germany in 1914 was in breach of the former's declared neutrality which was in turn guaranteed by treaty. This action created a groundswell of public concern which led the British Government to declare war on Germany, and to commit the British Army to a European land war. While acknowledging the underlying considerations relating to the prevention of a German hegemony in Europe, the attack on Belgium created legitimate and moral arguments in support of Britain's entry into the war. The victories of the British Second Army in 1918 were a direct contribution towards achieving a clear war aim and also satisfying public demand – for a Belgium free of German invaders. Victory also supported wider strategic issues including Britain's economy and ability to trade.[29] Britain had not chosen the battleground of the Western Front and yet it continued to stand by its French and Belgian allies who

25 Reynolds, *The Long Shadow*.
26 Reynolds, *The Long Shadow*, p. 305 and p. 428.
27 Reynolds draws this point from a paper by Hannah Arendt: 'Nightmare and Flight', *Essays in Understanding, 1930-1954*, ed. Jerome Kohn (New York, 1994), p. 134.
28 Reynolds, *The Long Shadow*, p. 351.
29 For examples of the different views on the importance of the breach of Belgium's neutrality by Germany to the decision of the British Government to declare war on Germany, see N. Ferguson, *The Pity of War* (London: Allen Lane, 1998), who sees underlying reasons based upon flawed political and economic considerations (Some Conclusions, pp. 443-4); or Sheffield, *Forgotten Victory*, who views the invasion of Belgium as the clinching argument for Britain's entry to the war (chapter 2, pp. 40-42).

had no other option but to fight to remove the German occupiers from their lands.[30] For this, if for no other reason, there was a moral case in support of Britain's role in the war.[31]

In September 1918 British Second Army held a sixteen mile front line in Flanders. This ran from west of Armentières, at a junction with the River Lys, reaching northwards to above the town of Ypres (the salient); there it linked with the right of the Belgian Army front. Within weeks Second Army was to become part of a coalition army group under the overall command of Albert, King of the Belgians. Together with the Belgian forces and two French Army Corps, it would make up the *Groupe d'Armées des Flandres* (Army Group, Flanders) (GAF).

What proved to be the final Battle of Ypres opened on 28 September 1918, with the ten divisions of British Second Army assaulting between five and six divisions of the German Fourth Army; in cooperation with the simultaneous attack to the north by the Belgian Army.[32] This was a combined arms assault – the previous night had seen squadrons of the Royal Air Force's II Brigade undertake reconnaissance missions and bombing raids on enemy supply dumps and communications; over the next week the RAF would drop almost 7,000 bombs on German sectors.[33] The British troops attacked following a surprise artillery barrage targeted on enemy batteries and specified targets, utilising smoke and gas shells to neutralise defenders. A field artillery creeping barrage in front of the attacking infantry was complemented by a rolling barrage from heavy artillery to disrupt communications and any attempts by the Germans to move reserves forward. The successful advance that day of between four and six miles was also supported by the swift manoeuvring forward of artillery to exploit early gains, regular ground attacks by the RAF, and flexible troop deployment including advance squads, encircling attacks, and immediate fire support by Lewis light machine gun teams.

Second Army can therefore present its own case in support of the improved integration of arms and tactics achieved by the BEF in 1918, the 'learning curve' regularly referred to by military historians.[34] There are, however, a number of particular questions and issues which arise from the history of Second Army during the Final Advance in Flanders.[35]

To begin with there is the career position of the army's commanding officer, General Sir Herbert Plumer, and his relationship with the leader of the BEF, Field-Marshal Sir Douglas Haig. At the start of 1918 Haig negotiated for Plumer's return from Italy as part of a trade-off for the former's failure to obtain requested reinforcements and replacements for the British armies; linking the move to Haig's agreement to transfer Second Army's then commander General

30 For example, see the preface of Brown, *Book of the Western Front*, p. xvi.

31 This point is made in Reynolds, *The Long Shadow*, pp. 421-2.

32 This summary of the Battle of Ypres 1918 is drawn primarily from J. Edmonds, *Official History, Vol .V*; supplemented by other secondary works, primarily J. P. Harris with N. Barr, *Amiens to the Armistice.*

33 Figures taken from TNA WO158/218, *Operations on the Second Army Front.*

34 For example see R. Prior and T. Wilson, *Command on the Western Front: The Military Career of Sir Henry Rawlinson 1914-18 (*Oxford: Blackwell, 1992); P. Griffith, *Battle Tactics of the Western Front: The British Army's art of attack 1916-18 (*London: Yale University Press, 1994); and the two books at the start of the 1980s which are seen to have launched this revisionary approach to the assessment of the British Army's performance during the war, S. Bidwell and D. Graham, *Firepower: British Army Weapons and Theories of War 1904-1945* (London: Allen & Unwin, 1982); J. Terraine, *White Heat: The NewWarfare 1914-18* (London: Sidgwick & Jackson, 1982).

35 The term 'Final Advance in Flanders' is that adopted for the campaign by J. Edmonds for the *Official History.*

Rawlinson to be his representative at Versailles. His original release of Plumer to Italy in the autumn of 1917 receives limited coverage in Haig's diaries. Given his willingness at other times to record his views upon similar manoeuvrings regarding senior officers, this appears to be a surprising omission. It can be equally perplexing to try and understand his subsequent actions in firstly bargaining to bring Plumer back to the Western Front; and then within six months transferring him again to operate under foreign command. Having seen Plumer and Second Army fight a vital and successful defence in Flanders against the German Army's Georgette Offensive in spring 1918, Haig was then prepared to release this force and its commander to undertake what was, on paper, a subordinate role within a coalition army group. Second Army became part of a tripartite force under Albert, King of the Belgians, with a French Chief of Staff controlling the main lines of command. Haig's diaries say very little about this arrangement. There is subsequently a further paradox whereby, having apparently acquiesced to releasing Second Army to the GAF and it being of little note as far as his diary is concerned, Haig is at very great pains to have the Army returned to his command as a matter of the greatest urgency – this coming after the initial success of the campaign in Flanders.[36]

This book describes the rationale behind the decision to create the GAF, and considers the reasons for the attachment of Plumer and Second Army. There can be no question of Plumer lacking status, as he would subsequently assume overall command of British forces in Germany for the period following the Armistice; this appointment coming on the recommendation of Haig. Later the book looks in detail at the serious falling out between Haig and the allied *Generalissimo* Ferdinand Foch over the return of Second Army to Haig's command at the end of October 1918.

With regard to Plumer there is also the question of his performance as an army commander during the second half of 1918. Such consideration takes place within the context of the common denigration of British army command during the First World War, which has been a dominating feature of modern commentary and public perception. As one historian has summarised it: '…the historiography of the of the Western Front during the middle years of the twentieth century was dominated in Britain by debates over the standard of senior command…'.[37]

Together with Plumer's initial experience of army command at Second Ypres in 1915 and the high point of his victory at the battle of Messines in 1917, there are the second stage successes during Third Ypres 1917, his experience in Italy, and his resistance to the German offensives in spring 1918. Each of these has been referred to by military historians and others as evidence of his abilities. This book assesses the record of Second Army and the GAF to determine whether his leadership in the final months of the war enhances Plumer's standing as one of, or perhaps the most, consistent and successful British commanders in the First World War.

Second Army operated for most of the final months of the war as part of a coalition force. Within any coalition there are the internal politics to be considered and the implications of these for military operations. Plumer had experience in Italy of working within such an environment,

36 See the relevant sections of G. D. Sheffield and J. Bourne, ed., *Douglas Haig: War Diaries and Letters 1914-1918* (London: Wiedenfeld & Nicolson, 2005).

37 D. Todman, 'The Grand Lamasery Revisited', from G. Sheffield and D. Todman, ed., *Command and Control on the Western Front: The British Army's Experience 1914-18* (London: Spellmount Ltd, 2004), p. 40; the introduction to this book is also a useful summary of prevailing attitudes and misconceptions.

and he was to have every opportunity to show his ability to operate in a highly charged political situation with his subsequent appointment in charge of British forces after the Armistice, and his later posting in Palestine. Although many British historians have commented upon the allied relationships at a strategic level throughout the war,[38] particularly those between Haig, the politicians at home in Britain, and the French military commanders, there is very little reference to the relationship with the Belgian leadership. This also applies to the links at a campaign level, corps command and below.

There has also been very little reference in the war's historiography to Anglo-Belgian relationships after 1914, particularly military liaison. Information about or references to the Belgian Army, particularly English language studies, rarely go beyond the valiant resistance to the German invasion during the first few months of the war – and often the focus is on the actions of the German troops and their alleged atrocities, rather than the performance of the Belgian Army. In looking at the operation of the GAF in 1918 it is necessary to understand the views of the Belgian leadership, and to take account of the development of the country's army after 1914.

The joint offensive with Belgian and French forces placed particular requirements upon Second Army commanders and troops. This book considers these demands and their implications, looking at how Second Army responded and with what success. Did the tripartite coalition that was the GAF produce a sum greater than its parts, or was Second Army constrained in its actions in order to support or assist its partners? The lessons from this experience of coalition warfare, the successes and failures, perhaps could and should have been taken note of a generation later, when an allied force once again fought for the future of Europe.

A feature of the more recent historiography regarding the Western Front has been the attempts to provide an objective and reasoned analysis of how the British Army performed and why.[39] These assessments do not all reach the same conclusion: witness the generally positive views of writers such as Paddy Griffith and Gary Sheffield, in comparison to the more critical Tim Travers (who stresses the deterioration in the strength and condition of the German Army during 1918) and Robin Prior and Trevor Wilson (who tend to view the subsequent British army successes as being due more to accident than design).[40] Studies on the organisation and tactics of British forces during the final months of 1918 have tended to concentrate on Fourth Army, the Battle of Amiens (with the deployment of 400 tanks) and the headline-catching (and undoubtedly magnificent) achievement in breaching the Hindenburg line; more recently Jonathan Boff

38 Most notably, W. J. Philpott, *Anglo-French Relations and Strategy on the Western Front 1914-18* (London: Macmillan, 1996); see also, E. Greenhalgh, *Victory through Coalition: Britain and France during the First World War* (Cambridge: Cambridge University Press, 2005). Of particular interest is W. J. Philpott, 'Britain, France and the Belgian Army', in Bond, B.et al, *'Look to your Front' Studies in the First World War by The British Commission for Military History* (Staplehurst: Spellmount, 1999).

39 Some prime examples include: S. Bidwell and D. Graham, *Firepower: British Army Weapons* and *Theories of War 1904-1945* (London: Allen & Unwin, 1982, 1985); P. Griffith, *Battle Tactics of the Western Front: The British Army's Art of Attack 1916-18* (New Haven, Connecticut: Yale University Press, 1994); Griffith, P. ed., *British Fighting Methods in the Great War* (London: Frank Cass, 1996); Sheffield, *Forgotten Victory*; T. Travers, *The Killing Ground: The British Army, the Western Front and the Emergence of Modern Warfare 1900-1918* (Barnsley: Pen & Sword, 2003; first published, London: Allen & Unwin, 1987).

40 For a recent summary of these arguments see J. Boff, *Winning and Losing on the Western Front: The British Third Army and the Defeat of Germany in 1918* (Cambridge: Cambridge University Press, 2012), pp. 10-15.

has produced a detailed analysis of Third Army in the Hundred Days.[41] The achievements of the Australian and Canadian forces have also frequently been highlighted, with these formations often viewed as 'elite'.

Historians have emphasised to varying degrees the combined arms nature of the British Army's offensive, and the development of a 'modern' style of warfare.[42] The circumstances in which Second Army operated had certain obvious differences – for example, it had no tanks of its own, and faced particular challenges by way of terrain and climate. However, the Army was subject to the same direction and guidance on tactics and operations as other British armies. Given that 'For surely the [British] Army learned from its experience…',[43] then there should be evidence that this applied equally to Second Army; whether the battlefield successes of Second Army formations arose from similar modus operandi to the other British armies.

The quality and composition of the units it commanded is another potentially distinguishing feature of Second Army in the Hundred Days. Of the British armies fighting in those final months of the war, Plumer's force included the largest number of units which had suffered severely during the German offensives earlier in the year, before being re-formed and re-built; in at least one case within a few weeks of the opening of the Battle of Ypres at the end of September 1918.[44] In common with other British formations its frontline fighting strength came under increasing pressure as the campaign continued and the casualty list grew; placing increased demands on the capability of those who remained and on the replacements that could be made available.

This final campaign in Flanders was a war of liberation first and foremost – particularly for its Belgian contingent. Second Army and its coalition partners advanced over fifty miles in those three months, reclaiming land that had been under an occupying power for four years. This is a vital part of Belgian history; it was certainly an event of the greatest significance for the civilians released after years of German rule. The topic is one which has been neglected within First World War writing by British historians and requires more investigation. It cannot be a primary focus for this book on Second Army but provides an essential context within which to set and evaluate the Army's achievements.

Telling the forgotten history of Second Army in Flanders in 1918 provides an opportunity to revisit some of the myths regarding the First World War. The unique elements of coalition warfare and the liberation of western Belgium also provide an opportunity for a different perspective on some of the preconceived ideas in Britain on the war and its aims, its conduct and the outcomes.

In their book on the British Army's approach to war during the first half of the 20th century,[45] Shelford Bidwell and Dominick Graham discuss the role of the historian relative to the perspec-

41 Boff, *Winning and Losing on the Western Front.*
42 For an example refer to J. B. A. Bailey, 'The First World War and the Birth of Modern Warfare', in M. Knox and W. Murray, ed., *The Dynamics of Military Revolution, 1300-2050* (Cambridge: Cambridge University Press, 2001).
43 Bidwell and Graham, *Fire-Power*, p. 65.
44 The unit was 28 Brigade, 9th (Scottish) Division (referred to in, for example, J. Terraine, ed., *General Jack's Diary: War on the Western Front 1914-1918 – The Trench Diary of Brigadier-General J. L. Jack, D.S.O.* (London, Cassell & Co., 2000 edition); Jack only assumed command of 28 Brigade on 8 September 1918, with its new battalions and other constituent units still in transit.
45 Bidwell and Graham, *Fire-Power*, pp. 64-5.

tive of those who lived (and died) during the fighting. They point out the very limited view of the direct participants: 'Once a battle started, no one knew much more than was within his sight and hearing; nor would they until an historian reconstructed the scene'. There are also 'discontinuities' between a series of battles over time: 'Improvements in methods between one battle and the next went almost unnoticed because so many survived or fought in but one episode of a long ordeal… [soldiers] could not write historically about the changes in the way battles were fought'. This book responds to that statement by taking the long view of what was happening during the fighting by Second Army in the final period of the war. I have pointed out previously that the *Official History* represents the only previous serious and detailed account of this episode. However, as Bidwell and Graham point out: '… as that memorial is dull and seldom visited it has not preserved the memory of how the victory was won, what it took to win it or why the sacrifice was necessary'.[46] *Pouring With Rain* will hopefully start to provide some answers to those questions.

This view by Bidwell and Graham is extended in the desire to 'continue to campaign vigorously to the wider public a sense of the 'real war' in all its complexity'.[47] This cry was issued by Brian Bond at the time of the eightieth anniversary of the war, in his introduction to a series of papers by writers with a 'common conviction that the time is at last coming when the First World War can be treated as history (like earlier wars) rather than be approached emotionally and polemically in terms of 'futility', 'horror' and 'national trauma'.[48] The roots of modern warfare in terms of strategy, tactics and weaponry are there in the final battles of 1918.

This book recounts the lost story of British Second Army during the final Hundred Days campaign of the First World War; it provides a chronological military history of the army and its troops from September to November 1918. As such the relevant volumes of the *Official History* were an essential read.[49] As also was the 1998 book by J P Harris with N Barr, *Amiens to the Armistice*,[50] the one notable exception of a modern work that includes specific coverage of Second Army and the Liberation Offensive in Flanders.

My next step was to review the writings on 1918 and in particular to find any and all references regarding Second Army. This subsequently confirmed, if there had ever been any doubt, that there were very limited references to the operations of British Second Army and the GAF within descriptions and assessments of the final period of the War. There were acknowledgements of advances being made in Flanders, and often the opening of the Battle of Ypres on 28 September 1918 was referred to, mainly because of its place in the sequence of timed offensives by allied forces across the Western Front at that time. It became clear that my task would involve the researching and putting together of a military history of Second Army's campaign, drawing upon the evidence from those that were there.

46 Bidwell and Graham, *Fire-Power*, p. 65.
47 From the Foreword to B. Bond et al, *Look to Your Front: Studies in the First World War by The British Commission for Military History* (London: Spellmount, 1999), p. vii.
48 Bond, *Look to Your Front*, p. vii.
49 As referred to earlier, these are, J. Edmonds, *Military Operations France and Belgium 1918 Vol. IV, 8th August-26 September (Official History)* (London: HMSO, 1947); J. Edmonds with R. Maxwell-Hyslop, *Military Operations France and Belgium 1918 Vol. V 26 September – 11th November (Official History)* (HMSO, 1947).
50 Harris with Barr, *Amiens to the Armistice.*

Thus the initial material was revised, developed and expanded through contemporary documents and original writings. The key sources for this book have been the official papers, reports and war diaries of those formations and units which took part.

Unit war diaries are contemporary documents written during or very soon after the events described therein, by someone directly involved in or close to the operations. They are produced at each level of army command from the battalion through to army HQ. These diaries therefore provide the most current, and in general the most accurate record of what actually took place.

There are however, some important reservations regarding their use of which one must be aware, as the following description of battalion war diaries makes clear:

> A War Diary is an official daily record of operations, intelligence reports and other events, kept for each battalion by an appointed junior officer. They are not personal diaries... the information and quality of each war diary varies, often quite substantially. Some diaries will record little more than daily losses and map references whilst others will be much more descriptive... Units of infantry battalion / artillery brigade size were obliged to keep such a record once they were on active service overseas. Often they are the most detailed surviving record of the movement and activities of a unit.[51]

It is also important to acknowledge the circumstances in which the diary may have been completed:

> Writing such documents in the trenches would have been a difficult enough job in its own right but amid the clutter and confusion of battle it must have been doubly so.[52]

For this period of the history of Second Army, many diary entries will have been written while the writer was on the move as part of the general advance; or a few days later at the conclusion of an operation. The amount of detail can also vary considerably between diaries, leading to the evidence from certain units being made greater use of. In some cases the diary has been hand written – the importance to the researcher for the officer concerned to be able to write legibly should not be underestimated. Throughout my aim has been to ensure that there is a balanced and well-informed picture presented of the operations undertaken by the Army through drawing from information and commentary at all command levels and across all constituent parts.

I have read and analysed the war diaries produced at battalion, brigade, division and corps levels, as well as Second Army HQ records. All the diaries also contain, irrespective of the varying levels of detail or quality of writing, additional papers and documents. These normally include the reports of particular actions, maps and diagrams, correspondence, reports on unit circumstances and activities, and copies of orders and administrative memoranda both issued and received. Thus the diary and its associated papers allows for an informed and rounded record and assessment of the unit's history and operations to be put together.

51 M. Mace and J. Grehan, '1 July 1916 – The Somme War Diaries: Unvarnished Accounts of the British Army's Worst Day', *Stand To! The Journal of the Western Front Association*, 98 (September 2013), p. 23.

52 Mace and Grehan, 'Somme War Diaries', p. 23.

I have also made use of certain first-hand accounts by individual participants where these add texture to the description of an event or help to emphasise a piece of information or commentary. Such memoirs have usually been written some years after the events described, although they may be based upon contemporary diaries and other papers. I have been very selective in the use of such records as my focus has been to present a narrative and analysis of the military campaign; and to do this as objectively and impartially as possible. Eye-witness testimony can provide a snap-shot of an incident or event at the very sharp end but does not allow for context or give an overview of what was happening generally. There are an accelerating number of books that are based on one individual's memoirs of the First World War or, increasingly, collect together extracts from a range of personal written or audio accounts. David Reynolds has pointed out the pitfalls of such records:

> This is, however, a problematic approach to the writing of history. Although the recollections of ordinary participants can often provide fascinating and important historical detail that is not recorded in official archives, scholars cannot treat such 'testimony' as intrinsically more reliable than any other source.[53]

For this book I have therefore interpreted and analysed these primary and first-hand eyewitness sources through researching selected and relevant secondary writing and commentary. Examples of these include:

- Histories of formations including units which formed part of Second Army at the time; two particular classic accounts are the book on the 36th (Ulster) Division by Cyril Falls, and David Bilton's history of the Hull Pals (92 Brigade, 31st Division).[54]
- Books which include references to Second Army during 1918 and particularly the Hundred Days; the two titles which have provided the most useful pointers on the strategic import of the GAF victories were written thirty years apart: John Terraine's summary account of 1918, written at the end of the 1970s in his drive to have the military history of the First World War looked at afresh; and the recent comprehensive history and analysis of that year by David Stevenson.[55]
- Commentaries and assessments regarding the British Army in 1918, its composition, doctrine and tactics, logistics and supply, weaponry and resources; in particular Bidwell and Graham's book on the development of artillery and its place in the all-arms battle;[56] Paddy Griffith's analyses of the British Army's fighting tactics.[57]
- Revisionist writings on the British Army's performance during the war and in 1918 in particular; the principal starting point being Gary Sheffield's *Forgotten Victory*, plus Gordon

53 Reynolds, *The Long Shadow: The Great War and the Twentieth Century*, pp. 367-370.
54 C. Falls, *A History of the 36th (Ulster) Division* (London: Constable, 1996; first published, Belfast: McCraw, Stevenson, 1922); D. Bilton, *Hull Pals: 10th, 11th, 12th & 13th (Service) Battalions of the East Yorkshire Regiment: A History of 92 Infantry Brigade, 31st Division* (Barnsley: Pen & Sword, 1999).
55 Terraine, *To Win A War*; Stevenson, *Backs To The Wall.*
56 Bidwell and Graham, *Firepower.*
57 Griffith, *Battle Tactics*; Griffith, ed., *British Fighting Methods.*

Corrigan's *Mud, Blood and Poppycock*, an excellent re-examination of the various myths and misperceptions regarding the War.

The most useful and relevant of these works are referred to within the text and listed in the accompanying bibliography.

My research also led me into areas where there is very limited writing and analysis on which to draw. Books which concentrate on the allied coalition are few in number and these focus primarily on the links between Britain and France, and with the USA; there are few references to Belgium other than at the beginning of the war and the German occupation in 1914. One exception is the book on the relationship between Britain and France by Elizabeth Greenhalgh,[58] which provides a valuable description of Haig's dispute with Foch regarding the return of Second Army to the former's command.

Of the conscript army of 1918, there has only been one general study so far. Written in 1999, Ilana Bet-El's excellent 'ground-breaking' description of the conscript experience describes the reality of army life for the new troops.[59] Fourteen years later, Tim Lynch published his study of a Yorkshire draft, which also provides a brief social and military history of the conscript generation, and their combat experience. Lynch's analysis makes the challenging claim that 'More attention has been paid to pets in the trenches' than to the conscripted soldiers.[60]

English language writing on the performance of the French Army in the First World War is generally available, often as part of accounts of particular battles where the British Army was also involved; or within writing on certain periods of the war, often complementary to the British experience. The one exception is the iconic Battle of Verdun. There is very little information on the French forces supporting the GAF. There is no comprehensive account in English regarding the Belgian Army in the First World War; most writing has dealt mainly with 1914 and little thereafter. Given the emphasis within this book on uncovering the lost story of British Second Army then I have opted to rely primarily on the information from its own sources in order to describe the deployment and operation of allied and German formations. Their actions and the consequences of these are therefore presented as seen and experienced by Second Army commanders and troops.

This book is based upon the contemporary records of the British troops and units which fought in Flanders during the autumn of 1918. In tribute to their bravery and sacrifice this is

58 E. Greenhalgh, *Victory through Coalition: Britain and France during the First World War* (Cambridge: Cambridge University Press, 2005); also valuable is her later book on Foch: E. Greenhalgh, *Foch in Command: The Forging of a First World War General* (Cambridge: Cambridge University Press, 2011); and W. J. Philpott, *Anglo-French Relations and Strategy on the Western Front 1914-18* (London: Palgrave Macmillan, 1996).

59 I. R. Bet-El, *Conscripts: Forgotten Men of the Great War* (Stroud, Gloucestershire: The History Press, 2009; first published under the title *Conscripts: Lost Legions of the Great War* by Stroud, Gloucestershire: Sutton Publishing, 1999); the term 'ground-breaking', while taken from the paperback edition's sleeve notes, is a warranted description.

60 T. Lynch, *They Did Not Grow Old: Teenage Conscripts on the Western Front, 1918* (Stroud, Gloucestershire: Spellmount (The History Press), 2013), p. 230. This book is a wonderful read, combining social and military history, and providing a concise history of the British Army's development during the war years. Lynch's ability to combine readability with academic rigour, to provide first hand experiences within a meaningful context – not always the case with such forms of history writing on the First World War – is to be admired .

their story told from their perspective via the official war diaries completed at the time. In so doing there is the opportunity to analyse and comment on the performance of the Army, its troops and commanders; the strategy and tactics adopted; and the wider implications of the Army's victories. The aim is to place on record an assessment of the achievements of Second Army, within the coalition force *Groupe d'Armées des Flandres* and in the liberation of Flanders, and its role in the defeat of the German Army on the Western Front.

This book is intended to make some small contribution to the history of the First World War; and in particular to bring the forgotten story of the achievements of British Second Army in the liberation of Flanders in 1918 to wider attention.

Dennis Williams

Prologue

In April 1918 General Sir Herbert Plumer faced what was possibly the hardest decision in his military career: to withdraw his British Second Army troops from the Passchendaele Ridge in Flanders.

On 9 April 1918 the second stage (operation 'Georgette') of the German Army offensives on the Western Front had commenced with an assault on the lines of British First Army immediately south of Plumer's forces. The initial breakthrough achieved by the attack threatened Second Army's right flank, thereby drawing it into the battle. First the Messines Ridge and then Kemmel Hill were lost as the German forces advanced to try and finally take out the bitterly held salient around the city of Ypres. Second Army was being inexorably driven back from ground it had won with the loss of the lives of so many British soldiers during the attrition of the 1917 Battle of Third Ypres – known more commonly today through the single word *Passchendaele*.

General Sir Herbert Charles Onslow Plumer had led Second Army in the prelude to that campaign at the Battle of Messines on 7 June 1917. This '*piece de resistance* of methodical generalship'[1] captured the ridge and high ground that dominated the skyline overlooking Ypres. Post-war writers have subsequently referred to this 'most complete Allied victory since [the] siege-warfare [of the Western Front] had begun' as a 'siege-warfare masterpiece' and 'a masterpiece of modern tactics'.[2]

Plumer was however overlooked by Sir Douglas Haig, commander of British forces on the Western Front, for the first phase of the subsequent Third Battle of Ypres. General Gough, considered a more 'thrusting' commander by Haig, was handed the responsibility for operations on the northern sector of the Second Army front.[3] The subsequent lack of progress achieved by Gough, culminating on 22 August 1917 in a series of failed attacks, forced Haig to reassess the offensive. He turned back towards Plumer, who proceeded to carry out a programme of planned set-piece attacks, each adhering to the concept of 'bite and hold': to achieve a short advance and consolidate the taken ground securely. The subsequent battles of Menin Road (20-25 September), Polygon Wood (26 September-3 October), and Broodseinde (4 October), brought

1 N. Steel and P. Hart, *Passchendaele: The Sacrificial Ground* (London: Cassell Military Paperbacks, 2007; first published 2000), pp. 55-6.
2 In order these quotes are from G. Powell, *Plumer: the Soldiers' General: a Biography of Field-Marshal Viscount Plumer of Messines* (South Yorkshire: Pen Sword Military Classics, 2004), p. 191; B. H. Liddell Hart, *A History of the World War 1914-1918* (London: Faber, 1930), p. 417; Field-Marshal Sir William Robertson, *From Private to Field-Marshal* (London: Constable, 1921), p. 311.
3 Steel and Hart, *Passchendaele*, p. 37.

a 'relentless advance' although any previous strategic ambitions which Haig had fostered had now become much more focused. Tactically, and to improve the security of the British positions for the forthcoming winter, it was essential that Second Army capture the Passchendaele Ridge from which the Germans overlooked their enemy's lines.[4]

Accordingly, and despite the worsening weather conditions of heavy constant rain and increasing cold, further attacks were launched. The desperate fighting at Poelcappelle (9 October), the First Battle of Passchendaele (12 October) and the Second Battle of Passchendaele (26 October – 10 November) ultimately saw Canadian troops capture the 'blasted remnants' of Passchendaele village and the crest of the ridge on 6 November, four days later extending their hold on the position.[5]

The series of battles that autumn, the brutal conflict that has become known through the term 'Passchendaele', saw over a quarter of a million British and Empire soldiers become casualties. While around 80% of these would return to active service or in support roles – and the daily casualty rate could be compared favourably with the figures for the Normandy campaign in 1944 for example – the toll in misery and suffering for the troops involved was immense. The campaign remains mired in controversy in spite of Plumer's success at Messines and his subsequent series of limited victories in September and October. It is argued that the British efforts were nonetheless crucial in saving the French Army from itself: an army attempting to recover from the failures of its spring 1917 offensives and the subsequent series of mutinies by French troops. Throughout it all Plumer is considered to have remained loyal to Haig, demonstrated through his driven commitment to following Haig's orders to capture Passchendaele.[6] Charles Harington, Plumer's Chief of Staff during the campaign, subsequently wrote that the fighting had 'always been a nightmare' for himself and his commander: 'No words can ever express what those gallant troops had gone through to get it [Passchendaele]'.[7]

By April 1918 Plumer had already weakened his Second Army through offering to release most of its rested divisions – in order to move these south to strengthen the resistance against the enemy's initial 'Michael' offensive. In return he received forces which had already suffered considerably in the face of the earlier German attacks and breakthrough against British Fifth Army – '...shattered formations, mere skeletons of divisions that had lost seventy to eighty per cent of their infantry'.[8] Where it had been possible to start bringing units back up to strength the majority of the new drafts were composed of conscripted nineteen year olds together with men 'combed out' from former placements behind the front line or soldiers previously wounded and returning to duty.

As the Germans continued to threaten to cut the Second Army's communications and supply lines it became increasingly clear that a further withdrawal was necessary – thus the awful prospect of confronting the decision to concede the hard-won ground at Passchendaele – 'for which so many lives had been given'.[9]

Plumer's chief of staff, Charles Harington, subsequently wrote of the event:

4 See the relevant chapter in Steel and Hart, *Passchendaele*, pp. 210-56; the term 'relentless advance' is used on p. 255.
5 Steel and Hart, *Passchendaele*, pp. 257-301; the term 'blasted remnants' is used on p. 298.
6 G. Powell, *Plumer*, pp. 227-30.
7 Sir Charles Harington, *Plumer of Messines* (London: John Murray, 1935), p. 133.
8 G. Powell, *Plumer*, p. 259.
9 Harington, *Plumer of Messines*, p. 161

> One day, however, after consulting with the Corps Commander holding Passchendaele (Hunter-Weston), I decided to suggest to the Chief that we should have to withdraw from Passchendaele. I know how it stung him. 'I won't have it,' and he walked out of my room. A few moments afterwards he came back and laid his hand on my shoulder, saying, 'You are right, issue the orders.'[10]

We can only guess at the extent of the despair that Plumer must have felt. Even at the last minute he attempted to have second thoughts as the orders were prepared – but the die was cast. Plumer demonstrated in these most difficult of circumstances that he was a commander who accepted the 'tactical realities' of war.[11] Harington reflected on the scene that he would 'never forget':

> There was the man, who by sheer determination and pluck had held the Ypres Salient for years against all comers and who had gained Messines and Passchendaele, being forced to withdraw. How he hated giving it up. He knew it had to be. He knew that it was necessary for the safety of his men.[12]

As one recent writer has summarised: 'In the course of 48 hours almost all the gains made in 1917 were lost, including Messines and even Passchendaele'.[13] What General Sir Herbert Plumer could not know at that time – and probably could never have anticipated – was that less than six months later he would lead Second Army as part of an allied coalition preparing for a final attempt to break out from Ypres and the salient; and to successfully drive the German forces from Passchendaele Ridge.

10 Harington, *Plumer of Messines*, p. 161
11 As summed up by P. Simkins, 'Herbert Plumer' in I. F. W. Beckett & S. J. Corvi, ed., *Haig's Generals* (Barnsley: Pen & Sword, 2006), p. 143.
12 Harington, *Plumer of Messines*, p. 161.
13 A. Palmer, *The Salient: Ypres, 1914-18* (London: Constable, 2016), p. 187.

1

Fall In – British Second Army: July-September 1918

> [Captain Baron] liked a well-planned unalterable routine … He petulantly disapproved of the open warfare which had suddenly come after years of trench routine: unexpected things kept happening and decisions had to be made at once without any guiding precedent – which was most incorrect.[1]

Flanders

Flanders is the ancient name for the area of land along the North Sea coast in Belgium adjoining the French coast along the English Channel. The name means literally 'flooded land', reflecting the elaborate drainage system which channels most of its heavy rainfall into the river Yser. The area is largely flat and therefore the series of relatively low ridges (no more than 160 feet high) east of the main town of Ypres, provide a commanding view of the entire plain; hence the strategic value of these ridges and the small villages and key pieces of ground in and around them. Many of the names subsequently achieved notoriety as the record of key battles and actions. Control of each was bitterly contested at various points during the war: the villages of Messines and Wytschaete, Ploegsteert and Hollebeck; features such as Polygon Wood, Hill 60, and Passchendaele Ridge.[2]

Ian Beckett has described Flanders area as:

> … a level plain broken only by a line of undulations rising to slight, almost imperceptible, hills which ran first west to east from Cassel to Mount Kemmel then, as gentle ridges, east to north-east through Wytschaete, Gheluvelt and Passchendaele, finally curving north to Dixmude. Technically the plain was mostly heavy marine clay known as Ypres clay, the hills of Ypresian and Paniselian sand sediments overlying the clay. The hill line stood at about 400 feet at Kemmel, but not much more than 100 or 150 feet at Wytschaete and

1 From the opening page of R. Aldington, 'Victory', a short story in B. Korte, ed., *The Penguin Book of First World War Stories* (London: Penguin Books, 2007), pp. 41-48.

2 A useful pen picture is given at the start of chapter 3 of W. Groom, *A Storm in Flanders: The Ypres Salient 1914-1918: Tragedy and Triumph on the Western Front* (London: Cassell, 2003); see also the various battlefield guides which are available for anyone wishing to visit the sites.

> Gheluvelt, and only 70 feet at Passchendaele. From Kemmel it was possible to see the whole countryside from Lille to Menin and Dixmude. Various spurs extended from the ridge line, as at Messines… given the low-lying nature of much of the plain, these gentle slopes took on the appearance of dominant features, a saucer-like rim appearing to the observer from Ypres lying at the centre of the plain. Gradients were gentle nearly everywhere…[3]

In a subsequent volume, Beckett referred to the description of Flanders in 1914 by one French general as 'a monotonous countryside with an air of melancholic sadness melting almost imperceptibly into the grey waters of the North Sea'.[4]

Another feature of Flanders – which achieved infamy amongst the soldiers who fought there – was its climate: '…the relentlessly flat, low-lying Flanders was wet'.[5] This same writer quotes the conclusion of a British Lieutenant stationed there:

> The appearance of the countryside suggested that it has been raining since the beginning of time.[6]

As had been the case in previous battles, the weather would make its mark on the fighting in prospect during the campaign in the autumn of 1918.

The majority of Belgium had been under foreign occupation and military rule for four years. The Belgian Government had rejected Germany's insistence on 2 August 1914 that Belgium adopt a stance of 'benevolent neutrality' and allow free access across its borders for the German Army: invasion followed. Because its overarching *Schlieffen Plan* required an attack on France from the direction of Belgium, the German Army had already commenced crossing the border before the ultimatum expired. To the fury of the German leadership, the Belgians then attempted to put up as much resistance as possible, with an inevitable outcome such was the imbalance of the opposing forces.[7]

A subsequent attempt by the invaders to set up an independent Flanders under German influence and with a force to fight alongside the German Army failed, as most Flemish-speakers remained loyal to the country of their birth. Between October 1916 and June 1917 around 170,000 Belgians (including 4,000 women and 3,000 children) were deported for labour in Germany, although this was not seen as a successful policy and repatriation began in 1917.[8]

3 I.F.W. Beckett, *Ypres: The First Battle, 1914* (Harlow: Pearson Education Limited, 2004), pp. 42-43; Beckett's references include P. Doyle, *Geology of the Western Front, 1914-1918* (London: Geologists' Association, 1998), pp. 11-14, 29-32; J. Hussey, 'The Flanders Battleground and the Weather in 1917' in P. Liddle, ed., *Passchendaele in Perspective: The Third Battle of Ypres* (London: Leo Cooper, 1997), pp. 140-158.

4 I.F.W. Beckett, *The Making of the First World War* (New Haven and London: Yale University Press, 2014), p. 1.

5 J. Lewis-Stempel, *Where Poppies Blow: The British Soldier, Nature, The Great War* (London: Weidenfeld & Nicolson, 2016), p. 20

6 C. Douie, *The Weary Road* (London: J. Murray, 1929), p. 62; quoted in Lewis-Stempel, *Where Poppies Blow*, p. 20

7 M. MacMillan, *The War That Ended Peace: How Europe Abandoned Peace for the First World War* (London: Profile Books Ltd., 2013), pp. 584-6.

8 M. Derez, 'The Experience of Occupation: Belgium', in J. Bourne, P. Liddle, I. Whitehead, eds., *The Great World War1914-45: Volume 1: Lightning Strikes Twice* (London: Harper Collins, 2000),

However, forced labour for German interests either in Belgium or occupied France continued.[9] The Belgians were forced to conform 'to German rules and German ways of life (even… to German time of day)'.[10]

Resources were seized for German consumption leading to homelessness and starvation as increasing facts of life for many Belgians, despite humanitarian aid from allied and neutral countries. Germany requisitioned all manner of goods from the populace such that 'From 1917 Belgium's industry was systematically dismantled… and its machines were melted down to make weapons'.[11] In his article giving an insight into life under German occupation – describing the operation of the American-based aid agency, *Commission of Relief for Belgium* – Garcia has pointed out that there is still very little research available into the experiences of the civilian population during the war.[12]

The majority of occupied Belgium was under the administration of a Governor General. However the areas in the vicinity of the front line, and where the majority of the fighting took place, came under military administration. It has been estimated that total Belgian deaths during the war, military and civilian, were around 50,000; the army recorded 13,716 soldiers killed, 44,686 wounded, and 34,659 captured or missing in action.[13]

The British Army had been committed to fighting for Belgium since the dogged resistance by the 'Old Contemptibles' of the BEF at the end of 1914.[14] In the defence of the city of Ypres – the principal remaining city of Belgium not subject to German occupation – and its surrounding environs, Malcolm Brown has noted the determination of the British 'to hang onto this piece of torn and battered territory'. He goes on to explain this commitment, given that the resulting salient was of little or no military value:

> Not yielding ground to the enemy was part of the ethos of the time. Additionally the Belgians had lost so much of their homeland to the Germans that to concede even more – and by doing so to allow the Germans to advance to the very walls of Ypres – would not have been just a geographical adjustment, it would have been a psychological one, indeed almost a gesture of defeat.[15]

The Ypres Salient, pushing out into the German front line, would be the subsequent focus for major clashes in 1915, 1917, and the German spring 1918 Georgette offensive. This protracted conflict was such that a parallel has been drawn between the salient and the epic

pp. 511-532; Stevenson, *Backs to the Wall*, p. 279, states that 'during the war [Germany] used some 120,000 Belgian workers in France and Belgium.

9 P. Haythornthwaite, *The World War One Source Book* (London: Arms & Armour Press, 1992), pp. 148-9.

10 A. Garcia, 'Soup and Stoicism – Feeding occupied Belgium during the Great War', *Stand To! The Journal of the Western Front Association*, 82 (April/May 2008), pp. 57-60.

11 Derez, 'Experience of Occupation', p. 519.

12 Garcia, 'Soup and Stoicism', pp. 57-60.

13 Haythornthwaite, *World War One Source Book*, pp. 149-152.

14 It is alleged that the Kaiser had dubbed the small British Army in 1914 a 'contemptible little army' – the original BEF proudly adopted the term as a compliment.

15 From the introduction by M. Brown to *The Wipers Times: The Complete Series of the Famous Wartime Trench Newspaper* (London: Little Books Ltd., 2006), p. xv.

Franco-German battles for Verdun.[16] A modern writer has summarised it thus: "Men called it Hell. Even the earth seemed dead. Modern war's weaponry, the shells and the chemical gases, did its damnedest in the Salient."[17]

In purely military terms the salient was a hopeless case – but the retention of Ypres was a symbol of resistance to German attrition. Fittingly, the Ypres salient would provide the platform for the successful breakthrough into the German defences by Second Army at the end of September 1918.

British Second Army

The *Official History* sets the scene for British Second Army in the summer of 1918, pending the forthcoming *Advance in Flanders*:

> The preparations of the enemy had been very carefully watched, complete air photographs being obtained week by week; and as the same formations, with the same staffs and same intelligence organisation had remained on the front since the battle in April, any change in the German situation had been at once noticed. Early in June, when an attack [by the Germans] seemed imminent, a systematic destruction of the enemy's establishments by bombardment was begun, and harassing fire had since been ceaselessly employed.[18]

Following the heavy fighting in April as a consequence of German chief of staff Ludendorff's *Georgette* offensive, this part of the northern sector of the Western Front had been relatively quiet. However even the relatively limited actions of both sides, consigned primarily to raids and artillery shoots, meant that casualty levels remained high, as the following table shows:

British Second Army: Casualties 5 August-7 September 1918[19]

II Corps	346*
X Corps	2,392
XV Corps	4,832
XIX Corps	2,867**
TOTAL	10,437
Prisoners taken	1,790

* Includes the American 30th Division
** Does not include the American 27th Division – losses not known

In July 1918 Ludendorff had still harboured hopes of a further offensive in Flanders, believing that the prospect for a breakthrough remained; resources including heavy artillery and aircraft had been directed to the area in readiness. However the losses further south at the Battle of the

16 The analogy is drawn by M. Brown, *Verdun 1916* (Stroud, Gloucestershire: Tempus Publishing, 2003; first published 2000), pp. 21-2: 'The city of Ypres, determinedly defended with the kind of 'they shall not pass' mentality which pertained at Verdun, is the only possible British equivalent'.
17 Lewis-Stempel, *Where Poppies Blow*, p. 21.
18 Edmonds, *Official History Vol. IV*, p. 428.
19 Edmonds, *Official History Vol. IV.*

Marne dealt a final blow to this plan and the attack was cancelled.[20] That Flanders had retained this level of importance for so long in the thinking of the German High Command is an indication of its strategic importance, guarding as it did access to the coast and the supply routes for the British and Empire forces; as well as securing the Belgian Army line and the left flank of the allied front along the Western Front.

During this period the Germans continued to mount occasional raids and limited attacks on parts of the Second Army front, operations that do not suggest an enemy suffering from low morale or contemplating defeat.

On 11 August 1918 the diary of 18th Battalion (Arts and Crafts), King's Royal Rifle Corps (18/Art and Crafts) (122 Brigade, 41st Division) records its troops manning the forward line of trenches and coming under a severe enemy barrage; the battalion was then hit by a German attack in force. The consequence was that its troops were required to carry out a counter-attack to recover lost ground, with the resulting casualty list shown in the table below:[21]

18th Kings Royal Rifle Corps: Casualties 11 August 1918

	Officers	Other Ranks
Killed	3	4
Wounded	2	20
Missing	1	19
Total	6	43

At the start of August the front of British Second Army (with Fifth Army to its right), ran from three miles north of the La Bassee canal along to the northern side of Ypres. To the Army's left was the Belgian line, extending through to the coast. The *Official History* comments on the condition of the units comprising the British armies at that time:

> All the British divisions of the Second and Fifth Armies had taken part in heavy fighting during the early part of the year and were regarded as not so forward in their recovery as those of the First, Third and Fourth Armies.[22]

This reference to possible questions regarding the combat readiness of Second Army at the start of August 1918 is an important context for any analysis of its subsequent performance during the Hundred Days. This is discussed in more detail in chapter two.

Over the course of the month, the Germans in Flanders gradually withdrew their line and reserve formations from the Lys salient, which had been created as a consequence of the enemy's advance during the April offensive. Half of these troops were redeployed south to assist with the defence of the German line from attacks by the other British armies. British Second Army successfully followed up these evacuations, in accordance with General Plumer's instructions 'to exert continuous pressure upon [German] retiring forces, acting vigorously against his

20 Terraine, *To Win A War*, pp. 94-5, 100.
21 TNA WO95/2365, War Diary of 18th Battalion, Kings Royal Rifle Corps.
22 Edmonds, *Official History*.

rearguards and thus hampering his choice of defensive lines, whilst making his retirement as costly as possible.'[23]

A practical example of the carrying out of these orders is an operation by 9th Battalion, Royal Irish Fusiliers (9/Royal Irish Fusiliers) (107 Brigade, 36th Division) on 24 August. Its troops seized a section of the enemy trench line and also secured *Tomlin Farm*, capturing 60 prisoners and five machine guns.[24]

Throughout July and August 1918 the troops of Second Army undertook a range of duties and actions, reflecting the various demands upon units at that time. The Army was engaged in the induction of mainly young conscript replacements and men re-categorised as fit for front line duty into its differing arms; developing the skills and abilities of its troops with the focus on an anticipated (though as yet unplanned) assault to break through the German defensive lines. At the same time its units were increasingly prompted to maintain pressure upon an enemy carrying out a planned withdrawal designed to strengthen the defenders' ability to resist assault.

Typical of the experiences on the Second Army front during this period of "The Advance in Flanders" (as designated by the post-war Battles Nomenclature Committee), are those described in the war diary of 105 Brigade (35th Division).[25] The brigade comprised 15th Battalion, Cheshire Regiment (15/Cheshires), 15th Battalion, Sherwood Foresters (15/Sherwood Foresters) and 4th Battalion, North Staffordshire Regiment (4/North Staffords). During the course of 5-6 July 1918, the brigade relieved the 358 French Infantry Regiment along a stretch of the front in the Locre Sector, Mont Rouge, to the south-east of Ypres.

The exercise proceeded smoothly and without incident. 15/Cheshires relieved the French front line units; 15/Sherwood Foresters took over the support positions; 4/North Staffords moved into place as brigade reserve. It was common policy across BEF formations for these three roles to be rotated at regular and frequent intervals, to ensure that all troops had an equitable share of the responsibilities of the front line, and opportunities for training and recreation. The following extract from the brigade's war diary illustrates the varied range of activities taking place over a three week period during that summer of 1918:

From the war diary of 105 Infantry Brigade, 6-25 July 1918 (1)

6	Quiet day in the line. Hostile Artillery heavily shelled Battery positions W of Mount Rouge [sic] in the evening.
night 6/7	Patrols were out during the night but no enemy were encountered. Our wire was examined and was found to consist of rows of plain French Concertina wire. Hostile M.Gs. were very active during the night sweeping the forward slopes of Mont ROUGE.
night 7/8	Three of our Patrols were out during the night and reconnoitred our own and enemy wire. One of our patrols on approaching the enemy lines was fired at with rifle grenades but withdrew without casualties.

23 Edmonds, *Official History Vol. IV.*
24 Noted in the War Diary of 1st Battalion, Royal Irish Rifles, TNA WO95/2502/3.
25 TNA WO95/2486, War Diary of 105 Infantry Brigade.

8	Hostile Artillery was fairly active during the day... shelled continuously with Gas and H.E. Provisional Defence instructions for the Centre sub-sector... were issued.
night 8/9	Standing patrols were out... [This activity, checking own and enemy defence arrangements, was routine for the battalion holding the front line positions; as was the experience of occasional bouts of enemy artillery and machine gun fire.]
10	Our Trench Mortars registered enemy positions during the early morning...
13	Hostile Artillery was unusually active on the Brigade Sector during the day. [My emphasis – much more intense and prolonged artillery fire by the Germans, perhaps indicative of the forthcoming night-time operations.]
night 13/14	[a patrol of one NCO and three men] went out from our lines, and after proceeding some distance the N.C.O. gave orders for the men to remain behind. He went forward himself and ran into a party of 30 Germans, apparently forming up for a raid. The patrol being warned attempted to get back to bring up a Lewis Gun but were pursued by the enemy and bombed while taking cover in a building. The N.C.O. being wounded the 3 men made a dash for it and have not been seen since. When the enemy party were first discovered a heavy barrage of shells of all calibres was put down on Locre and our front line causing several casualties.
14	Enemy artillery fired crashes of mixed calibre on Locre during the day... The sunken road occupied by the Front Line Battalion Headquarters was heavily shelled for an hour... direct hits on the road being obtained and casualties caused. [These last entries show the ongoing danger for troops manning the front lines.]

From the war diary of 105 Infantry Brigade, 6-25 July 1918 (2)

night 14/15	A patrol of two other ranks reconnoitred our wire and located an enemy post at about 60 yards from our trench, probably a listening post. A minor operation was carried out by [104 Brigade, on the left of 105 Brigade's position].
night 16/17	A fighting patrol of 1 Officer and 21 other ranks attempted to rush an enemy post but were held up by wire. The enemy trench appeared to be held by 20 men. Machine Gun fire and bombs greeted the patrol, and during withdrawal trench mortar fire was opened on them.
18 night	Our lines especially Locre and vicinity were heavily shelled in retaliation for the activity of our Artillery supporting a raid by the right flank Division. A patrol of one Officer and two men reconnoitred the ground
18/19	in front of Right Company Sector. Portions of the ground covered were very marshy and all shell holes were full of water. This patrol also reconnoitred enemy wire drawing rifle and Machine Gun fire. [The description shows the problematic nature of the ground over which the forthcoming action would take place. It is also another example of the

ongoing resistance by the German defenders, not suggestive of an opponent losing his fighting qualities.]

19 Orders were issued for the 15th Cheshire Regt. [holding the front line] to advance their right and establish five posts to conform with new line being established with the right flank Brigade.

night 19/20 The ground along which the new posts were ordered to be established was reconnoitred by 2 Officers and 2othyer ranks.

night 21 The operation entailing the establishing of five posts was carried out without interference from the enemy and the posts were consolidated and wired. Covering patrols were out…

Orders were issued for a small raid to be carried out by the 4th North Staffordshire Regt. On night 22/23rdJuly, with a view to capturing an enemy Machine Gun Post. Strength of raiding party one platoon…

night 21/22 At 12-53 a.m. the enemy put down a barrage on our left flank, and working through centre to right flank. The S.O.S. was reported to have been sent up, and our Artillery retaliated, firing for fifteen minutes after which fire died down all being quiet by 1-40 a.m. …

night 22/23 A fighting patrol of one Officer and a platoon left our lines under cover of 18 pounder barrage, with the object of capturing a machine gun and killing Germans. On reaching their object the post was found to be unoccupied and after remaining for five minutes in the position the patrol withdrew without casualties.

From the war diary of 105 Infantry Brigade, 6-25 July 1918 (3)

night 23/24 A patrol of One Officer and 14 men reconnoitred approach from BALLEIL Road to LONG WOOD. An enemy Strong Point was located and found to be strongly protected by wire. Another of our patrols, was observed by the enemy, after proceeding about 100 yards from our lines, and were heavily fired on by Machine Guns and rifles… the S.O.S. signal was put up… but no attack developed.

night 24/25 Our front was actively patrolled during the night. A hostile party of about 30 men were reported by one of our patrols, and were dispersed by Machine Gun fire. Another of our patrols attempted to force their way through the wire of a German Strong Point but were met with bombs, rifle and machine gun fire. This patrol then attempted to withdraw, and a small encounter ensued, one German being shot at 15 yards range. After withdrawal the patrol leader and two wounded men were missing.[26]

A similar routine persisted for the remainder of the month, with increased regular patrolling by troops from the front line battalion, occasionally generating small arms, machine gun or artillery fire from the German positions; punctuated by prepared bouts of enemy artillery fire, day

26 TNA WO95/2486, War Diary of 105 Infantry Brigade.

and night, often intense and for a prolonged period. The sobering consequences of the German activity, during what might be described as a reasonably quiet period, are evident from that month's casualty figures for the brigade:

105 Brigade: Casualties July 1918[27]

	Killed		Wounded		Missing	
	Officers	Other Ranks	Officers	Other Ranks	Officers	Other Ranks
15/Cheshires	1	8	1	31	–	3
15/Sherwood Foresters	1	16	–	43	1	10
4/North Staffs	–	7	1	34	1	13
Totals	2	31	2	108	1	13

August brought some changes in the brigade's arrangements including representation at special events. For instance, on 4 August:

> Representatives of the Brigade attended a special Commemoration Service at which the Second Army Commander was present. After the service the troops marched past the Army Commander who took the salute.[28]

At the end of the first week in August, 35th Division, deployed in the Locre Sector, was relieved by 30th Division. Accordingly, 90 Brigade replaced 105 Brigade in line, with the latter moving back to billets in the area of Sylvestre Cappel.

On 11 August the brigade was represented at a church service attended by royalty:

> A Special Church Service was held at TERDEGHEM, on the occasion of a visit by His Majesty the King. Twelve representatives from Battalions of 105th Infantry Brigade formed part of a contingent from Second Army which attended the Service at 11.0 a.m. and subsequently marched past his Majesty. The Brigadier-General Commanding [A. J. Turner, C.M.G., D.S.O.] attended this parade.[29]

The war diary proceeds to describe the subsequent training and work duties undertaken by 105 Brigade's troops. Much of the content can be seen in retrospect as the preparations for offensive action:

27 TNA WO95/2486, War Diary of 105 Infantry Brigade.
28 TNA WO95/2486, War Diary of 105 Infantry Brigade.
29 TNA WO95/2486, War Diary of 105 Infantry Brigade.

From the war diary of 105 Infantry Brigade, 9-22 August 1918

August 9	… One platoon from each Battalion, detailed for work in the forward area under No. 1. Foreways Company…
10	The Units of the Brigade spent the day re-organizing and refitting.
12	Orders were issued relating to a practice attack on the TERDEGHEM SWITCH by 15th. Sherwood Foresters and the 4th. North Staffordshire Regiment, to take place on Wednesday, 14th. August. Only Signallers on Brigade Headquarters and of each Unit to take part – assisted by a contact aeroplane of 53rd. Squadron R.A.F. [An exercise demonstrating the crucial need for effective communications during an assault – and the importance of this within Second Army preparations.] Battalions carried out training according to programme. [15th Cheshires ordered to undertake] 4 days Range Practice. [Brigadier-General Turner went on a short leave to England.]
13	The 105th. Brigade Headquarters Staff… attended a Lecture… on 'Counter-Battery Work'. A closer co-operation between Infantry and Artillery was advocated, and facilities for more immediate action were promised. [This could have been in part a response to the number of casualties being caused to the troops manning front line positions – and the concerns of their immediate commanders.]
14	[Practice attack on the TERDEGHEM SWITCH by Signal troops carried out.] The object of the practice exercise was to improve the efficiency of Signal Personnel in the use of the 'T' POPHAM PANEL' and other means of communication (without cable). Communication between Headquarters of Assaulting Battalions and Headquarters of 105th. Infantry Brigade was satisfactorily established and maintained by means of (a) 'T' POPHAM PANEL', (b) Visual and (c) Runner.
16	Instructions (105th. Infantry Brigade G.1427) shewing 'Action of 105th. Infantry Brigade while in 10th Corps Reserve' issued.
19	A short Brigade Tactical exercise (in which Officers only took part) was carried out during the evening.
22	Second Army Commander visited 15th. Cheshire Regiment and 15th. Sherwood Foresters and inspected them while training.[30]

On 15, 17, 20, 21, 23, 25, and 27 August, the diary simply refers to training continued.

These extracts from the record of one brigade give a representative picture of the range of activities which Army units engaged in during the periods when they were withdrawn from the line. It is suggestive of what might now be termed 'a learning organisation' and demonstrates Second Army's commitment to training. You will note also the visit by General Plumer on 22 August, indicative of the importance he attached to this side of the Army's activities.

30 TNA WO95/2486, War Diary of 105 Infantry Brigade.

The system of rotation of units between rear and front-line positions was an institution in the British Army and one of its strengths.[31] In essence, this is combat as shift-work, an analogy appropriate for the new industrialised warfare; and a routine not unfamiliar to those men drawn from life amidst the factories and mills. As one rota of men completed its 'shift' in the front line another 'clocked on' to take its place; thus the productivity of the workplace – in this case, the fighting capability to sustain the battle – was maintained.[32]

There are very few references to troops being used for work duties such as road repairs (a common grouse of the men) or similar; or taking part in recreational activities such as inter-unit sports competitions. The emphasis appears to be very much on developing and improving the skills of soldiery in the new troops while there is time and opportunity to do so. Reflecting the time spent behind the lines, the monthly casualties' report showed no soldiers killed or missing; two officers and 20 men were recorded as wounded.

There is plenty of evidence to show that units and their commanders were working hard to learn lessons from minor operations and apply the experience gained in planning and preparing for future action. Much of the emphasis was on strengthening the firepower of the fighting infantry group on the ground and improving its ability to operate on its own initiative. The following war diary extract gives some examples of another brigade's application of such learning:

From the war diary of 86 Infantry Brigade, 4-5 September 1918

Trench Mortars
At present owing to the establishment of personnel, they are practically useless, immobile. It is suggested as a temporary measure that 6 pack animals per Battalion be used as transport for Trench Mortars when they are required to come into action in mobile fighting.
18 mules will carry 4 Stokes Trench Mortars and 56 rounds per gun…

Maps
In mobile fighting it seems that more maps should be issued so that senior N.C.O.s may be in possession of a map of the immediate area – more instructions in map reading for all ranks appears to be necessary.

S.O.S.
A larger supply is necessary, so that the fighting troops may carry at least 4 rockets per Company and obviate the necessity of sending rockets to the Front Line at night time.[33]

31 Corrigan, *Mud, Blood*, pp. 89-94, provides a concise summary of how the system operated and describes its advantages for the troops and the Army as a whole.

32 My thanks to Thomas Keneally, from his novel about two Australian sisters working as nurses during the First World War, *The Daughters of Mars* (New York: Atria Books, 2012), for the idea of the shift-work analogy.

33 TNA WO95/2299, War Diary of 86 Infantry Brigade, Notes On Minor Operations 4 and 5 September, 7/9/18.

Inspections were also a regular feature of the Army's routine, particularly as the build-up to a forthcoming offensive gained momentum.

> Transport inspected by the Brigadier at 10a.m. The state of the transport was by no means satisfactory, and the whole inspection was too painful to describe.[34]

True to his word, the writer provides no details. The saying of no gain without pain was clearly demonstrated here.

Second Army had a number of units which had been reconstituted or reorganised during the summer of 1918, in some cases from an initial training cadre. Chapter two provides a detailed examination of this particular feature of Second Army. This meant that some units required a new set of administrative orders to provide a comprehensive outline of their deployment and organisation when ordered forward on active service. An example of this rebuilding is provided by the experience of 120 Brigade in 40th Division. After its losses in the Battle of Hazebrouck during the German offensives in spring 1918, the division had been reduced to a training cadre until its restructuring; it was declared ready for a return to front line action again by 18 July later that year. 120 Brigade was re-formed in June 1918 comprising 15th Battalion, the King's Own Yorkshire Light Infantry (15/ KOYLI); and two former Garrison battalions: 10th Battalion, the King's Own Scottish Borderers (10/KOSB) (formerly 9th Garrison Battalion) and 11th Battalion, the Cameron Highlanders (11/Cameron Highlanders) (formerly 6th Garrison Guard Battalion). In 'Brigade Administrative Order No. 207, 10th August 1918',[35] issued pending the brigade taking over the forward positions for the division from 121 Brigade, there are four closely typed pages giving details of the location of all its constituent elements, with associated arrangements for supplies and support. Some of the specific supplies or supply points (for example, clean clothing) were made available through 31st Division; this was the other division under the command of XV Corps at that time, and these arrangements reflect the newly constituted nature of 40th Division and the greater experience of its partner division.

In section 1, the administrative order lists (by map reference) the sites for the headquarters of the brigade, for the headquarters of each of the battalions when deployed respectively in one of the three active positions (front line, support or reserve), and for the brigade's trench mortar battery and RE company. The section also gives map references for the transport lines of the brigade and battalions (from 121 Brigade) plus the locations of the company train, the brigade post office, and the refilling point. The order goes on to provide information covering particular services and arrangements, as set out in the following table:

From the war diary of 120 Infantry Brigade, Administrative Order No. 207, 10 August 1918 (1)

Railhead	location map reference; also stating that reinforcements will be sent to Battalion Transport Lines

34 TNA WO95/1765, War Diary of 7th Battalion, Seaforth Highlanders, 27 August 1918.
35 TNA WO95/2610, War Diary of 120 Infantry Brigade, Administrative Order No. 207, 10 August 1918.

Rations	transport and delivery arrangements for food and water
Ammunition	locations of the Divisional and Brigade Ammunition Dumps; plus the rules for the issuing and handling of ammunition supplies
R.E. Dumps	location of the Divisional R.E. Dump and other forward Dump; plus rules for requisitioning R.E. 'Material'
Medical	location of medical posts; 31st Division is responsible for evacuating casualties
Cemeteries	location of two cemeteries. 'Burials in other than authorised cemeteries are strictly forbidden'
Receipts	receipts – in duplicate, for all stores and supplies – 'must be exchanged… at all inter-unit reliefs… [and] copies sent to Brigade. Headquarters… any shortage subsequently discovered must be accounted for…'
Trench Foot	'In the event of continued wet weather, trench foot preventative measures will be carried out'; whale oil and clean socks can be requisitioned
Baths	The battalion in reserve can make use of a designated bath ('capacity of 100 men per hour'); battalions can also 'improvise' by using 'tarpaulin sheets'
Clean Clothing Store	locations provided
Gassed Clothing	There is a Divisional Reserve of '500 S.D. [service dress] jackets and trousers together with underclothing' for men affected by Yellow Cross gas, who will require a certificate signed by an officer

From the war diary of 120 Infantry Brigade, Administrative Order No. 207, 10 August 1918 (2)

Salvage	all soldiers have a duty to send back to the rear any damaged equipment 'however muddy or apparently useless'; 'no man moving away from the line for any distance however short, on any duty whatsoever, should do so empty-handed'
Economy	'waste paper, jam cartons, dripping; tea, biscuit and other large tins, etc. will be returned to the Base…'
Sanitation	'systematic burial of excreta is essential'; 'disciplinary action is to be taken against any man found throwing food refuse or tins over the parapet…'
Ordnance	details of administration
Canteens	details of the locations of two canteens, plus the YMCA
Transport	details regarding baggage wagons
Armourer Sergeant	arrangements for work
Communication	arrangements for telephone lines, cyclist and dispatch riders
Baggage Wagons	arrangements for the day of changeover for battalion responsibilities.[36]

36 TNA WO95/2610, War Diary of 120 Infantry Brigade, Administrative Order No. 207, 10 August 1918.

The arrangements and instructions referred to here would be familiar to any troops in the British Army on active duty at this time. There is an emphasis upon encouraging and maintaining the health and welfare of the men, whether by strict rules on sanitation and trench foot, or through the careful planning to deliver rations and provide clean clothing. Very much a 'stick and carrot' approach. These arrangements, as the example summarised above shows, were also underpinned and made feasible by the supporting material resources and logistics. There are detailed systems in place, with specified locations and transport routes, to maintain effective communications and deliver or permit access to supplies and provisions. Equally important is the plentiful availability of the variety of goods required in order to meet the needs of the soldier deployed on active service. Food (hot rations inclusive) and water, baths for a clean body and clean clothes to put on when necessary, medical facilities, mail services, and ammunition. In addition the Army, being the Army and also a very large and complex organisation, has its share of bureaucratic rules and requirements – the signing of duplicate receipts, accounting for supplies and looking to salvage damaged equipment at all times. The grim business of using the authorised cemeteries was a further routine arrangement – but of immeasurable importance in the future for the families of those who lost their lives while serving.

That the British Army continued to operate efficiently and effectively after the four years of grinding warfare, with a generally cohesive and motivated body of men, was in itself a notable achievement. This is particularly so by 1918 when an increasing proportion of the troops were made up of younger men, conscripts and soldiers re-categorised as fit for front-line duty. These personnel, many with potentially less obvious commitment than the volunteers of 1914 and 1915, had a greater need to be inducted into an organisation that might today be described as 'still fit for purpose'. For Second Army there was an extra element of importance in these circumstances. In comparison with the other armies making up the BEF in the autumn of 1918, Second Army had a higher proportion of units which had been rebuilt over the summer months through making use of the extra steps taken to comb out additional manpower for the armed forces. There were also units newly transferred to Second Army formations from service in other theatres; hence these were unfamiliar with the circumstances and demands of the Western Front. A well-resourced and efficiently organised structure was a very important prerequisite for attempting to bring these various elements together as a coherent fighting force within a short space of time.

This cohesion would be crucial for Second Army given its pending role as a partner in a coalition army group alongside forces from two other nations. The ability of its troops to operate effectively would be open to close scrutiny by its allies. It was particularly important given the Army's original planned role, that of securing the right flank of the coalition force when operations began, was intended to provide sufficient confidence to the Belgian Army for the latter to take up the fight with the opposing German forces. There could not be cause for doubt or uncertainty in the conduct of Second Army's operations – a visibly effective fighting force was required.

Outtersteene Ridge: 18 August 1918

In mid-August, XV Corps of Second Army led a well-planned and successful operation to seize the *Outtersteene Ridge*, described by John Terraine as 'a smart little victory'.[37] This demonstrated that units of Second Army were capable of applying successfully the planning, tactics and weaponry typical of the British Army in 1918.

The ridge was the last remaining piece of high ground still held by the Germans in front of XV Corps, following the initial advances that month. The capture of this objective was considered to be an important pre-requisite for further advances.

The chart below lists the key features of the plan of attack:

Outtersteene Ridge 18 August: Preparations for attack (1) XV Corps: 9th Division, supported by 29th Division

- Main attack: XV Corps: 9th Division, supported by 29th Division
- One section of machine guns attached to each attacking battalion of 9th Division
- Creeping barrage
- First round: smoke shells – to be fired at Z-1 minute*
- Infantry to advance at Z+3 minutes*
  - The timings were subsequently changed to Z+1 minute for the opening of the barrage, with troops leaving the trenches after counting to ten from the opening of fire – this was due to captured German documents which reported lessons from a previous successful attack by Second Army troops using an initial smoke barrage; therefore as soon as a smoke barrage was applied, the British front line was to be hit by artillery and machine gun fire – hence XV Corps decided on the slight alterations in timing
- Second round onwards: 25% smoke, 75% high explosive
- Advance of 50 yards per minute
- To halt as a protective barrage 200 yards beyond first objective (until advance resumed)
- Four companies of machine guns to fire enfilade and creeping barrages

Outtersteene Ridge 18 August: Preparations for attack (2) XV Corps: 9th Division, supported by 29th Division

- On the left flank, smoke barrage to hide attack from enemy observation
- On the right flank, an enfilade barrage
- plus a rolling barrage across the front of 9th Division, from right to left
- XV Corps heavy artillery (57 guns and howitzers) to target specific enemy points
- plus put down a final protective barrage
- Z-hour set as 1100, with the aim of surprise

37 Terraine, *To Win A War*, p. 124.

- To conceal the assembled troops, trenches were covered with cocoa matting, with a black band painted on to represent the shadow of the trench
- A rehearsal of the attack (27th Brigade) was carried out beforehand
- Each battalion advanced on a two company frontage
- Each company adopted a two platoon frontage
- First wave in extended order
- Subsequent waves in file
- Achievement of the objective to be signalled by blue smoke rifle grenades
- Red flares to be used to signal achievement of the objective to RAF patrols[38]

The operation was launched on 18 August when 27 Brigade (9th Division) together with 9th Battalion, Cameronians (9/Scottish Rifles) (then with the South African Brigade)[39] attacked Hoogenacker Ridge; 87 Brigade (29th Division) cooperating on their right. This ridge overlooked the Flanders Plain, including to the right the valley of the Meteren Beque; on the left was the village of Meteren offering a good view of the surrounding country. With the prime aim of seizing and holding the high ground, the orders included arrangements for a defensive barrage to be established as soon as the objective was achieved; together with the immediate establishment of Lewis gun positions as far forward as possible, to cover the trench preparations and wiring operations. Despite a level of enemy resistance, the attack was a success – in many cases, troops were reported to have advanced beyond the line of the objectives. Consolidation began during the early afternoon, with units reported to be entering Outtersteene at 1248 hours. Although a counter-attack was anticipated this did not result, although there was some heavy enemy shelling and machine gun fire.[40]

The next day, units of the 9th (Scottish) Division mounted an operation to capture the village of Meteren and secure the position by establishing a line approximately 400 yards to the south. 5/Cameron Highlanders and 8/Black Watch of 26 Brigade took part, together with forces from the South African Brigade which was attached to the division at this time.[41] Under a barrage of HE and smoke shells, together with the throwing of 'some hundreds of drums of burning oil' the assault was successful. Initial fire from enemy machine gun posts was tackled by taking out each post using small arms fire and bombs. The advance troops dug themselves in quickly but the expected counter-attack did not materialise. There was however some shelling from the Germans which continued for a number of days, including occasional gas shells, plus active

38 Taken from Edmonds, *Official History Vol. IV* and archive sources, notably: TNA WO95/2303, War Diary of 87 Infantry Brigade.
39 The South African Brigade reported to 9th Division from 22 April 1916 to 13 September 1918. On 24 April 1918, due to heavy casualties, 1st, 2nd and 4th Battalions were amalgamated – forming the South African (Composite) Regiment; they were reformed by 1 September 1918. The 9th (Service) Battalion, Cameronians (Scottish Rifles) and 2nd Battalion, Royal Scots Fusiliers were transferred to the Brigade in April 1918 to bring it up to strength; 9/Scottish Rifles and 2/Royal Scots Fusiliers were restored to 28 Brigade when this was re-established in September 1918, prior to the Battle of Ypres.
40 TNA WO95/1771/4, War Diary of 27 Infantry Brigade, diary entries; Brigade Order No.256, 15/8/18; Defence Scheme (Provisional), 22 August 1918.
41 As described in an earlier citation.

sniper fire. It was thought that the Germans suspected that new forces were being prepared for a further attack, and they were attempting to disrupt this. The new positions remained secure.[42]

An important component when defending ground recently gained was to ensure that effective methods of communication were put in place as soon as possible between the various levels of command. Historian Jonathan Boff has observed:

> The return of relative mobility [as opposed to trench warfare] confronted commanders with a series of new challenges. One of the most pressing was the exercise of command and control… [placing] a premium on rapid intelligence and speedy decision-making. However communications remained a major constraint.[43]

For the newly re-established 43 Brigade, a briefing note on defensive arrangements issued at the end of July included a list of the communication methods to be employed, outlined in the following table:[44]

43 Brigade, 28 July 1918. Provisional Instructions for the Defence of portion of WINNEZELLE-HAZEBROUCK Line

Line communications:	Cable routes (buried and otherwise) for telephone communication between Brigade HQ and Battalion HQs NB Instruments forward of Brigade HQ are potentially able to be overheard by the enemy – all messages will be sent in morse by Fullerphone, the exceptions being messages in code or cypher.
Visual communications:	Brigade and Battalion Stations to be positioned as close to their respective HQs as visibility and cover will allow.
D.R. (Dispatch Rider) and Runner Services:	Once Battalions are in position in the line, runners will be sent from Brigade to Battalion HQ; Battalion runners should then return with these in order to learn routes. HQs down to company level will be marked by a board and by a lamp or lantern at night.
Wireless, Power Buzzer etc.:	Wireless communication will link Brigade HQ with Division HQ. Power Buzzers and Wireless Loop Sets will be issued to Battalions subject to the availability of sets and to trained personnel.
Other forms of communication:	To be used as available and appropriate: dogs, pigeons, rockets, etc.

42 TNA WO95/1767, War Diary of 5th Battalion, Cameron Highlanders.

43 J. Boff,'Command Culture and Complexity: Third Army during the Hundred Days, August-November 1918', in G.D. Sheffield and P. Gray, ed., *Changing War: The British Army, the Hundred Days Campaign and the Birth of the Royal Air Force, 1918* (London: Bloomsbury Academic, Birmingham War Studies, 2013), p. 19.

44 TNA WO95/1905, War Diary of 43 Infantry Brigade, Provisional Instructions for the Defence of portion of WINNEZELLE-HAZEBROUCK Line, 28/07/1918.

Meanwhile for 87 Brigade, one or two 'messenger dogs' were allocated to each of its battalions, capable of working their way back to brigade HQ.[45] As will be seen regularly throughout Second Army's operations, the maintenance of effective communications was both a constant worry and an increasing challenge for the advancing troops.

Equally important for the defence of captured ground was to ensure that artillery support was available and could fire to maximum effect. In this regard the counter battery arrangements were important, and would become more so in the planning and execution of forthcoming offensives. The collection and feeding back of the necessary intelligence from the front line became more problematic as the line advanced and troops were no longer in fixed positions. Hence, on 6 September, XV Corps found it necessary to write to its units reminding them of the value of feeding back information on enemy shelling.[46] The original instructions, issued on 13 December 1917, stated:

> 1 The Counter Battery organization exists for the benefit of the Corps as a whole.
> All units, Infantry and Artillery, should understand the necessity of sending to the Counter Battery Office, at all times, such information as exists, concerning enemy Artillery fire.
> All shelling must be reported at its commencement or as soon after as possible. Officers should not wait to see if it becomes heavy or damaging.
> Reports should be made by telephone direct to the Counter Battery Office – not to the Heavy Artillery – in the following form:
> 1 Time of first round.
> 2 Area shelled.
> 3 Nature of Gun or Howitzer firing.
> 4 Rate of fire.
> 5 Rough sound bearing of report of gun.
> 6 Point from which sound bearing is taken.
> 7 Code word HELP if neutralisation is required. Code word HARMLESS if hostile shells are doing no damage.
>
> 2 All bearings to be Grid Bearings.
>
> 3 It is important to report always when shelling has ceased.

These were reissued on 19 April 1918 with a covering note:

> … information concerning the enemy artillery is specially desired at the present time. This can best be obtained at the moment by a careful analysis of all shelling reports, and it is therefore of first importance that these should be complete.

45 TNA WO95/2303, War Diary of 87 Infantry Brigade, Brigade Communications Circular No. 7, 1 September 1918.

46 The following three extracts are to be found in TNA WO95/2610, War Diary of 120 Infantry Brigade, XV Corps, No. 100/70 G. 13 December 1917; No. 100/84 G. 19/4/1918; No. 100/90 G. 6/9/1918.

> Endeavours must be made that no shelling, whether damage is done or not, passes without being reported to the Counter Battery Officer.

Both sets of instructions were once again reissued at the start of September 1918, with a covering note acknowledging the new circumstances created by the extent of the advances being made by Army forces, and reminding officers of the importance of providing details of enemy artillery fire:

> Attention is directed to [previous instructions] (Copies attached).
> No doubt largely owing to difficulty of communications under existing conditions very few reports of hostile shelling are at present being forwarded by units to the Counter Battery Office. This absence of information handicaps the efforts of the Counter Battery Staff. Additional Heavy Artillery is now being brought forward and it is of the utmost importance that shelling reports should be forwarded as regularly as possible. Every effort should be made to keep the Counter Battery Office fully supplied with information.[47]

It is probably no coincidence that this reminder was being issued only a few weeks before the opening of the Battle of Ypres. Information on the deployment and operation of enemy artillery would be crucial for the development of the artillery fire-plan to support the initial infantry assault and subsequent attacks; and to provide fire cover in defence of the ground gained. While at a practical level it would not be the immediate priority for an officer subject to an artillery barrage to begin writing up details in his notebook (the maintenance of life and limb being foremost in his thinking at such a time), there is no doubt that the central collation of this information would be viewed as of essential value to HQ.

These circumstances would change in due course as the forward advance of Second Army units meant that the location of the front line at any one time became far more fluid. For a number of reasons, intelligence on the location of enemy artillery became a lower priority. The forthcoming campaign would see problems in getting the supporting artillery forward sufficiently quickly to cooperate with new attacks once the initial assault had been launched and early objectives achieved. At the same time enemy artillery positions were facing the prospect of either withdrawing or being overrun. In practice this meant that the locations of both British and German artillery batteries would change far more frequently, albeit for these different reasons. The prospects for successful counter battery pre-planning and firing would be reduced as a consequence.

As the 'war of movement' returned for the British forces, it was a constant priority to ensure that ground claimed following assault was retained. As British forces advanced from previously established defence lines (British or captured German) then arrangements were needed to ensure that the new front could be made secure as quickly as possible. This included operational arrangements to support the infantry in the advance trenches (which could take the form of smaller foxholes, hastily adapted shell holes, or modified strongpoints utilising the terrain or available buildings, or the remains of the latter). The ability of the divisional pioneer battalions

47 TNA WO95/2610, War Diary of 120 Infantry Brigade, XV Corps, No. 100/70 G. 13 December 1917; No. 100/84 G. 19/4/1918; No. 100/90 G. 6/9/1918.

to keep pace with an attack, and to be available for the building of communication works and temporary defences, was an important factor in the securing of captured ground.

On the night of 20-21 August, 6th Battalion, South Wales Borderers (6/South Wales Borderers), the pioneer battalion of 30th Division, supported an operation to attack and secure the line of the Dranoutre Ridge; the pioneers were attached to 2/14th Battalion (London Scottish), London Regiment (2/14 London Scottish) (21 Brigade, 30th Division), under the command of its CO. Reaching the objective by 0250 hours, the troops were then involved in a number of associated tasks including digging in and ‘wiring’ (laying out and fixing barbed wire defence lines) along the advance line; plus ‘consolidating the support line by digging and wiring three strong points’. During these operations the battalion sustained six casualties.[48] The war diary of 2/14 London Scottish recorded that the pioneer battalion had ‘aided materially in the work of consolidation’.[49]

It was also important for front line troops to be able to call for assistance when danger threatened. The following example is from a set of ‘defence orders’ issued to 121 Brigade of 40th Division:

121 Brigade, July 1918 Centre Sector Defence Orders (extract) ***S.O.S. Signals***

1 USE
The signal operates automatically as an order to the Artillery and Machine Guns to lay a barrage in front of our lines, or on the enemy’s lines, to assist the infantry in breaking down an enemy attack.

2 WHEN USED
The signal will only be used when the enemy actually attacks our lines in force, or is undoubtedly about to do so immediately…

3 DEFINITION OF AREA…

4 BY WHOM MADE
The S.O.S call may be sent by any officer, Infantry or Artillery, who has assured himself that [the stated conditions apply]… In very exceptional circumstances, a senior N.C.O. may send an S.O.S. call, but he may not do so if an officer is present or within reasonable distance.

5 The S.O.S. signal can be made in three ways:
a) By signal communications.
b) By S.O.S. light signal.
c) By a series of short blasts on the strombos horn…

48 TNA WO95/2323, War Diary of 6th Battalion, South Wales Borderers, Report on Operations carried out on the night of 20/21 August 1918.
49 TNA WO95/2340, War Diary of 2/14th Battalion (London Scottish), London Regiment.

> [The order continues with precise details of the various signalling arrangements and when and how various units and officers should be informed... conditions for repeat S.O.S. signals... test S.O.S. calls... and for cancelling the S.O.S. fire].[50]

In this epoch of modern warfare when wireless signal communications were in their infancy, such pre-planning for emergency artillery support, as set out in the above extract, was essential. Commanding officers were required to place great emphasis upon maximising the pre-planning of operations. Because of the limitations of communications technology, they recognised that once an action was underway they were restricted in their ability to influence subsequent events. Empowering a junior officer, or an NCO, to signal for a defensive artillery barrage, is indicative of the need to allow such decisions to be taken at the sharp end of the fighting. Such fire support could prove decisive in enabling the advance troops to beat off an enemy attack. This represented a considerable delegation of authority to the junior officer or NCO in the front line. There was an increased acceptance at senior levels of the need for section leaders to exercise initiative. Over the course of the forthcoming advance there would be a corresponding increase in the confidence of commanders in those in charge at the sharp end of the fighting.

In the same division, 23 August saw action by 119 and 120 Brigades, in cooperation with neighbouring units, to 'advance their line by means of strong fighting patrols' with artillery support available if any significant hold-up occurred because of enemy action.[51] The resulting attack was only a partial success and so planning was quickly commenced for a further attempt on 27 August. Artillery support was pre-planned on this occasion with a fire plan to include a creeping barrage to provide cover for the troops during the initial advance; together with a subsequent protective barrage to prevent any immediate counter-attack, and a standing barrage to help secure the left flank of the assault. The second assault met heavy resistance from the German defenders, primarily in the form of heavy machine gun fire, and it took concentrated fighting over the next two days to finally take the objective. On the evening of 28 August there had been a defensive barrage from the German artillery incorporating gas shells, which forced the British troops to put on their respirators (the attack stalling as a consequence). A set-piece attack was then planned and launched on 29 August, again including a creeping barrage, which finally secured the Bowery Cottages objective.

On 25 August, details were received by 105 Brigade (35th Division) of the arrangements for its division to relieve 36th Division in the line (St Jans Cappel sector); the move was completed successfully four days later. That evening the brigade recorded 'fires and explosions in rear of the German lines', which were interpreted as signs of a likely enemy withdrawal.[52] This was confirmed the following day by division, reporting that the Germans did indeed appear to be pulling back, and that 31st Division now held part of Bailleul. Wired reports later that day stated that the enemy was carrying out a measured withdrawal across the whole of what was then the X Corps front, with machine gun teams deployed in order to cover the manoeuvre.[53]

On 31 August, news reached the HQ of 14th Division that the enemy was evacuating the Kemmel area. In consequence patrols were ordered forward, operating in conjunction with 27th

50 TNA WO95/2614, War Diary of 121 Infantry Brigade, Centre Sector Defence Orders, Appendix I.
51 TNA WO95/2610, War Diary of 120 Infantry Brigade.
52 TNA WO95/2486, War Diary of 105 Infantry Brigade.
53 TNA WO95/2486, War Diary of 105 Infantry Brigade.

and 30th American Divisions on the right and 12th Belgian Division on the left. The opportunity was taken to move the division's artillery into more advanced positions. New orders required that the enemy was to be 'pressed' but not 'actually attacked'.[54] 43 Brigade of 14th Division sent forward patrols to check if the enemy was withdrawing and to maintain contact if this was so. The patrols reported that 'the enemy was holding his usual positions in at least normal strength'.[55]

Opposite Second Army, Crown Prince Rupprecht, commander of the German forces from Albert through to the sea, eventually called a halt to the withdrawal, initially securing a line to the east of Ypres, on La Bassée. The enemy continued to hold Messines Ridge and the town of Armentières.

Operations in Flanders

To the west of Armentières, September 1918 saw British Second Army holding a sixteen-mile front from a junction with the River Lys, northwards to just beyond Ypres, where it joined up with the Belgian line. With the breakthrough of the Drocourt-Queant Line by British First Army with Third Army on 2 September 1918, German forces had commenced a general withdrawal across the Western Front, pulling back from ground won during the March and April offensives.[56] As the enemy retired to their front, the early days of September saw the British forces in Flanders continue their methodical pursuit. However the enemy soon started to increase the intensity of its resistance through prepared fire positions and set-piece counter-attacks. The situation is described through a classic piece of military understatement in Second Army's monthly 'Operations Summary':

> Opposition stiffened considerably on the 4th [September] and subsequently, and the reluctance of the enemy to suffer the dislocation of his scheme of defence found frequent expression in counter-attacks. A sturdy opposition has been offered by the troops fronting us, and they have shown no signs of yielding positions of value without fighting. It was with increasing reluctance, from 10th September onwards, that the enemy gave ground, and our rate of progress thenceforward was appreciably lessened.[57]

There is a notable trajectory in the intensity of the fighting, with British troops increasingly required to battle their way forward objective by objective. One of the most difficult aspects of these operations was the unpredictability of the enemy opposition. As a unit advanced it might face no resistance or experience largely harassing fire, or suddenly be confronted by the heavy fire-power of machine gun posts or artillery, or even be on the receiving end of a full scale counter-attack. The psychological pressure which this uncertainty created – as much as the physical risk of injury and death – placed very heavy demands upon the men and their commanders. This 'staccato' pattern of warfare – short advances punctuated by the varying

54 TNA WO95/1876, War Diary of 14th Division: General Staff.
55 TNA, WO95/1905, War Diary of 43 Infantry Brigade.
56 Terraine, *To Win A War*, p. 143.
57 TNA WO158/218, Operations on the Second Army Front: 1st September to 27 September 1918.

forms of enemy resistance and delaying tactics – was to be a distinctive feature of the Final Advance in Flanders.

The follow-up and harassment of the German forces as they carried out their fighting withdrawal during the latter part of August and through September, required Second Army units to proceed carefully and with due preparation. The war diary of 36th Division recorded operations by 108 Brigade from 1-5 September 1918. The record includes references to 'a lot of house-to-house fighting', particularly in Neuve Eglise; and a call made for artillery assistance when 9th Battalion, Royal Inniskilling Fusiliers (9/Royal Inniskilling Fusiliers), was caught by the enemy in an 'exposed forward position'.[58]

On 12 August 1918, 1st Battalion, Lancashire Fusiliers (1/Lancashire Fusiliers) had carried out an operation to advance its forward line by 400 yards and seize a line of trenches east of a point designated as Celery Copse. The fierce fighting which resulted, the strength of the enemy defence and its subsequent counter-attack, led to battalion casualties of over 80 soldiers killed or wounded. The battalion's war diary remarked that 'This operation, though costly, established the position of the enemy's main line of resistance, which was required by higher authority'.[59]

On 30 August, 2nd Battalion, Royal Inniskilling Fusiliers (2/Royal Inniskilling Fusiliers), deployed on the right of 109 Brigade (36th (Ulster) Division), passed on a report to brigade HQ that the Germans (118th Regiment) were undertaking a withdrawal. There had been some anticipation of this the previous night, following a number of fires south and east of Ballieul, sight of an enemy working party, and defensive covering fire from German machine guns. The origin of the report was 94 Brigade (31st Division), on the right flank of the Fusiliers, which had already set in motion an advance by its troops in response. To the left was 89 Brigade (30th Division). Scout patrols were sent forward by 109 Brigade, each one with an attached Stokes Mortar. Despite some defensive machine gun fire, there was overall progress forward during the day across the divisional fronts.[60]

This was considered to be a part of a carefully planned operation by the Germans:

> Definite information could not be gathered regarding the intention of the enemy but from situation reports he was thought to be fighting a rearguard action according to a definite plan as his withdrawal up to the time had been methodical and not hurried.[61]

The next day saw further advances by British forces including Kemmel Hill and the village of Ravelsberg. Each of the forward battalions had a machine gun section attached plus a unit of field guns deployed in support. An artillery officer was available in order to call for covering fire or to direct fire onto an enemy strongpoint as circumstances required. In the event, the poor state of the roads impeded the progress of the artillery. The resistance of the Germans increased, with light shelling of the high ground and fire from machine gun posts; the village of La Crèche was particularly strongly held. The advancing soldiers found that the ground south of the ridges

58 TNA WO95/2492, War Diary of 36th Division.
59 TNA WO95/2300, War Diary of 1st Battalion, Lancashire Fusiliers.
60 TNA WO95/2509, War Diary of 109 Infantry Brigade, Summary of Operations (30 August-1 September).
61 TNA WO95/2504, War Diary of 108 Infantry Brigade, Report of Operations carried out by 108th Infantry Brigade 1st to 5 September.

was quite open with any movement easily visible. In spite of this some limited progress was possible along the Ravelsberg Road and, in the evening, along Waterloo Road.[62] In accordance with orders from 36th Division, during 1-2 September, 108 Brigade moved through 109 Brigade, heading in the direction of Neuve Eglise, in order to sustain the momentum of the advance and continue to press the retreating enemy forces. Light mortars, machine guns and also a section of cyclists and a section from a tunnelling company, were attached to the brigade to support the operation.[63]

On 1 September, units of 29th Division had moved up into the space created on the right of 36th Division, with 30th Division remaining on the left. The problems of crossing open ground once troops had occupied the various ridges still persisted. A number of casualties resulted, including the intelligence officer of 109 Brigade killed by a shell, and the CO, Lieutenant-Colonel J Knott, of 2/Royal Inniskilling Fusiliers severely wounded. Progress was made in the direction of Neuve Eglise such that a new line was established east of the village by dusk; linking north along the Neuve Eglise–Kemmel road, and south west of La Crèche.[64]

On 2 September, 41 Brigade was in the line for 14th Division. Reports were received that:

> … the enemy might withdraw his line owing to his having relinquished Mount KEMMEL. This necessitated sending out strong patrols day and night in order to locate the enemy's position. [There was] No change in enemy's positions.[65]

Elsewhere on the front, at dawn on 2 September, despite enemy machine gun fire, the advance battalions of 108 Brigade (36th Division) – 12/Royal Irish Rifles and 1/Royal Irish Fusiliers – moved forward in the direction of the Neuve Eglise – Nieppe road. There was some fierce fighting for the possession of a small number of houses in the area, these only being cleared with the assistance of supporting mortar fire. Beyond this point the British troops, including forces from 89 Brigade to the south, ran into intense machine gun fire from the Germans. The advance now paused here to take stock. The priority was to clear Neuve Eglise, with 12/Royal Irish Rifles tasked to advance from north west of the village. The result was 'stiff house-to-house fighting' and the step by step clearance of enemy machine gun positions, causing the fighting to continue over the next few days.[66] These were very different challenges from those presented by the trench warfare familiar to the more experienced soldiers.

The need for artillery support for particular operations remained a priority throughout. The subsequent report by 108 Brigade, extracts of which are contained in the following table, illustrated the nature of the advance; from its record one can visualise the street by street, house by house, fighting progress of the infantry – familiar images perhaps but ones usually associated with the urban combat of a later war.

62 TNA WO95/2509, War Diary of 109 Infantry Brigade, Summary of Operations (30 August-1 September).
63 TNA WO95/2504, War Diary of 108 Infantry Brigade, Report of Operations carried out by 108th Infantry Brigade 1-5 September.
64 TNA WO95/2509, War Diary of 109 Infantry Brigade, Summary of Operations (30 August-1 September).
65 TNA WO95/1894/6, War Diary of 41 Infantry Brigade.
66 TNA WO95/2504, War Diary of 108 Infantry Brigade, Report of Operations carried out by 108th Infantry Brigade 1-5 September.

108 Brigade 1-5 September 1918 (1) *Report of Operations* (extract)

2 September, from 1230 hours]

[orders]... to seize LA THORPE CAB. and make good the house...and houses...

The enemy still stubbornly held on to their line in the houses on roadway... a frontal attack on this line with artillery support was organised...

An attack was [successfully] carried out by 88th Inf. Bde. on the Right at 3.45 p.m...

At 4 p ... 12th R.I.Rifles... attacked under cover of an artillery barrage... Heavy M. G. fire from the direction of ENGLISH LINES... interfered with this little operation. Ground was gained however and the attackers by a very good effort reached the line of the track...

At 8 p.m. 12th R.I.Rifles pushed forward. The Centre & Left Coys. were ordered to take the objective [described as 'the old GHQ line', east of Neuve Eglise] by working round the North of the Line held by the enemy along roadway... to the South. These Coys. were able to get close to the G.H.Q. line opposite their objective without much opposition. The G.H.Q. line was found to be strongly held by the enemy. Sharp fighting ensued & it took some time to dislodge the enemy from these positions.

The Right Coy. 12th R.I.Rif. pushed forward at the same time... The enemy still held the houses on this Road with M.Gs In the dark the troops managed to get to close quarters with the enemy who put up a stubborn resistance. Hand to hand fighting took place until the houses were finally cleared. Most of the teams of the M.Gs. were killed and 2 heavy and 2 Light M.Gs were captured.

At 10-30 p.m. 1st. R. Irish Fusrs. made a night advance to capture the G.H.Q. line opposite their front. Very little resistance was met on this flank.

108 Brigade 1-5 September 1918 (2) *Report of Operations* (extract)

At 6.40 a.m. [3 September] the Brigade objective along the old G.H.Q. line was in our hands...

At 6.41 a.m. [90 Brigade on the left] reported that their advanced troops had reached WULVERGHEM from the North...

At 9.30 a.m. 12th R. Irish Rifles. and 1st R. Irish Fusrs. advanced... Heavy M.G. fire... The houses and hedges in several places on the immediate front were also held by enemy M.Gs.

The advance developed into a series of sharp encounters with enemy M.Gs. which were tackled separately.

Each post was dealt with first of all [by] bringing fire to bear on them with our Lewis Guns & Vickers guns from the flank and then rushing them with the bayonet...

1st R. Irish Fusrs. on left advanced in artillery formation [and] made rapid progress until reaching the roadway... when front [company] gained touch with the enemy and came under heavy fire from enemy M.Gs. and artillery.

Coy. at once opened out into extended order. The advance then continued slowly. Each platoon advanced supported by covering fire from the remainder. By this means the enemy were forced to retire from their forward positions.[67]

Over the course of the next two days the chasing down of the German retirement was maintained, in the face of an increasing strength in the resistance offered. Fierce fighting saw British troops counter-attacked on occasions and forced to withdraw temporarily. When necessary, 'Artillery assistance was called and promptly given'. At times touch was lost between the forward elements of one or more of the brigades involved in the operation, and the circumstances facing the advance troops became very fluid. The relief of 108 Brigade by 107 Brigade (also from 36th Division) was completed at 1430 hours on 6 September, when the former was withdrawn into divisional reserve. The determination of the German defenders to carry out an effective fighting withdrawal, and the resulting intensity of the fighting that the attacking forces were engaged in, is illustrated by the casualty figures. During the five day series of actions, 108 Brigade sustained over 400 casualties across its three battalions:[68]

108 Brigade: Casualties 1-5 September 1918

	Killed		**Wounded**		**Missing**	
	Officers	**Other Ranks**	**Officers**	**Other Ranks**	**Officers**	**Other Ranks**
108 Bde				1		
12/R I Rifles	2	26	4	103		6
1/R I Fusiliers		22	4	95		9
9/R I Fusiliers		20	4	103		19
108 T M Batt				1		
Totals	2	68	12	303		34

67 TNA WO95/2504, War Diary of 108 Infantry Brigade, Report of Operations carried out by 108th Infantry Brigade 1-5 September.
68 TNA WO95/2504, War Diary of 108 Infantry Brigade, Report of Operations carried out by 108th Infantry Brigade 1-5 September.

The progress of the advance, the nature of the fighting and the tactics employed by both sides, gave the troops some experience of what they would face in the forthcoming campaign to liberate Flanders. What I have described as the 'staccato' rhythm of the advance, as advancing units paused to allow for artillery support, the passing through of fresh troops, or for assistance from forces on the flanks, (or in the face of deteriorating weather conditions, not a factor in this example) is a repeating feature of the combat throughout this final period.

The report of 108 Brigade for 1-5 September also included, as was common practice, an analysis of the operations. This included praise for the support from the machine gun company which had been organised with one machine gun section attached to each battalion, an arrangement which had 'worked very well'. The company's OC had been based at brigade HQ together with one machine gun section acting as reserve. In conclusion the guns had been deployed very quickly when needed and ammunition supply had been carried out efficiently.[69] In addition an artillery liaison officer was attached to the brigade which had 'proved very useful'. The delivery of a protective barrage had been arranged successfully when troops were halted for a length of time; there had also been useful harassing fire when called upon. The report added the suggestion that a 'sniping' field gun attached to each battalion 'would have proved useful' – perhaps a reflection of an infantryman's innate attraction to having direct firing artillery alongside him whenever possible. The brigade identified some valuable prerequisites to maximise the effectiveness of such an arrangement:

> The use of the gun would of course depend on conditions. The conditions from an infantry point of view were thought to be very good on this occasion. I think a certain amount of preliminary training is necessary before a gun is employed in this way and it is absolutely essential that perfect liaison should exist between the Battn. Commander & the officer i/c of the gun, if the gun is to prove of any use.[70]

Each battalion had also had one trench mortar attached to it; the gun was deployed in the relatively new 'mobile' manner – with only the mortar tube, its body bed plate and ammunition being carried forward by the troops. The report commented that this was the first time that the brigade troops had operated with the trench mortar used in this way, 'and probably had teams been better trained the results would have been far better':

> Teams require to be well trained and a capable officer is needed to handle the section and control the gun. The general use of the 'mobile' L.T.M. can be developed with advantage. Its power when used to the full should prove the gun a very effective weapon and a valuable asset in this kind of warfare.[71]

69 TNA WO95/2504, War Diary of 108 Infantry Brigade, Report of Operations carried out by 108th Infantry Brigade 1-5 September.
70 TNA WO95/2504, War Diary of 108 Infantry Brigade, Report of Operations carried out by 108th Infantry Brigade 1-5 September.
71 TNA WO95/2504, War Diary of 108 Infantry Brigade, Report of Operations carried out by 108th Infantry Brigade 1-5 September.

A tunnelling section had accompanied the advance, for the purpose of searching and clearing captured dug-outs. As was becoming a more common feature following enemy withdrawals, the section discovered a number of booby traps left by the retreating German soldiers, all of which were made safe and removed. Supplies of rations and water, and ammunition, to advanced troops had been successfully provided, though it was noted that the good conditions of the roads during this operation had been an important factor in this. This would not always be the case in the future.

The report also referred to the ongoing problem of communications, caused in part through this more open warfare which the advancing forces were being required to wage. As already noted, the technology of communications had not kept pace so far with the advanced developments in weaponry. Hence the plethora of methods used – adopting a form of 'belt and braces' approach on the basis that at least one method would be successful – for conveying messages between HQ advance bases, central HQ and its subordinate units, and with the advance units in the field. In this operation the liaison with flanking brigades had not been good; the telephone lines had been used so frequently that there had often been difficulty in 'getting through'. Other means of communication had been 'seldom used' or not practicable. However there was no obvious solution available as the report concludes:

> A better liaison with flank Brigades would have proved most useful at times during the operation. The only solution appears to be that flank Brigades should be 'united' where possible. It is realised that there are difficulties in the way especially when Divisions are operating on a one Brigade Front.[72]

On 4 and 5 September, 86 Brigade, with 1/Lancashire Fusiliers and 1/Royal Dublin Fusiliers leading, was part of a number of attacks undertaken by 29th Division (alongside 36th Division, attacking Neuve Eglise); the brigade's principal targets were the village of Ploegsteert and the adjacent Ploegsteert Wood. On its left, 88 Brigade attacked the objective of Hill 63, with 2nd Battalion, The Hampshire Regiment (2/Hampshires), on the left and 2nd Battalion, The Leinster Regiment (2/Leinster Regiment), on the right. It was a 'brilliant hot day' with an early mist providing valuable cover for the attacking troops, though it caused some problems for the artillery. Despite a number of German counter-attacks the objectives were taken and held, but with a large number of casualties.

On the night of 4 September, 1/Royal Dublin Fusiliers advanced east of Ploegsteert. The acting commander of 86 Brigade, in a letter praising the subsequent performance of the troops 'under very trying circumstances', expressed his sadness at 'the heavy losses that the Lancashire Fusiliers and Royal Dublin Fusiliers sustained'; while acknowledging that the action had led to the capture of '160 odd prisoners and many machine guns and trench mortars'.[73]

72 TNA WO95/2504, War Diary of 108 Infantry Brigade, Report of Operations carried out by 108th Infantry Brigade 1-5 September.

73 TNA WO95/2300, War Diary of 1st Battalion, Lancashire Fusiliers, letter 86th Inf. Bde. No. 5c.C/21 from Staff Captain C. Barrington Brown; TNA WO95/2307/4, War Diary of 88 Infantry Brigade, 88th Infantry Brigade Order No. 199, 3 September 1918; TNA WO95/2285, War Diary of 29th Division.

The initial orders for the operation had specified the objectives as Hill 63 and Ploegsteert village;[74] prisoner statements had identified these points as part of the German army's line of resistance within its planned withdrawal and the defenders were ordered 'to hold it at all costs'. The cover of an artillery barrage was arranged for the assault, with the two attacking brigades (86 and 88), each deploying two advance battalions with the remaining battalion in reserve. There were initial problems overnight when enemy forces were encountered along the roadway identified as the 'jumping off' point: only the 1/Lancashire Fusiliers (86 Brigade) managed to secure their portion of the road, and to hold onto this despite a counter-attack before dawn. 88 Brigade withdrew 500 yards to allow for a 12 minute barrage of enemy forces along the road; then proceeded to follow the barrage, encountering only limited resistance at first. Subsequently the troops met artillery fire from the western slopes of Hill 63, plus enfilade machine gun fire from the south. The assault was pushed home by 2/Hampshires and 2/Leinsters, despite the defenders' fire and encountering large amounts of wire. Two subsequent counter-attacks were beaten off with little difficulty.

For 86 Brigade, the artillery preparation had concentrated on predicted centres of enemy resistance, rather than providing a covering barrage. The Lancashire Fusiliers, from its starting line, had successfully advanced along the left flank of the attack. On its right, 1/Royal Dublin Fusiliers was facing heavy machine gun fire to both its front and from its right flank; it was therefore decided to delay its assault until 1500 hours, pending the cover of an artillery barrage. In the event the battalion advanced such that it was able to secure a line east of Ploegsteert. It was relieved by 2/Royal Fusiliers, who drove off a counter- attack upon its right flank at noon on the following day. The right company of the Lancashire Fusiliers was halted short of the village but by 1100 hours on 5 September it too had reached its objective.

In its concluding remarks on the operation, the division's summary notes that the success owed much to the initiative and leadership on the ground of the company and platoon commanders. The artillery barrage was delivered as 'a map shoot' without preparation (most of the guns had only moved into position on the evening of 3 September); the infantry also received valuable covering fire from machine guns and mortars (particularly important in tackling enemy machine gun posts).[75] This example of Second Army operations during September illustrates the potential strength of the German resistance once the latter was committed to holding a defensive line. Such strength in defence does not support comments that by this stage of the war the enemy's capabilities had been reduced. While the Germans may no longer have had the capacity to mount major offensive operations they were able to carry out defensive actions in strength. What these operations by Second Army also show is that its units were becoming more confident in the art of attack and in their ability to sustain or remount assaults, successfully combining arms to achieve identified objectives.

On 6 September the CO of 29th Division, Major-General D. Cayley, wrote to all his immediate subordinate commanders in order to 'congratulate all ranks of the Division on their

74 The British Tommy's celebrated 'Plugstreet Wood'.
75 TNA WO95/2285, War Diary of 29th Division, Report on Operations by 29th Division on 4 September 1918.

excellent work during the last seven days, while following up the retreating enemy'.[76] In his letter he made particular reference to:

- The advance by 87 Brigade to capture La Creche, Steenwerck and Nieppw
- The attack by 88 and 86 Brigades (4 September) to secure Hill 63 and Ploegsteert;
- The 'skilful co-operation' between the artillery and the infantry, with the assistance of the Division's Machine Gun Battalion
- The setting up and maintenance of communications by Signals
- The work of Engineer and Pioneer sections in repairing and maintaining roads and bridges, allowing the supply of the large quantities of the ammunition required
- The good organisation of the Field Ambulances.

This last point is important to note, given the high number of casualties that were sustained in a relatively short period of time; even though the soldiers were pursuing an enemy that was carrying out a withdrawal rather than defending an established line of defence. The following table provides details:

29th Division: Casualties 3-5 September 1918

	Killed		Wounded		Missing	
	Officers	**Other Ranks**	**Officers**	**Other Ranks**	**Officers**	**Other Ranks**
86 B[de]	3	45	12	175	1	24
88 B[de]	4	57	10	309		17
1/2 Monmouth (Pioneers)				2		
29th Machine Gun		7	1	34		1
Totals	7	109	23	520	1	42

These figures, over one hundred soldiers killed and five times that number wounded, during a three day period, indicate the continuing determination of the German resistance and their intention to maintain an orderly withdrawal having pulled back from the Lys Salient. The preparation and tactics employed by the division, while drawn up at short notice, evidence sensible and careful planning. The resulting casualties do not appear to result from faulty work at command or staff level. 29th Division was the one former regular army division within Second Army.

Another example of the developing expertise of Second Army units, particularly regarding small scale infantry tactics and the co-operation with artillery support, was an operation carried out by 93 Brigade on 18 September. The attack was designed to capture Soyer Farm in the area east of Ploegsteert, thereby allowing the line to be advanced towards a stretch of the River

76 TNA WO95/2285, War Diary of 29th Division, letter 29th Division No. G.S. 51/14 from Major-General D Cayley.

Warnave. Two companies from each of the two battalions, 15/West Yorkshires (operating on the left) and 13/York and Lancaster (operating on the right), were involved. It subsequently transpired, from prisoner interviews and evidence on the ground – which included the presence of enemy pioneer troops with mobile charges – that the Germans had themselves been intending to carry out a raid on 93 Brigade positions. They had become concerned at the proximity of the British advance posts and the raid was intended to provide greater security for the defenders at the farm. Overall, the fact that the Germans in that area were planning operations to improve their defensive position, suggests that their intention at that time was to resist actively any assault on their positions; and steps would be taken where possible to disrupt any preparations regarding this.[77]

The attack by 93 Brigade was a complete success. In addition to the capture of the farm, 59 prisoners were taken and heavy enemy casualties (from 186 and 118 Infantry Regiments and 118 (Pioneer) Regiment) resulted. The brigade suffered 75 casualties of which 30 men were killed. Soyer Farm had been protected with large concentrations of wire, and heavily defended, particularly to the north and west. Thus the aim of the plan was to get troops around the flanks and able to strike at the rear of the farm, where defences were relatively weaker. Sketch maps were drawn to show the deployment and manoeuvres for each platoon involved in the attack. In the event, although the farm seemed 'to have been held abnormally strongly [reflecting the Germans' intentions] to attack [British positions] at about the same time that [the attack by 93 Brigade] was launched',[78] the operation appears to have been carried out with minimal problems and in accordance with the plans prepared by the brigade and battalion commands.

The key elements of the operation included:

- Incorporation of a machine gun barrage within the covering fire support
- Enemy outposts to the east of the farm to be subject to a standing barrage throughout the operation
- The creeping barrage to cover the attack:

  ... instead of moving forward on parallel lines was pivoted on the farm and moved fanwise, thus ensuring that the farm and enclosures remained under fire until the attacking force had reached a position in rear of it. This barrage then lifted and joined the standing barrage whereupon the attacking troops at once rushed the farm from the rear.
- The soldiers were equipped in full 'fighting order':
  - Full water bottle, one day's rations plus Iron Rations
  - Each man carried
    - 2 No. 36 Rifle Grenades
    - 1 Flare
  - Each Rifle Grenadier carried
    - 5 No. 36 Rifle Grenades

77 The details of this operation and its execution are taken from: TNA WO95/2360, War Diary of 93 Infantry Brigade: Brief Report of Operation carried out by 93rd Infantry Brigade on Morning of 18 September 1918; 13th York and Lancaster Regiment, [Summary of] Attack on Soyer Farm 18 September 1918; Narrative of Operations carried out by the 15th Battalion West Yorkshire Regiment in the Left Battalion, Left Division, Ploegsteert Sector from the 13-18 September, 1918.

78 TNA WO95/2360, War Diary of 93 Infantry Brigade, 13th York and Lancaster Regiment, [Summary of] Attack on Soyer Farm 18 September 1918.

        - 12 Cartridges
    - Each Lewis Gun carried
        - 18 L.G. Pans
    - Each Platoon carried
        - 2 pairs of Wire Cutters
        - 2 Day S.O.S. Grenades
        - 2 Night S.O.S. Grenades
        - 4 R.G. Discharger Cups
        - 1 Very Pistol
        - 12 Rounds 7 P.A.
        - 5 Shovels
- The value of the No. 36 Rifle Grenade in providing additional firepower on the ground was noted.
  [Rifle Grenades] were employed with great effect against M.G. posts which attempted to put up a fight.[79]

Zero hour was 0530 hours and the light signal to indicate the capture of the farm was observed at 0638 hours.

The method of attack and its successful execution show the level of detailed planning of which some Second Army units were now capable. This was to be essential in the forthcoming campaign, enabling the mix of new and experienced troops to deploy successfully on the battlefield. There is evidence of innovation and creativity in the delivery of the artillery support, and the infantry demonstrated a confidence in the ability of the artillery to provide the planned barrage efficiently; this co-operation between the two arms allowed the troops on the ground to carry out their actions in an organised and effective manner. The tactics of the advancing infantry, the use of Lewis guns and rifle grenades, all point to a doctrine of 'fire and movement' with which the troops were becoming familiar.

One point of post operation criticism concerned the lack of photographs of the target and the surrounding area. The report on the attack pointed out that 'Most of the men and nearly all N.C.O.'s are now capable of appreciating a photograph, and explanation is much assisted by their use'.[80] This comment indicates the positive view which commanding officers held of the soldiers they led, and their confidence in the men's abilities; it also shows how the application of aerial photography was now considered to be an integral part of operations at all levels within the army. This increase in expectations regarding the initiative of NCOs and the private soldier was demonstrated to be well-placed as illustrated by a practical example of initiative in command and control during the operation:

79 TNA WO95/2360, War Diary of 93 Infantry Brigade, 13th York and Lancaster Regiment, [Summary of] Attack on Soyer Farm 18 September 1918.
80 TNA WO95/2360, War Diary of 93 Infantry Brigade, 13th York and Lancaster Regiment, [Summary of] Attack on Soyer Farm 18 September 1918.

> The importance of practising chain of command was also made clear. One platoon lost its Officer and all senior N.C.O.'s and was commanded with success by a young Lance Corporal assisted by a Senior Private.[81]

The success of the operation was sealed with rum:

> A rum ration for each Platoon was sent forward in water bottles and issued to the men when consolidation was well advanced. This was much appreciated by the men and did them good.[82]

However good the planning, there was always the prospect of the local geography and climate undermining the best laid schemes. There were three particular features of Flanders which impacted on operations and would influence the forthcoming offensives:

1 The notorious Flanders weather. This was able to produce stifling dry heat on one day, yet change to torrential rain within twenty-four hours. The consequences for the advancing forces would be considerable – and referred to regularly in contemporary writings and in the *Official History*.

> [27 July 1918]
> Inspection by Divisional Commander cancelled owing to rain.
> [Rearranged for, and carried out on 29 July][83]
> [6 August 1918]
> Rain fell continuously until Dawn, and trenches are very muddy and uncomfortable.[84]

2 The variable weather exacerbated the transport problems created by the poor quality of the roads in the area. Sustaining supply lines, and in particular the bringing forward of artillery support for advancing forces, had been a major factor throughout the war. This undermined the ability of troops on either side, to maintain the momentum of an advance; to convert a *breakthrough* into a *breakout*. This would be the main challenge facing the coalition force as the offensive progressed.

3 The Flanders terrain was divided by a series of rivers, generally running north to south, which created a succession of natural defensive lines.

> The partially canalised River Lys bisected the area, running west then south-west from Ghent to Armentières via Menin some 15-20 yards wide and 5-6 feet deep

81 TNA WO95/2360, War Diary of 93 Infantry Brigade, 13th York and Lancaster Regiment, [Summary of] Attack on Soyer Farm 18 September 1918.
82 TNA WO95/2360, War Diary of 93 Infantry Brigade, 13th York and Lancaster Regiment, [Summary of] Attack on Soyer Farm 18 September 1918.
83 TNA WO95/1765, War Diary of 7th Battalion, Seaforth Highlanders.
84 TNA WO95/1767, War Diary of 5th Battalion, Cameron Highlanders.

> and passable only by bridges. There was also a network of other canals originally constructed both for communication and defence, while numerous streams like the Steenbeck, Stroombeek and Kornebeek,and willow-lined dykes intersected the plain, fed by springs at the junction of the permeable sands and the impermeable clay. The Yser Canal connected to the Lys at Comines.[85]

These were important planning considerations for the advancing forces, impacting on transport, communications and logistics. Mitchinson, writing about the experiences of the Pioneer Battalions on the Western Front, has pointed out the additional problems in building railways and laying roads within the region of Flanders.[86]

The changed nature of the fighting as Second Army advanced would also be reflected in changes in the nature of the terrain. Much of the initial ground regained was pitted by the detritus of battles previously fought and the enduring pock marks of no man's land. As new ground was reached then different challenges could present themselves. On 5 July 1918 the following order was issues to units of 121 Brigade:

> Amendment No. 4 to 121st Infantry Brigade Instructions No. 2:
>
> No.2 of each Lewis Gun will go forward with two sandbags tucked into the belt. When necessary these sandbags are to be filled and used to raise the tripod so as to enable the guns to be fired over standing crops.[87]

While at first reading this statement may seem self-evident it does illustrate two important points – about the soldiers, and the battlefield terrain. The most obvious reason for the instruction was a likely reaction to the fresh composition of much of the brigade's troops, such that orders were required to ensure that small levels of detail in weapon handling were known and complied with. The other more general item to note is the reference to 'standing crops' – it is highly unlikely that experienced troops on the Western Front would have had cause to manoeuvre or fight in terrain still covered with crops, whether standing or otherwise, for a period of years. One feature of the new context for the fighting to come would be cultivated farmland (and also the people responsible for the cultivation).

The Commander

Second Army had been formed in France in December 1914, initially commanded by Sir Horace Smith-Dorrien. Sir Herbert Plumer assumed command of V Corps at Christmas 1914, subsequently replacing Smith-Dorrien as C-in-C of Second Army in May 1915 during the fighting of Second Ypres.

From the start Plumer developed a reputation for success via careful planning, effective support and preparation, of which there was strong evidence during the Final Advance

85 Beckett, *Ypres: The First Battle,* p. 43; also reference TNA WO95/668, 'Notes on the River Lys'.
86 K. W. Mitchinson, *Pioneer Battalions in the Great War: Organized and Intelligent Labour* (Barnsley: Pen & Sword Military, 2014), pp. 116-7 (railways) and 130-2 (roads)
87 TNA WO95/2614, War Diary of 121 Infantry Brigade.

in Flanders.[88] The regular availability of drinking water, and the ready provision of food and supplies for units in action, are both examples of the importance he attached to effective material support for the front-line troops. Organisation and logistics were a high priority. He set great store by the co-ordination of artillery fire-plans, the planned preparation of defensive positions, and the drawing-up of operational plans to cope with emergencies. Army HQ liaison officers were attached to each Corps, charged with getting to know each of the Corps battalions and spending time in the trenches with their troops. Training was seen as a vital tool and troops were released as often as opportunity would allow.

Joseph E Persico summarises the outward appearance of Plumer as being deceptively suggestive of:

> ... a caricature of the British armchair officer, an early incarnation of Colonel Blimp. The sixty-year-old was squat, pot-bellied, jowly, chinless, with a veinous red face, snow-white hair, and a matching mustache. The comic appearance, however, belied the man. Plumer's manner lacked fire, but he was a meticulous planner, not without imagination, and unflappable under the severest pressure. His men trusted him implicitly and felt genuine affection for their commander, calling him 'Daddy'.[89]

An early example of Plumer's considered approach to command and his preference for careful planning is his response to the creation of pioneer battalions in 1915. He disagreed with the simple expedient of identifying one existing unit to be converted to a division's pioneer battalion,

> ... preferring instead the idea that divisional commanders should be allowed to build up a Pioneer unit. Such a formation should, he suggested, begin with a small establishment and then be gradually expanded by the transfer of officers and men within their divisions.[90]

Second Army held part of the front in Flanders and Plumer became directly associated with that area for the period of the war. During winter 1916, his staff produced four training manuals, looking to take account of the lessons from Arras and the Somme. He achieved the success for which he is most noted on 7 June 1917 with the attack on Messines, 'one of the completest victories of the war'.[91] Although initially overlooked by Haig for the subsequent Third Ypres (Passchendaele) offensive, despite commanding continuously in the area since 1915, he took over responsibility after the failures of August 1917. Applying the concept of 'bite and hold',

88 The sources for this section on Plumer include G. Powell, *Plumer: The Soldiers' General: A Biography of Field-Marshal Viscount Plumer of Messines* (Pen & Sword, 2004); T. Harington, *Plumer of Messines* (London: John Murray, 1935); J. Terraine, *The Western Front 1914-1918* (London: Hutchinson, 1964) (Barnsley: Pen & Sword, 2003); P. Simkins, 'Herbert Plumer' in I. F. W. Beckett & S. J. Corvi, ed., *Haig's Generals* (Barnsley: Pen & Sword, 2006) – which provides an excellent summary biography; websites: The Long, Long Trail <www.1914-1918.net>; The Trench <www.worldwar1.com>.

89 J. E. Persico, *11th Month, 11th Day, 11th Hour: Armistice day, 1918 – World War I and its Violent Climax* (London: Hutchinson, 2004), pp. 168-9.

90 K. W. Mitchinson, *Pioneer Battalions in the Great War: Organized and Intelligent Labour* (Barnsley: Pen & Sword Military, 2014; first published by Barnsley: Leo Cooper, 1997), pp. 58-9; the author points out that Plumer's advice was not always heeded.

91 Terraine, *The Western Front.*

he planned, fought and won three consecutive battles – Menin Road Ridge, Polygon Wood and Broodseinde.[92] The results of two subsequent actions with II Anzac Corps at the start of October 1917, Poelcappelle and First Passchendaele, were less successful and more controversial. Following the winning of Passchendaele Ridge with Canadian forces in November, the infamous Flanders' weather led to Haig calling a halt to the actions. The Second Army staff then moved to Italy with General Plumer between 13 November 1917 and 17 March 1918 (during which time Fourth Army was re-titled Second Army, reverting back in March 1918); where Plumer assumed command of the British forces deployed to support the Italian army, following the calamitous defeat of the latter at Caporetto. He was 'as shocked and 'sick' to be sent to Italy… as Haig was to see him depart'.[93]

Plumer arrived back in Flanders on 13 March 1918, his sixty-first birthday, together with most of his staff. Haig had negotiated his return – 'a great satisfaction to me to have you again at the head of an Army here'[94] – plus two British divisions, in return for agreeing to release General Rawlinson to Versailles (a consequence of the ongoing attrition between Haig and the British government over issues of BEF command and troop supply).

In response to the crisis caused by the German spring 1918 offensive, which opened on 21 March, it was Plumer who made the unconditional offer of a transfer of additional troops from the Second Army front, including four Australian divisions and the New Zealand division, plus a full strength British division. Haig recorded in his diary on 23 March 1918:

> I arranged with Plumer to thin down his front; then I shall be glad to see the divisions thus set free near the Somme! It is most satisfactory to have a Commander of Plumer's temperament at a time of crisis like the present.[95]

This view represented a major re-evaluation of Plumer from Haig's initial judgement, made shortly after the latter assumed the full command of the BEF.[96]

In exchange for the troops redeployed from Flanders, it was agreed with the Belgians that they would slightly extend their frontage. Exhausted divisions from the southern fighting were now to be transferred north to Second Army as an opportunity to recuperate on what had been up to that stage a quieter front. (This would have further repercussions as events unfolded.) All but three of Second Army's divisions were moved to the south, replaced by divisions who had suffered up to 70 per cent or more casualties during the first German offensive. Replacements largely comprised 19-year olds with a minimum of training and existing soldiers previously considered short of the A1 frontline requirements; plus returnees recovered from wounds. New

92 Prior and Wilson, in their assessment of Passchendaele (R. Prior and T. Wilson, *Passchendaele: The Untold Story* (New Haven: Yale University Press, 1996)), are more critical of Plumer than has previously been the case, arguing, from their analysis, that his achievements were more in line with previous commander Gough's results and that he benefited greatly from improved weather conditions; this view contrasts sharply with Terraine's praise of Plumer and with the conclusions drawn by Simkins.
93 Simkins, 'Herbert Plumer', p. 147.
94 Harington, *Plumer*, p. 147.
95 Sheffield, G. D. and Bourne, J. eds., *Douglas Haig: War Diaries and Letters 1914-1918* (London: Wiedenfeld & Nicolson, 2005), p. 391.
96 On 18 February 1916, Haig had criticised Second Army defences and Plumer had offered his resignation – see Haig's diary note in Sheffield and Bourne, *Haig Diaries and Letters*, pp. 180.

command teams were being hastily put together alongside the gradual replacement of lost or destroyed equipment and weapons.

On 9 April the German 'Georgette' offensive was launched against Horne's Third Army on the right of Second Army. Plumer's willingness to put the overall strategic priorities ahead of his own circumstances saw him immediately agree to move two of his three remaining full strength divisions to cover Third Army.

The following day, 10 April, the Germans extended their attack northwards in a drive towards the railway interchange of Hazebrouck, and around the Ypres salient. The bitter rearguard defensive actions are well documented.[97] The gravity of the position is evidenced by Haig's 'Backs to the Wall' order issued on 11 April. Plumer's actions as commander included daily visits to every divisional HQ and also some brigade HQs – a clear sign of his desire to provide tangible leadership and personal support to his officers. His experience also saw him taking charge of additional French troops sent as reinforcements. He did however have to take the undoubtedly hard – but tactically correct – decision to concede ground beyond the Ypres Salient in April, as part of a planned withdrawal to create a shorter and more defensible line (as described in the Prologue of this book). Around this time Harington is reported to have informed his commander that his Second Army was broken into three pieces; 'Well that is better than being in four' was Plumer's reply.[98] True British stiff upper lip!

In his biography of Plumer, Powell draws the conclusion that this was a battle that had to be won if the military credibility of the British forces on the Western Front – and their very purpose on the continent – was to be preserved:

> If Plumer's depleted divisions had failed to prevent that German breakthrough to the Channel ports, the war would almost certainly have been lost.[99]

In a recent history of 1918, referring to the defensive battles of April that year, David Stevenson observed that 'The British were… fortunate in their Second Army commander, Sir Herbert Plumer [who] ran an efficient headquarters'.[100]

Plumer was subsequently to take advantage of local German withdrawals in August to begin to reclaim the ground conceded. Through a series of small actions, the Second Army advanced slowly forward, and the Lys Salient had been cleared by 7 September.

Much of Plumer's success has been attributed to his Chief of Staff (and subsequent biographer) Major-General 'Tim' Harington, who had served with Plumer since June 1916. Summarising Plumer's career, Peter Simkins has written that Harington had a 'special bond' with Plumer which 'was an indispensable ingredient in Second Army's success in 1917'.[101] It was a successful partnership, perhaps the most effective of the war on the allied side, between CinC and MGGS.[102] Yet it ended before the final phase of the war. After the stalling of the German

97 For a recent summary of the German offensives including 'Georgette' see Stevenson, *With Our Backs To The Wall*, chapter 1 and particularly pp. 68-78.
98 Powell, *Plumer*, p. 264.
99 Powell, *Plumer*, p. 266.
100 Stevenson, *Backs To The Wall*, p. 74.
101 Simkins, 'Herbert Plumer', p. 148.
102 Harington had the sincerest respect and admiration for Plumer, evidenced most strongly by the praise contained within his 1935 biography: *Plumer of Messines* (John Murray, 1935).

offensives in Flanders, Harington had received promotion to become deputy to Wilson at the War Office. For the final phases of the war, Plumer had Jocelyn Percy as MGGS, who proved to be an effective replacement. A man of Harington's undoubted ability and intellect, and who had an uncanny ability to interpret his chief's thinking, was impossible to replicate. It would have been difficult for Plumer to have had the same confidence in Percy. Harington however was adamant that Plumer was always the man in command – it was his ability to lead, to attend to detail, to grasp the key points of plans and react decisively when engaged in action, which shaped the direction of Second Army.

In his command of Second Army in that summer and autumn of 1918, Plumer's central approach when issuing orders to his Corps commanders was to produce an initial written draft (complete with crossings out and amendments), probably following discussion with Percy and taking account of current intelligence reports and briefings. From September 1918, he had also to take note of the orders produced by the Flanders Army Group.[103] It was Percy's role to then arrange the final typed set of orders, including administrative numbering and circulation list, which he would sign off as MGGS.

An example is Second Army Order G452, issued 24 September 1918, which summarises the main objectives for each corps in Second Army for the pending Battle of Ypres: there is an initial draft – a handwritten sheet of A4 incorporating ink stains and corrections and initialled 'HP' ('Herbert Plumer') – then the final typed order with the order number and corps commander circulation list, signed off by 'J Percy'. [104]

Terraine has praised Plumer as a forward-looking general in a war in which such individuals were in short supply. In particular, he highlights Plumer's emphasis on planning and preparation, and the high level of organisation that Plumer demanded in order to manage the increasing complexity of warfare during the 1914-18 conflict. In such methods, Terraine detects a forerunner to the requirements of the Second World War and beyond:

> [Plumer was] one of the most modern soldiers of his generation... many of [his] methods became the standard procedure of the Second World War... Plumer's sense of organisation was therefore a cardinal principle, a sine qua non of modern war.[105]

These are personal and professional qualities which would be tested further during the final period of the war.

There is a common saying that 'imitation is the sincerest form of flattery'. Writing about Lieutenant-General (later Field Marshal) Bernard Law Montgomery, most famous of Britain's Second World War generals, at the time of his appointment as the commander of Eighth Army in August 1942, Jon Latimer commented:

> His [Montgomery's] models for future operations were the meticulously planned battles of Sir Herbert Plumer [My emphasis] – arguably the best British general of the First World

103 See Chapter 2.
104 These papers are located within 29th Division records: TNA WO95/2285, War Diary of 29th Division. The significance of these particular orders is discussed in more detail in chapter three.
105 Terraine, *Western Front*, pp. 200/201.

> War – particularly Messines Ridge in 1917, when artillery preparation was at its most thorough and well coordinated.[106]

Montgomery's biographer, Nigel Hamilton, observed:

> The lessons he would draw from [the First World War] were… those fundamental lessons implanted by General Plumer: namely that if offensives are planned on a sound tactical understanding; if the troops are well trained and have limited, realistic and identifiable objectives; and if the full weight of modern artillery is intelligently brought to bear on a concentrated front, there is almost nothing the enemy can do except withdraw.[107]

The references here to planning and realism are echoed in other assessments of Plumer. Simkins concludes that Plumer, owing to his instincts for promoting teamwork and practical approaches to problems, alongside a sound feel for tactics, 'did as much as anyone, and more than most, to encourage and develop the type of all-arms attack that proved the key to victory in 1918'. Such qualities also encouraged the delegation to lower levels of command and the encouragement of local initiative which were to prove essential during the more open warfare of autumn 1918.[108]

British Second Army: Order of Battle September 1918

A British Army in the First World War was composed of an army headquarters (HQ), at least two corps, plus units attached at army level for the purposes of management, supply and strategic firepower. This included artillery, engineers, transport, medical, machine gun, veterinary and labour units. Army HQ reported to general headquarters (GHQ).

From their original structure in 1914 of two divisions plus signals section, army corps grew and increased in complexity. The number of divisions could be more than two and, as these were moved around or in and out of the line, so they might be moved to different corps. By 1918 a corps HQ could consist of 50 officers and up to 150 other ranks. Attached corps units included heavy trench mortar batteries, signals, cyclists, motor transport and mobile workshops. The average soldier would know which army he was in and its commander, and usually his division, but was far less likely to know which corps due to the movement in the line of command and control of divisions and the resulting lack of a distinct corps 'identity'.

The largest tactical unit of the British Army was the division. It consisted of a division HQ, three infantry brigades, plus troops from all ground forces including artillery, engineers, signals, transport, and medical. At full establishment it could consist of 18,000 men and 5,000 horses.

The infantry brigade was an intermediate and largely administrative and command unit, placed between the division and battalions. An example of its function is the regular *Intelligence Summaries* which the brigade prepared for division HQ, recording information on its own and

106 J. Latimer, *Alamein* (London: John Murray, 2002), p. 96. It is not for this book to enter the on-going debate about Montgomery's abilities and achievements – however he remains the Second World War British commander best known amongst the general public, derived in large part from his success at the Battle of El Alamein in autumn 1942.

107 N. Hamilton, *Monty: The Making of a General 1887-1942* (London: Coronet, 1984), pp. 125-6.

108 Simkins, 'Herbert Plumer', pp. 154, 159.

enemy operations, plus other intelligence of use.[109] Its HQ would have a small number of officers and men, often drawn by secondment from constituent battalions. In early 1918, as a consequence of the manpower shortage, brigades were reorganised from four down to three infantry battalions (which is still the case today). The exercise saw a number of brigades and battalions wound up and men redeployed to other battalions, to ensure that most remaining battalions were as close to full-strength as possible. Battalions could be moved between brigades, usually within the same division, most often for tactical reasons or as part of particular command arrangements for a forthcoming operation.

The core tactical unit of the army was the infantry battalion. Its HQ comprised the battalion CO with senior and administrative officers and men; key responsibilities included such specialist roles as medical and transport. The battalion was drawn from the British system of regiments. With the exception of the Guards regiments, who had no Territorial or New Army battalions (though they did recruit from volunteers and conscripts), most County regiments had two Regular Army battalions, two Territorial battalions, and also subsequently raised battalions of the New Army.

All soldiers carried a rifle, the Short Magazine Lee Enfield (SMLE), and bayonet. By 1918 each battalion was also equipped with 36 Lewis light machine guns, plus small mortars and grenades. This significant increase in firepower was designed to address the falling number of overall troops; it also reflected tactical improvements through which small units of infantry would be more flexible and effective when attacking, carrying with them a range of personal fire support. Trench mortar and machine gun units were deployed at divisional level, increasing in number and scope during the war. There was a similar increase in heavy artillery at corps and army level.

As well as its HQ each battalion consisted of four companies of men; each company was made up of four platoons. To illustrate the practical make-up and deployment of a company under the 'open' style of warfare facing Second Army, the following description is from the operational instructions issued for the troops of 1/Lancashire Fusiliers (86 Brigade, 29th Division), as part of the preparations for the Battle of Ypres 1918:

> Platoon marching in file thus.
>
> | | |
> |---|---|
> | 1 | Platoon Commander and Runner |
> | 2 | Scouts |
> | 6 | Lewis Gun Team, Right |
> | 6 | Lewis Gun Team, Left |
> | 4 | Riflemen, Right |
> | 4 | Riflemen, Left |
> | 1 | Yukon Pack Carrier |
> | 2 | Platoon Sergeant and Runner |
> | -- | |
> | 26 | Other Ranks |
>
> --

109 TNA WO95/2364, War Diary of 94th (Yeomanry) Brigade HQ, July 1917–May 1919: 'Intelligence Summary' headings included Our Operations (Infantry, Artillery, machine-guns, trench mortars, aircraft, visibility), Enemy Operations (Infantry etc), and Intelligence (Movement, General).

Lewis Gun Team =	1 man for gun 1 man for spare parts as laid down 4 men with 4 magazines each
Rifle Section =	Each man to carry a P Bomb and 1 man to carry Wire Cutters

Yukon Pack to carry 8 Lewis Gun Magazines and 8 Bandoliers
[A special backpack mounted on a board]

Each platoon will march [in the column order shown above] and be capable of [spreading out into rank order, left and right as described – shown by diagram]

Co. H.Q. as above. Strength of co. = 4 × 26 =	104
	19
	123[110]

The composition of the platoon in the closing stages of the war, its weaponry and additional equipment, reflected the importance of even the smallest unit of soldiers having the ability to provide its own covering and supporting firepower; with additional supplies and ammunition such that it can occupy and 'dig in' on seized ground. The platoon had become,

> ... An army in miniature, the Lewis guns supplying the covering machine gun fire, the rifle grenadiers acting as artillery; and the riflemen making the infantry assault.[111]

The platoon had to be capable of altering its approach formation on command, to respond to circumstances as they arose. It was implicit that the platoon command was expected to use its initiative in dealing with, as a first response, whatever threat the enemy presented; and was expected to take appropriate steps should a firefight develop. These sorts of arrangements are relevant to the more open style of warfare, and the expectations of an Army that it is now moving onto the offensive. The instructions are a pragmatic reflection and demonstration of the changes that have taken place – the 'learning curve' – in the small arms tactics and delegation of command initiative within the British Army by these closing stages of the war.

The war diary of 87 Brigade (29th Division) refers to a new policy of attaching to each company one field gun, two machine guns, one trench mortar, and a section of cyclists (in the vanguard position – a forward scouting role).[112] There are also references in the war diaries to the use of bangalore torpedoes for the purpose of breaching wire barriers. For 104 Brigade, two torpedoes

110 TNA WO95/2013, War Diary of 1st Battalion, Lancashire Fusiliers, Operation Instruction No: 1, 24/25.9.1918.

111 Captain A.O. Pollard, VC, quoted in Simon Robbins, *British Generalship on the Western Front, 1914-18: Defeat into Victory* (London: Frank Cass, 2005), p. 98; this descriptive metaphor is used in Boff, J. 'Combined Arms During the Hundred Days Campaign, August-November 1918', *War in History*, 2010, 17(4), pp. 459-477, online at < http://wih.sagepub.com/content/17/4/459>

112 TNA WO95/2303, War Diary of 87 Infantry Brigade, 1 September 1918.

were used in a raid in the middle of July 1918.[113] On 27 July, 19/Durham Light Infantry (from the same brigade) carried out a large raid under the cover of a combined barrage from artillery, trench mortars and machine guns – a designated party carried four bangalore torpedoes.[114]

The following table shows the Order of Battle for Second Army command in August 1918, prior to its final realignment and the composition with which it joined the GAF:

British Second Army:
Order of Battle August 1918
General Sir H. C. O. Plumer

Corps	Commander	Divisions
II Corps	Lieutenant General Sir C. W. Jacob	**14th** **34th** **35th** 49th 30th AEF
X Corps	Lieutenant General R. B. Stephens	**30th** **36th (Ulster)**
XV Corps	Lieutenant General Sir B. de Lisle	**9th (Scottish)** **29th** **31st** **40th**
XIX Corps	Lieutenant General Sir H. E. Watts	6th **41st** 27th AEF

Divisions highlighted in **bold** remained with Second Army for the Final Advance in Flanders.

113 TNA WO95/2483, War Diary of 104 Infantry Brigade, addendum to Operation Order No. 201, 13 July 1918.
114 TNA WO95/2483, War Diary of 104 Infantry Brigade; the raid was deemed a success, with two prisoners and a light machine gun captured, and approximately 60 German soldiers killed.

2

Present Arms: The Groupe d'Armées des Flandres

> By Sunday 11 August, the last day of the Battle of Amiens, Haig had conceived the possibility of bringing the war to an end that autumn ... From mid-August a scheme for a general offensive [by all allied armies] was gradually developed...[1]

> To turn the present situation to account, the most resolute offensive is everywhere desirable. Risks, which a month ago would have been criminal to incur, ought now to be incurred as a duty. It is no longer necessary to advance in regular lines and step by step. On the contrary, each division should be given a distant objective which must be reached independently of its neighbour, and even if one's flank is thereby exposed for the time being. Reinforcements must be directed on the points where our troops are gaining ground, not where they are checked. A vigorous offensive against the sectors where the enemy is weak will cause hostile strongpoints to fall, and in due course our whole army will be able to continue its advance. The situation is most favourable; let each one of us act energetically and without hesitation push forward to our objective.
>
> Field Marshal Sir Douglas Haig, 22 August 1918.[2]

Map 1 denotes the overall position (July 1918) on the Western Front before the start of the Hundred Days, and the final line at the time of the armistice on 11 November 1918. The map illustrates the key deployment of Second Army in front of Ypres and holding the right flank of the Belgian line.

It had become clear to both Haig and Foch that operations in Flanders must be included in a scheme for a series of coordinated offensives across the Western Front, designed to stretch the resources of the enemy to the maximum extent; and that the Belgian Army had to be party to operations.[3]

1 Harris with Barr, *Amiens to the Armistice*, p. 182.
2 Field Marshal Sir Douglas Haig, Headquarters, BEF, 22 August 1918 (Day 2 of the Battle of Albert), quoted in Edmonds, *Official History Vol. IV*, p. 588.
3 W. J. Philpott, 'Britain, France and the Belgian Army', in Bond, B.et al, *'Look to your Front' Studies in the First World War by The British Commission for Military History* (Staplehurst: Spellmount, 1999), p. 130-1; Philpott points out that Petain had argued that the Belgian Army could improve its offensive capability through a reduction in its number of battalions and a corresponding increase in the number of divisions and artillery units.

> Foch proposed to Haig and to the Belgian CGS, Cyraique Gillain, a new attack in Flanders... Foch had been approached by Belgium's King Albert, who had nursed his army since 1914 but now wished it to participate in the final act. By abandoning the Lys salient the Germans had exposed their railways running north to the sea. The chance presented itself to over-run the heights east of Ypres that the British had assaulted in the previous year, and to establish a base for operations against the trunk line running through Roulers.[4]

The disillusionment with the strategic policies of the allies that had grown in Albert as the war ground on, and his despair that victory remained ever-distant, had begun to dissipate during 1918. His insistence on maintaining the Belgian Army's freedom of action, and his resistance to offensive action in Belgium given the potential devastation that could result, was now less marked.[5] The King's 'growing appreciation of Foch's leadership of the Allied forces and the recent battlefield successes' led to an 'ingenious compromise' to allow Albert to cooperate with the proposed joint offensive.[6] It should be noted that the Belgian Army would never come within the formal ambit of Foch as Generalissimo of the allied armies, not least because of constitutional obligations, as the formal commander of the Belgium Army was also the country's sovereign. However King Albert had become 'more amenable' to working in cooperation with Foch's authority.[7]

Following a positive meeting between French Premier Clemenceau and King Albert on 7 September, Clemenceau prompted Foch to meet the King as he believed that the latter 'would not sit idly by as the British and French advanced'.[8] Two days later, Foch and Albert met and the idea of the GAF was born; a series of meetings followed, involving Foch and King Albert, the Belgian Chief of Staff, Gillain, Haig (and Henry Wilson, at Haig's request) and Plumer. On 9 September, at Cassel, an agreement was reached on the establishment of a new army group. The *Groupe d'Armées des Flandres* (Army Group, Flanders – or GAF) would comprise the Belgian Army, the British Second Army and two French corps; the GAF would be led by King Albert with the French General Jean Marie Joseph Degoutte as Chief of Staff.[9]

Haig had therefore agreed, in the interests of the overall campaign to defeat the main German field armies on the Western Front, to relinquish operational control of Plumer and Second Army; British Second Army would operate within the new coalition army group, under the overall command of Albert, King of the Belgians.[10]

4 Stevenson, *With Our Backs To The Wall*, p. 131; Powell, *Plumer*, p. 272.
5 W. J. Philpott, 'Britain, France and the Belgian Army', in Bond, B.et al, *'Look to your Front' Studies in the First World War by The British Commission for Military History* (Staplehurst: Spellmount, 1999), pp. 123, 128, 130-1.
6 E. Greenhalgh, *Foch in Command: The Forging of a First World War General* (Cambridge: Cambridge University Press, 2011), p. 439.
7 Philpott, 'Britain, France and the Belgian Army', pp. 130-1.
8 Greenhalgh, *Foch in Command*, p. 439.
9 Degoutte, who with his staff would have responsibility 'pour assurer la direction des operations', was not happy with his new role and complained at the equipment shortages in the Belgian Army, Foch subsequently overriding Petain to ensure that Degoutte received his extra supplies (see E. Greenhalgh, *Foch in Command*, pp. 400, 445).
10 Sheffield summarises this event in his biography of Haig, G.D. Sheffield, *The Chief: Douglas Haig and the British Army* (London: Aurum Press Limited, 2011), p. 316; see also Greenhalgh, *Foch in Command*, pp. 439-440, and Terraine, *To Win A War*, pp. 153-4; for an introduction to King Albert

Subsequently, when a dispute arose over the return of Second Army to his command, Haig summarised his view of the original arrangement in a letter to Foch as follows:

> [At Cassel on 9 September] it was agreed by me that two divisions of the Second Army should be employed under the command of His Majesty the King of the Belgians for the purpose of covering the flank of the Army of Flanders operating in an easterly direction. It was further agreed that the whole of the Second Army should be used in the event of the enemy retiring from the MESSINES Ridge, and to exploit any success which might be obtained by following and pressing the German forces... The Second Army was not to be committed to any other operation than that of clearing the ground up to the LYS River. The whole scope of the operation had as its objective the 'clearing of the Belgian coast and the country between the coast and the River LYS'.[11]

As will be seen, in practice there were no two specified British divisions placed under King Albert's direct command; it was Second Army as a coherent entity which acted in concert with its army group partners. It is not clear whether Haig subsequently chose to reinterpret the agreement in this way or if Plumer perceived that the achievement of the overall objective was most likely if the whole of Second Army co-operated with the allied forces in the GAF. It was the latter course which Plumer followed, though he was to carry it out in single-minded fashion. In practice the operations of Second Army would be determined by its army commander in accordance with the strategic aims of the army group; the resulting deployment and performance of Second Army would go well beyond the limited deployment as recollected here by Haig.

At the same time as he wrote the above letter to Foch, Haig also wrote to the War Office on the same subject. In this more detailed letter he emphasises that his original agreement was for a 'temporary detachment of the Second Army under the King of the Belgians', and that Second Army 'was to be returned on the completion of the specific operation in hand'.[12] This may have been Haig seeking to add limited objectives to the attachment with the benefit of hindsight, or perhaps he had been satisfied from the outset that the agreement with Foch was explicitly short term and limited in nature. The resulting successes of Second Army and its increasing importance within the Army Group would lead to repercussions however, not least in terms of the relationship between Haig and Foch.

There can be no doubt from the resulting actions of both Haig and Plumer that the former had decided to transfer the command of Second Army to King Albert and the structures of the GAF, for the purposes of an assault on German forces in Belgium. This arrangement and the circumstances of its subsequent ending are considered in detail in Chapter 7.

and his relationship with the Belgian Army at the outset of the war, see B. Tuchman, *The Guns of August* (London: Penguin Books, 2014; first published MacMillan, 1962), pp. 113-122.

11 TNA WO32/5102, (General, Code 86(A)), Field Marshal Haig requests return of 2nd British Army to his command from the King of the Belgians, letter from Haig to Foch, 25 October 1918. See Appendix IV for the full text.

12 TNA WO32/5102, Haig requests return of 2nd British Army, letter from Haig to The War Cabinet, 25 October 1918. See Appendix V for the full text.

The Belgian Army[13]

In August 1914, the Belgian army had comprised a field army of 120,500 troops with 18,000 volunteers, organised into six divisions of either two or three brigades; together with around 130,000 garrison troops. This, as Ian Beckett has noted, was 'a conscript army though one of only recent creation', conscription only being introduced from 1909.[14] Each brigade included one machine gun company (Maxim or Hotchkiss guns). The Army consisted of the following front-line units:

Infantry
14 regiments of the line
3 light infantry regiments *(Chasseurs á pied)*
1 Grenadier regiment
1 Rifle regiment *(Carabiniers)*
1 Cyclists battalion *(Carabinier-Cyclists)*
Corps of Gendarmerie

Cavalry
2 regiments of guides
3 regiments of Mounted Rifles *(Chasseurs á cheval)*
5 regiments of lancers

Artillery
3 Field regiments (75mm Tir Rapide Krupp guns)
2 Horse groups
3 Fortress groups

Engineers
1 regiment

There was also a small aeronautical section. Belgium also had its own colonial troops but these were not deployed on the Western Front.

Following the initial resistance to the German invasion, and the Battle of the Yser, by the end of 1914, the Belgian army was an exhausted and demoralised force: only 85,000 of the original field army and the 80,000 Troupes de Forteresse reached the River Yser. Regiments that had been split on mobilisation to form a second unit had to be merged to maintain their strength. The army was desperately in need of new recruits. In a first appeal

13 The majority of the material in this section is drawn from Haythornthwaite, *World War One Source Book*, pp. 149-153; R. Pawley & P. Lierneux *The Belgian Army in World War I* (Osprey Publishing, 2009); W. J. Philpott, 'Britain, France and the Belgian Army', in Bond, B. et al, *Look to your Front: Studies in the First World War by The British Commission for Military History* (Staplehurst: Spellmount, 1999), pp. 121-135; and the website Brave Little Belgium – a website of summary information on the Belgian Army during the First World War <http://www.belgianarmy.freeservers.com/> (other useful websites are included in the bibliography).
14 I.F.W. Beckett, *Ypres: The First Battle, 1914*, (Harlow: Pearson Education Limited, 2004), pp. 40-41.

(26 October 1914) King Albert asked every Belgian male between the ages of 18 and 30 to volunteer. The government in exile decided on 1 March 1915, that every male between the ages of 18 and 25 and living in Belgium, France or England was obliged to enlist (although there were also volunteers from Belgians living abroad); on 21 July 1916 this was extended up to the age of 40.

As a boost to numbers, many Belgians living in occupied territory made the risky journey across the Belgian-Dutch border to enlist. This was an extremely dangerous task, and many who tried were shot by German patrols. Eventually the Germans erected electrified fences along the entire length of the border, although many Belgians still made the attempt. From Holland they went to England and then to training camps in France.

Lacking a strategic reserve, the extent of the front held by the Belgian Army meant that none of its divisions could be wholly relieved. From 1915 onwards the army maintained its 'Watch on the Yser', where the most common enemy was the water undermining the defence works. Although sniping was a constant feature, there was little other action beyond occasional raids. Further south towards Ypres the flooded area between the lines became less intense and the terrain was more typical of the rest of the Western Front.

The German Spring offensives of 1918 involved the reconstituted Belgian Army in direct action, notably the fighting near Merkem in April. Despite the initial German attack breaking through to the Belgian support line, the advancing troops were halted by artillery fire directed at them and their reserves. Under the cover of a moving barrage the Belgian infantry then counter-attacked. Gradually the German forces were pushed back – 'Battalions broke, and the fighting degenerated into a number of smaller local battles' – and by the evening all of the lost ground had been recovered.[15] The action demonstrated that the Belgians had the potential to take the offensive as well as defend ground. Terraine states that 'the well-rested and up-to-strength Belgian Army had a good day north of Ypres on 17 April'.[16]

In January 1918 the Belgian Army had been reorganised: the initial brigades were abolished and each of the six *divisions d'armée* was to consist of two *divisions d'infanterie* (each comprising 3 regiments). The cavalry division had three brigades with two regiments each, one group *d'auto-canons mitrailleuses*', two battalions of cyclists, three batteries of 7.5 cm guns, one company of engineers, and a platoon of *télégraphistes sur cycles*.

By the time of the Final Advance in Flanders, the Belgian army, under its commander and Chief of Staff General Gillain, comprised:

170,000 soldiers
5,700 officers
38,000 horses
850 artillery pieces (not including trench mortars)

(A further 30,000 troops were employed in factories, hospitals etc.)

Belgian troops had undertaken little action since the retreat in 1914. They had experience of trench warfare to the extent of maintaining and defending their positions, but were composed predominantly of fresh soldiers. Their preparation and readiness for action in 1918 bears closest

15 Pawley & Lierneux, *The Belgian Army*, p. 35.
16 Terraine, *To Win A War*, p. 67.

comparison with the new American troops arriving in France at this time. They offered enthusiasm and energy, together with the added incentive of the prospect of fighting to rid their country of the German invaders. They lacked the experience of practicing the modern warfare of 1918. At the same time, British forces were aware that the Belgians needed to become accustomed to the rhythms of trench warfare, with its constant potential for danger within periods of tedious routine. In the build-up to Fourth Ypres, one British war diary recorded:

> Heavy barrage on the Belgian line on our immediate left, previous to enemy attempting a raid on Belgian posts.[17]

The appearance of the troops had also changed from the 19th century uniform worn in 1914. The revised uniform was a curious hybrid of French and British influence: a French Adrian helmet, a greatcoat, a uniform of khaki serge procured from Britain, and equipment made by the Mills Company and similar to the British 1908 pattern web equipment.

> At any distance [the Belgian soldier] resembled a soldier of the French Colonial and Moroccan divisions… M1915 Adrian helmets with cloth covers [and] M2 gasmasks.[18]

Control of most of Belgium by Germany meant however that the army had no large pool available for new recruits or replacements; Belgian units, while relatively fresh, were often below their paper strength. Conscription now operated for all Belgians aged 18-40 years, living in the retained part the country, France and Britain and, from the middle of 1916, in allied or neutral countries.

French Forces

The French Sixth Army was commanded by General de Boissoudy.

Though the French Army had mostly recovered from the mutinies and discord of the previous year it faced serious manpower problems in 1918, exacerbated by the casualty rates during the Germans' spring offensives. Despite such steps as bringing forward the 1919 draft to April 1918, the recall of certain categories of reservists, and the enlistment and deployment of foreign recruits, considerable deficiencies remained: 'Some front line units were composed almost entirely of men in their forties, some as old as forty-eight'.[19] Many divisions were under strength and there were ongoing issues regarding supplies, replacements and casualty rates. Morale remained brittle and it was all too clear to the French soldier that he lacked the material support which the British and in particular the Americans enjoyed.[20]

In his 2011 biography of Haig, Sheffield points out that 'Haig had already discussed with Plumer the possibility of co-operating with the Belgians and joint operations with the Royal

17 TNA WO95/1765, War Diary of 7th Battalion, Seaforth Highlanders, 23rd September 1918.
18 Pawley & Lierneux, *Belgian Army*, p. 36.
19 A. Clayton, *Paths of Glory: The French Army 1914-1918* (London: Orion Publishing, 2007; first published London: Cassell, 2003), p. 181.
20 This summary is based upon a more detailed account in Clayton, *Paths of Glory*, pp. 180-196.

Navy'.[21] However a suggestion by Plumer on 5 September for an assault to recapture Messines (conceded to the enemy following withdrawal during the spring 1918 fighting), was rejected as not sufficiently ambitious. Stevenson explains Haig's reasoning as follows:

> Plumer had wanted to by-pass the [Ypres] Salient and attack towards Wytschaete and Messines, but Haig refused to press the case, as his main concern was to get the Belgians into action.[22]

With agreement that the general offensive would include action on the northern stretch of the Front, the aims of this particular operation would include the clearing of ground between the River Lys and the coast; the clearance of the Flanders coast; and the establishment of a line through Ghent to the Dutch frontier. Haig subsequently told Plumer that he should 'be prepared to move a Division by sea to Ostend and occupy Bruges with left on the Dutch frontier, and connecting with Anglo-Belgian Army on the line Thourout – Roulers'.[23] Judging from subsequent events this advice appears to have been treated by Plumer with the same degree of importance as the guidance from GAF Chief of Staff Degoutte; that is, noted with respect, but not deflecting Plumer from what he considered to be the correct course of action.

Plumer had good experience of working with allied forces and commanders. As well as the experiences early in his career of commanding colonial and volunteer troops, he had the more recent Italian experience to draw upon. There he had made a good impression upon the Italian leaders despite his reservations about the lack of concern for their troops shown by some officers. During the spring 1918 fighting he maintained good relations with both Belgian and French allies, despite some frustration with the latter. Haig remarked that 'The French have been very trying and poor old Plumer has had a most anxious time'.[24] The evidence is that the Belgians had particular respect for Plumer. The Earl of Athlone, Head of the British Military Mission to King Albert's HQ, writing to his brother-in-law King George V in April 1918, is quoted as stating that the Belgians 'would do anything for General Plumer'; the same source also claims that the Belgians did not have the same liking for the French.[25]

During June-August two American divisions served under Second Army. The commander of American 27th Division wrote how Plumer'... became a very good friend of the 27th Division ... [all who met him] will always remember his kindness of heart and his interest and confidence in American troops'.[26] The *Ypres Times* makes a reference to the British, or certainly 'Plumeresque', method of issuing orders from the American perspective. Over tea Plumer made the casual remark 'Oh, by the way, O'Ryan [27th Division commander], how would you like to have a go at our friends on the ridge?' Major-General O'Ryan, having indicated his willingness, then found that the details of the plan and the draft orders had already been drawn up for discussion.[27]

21 Sheffield, *The Chief*, p. 316.
22 Stevenson, *With Our Backs To The Wall*, p. 135.
23 Reported in Sheffield, *The Chief*, p. 316; reference *Douglas Haig Manuscript Diary*, 9 September 1918.
24 Quoted by Powell, *Plumer*, p. 266, from Edmonds, *Official History Vol. 1V*, p. 484 .
25 Powell, *Plumer*, p. 267.
26 Major-General John F O'Ryan, *The Story of the 27th Division* (New York: Wynkoop Hallenbeck Crawford Company, 1921), p. 196.
27 Quoted by Powell, *Plumer*, p. 271; from the Plumer Papers, an extract for the *Ypres Times*, quoted by the Rev 'Tubby' Clayton in an unnamed Toc H publication.

Simkins has referred to Second Army's flank role for the GAF, a coalition force under foreign command, as a downgrading for Plumer within the final Allied Offensive.[28] There is a more positive take on the arrangement. The setting up of the GAF was certainly a political compromise negotiated through Foch as Supreme CinC. It allowed him both to incorporate the Belgian Army into the final series of offensives, and to respond to pressure from King Albert for his soldiers to play a visible role in the liberation of their country. This represented a major shift in Albert's position regarding his country and the army. In the past he had always wanted to see his army as independent of the Allied forces, and, whilst stating his willingness to work cooperatively, was single-mindedly committed to maintaining the neutrality of his country. He had initially feared that his troops could be absorbed into the French Army with implications for the relationship of his country with France after the war.[29] Wishing to avoid further devastation to his country, he had even been prepared to consider a unilateral negotiated peace with Germany during the winter of 1915-16. The views of his cabinet prevented any such manoeuvre and the influence of the Foreign Minister, Paul Hyams (former ambassador to Britain), together with the attractive prospect of leading the Belgian Army in the liberation of his country, persuaded him to finally agree to cooperation with the allies in the final push in 1918. It is reasonable to consider that the inclusion of Plumer was an important component in securing Albert's agreement.

It was now important that Belgian soldiers were seen to be leading the fight to drive the invaders from their country. In his diary for 5 September 1918, Haig reports his meeting with Plumer regarding 'the instructions I sent him for co-operating with [the] Belgian Army... I told [Plumer] the most important object was to get the Belgians to advance!'.[30] The British stance, influencing Haig's thinking, was one of concern to ensure that France did not claim the credit for liberating Belgium, and that French troops did not lead an advance that British troops had fought to create the conditions for. It can therefore be argued that Haig wanted and needed to keep Plumer in situ because of his proven ability to manage his way successfully through the political complexities of coalition warfare. As well as his successful experience in Italy, Plumer had past and current experience of liaising with the Belgian Army and there had been warm praise for him from the Belgians.

Haig was anxious to ensure that the Belgian Army would actively commit to the forthcoming series of attacks; at the same time he was also sceptical of the potential fighting value of the Belgian forces. Thus Plumer and Second Army would 'stiffen the Belgian Army with two British divisions on [the Belgian Army's] right flank'.[31] One can see that the presence of a British Army under a commander known to and respected by the Belgians – and with a thorough knowledge of the region – had the potential to provide the necessary reassurance.

Another consideration for Haig should have been the condition of Second Army. This was a weakened force, now just ten divisions, many depleted through the demands of the fighting in the spring. It is probable that Haig was worried that the Army, even with Plumer's proven capability and leadership, was not capable of an independent offensive role beyond that of securing

28 Simkins, 'Herbert Plumer', p. 148.
29 For a broader discussion of King Albert's considerations see P. Van Pul, *In Flanders' Flooded Fields: Before Ypres there was Yser* (Pen & Sword, 2006), including pp. 39/40.
30 Sheffield and Bourne, *Haig Diaries and Letters*, pp. 456-7.
31 Sheffield, *The Chief*, p. 316.

the flank of the GAF. This would give added weight to his reasoning, even though his priority remained that of persuading the Belgians to advance. He needed to provide a practical means by which to instil confidence in Albert and his army. The advantage of Plumer's diplomatic abilities in this regard was obvious – but Haig also needed an experienced commander who could nurse a weakened British Army through the fighting to come.

Plumer, perhaps showing understandable apprehension regarding the readiness of Second Army for a major offensive, and given the unproven potential of the Belgian Army, displayed initial caution regarding whether the GAF could meet the expectations placed upon it. He was wary of the pressure for Second Army to provide the necessary support for its Army Group allies. On 13 September, Plumer told General Sir Herbert Lawrence (Haig's Chief of Staff) 'that he doubted that he would be able to advance towards Menin and Courtrai unless the German defenders suffered a major collapse'.[32]

The allied front line in Flanders on 28 September, the date set for the GAF to commence its attack, is marked on Map 2; this would bring operations in Flanders within the allied grand offensive as conceived by Haig and Foch. The map also shows the progress of the subsequent advance in Flanders up to the conclusion of the Battle of Courtrai, the liberation of the coast through to the border with Holland, and the state entry of King Albert into Bruges.

German forces in Flanders: September – November 1918

The Second Army Intelligence Summary at the start of September identified eleven German divisions in line but only one in reserve,[33] following the enemy's withdrawal from the Lys Salient. These belonged to the German Fourth Army under General Sixt von Armin.

German Divisions facing British Second Army: Battle of Ypres
Opening Day – 28 September 1918

(Please refer to subsequent chapters for more details on German forces deployed during the campaign; and Appendix I Orders of Battle for the German ORBAT)

Division	Comments
12th Bavarian	(mainly opposite the Belgians). Largely rested
6th Bavarian Reserve	(south of Comines canal). Fought near Bapaume in August
40th Bavarian Reserve	(south of Comines canal). Involved in 18 July offensive
11th Reserve (Fourth Army)	Largely rested
4th	Believed to be a good division. Largely rested
56th	Largely rested

Sources: Edmonds, *Official History Vol. V*; TNA WO157/128, Second Army Intelligence Summary, 28 September 1918

32 Sheffield, *The Chief*, p. 316, reference Australian War Memorial (unpublished primary source), pp. 51/56, 'Record of a meeting … between … Plumer and… the CGS'.
33 TNA WO157/128, Second Army Intelligence Summary, 4 September 1918.

A German division normally comprised three regiments (battalions). By this period of the war, the average fighting strength of a battalion was three companies, each company of between 70-80 men.[34]

The mixed nature of the troops, in terms of experience and quality, is notable. Most had been able to undertake a period of rest following the fighting earlier in the year, which should have meant some improvement in their capability and morale. For instance, on 10 August 1918, the war diary of 121 Infantry Brigade (40th Division) notes information received that there was now a fresh German division (52nd Infantry) on the opposite side of no man's land:

> As their moral [sic] and fighting qualities were probably high... patrols to be more vigilant than when the 207th German Division was in the line.[35]

Though troop numbers meant that Second Army (ten divisions including two in Army reserve) enjoyed almost a 2:1 majority at the start of the battle, the German positions were well-organised. Pill-boxes, dug-outs and wire from earlier fighting were made maximum use of, in order to provide for effective defence in depth. Machine gun positions were heavily concealed, and the wide deployment of snipers provided further problems for the British. The enemy also held high ground giving clear lines of sight across the ground over which the British forces would advance. The ground itself was another factor in favour of the defenders. The shell-torn terrain, pock-marked by craters and former trenches, was littered with the debris of previous conflict – '... wire, wood and broken war material and equipment...'[36] – impeding the movement of men, animals and machines.

Two German reserve divisions were brought up to the line on 28 September, mainly in the Belgian sector and where the allied forces linked. In addition a further four divisions were put in against the British on 29 September, with one more division (1st Bavarian Reserve) on 2 October. The Battle of Courtrai opened on 14 October with the ten British divisions of Second Army opposed by three German divisions, plus three in reserve, and two infantry regiments. On 15 October, two further German divisions were moved up into the line.

The Operational Readiness of Second Army: Troops

> At the beginning of May 1918 [following the German Spring offensives]... of the sixty British infantry divisions then in France, ten were marked with a red circle, indicating they had been reduced to cadre divisions and could not be made up to strength, at least not for some considerable period of time.[37]

This situation was subsequently made worse by the German attacks on the French Army, and the additional British casualties which resulted from the support provided to its ally. Five (14th, 30th, 31st, 34th, 40th) of these 'reduced to cadre' divisions would be part of Second Army for the final campaign in Flanders.[38] John Terraine has described a retained cadre as follows:

34 TNA WO157/128, Second Army Intelligence Summary, 28 September 1918.
35 TNA WO95/2614, War Diary of 121 Infantry Brigade.
36 Edmonds, *Official History, Vol. V.*
37 A.B.D. Dewar, assisted by Lt.-Col. J.H. Boraston, *Sir Douglas Haig's Command: December 19, 1915, to November 11, 1918* (Two volumes) (London: Constable and Company Ltd, 1922), Vol. II, p. 277.
38 The other five formations were 16th, 39th, 59th, 61st and 66th divisions.

> In effect, the infantry ceased to exist, the battalions being reduced to mere 'caretaker' companies of ten officers and forty-five other ranks; artillery, machine-gunners and engineers remained available for action with other divisions.[39]

Following representations made by Foch to the Prime Minister Lloyd George at a meeting on 1 June, there were improvements in the reinforcement programme such that nine of the divisions were reconstituted.[40]

By the time of the Final Advance in Flanders there had been yet further changes to the composition of Second Army, including the withdrawal of the American 27th and 30th Divisions. Second Army was made up of four Corps: II, X, XV and XIX. However there were now just ten divisions in total, nine of which had been with the army during the summer. The additional division was the 14th (Light) which was initially attached to II Corps; it served under XIX Corps for the Battle of Ypres, before transferring to XV Corps for the Battle of Courtrai. 29th Division was originally a Regular Army Division. All the rest: 9th (Scottish), 14th (Light), 30th, 31st, 34th, 35th, 36th (Ulster), 40th, and 41st, were New Army Divisions, i.e. created out of Kitchener's volunteers and subsequent conscription.

British Second Army: Order of Battle: Army and Corps
Final Advance In Flanders
28 September 1918 (with subsequent changes)
General Sir H. C. O. Plumer

Corps	**Commander**	**Divisions**
II Corps	Lieutenant General Sir C. W. Jacob	9th 29th (to X Corps wef 25 October) 36th (Ulster) (to X Corps wef 31 October) 31st (from XV Corps wef 25 October) (to XIX Corps wef 2 November) 34th (from X Corps wef 28 October)
X Corps	Lieutenant General R. B. Stephens	30th 34th (to II Corps wef 28 October) 36th (from II Corps wef 1 November) (to XV Corps wef 9 November) 29th (from II Corps wef 25 October)
XV Corps	Lieutenant General Sir B. de Lisle	14th 31st (to II Corps wef 25 October) 40th 36th (from X Corps wef 9 November)
XIX Corps	Lieutenant General Sir H. E. Watts	35th 41st 31st (from II Corps wef 3 November)

39 Terraine, *To Win A War*, p. 79.
40 Terraine, *To Win A War*, pp. 79-80.

A comprehensive listing of the Orders of Battle of British Second Army throughout 1918, concentrating on the period September-November 1918, is attached as Appendix I Orders of Battle. The appendix also includes summary orders of battle for Belgian and French forces within the GAF.

British Second Army was made up completely of British troops – there were no colonial or dominion units. The Canadian and Anzac troops, who have often been referred to as the most effective formations within the BEF, were all deployed in other armies. There was no obvious 'elite' or similar unit or division within Second Army at this time. 9th and 29th divisions have been described subsequently as high performing divisions but this assessment includes their performance in the final months of the war.[41] Furthermore a British division was also smaller in size than its Dominion equivalent:

> Following the reduction of the B.E.F.by 141 battalions [at the start of 1918], in view of the alleged manpower shortage, British divisions were reduced to 9 battalions, 3 to a brigade. This reduction did not apply to the Dominion divisions, which partly accounts for the great part played by those formations in the subsequent fighting [during 1918].[42]

With Second Army wholly comprised of British divisions, and containing a number of reformed, rehabilitated or potentially less effective units, it was in theory the least strong of the armies making up the BEF at that time.

During the final year of the war, the British Army faced an increasing manpower challenge. While the reduction in the size of British divisions was justified by reference to the increased firepower available to the infantry, the consequences for the troops involved need to be acknowledged. Any assessment of the performance of British units during the spring 1918 German offensives and afterwards must take these changes into consideration. Implementing the reorganisation meant the breaking up of certain units and the dispersal of troops into unfamiliar groupings. It also impacted upon the amount of time available to divisions to provide reliefs and to release troops for training and refreshment.

Many divisions which had faced the Michael offensive in March had subsequently been redeployed to the north in order to recuperate. Instead they had found themselves repeating their experience in response to the Georgette offensive in northern France and Flanders. Battalions and brigades had faced the experience of having survivors pulled together in composite formations, to allow for some continuing cohesion in command and control. Subsequently a number of units were formally reduced to cadre status, from which some were rebuilt to be restored to active duty.

It is important to consider the experiences of certain units and divisions prior to joining Second Army during the summer of 1918, in order to appreciate the potential readiness or otherwise of the Army's operational formations. This information also helps in understanding

41 It has been argued by P. Griffith, *Battle Tactics of the Western Front: The British Army's Art of Attack 1916-18* (New Haven: Yale University Press, 1994), pp. 80/81, that 9th and 29th Divisions can be described as possible 'elite' or 'highly regarded' divisions; this assessment takes into account their performance during the final campaign in Flanders.

42 From an editor's note in J. Terraine, ed., *General Jack's Diary: War on the Western Front 1914-1918 – The Trench Diary of Brigadier-General J. L. Jack, D.S.O.* (London, Cassell & Co., 2000 edition), p. 244.

the condition and potential combat effectiveness of many of the troops prior to the commencement of the major offensives from the end of September.

2/15th Battalion (County of London) (Prince of Wales' Own Civil Service Rifles), London Regiment (2/15 Civil Service Rifles), only joined 90 Brigade ('The Grey Brigade'), 30th Division, at the start of July 1918. Prior to that, it had been part of 60th Division in the Middle East, only embarking from Egypt in June.[43] It was therefore inexperienced in the demands of warfare on the Western Front.

34th Division was reconstructed in June 1918, taking in units from India and the Middle East. 'They had no experience of the war as waged in France' complained the divisional history.[44] The division was soon placed under French XXX Corps and took a major part in the Battle of the Soissonnais and the Ourcq, and the Capture of Beugneux Ridge. One of its subsequent battalions, 2/Loyal North Lancs, had entrained to Alexandria, en route to France, on 23 April 1918 with 33 officers and 941 ORs. By 1 August it had been reduced to 7 officers and 380 ORs. The division was not ready for the intensity of the fighting into which it was plunged. It had

> … no experience of war as waged in France, except in one respect, this was no great drawback, as open warfare was expected. The one exception was that they knew nothing of gas. So they were slow to recognise gas shelling. This caused casualties which troops accustomed to gas would have avoided.[45]

The divisional history lists the various challenges facing this new formation, prior to its first action. These include:

- It was a newly re-formed division
- troops had no previous experience of action on the Western front
- troops had just completed a long journey by rail, bus and march
- the country was entirely new to them
- there were no organised trench systems on either side
- no time was available for reconnaissance
- the positions of the enemy were only fully known once captured
- it was acting in cooperation with allied troops, and for the first time.[46]

So Second Army, to which 34th Division was subsequently transferred, was not receiving an up-to-strength division, or one experienced in fighting on the Western Front. The arrangements for its reconstitution 'as a first line division in the Second Army area and under arrangements to be made by Second Army' were set out in a memo from GHQ on 24 June 1918.[47] This detailed

43 TNA WO95/2340, War Diary of 2/15th Battalion, London Regiment.
44 Lieut.-Colonel J. Shakespear, *The Thirty-Fourth Division, 1915-1919* (London: HF & G Witherby, 1921), p. 253.
45 A. Crookenden, *The History of the Cheshire Regiment in the Great War* (Chester: W H Evans Sons and Co., 1938).
46 Shakespear, *Thirty-Fourth Division* .
47 TNA WO95/2437, War Diary of 34th Division, memo O.B./2231, 24th June 1918.

the constituent battalions for the division and also its supporting units,[48] together with the initial steps for bringing these together. Second Army was required to distribute the battalions to brigades and nominate one for conversion to pioneers.[49] The battalion selected for the latter attachment to the division was 2/4 Somerset Light Infantry. This had been one of the first units attached to the newly re-established division, initially part of 101 Brigade for training and administrative purposes.[50]

This choice was not without its problems, as shown in the following report, filed on 25 June 1918, on the health of the battalion's troops:

> REPORT ON THE HEALTH OF THE 2/4TH BATTALION OF THE SOMERSET LIGHT INFANTRY
>
> 1 This Battalion is not at the moment suffering from a high Malarial incidence, but a few cases are occurring daily, and there are known to be 182 Malarial Subjects in the Battalion, of whom 50 are at present unfit for duty.
>
> 2 There is a large number of men in the Battalion who have not had leave for periods varying from 18 months to before 1914.
>
> The general standard of health is rather low, rendering men more susceptible to any form of disease, and at the present time a large number of influenza cases are occurring.
>
> 3 To render the Battalion fit for Active Duties in the field, I would recommend that they be removed to a seaside camp; that the training be of a very light nature, not lasting after mid-day, and that men who in the opinion of the Medical Officer are unfit for training, be excused.
>
> I would further recommend that a liberal leave allotment be granted as this would benefit the health of the men and improve morale.
>
> (Sd) G. W. Bliss
> Colonel, A,M.S.
> A.D.M.S. 34th Division
> D.H.Q.
> 25/6/18[51]

This assessment of the soldiers and the recommended actions highlight some points of general interest as well as providing valuable background on Second Army's composition:

a) The incidence of the symptoms of malaria is an ongoing concern of the medical authorities.

48 Three of the battalions already posted to the division, all of them of Irish origin, 6th Battalion, Royal Inniskilling Fusiliers, 5th Battalion, Connaught Rangers, and 6th Battalion, Leinster Regiment, were now withdrawn 'for medical reasons'.
49 The final composition of 34th Division is contained in the relevant entry in Appendix I.
50 The Battalion was, prior to taking on attachment to the division (TNA WO95/2456, War Diary of 101 Brigade, Order No. 205, 29 June 1918).
51 TNA WO95/2437, War Diary of 34th Division, memo 25th June 1918.

b) The reference to cases of influenza is a probable indication of the impending flu epidemic – itself a result in part of the poor health of soldiers and civilians; it was also starting to become a concern for the Army's medical staff with implications for maintaining unit strength.
c) The reference to the lack of leave taken by these troops, conflicts with the oft-referred to commitment by the BEF to ensuring its soldiers are regularly rotated out of the line and allowed opportunities for leave, as an important part of maintaining morale.
d) The recommendations by the division's medical officer, at a period of high activity for the Army, regarding an increase in leave entitlement, light training and a period experiencing sea air, are suggestive of a sympathetic and concerned approach to the welfare of the troops; this position does not match the common perception in current times of a heartless and disinterested top brass.
e) For Second Army, with a number of its units being reconstituted from cadres or receiving substantial numbers of replacement troops following severe casualty rates, this example shows the practical consequences.

The medical officer's recommendations were accepted by the division and referred up the chain of command to Second Army HQ for authorisation – reflecting the Army's commitment to maintaining, and where possible improving, the health of its soldiers.[52]

Initially placed under II Corps, the 34th Division would subsequently transfer to XIX Corps for operations in the Kemmel area 30 August – 6 September; and then to X Corps. It was under this latter command that it entered the Battle of Ypres.

35th Division, originally formed as a New Army Bantam Division,[53] had a chequered history prior to this final campaign, with concerns regarding its performance in combat at various points during the past two years. In the defensive battles along the Ancre at the end of March 1918, it had sustained more than 3,000 casualties. Despite its poor record, this action probably saved the 35th from reduction to cadre, showing it had potential fighting qualities.[54]

40th Division had also been intended as a New Army Bantam Division, although a number of its original units were non-Bantam. In 1918 it saw action during the German Spring Offensives, at the Battles of The Lys, the Battle of Estaires and the Battle of Hazebrouck. Following the scale of its losses in the fighting at Hazebrouck, the division was reduced to a training cadre. It then was subject to a major reorganisation, bringing together former Garrison Guard units which were converted to fighting units. On 10 June, Garrison Guard Battalions 6, 7, 8, 9, 10 and 11 were allotted to the division, initially as a brigade '... for work, and to man the line in case of necessity';[55]

52 TNA WO95/2437, War Diary of 34th Division, initial memo 25th June 1918, and subsequent memos 1st July and 2nd July.
53 The term 'Bantam' was used to describe specifically formed Battalions comprising men of short stature who did not meet the regulations regarding height and chest measurements. For further reference see S. Allinson, *The Bantams: The Untold Story of World War 1* (London: Howard Baker, 1981).
54 This summary is based upon P. Simkins, 'Each One A Pocket Hercules: The Bantam Experiment and the Case of the 35th Division', in Sanders Marble, ed., *Scraping The Barrel: The Military Use of Substandard Manpower 1860-1960* (New York: Fordham University Press, 2012), pp. 79-104.
55 TNA WO95/2594, War Diary of 40th Division.

from 12 June, each battalion was allotted a permanent designation.[56] Two days later, orders were issued for 40th Division to be reorganised as a 'Garrison Division' (semi-mobile) with support arms formed through Second Army and GHQ. As such, the division would be required 'to hold a quiet sector of the line' with training organised to support this role.[57] Via a divisional order, 13 July 1918, each battalion had the word 'Garrison' deleted from its title.

9th Garrison Battalion, the King's Own Scottish Borderers (9/KOSB) had been brought together at Buysscheure during the period 10-14 June 1918, many men being drafts from Labour Companies; the war diary refers to other ranks being equipped with '1914 equipment' at this stage. It began its battalion training on 15 June, when it was also renumbered as 10/KOSB. On 24 June, an inspection by the Inspector of Medical Services led to forty soldiers being classified as lower than B1 status, with the result that they were returned to labour companies.[58]

In the same 120 Brigade was 11/Cameron Highlanders. Originally 6th Garrison Guard Battalion, it had been established at Étaples in June 1918. Significant steps in its formation included:

9-10 June	Headquarters established.
11 June	Officers and four companies arrived – most men were category B1 drawn from 29 different labour companies.
14 June	Training commenced.
29 June	The GOC 40th Division 'decided to transfer Scotchmen to this unit' – the result was that there were 250 new transfers in, with 221 Englishmen and Irishmen transferred to other units in the Division (119, 120 and 121 Brigades). [No doubt this action was designed to assist in building a strong commitment to the regiment and a close bond between the new troops; given the fresh composition of the unit and the combat operations pending, this can be seen as a positive move, at least as far as 11/Cameron Highlanders was concerned.]
30 June	A new cadre of Scottish officers was received (from the Black Watch).
7 July	The battalion commenced a four day tour of duty in the West Hazebrouck line.

56 Nos. 6-11 GGBs were designated as Garrison Battalions (GB) 11/Cameron Highlanders, 13/Royal Inniskilling Fusiliers, 13/East Lancs, 10/ KOSB, 15/KOYLI and 12/North Staffs, respectively.

57 TNA WO95/2594, War Diary of 40th Division. Four GBs transferred in from 59th Division, First Army on 15 June: the organisation of Brigades (with deletion of the term 'Garrison' from 13 July) was:

119 Brigade	**120 Brigade**	**121 Brigade**
13/ Royal Inniskilling Fusiliers	11/Cameron Highlanders	8/Royal Irish (originally 2/)
13/East Lancs	10/ KOSB	23/Cheshires
12/North Staffs	15/KOYLI	23/Lancs Fusiliers

*Each Brigade also created one Light Trench Mortar Battery (3 officers, 47 other ranks)
*On 28 June, 17/Worcesters absorbed 12/Yorkshires (Pioneers) to become the Division's Pioneer Battalion.

58 TNA WO95/2611/4, War Diary of 10th Battalion, Kings Own Scottish Borderers.

	Three officers and six NCOs from 31st Division were attached to the battalion in order to provide instruction on trench duties.
15-16 July	'Garrison' designation deleted from the battalion title; now re-numbered as 11th Battalion, Cameron Highlanders.
	Training continued into August…
8 August	The battalion was inspected by the Army Commander, General Plumer.
17 August	The battalion returned to front line duty (relieving 15th King's Own Yorkshire Light Infantry, also of 120 Brigade, as part of the rotation policy of the Army).[59]

These entries give some insight into the steep learning curve which many of the soldiers making up Second Army had to climb. The new troops were not, in the main, keen volunteers with a long period of training behind them; they were young conscripted men, or from former garrison battalions, or transfers from labour companies. The evidence indicates that senior commanders were aware of this and there was a heavy emphasis on induction and training throughout June, July and August and beyond. The mentoring role above, using experienced soldiers from a neighbouring division, is indicative of the need to support these newly composed units; and that those units with a more established pedigree were willing and able to provide such support. Insofar as service demands and the actions of the enemy allowed, units were introduced to front line duty on a gradual basis, making full use of the Army's policy of the regular rotation of units between front line, reserve and support positions.

These arrangements are illustrated in the weekly 'Training Progress Reports' of 120 Brigade. The reports for July 1918 provide summary details together with some comments on progress; the series of headings for week ending 12 July 1918 include:

Musketry	Lewis Gun	Drill	P.T.
Marching	Gas Drill	Bombing	S.O.S.

Plus Instruction of Officers and reference to the Brigade Signalling Class for beginners [8 O.R.s per battalion].[60]

Other headings in subsequent weeks include:

Trench Duties B.F. [Bayonet Fighting].[61]

As has been noted above, 120 Brigade was newly constituted as part of the re-built 40th Division, and the comprehensive programme of training reflected this. Amongst the entries for the first week in July are:

59 TNA WO95/2611/4, War Diary of 11th Battalion, Cameron Highlanders.
60 TNA WO95/2610, War Diary of 120th Infantry Brigade, Training Progress Report 6-7-18.
61 TNA WO95/2610, War Diary of 120th Infantry Brigade, Training Progress Reports 12-7-18, 19th July 1918, 26/7/1918.

Musketry	Training has been continued in the Care of Arms, judging distances and rapid loading… Deliberate and rapid practices have been fired by all battalions on the range… Battalions report that the standard of shooting is fair.
Lewis Gun	The average number of men in each battalion under training is 120. Instruction has been continued in mechanism, drill and stoppages. All teams have fired on the 20 yards range with fairly satisfactory results.
P.T.	The younger men have improved considerably with the daily training. A number of the men however are unlikely to reach the standard of agility required for Recreational Training.
Bombing	Classes in bombing have been started by one battalion this week.
Instruction of Officers	Lectures have been given to junior Officers on Map Reading, Platoon Organization and on simple Tactical Schemes. The Brigade Signalling Class for beginners (consisting of 8 other ranks per battalion) has been running for a fortnight and satisfactory progress has been made in Visual Training (Flag) and in Buzzer Work.[62]

There are a number of points here worth highlighting. It is clear that the troops were in need of training across the range of skills and experiences which a soldier in 1918 required. Basic rifle shooting including care and reloading is a fundamental part of the programme. Alongside this there was the essential need for a trained core of Lewis gun teams to provide the mobile firepower to support advancing infantry. In subsequent weeks there would be training for a second team per gun as well as AA (anti-aircraft) shooting. Training in bombing has however only just commenced and there was much to do in terms of supporting skills such as signalling. Some concerns remained regarding the overall health and fitness of the men; a report later that month stated that there had been an improvement in marching with a reduction in the number of men falling out because of 'the worst cases having been evacuated to Base by A.D.M.S'.[63]

Improving the leadership abilities of the officers and NCOs was also a priority, indicative of the turnover in these positions and the overall shortfall in the initial combat readiness of many of the troops. The 19 July report, under the heading 'Drill', concludes that 'There is still considerable room for improvement one of the chief weaknesses being the lack of power of command on the part of both junior officers and N.C.O.s'. The training reports include reference to lectures 'to impress upon all Platoon Commanders the importance of handling their own platoon and the need of cultivating the power of command' as well as instruction in basic elements such as the writing of messages, saluting and march discipline.[64]

The following week saw the three battalions commencing four days occupation of the main front line for 'training in trench duties', carried out on a rotating basis. Troops from affiliated units – Labour, Tunnelling, RE – were also involved. The exercise was supported by experienced officers and NCOs from the neighbouring 31st Division, which was also under XV Corps command:

62 TNA WO95/2610, War Diary of 120th Infantry Brigade, Training Progress Report 6-7-18.
63 TNA WO95/2610, War Diary of 120th Infantry Brigade, Training Progress Report 19 July 1918.
64 TNA WO95/2610, War Diary of 120th Infantry Brigade, Training Progress Reports 12-7-18, 19 July 1918, 26/7/1918.

> Valuable experience was gained during these tours of duty in a trench system: but the standard of knowledge of actual trench routine as displayed by some companies was poor while there is also considerable room for improvement in trench discipline.[65]

The experience was also used to provide instruction for specialist roles including those of sniper, scout and observer.

That same week there were also lectures for officers on 'Trench Routine'. This was important for ensuring that units were at a level where they could be relied upon to take sole responsibility for a designated stretch of the front line. Despite the troops still undertaking training for combat, at the end of the second week of July the brigade HQ issued orders regarding the deployment of 120 Brigade should the Second Army front be attacked. The defence of the designated stretch of the West Hazebrouck Line would be:

> ... organised in depth, in accordance with S.S. 210 – 'The Division in Defence' – as far as troops are available but in any case troops will be disposed so as to hold both the Observation and the Main Line of Resistance. Where no Observation Line exists, already dug, battalions will push out Advance Posts in front of the existing Line of Resistance.
>
> In making their dispositions, Commanding Officers must realise the comparative lack of mobility of the troops at their disposal, and the small number of Lewis Guns which can be manned. It must be impressed upon all ranks that they are to hold the line in which they are posted, whether it be the Observation or Main Line, to the last man...

These orders indicate both the further progress required in up-skilling the troops, while stressing the utmost priority of holding the present front.

At the same time there remained the need to equip soldiers with the necessary skills for offensive manoeuvres, given the increasing anticipation that operations to advance the front are pending. Thus in the following weeks the brigade's training reports include reference to:

Musketry	Attention has been paid to rapid loading, to fire control and to the indication of targets.
Gas	Training in musketry etc... and other exercises... [have] been carried out while men are wearing masks
Drill	Training in the preliminary stages of the platoon in the attack has begun.
B.F. & P.T.	Instruction in Bayonet Fighting has been carried out daily.

The officers received lectures on 'the platoon in the assault'.[66]

August 1918 would see these operations begin to be carried out for real; although as late as 5-6 September 1918, 120 Brigade records that its units were 'practising' outpost and advanced guard operations, at battalion and brigade levels.[67] 40th Division orders include frequent refer-

65 TNA WO95/2610, War Diary of 120th Infantry Brigade, Training Progress Report 12-7-18; Brigade Order No. 204 8-7-18.

66 TNA WO95/2610, War Diary of 120 Infantry Brigade, Training Progress Reports 19 July 1918, 26/7/1918.

67 TNA WO95/2610, War Diary of 120 Infantry Brigade.

ences to 'advanced guard brigade' which comprised a brigade formation with attached field artillery and machine gun teams, under the command of the brigade CO.

In common with the rest of the BEF, Second Army was increasingly composed of conscripted men:

> By the Allied summer advance of 1918 a majority of the men fighting in the [BEF] were conscripts, and it was this force which won the war.[68]

The war diary of 7/Seaforth Highlanders states that on 7 July 1918 the battalion received reinforcements: 28 other ranks from 3rd Argyll & Sutherland Highlanders. It notes that the average age was 18-19 years, and none had previous service abroad.[69] In common with many other battalions, the Seaforth Highlanders continued to receive new drafts of men at various intervals:

10th July	22 ORs
	16 ORs
23rd July	20 ORs
27th July	2 Officers and 63 ORs

Following the original introduction of conscription through the Military Service Act of January 1916, there had been a further series of revisions which had widened the net from which new drafts were drawn. The changes in 1918 are indicative of the manpower problems faced by the BEF and demonstrate the very wide range of calibre of conscript which would make up the replacement drafts for units.[70] The Military Service Act (II) in February 1918 raised the age limit to 50 years, revised the schedules of reserved occupations, and gave the Ministry of National Service the power to cancel exemptions granted on occupational grounds. In July 1918 the Act was amended to raise the minimum age for exemption due to working in a protected occupation, to 23 years. While there had been developments in the medical inspection of recruits and revisions in the resulting classification system, there was consistent pressure to supply the army with new troops.

> Ultimately, fitness remained a relative term: such were the demands of war that military considerations nearly always overrode medical ones.[71]

The following table (also included as Appendix II) sets outs the medical categories applied to recruits and conscripts, noting the major change in October 1917 which removed Category C

68 I. R. Bet-El, *Conscripts: Forgotten Men of the Great War* (Gloucestershire: The History Press, 2009), p. 2.
69 TNA WO95/1765, War Diary of 7th Battalion, Seaforth Highlanders, 7 July 1918.
70 For an overview of conscription see Bet-El, *Conscripts*, Introduction pp. 1-24; from which the main information in this section is drawn.
71 Bet-El, *Conscripts*, p. 37; however, while this was a prime consideration for the authorities in Britain, the evidence suggests a more sympathetic and pragmatic approach closer to the front line – for example the approach adopted towards the soldiers in 2/4th Somerset Light Infantry (34th Division) described earlier.

and transferred all men so listed to the equivalent subdivision of Category B; thus increasing the potential pool of those who could serve on the Western Front in support of the BEF :

Medical Categories[72]

Category A – fit for general service	A1	Men for despatch overseas in all respects, as regards training, physical and mental qualifications
	A2	Recruits who should be A1 on completion of their training
	A3	Returned Expeditionary Force men who should be A1 once 'hardened'
	A4	Men under 19 years of age who should become A1 or A2 once they reach that age
Category B – fit for service abroad, but not general service	B1	In Garrison or Provisional units
	B2	In Labour units or on garrison or regimental outdoor employment
	B3	On sedentary work as clerks or store men only
Category C – fit for home service only	C1	In Garrison or Provisional units
	C2	In Labour units or on command, garrison or regimental outdoor employment
	C3	On sedentary work as clerks, storemen, batmen, cooks, orderlies, sanitary duties, etc.
Category D – temporarily unfit for service, but likely to become so within six months	D1	In command depots
	D2	In regimental depots
	D3	In any unit or depot under or awaiting medical or dental treatment, on completion of which will re-join their original medical category
Category E – unfit for service, and not likely to become fit within six months		

Notes:
In October 1917, following recommendations made in the report of Lieutenant General H. M. Lawson at the start of the year, under ACI 1606/17, Category C was abolished; men listed within this category were recategorised in the corresponding Category B subdivision
In addition, the following categories were applied in France and Flanders:
Class A – fit for general service
Class TB (Temporary Base) – temporarily unfit for general service
Class PB (Permanent Base) – unfit for general service at the Front, but fit for service on the lines of communication and in army corps areas and capable of being regraded Class A
Class PU (Permanently Unfit) – those in class PB who are never likely to become Class A, but employed in the same way as Class PB

72 The information in the table is taken from C. Messenger, Call to Arms: The British Army 1914-18 (London: Cassell, 2006), Appendix Two, pp. 521-2; which quotes the sources: *Statistics of the Military Effort of the British Empire During the Great War 1914-1920* (War Office, 1922; reprinted by Naval & Military Press, 1999); TNA WO32/5093, Lawson Report, The Number and Physical Categories of Men Employed out of the Fighting Area in France.

The new drafts into units were not always of the best quality. 14th Division had been reduced to a training cadre the end of April 1918. The division was subsequently reconstituted during June 1918, being 'mobilized with 'B' men'.[73] An administrative note on 5 July 1918 lists the infantry and specialist units which have arrived in the 'Concentration Area'; and confirms the arrival of the remaining units, including 43 Brigade HQ, its constituent battalions and the division's pioneer battalion, on the following day. The various supply arrangements are described – the note then ends with the following important commitment:

> Arrangements are being made to deliver S.A.A. and Grenades and the attendance of the Field Cashier as soon as possible.[74]

The new arrivals were therefore reassured that they would have ammunition for their weapons as well as being paid before becoming fully operational.

The importance of the rebuilding process for such units – and the pride to be gained in due course through achievements in the field – is shown by a subsequent note in the diary of 42 Brigade:

> [7th September 1918]
> The 14th [Argyll & Sutherland Highlanders] captured 1 NCO & 7 O.R. 12th Bavarian Division in a patrol encounter. These were the first prisoners captured by the reorganised 14th Division.[75] [My emphasis]

15/Loyal North Lancs (attached to the division as its pioneer battalion), from an initial cadre of about ten officers and forty ORs, was boosted by new drafts during June to 43 officers and 937 ORs – but on 2 July, 254 of the new arrivals were then 'boarded' as medically unfit and returned to Britain.[76]

The process of rebuilding the brigades which would make up 30th Division shows the amount of additional work and training which parts of Second Army had to undertake to make them fit for purpose. For 21 Brigade it began during June 1918, when the brigade HQ was involved in overseeing cadre battalions and also delivering training to American units. On 17 June its first battalion joined the brigade: 5/Royal Irish Fusiliers. However, just over a week later, the battalion left the brigade, 'having been found medically unfit for service'.[77] The brigade received (and kept) its three new battalions at the beginning of July: 7/Royal Irish Regiment (4 July), 1/6 Cheshires and 2/23 London Regiment (7 July).

73 TNA WO95/1880, War Diary of 14th Division, Administration Section, statement alongside period dated 17th to 30 June 1918.
74 TNA WO95/1880, War Diary of 14th Division, Administration Section, O.C.1 'A' and 'Q' NOTES 5.7.18.
75 TNA WO95/1899, War Diary of 42 Infantry Brigade.
76 War Diary of 15th Battalion, Loyal North Lancashire Regiment (Pioneers).
77 TNA WO95/2328, War Diary of 21 Infantry Brigade; 5/Royal Irish Fusiliers joined the Brigade on 17 June and left on 26 June 1918.

The different experiences of each of these three battalions leading up to their deployment as part of 21 Brigade provides a clear illustration of the variable make-up of formations within Second Army.

7/Royal Irish had only been rebuilt as a battalion at the end of June 1918:

> [26 June 1918]
> The training staff of the 7th (SIH) [South Irish Horse] Royal Irish Regiment arrived to take over Irish Reinforcements composed of 500 Royal Dublin Fusiliers, 250 Royal Munster Fusiliers, 85 Royal Irish Regt.[78]

A period of organisation and training followed, with the battalion allocated to 21 Brigade of 30th Division on 4 July. Symbolism can be all in building and maintaining the morale and spirit of a unit. Three days later the war diary records that 'Drums and fifes having been received, the Drums were organised and practice commenced'.[79]

Like a number of other battalions in Second Army, 2/23 London Regiment had been based previously in the Middle East. It formally joined 21 Brigade on 8 July, spending the rest of the month on training and inspections. On 31 July it carried out 'a practice attack'.[80]

While part of the 25th Division, 6/Cheshires had suffered significant losses earlier in the year as had another battalion from the same regiment, 11/Cheshires. During June 1918 the two were put together as a composite battalion. On 17 June the 11th Battalion was formally absorbed into the 6th; 6/Cheshires began its new life with 16 officers and 492 other ranks.[81]

Just two months later, 1-2 September 1918, 21 Brigade composed of its three transferred or rebuilt battalions took part in the action to capture Wulverghem.[82] The 30th Division also included two other 'new' brigades. On 6 June 1918, the records of 89 Brigade note that '... officers of the British Cadre Battalions carried out tactical exercises without troops'.[83] One week later an order was issued by the new 30th Division HQ stating that:

> [It has been decided] to reconstitute the 30th Division as a first line Division with Battalions due to arrive from Egypt about the end of this month. In the meantime the Division will continue to supervise the training of American Divisions in the Fourth Army area.[84]

After a further week the battalion training cadres under 89 Brigade HQ were transferred across to the 66th Division. The brigade was then put together with three battalions joining: 2/17 London Regiment and 2/South Lancashire Regiment (30 June); 7/8 Royal Inniskilling Fusiliers (3 July 1918).[85]

78 TNA WO95/2330, War Diary of 7th Battalion, Royal Irish Regiment.
79 TNA WO95/2330, War Diary of 7th Battalion, Royal Irish Regiment.
80 TNA WO95/2330, War Diary of 2/23rd Battalion, London Regiment.
81 TNA WO95/2330, War Diary of 1/6th Battalion, Cheshire Regiment.
82 TNA WO95/2330, War Diary of 7th Battalion, Royal Irish Regiment.
83 TNA WO95/2332, War Diary of 89 Infantry Brigade.
84 TNA WO95/2332, War Diary of 89 Infantry Brigade, 13 June 1918.
85 TNA WO95/2332, War Diary of 89 Infantry Brigade, 19 June, 30 June, 3 July 1918.

Preparations had been made in May 1918 for 90 Brigade to become a cadre brigade and to play a part in the training of American troops. The brigade consisted of a HQ establishment; by 19 May it had responsibility for five cadre battalions, each of which contained ten officers and 49 other ranks.[86] In July the brigade was formed with the addition of its three battalions from the London Regiment, all transferred from Egypt: 2/14 London Scottish (1 July); 2/15 Civil Service Rifles and 2/16 Queen's Westminster Rifles (2 July 1918).[87] All three battalions had been together since mobilisation at the start of the war (their popular titles reflect the volunteer arrangements during the early part of the war), together with 2/13 London Regiment prior to the reduction of brigades from four to three battalions.

Individual battalions each had their own tales of rebuilding. The losses of 25th Division had led to it being broken up and a cadre sent to the UK. 2nd Battalion, Prince of Wales' Volunteers (South Lancs Regiment) (2/South Lancs), which had been part of a composite unit following the Battle of the Aisne, stayed in France and received new drafts to bring it back up to strength. It was deployed to 89 Brigade, 30th Division, with X Corps of Second Army, where it was quickly brought into action and played a full part in the subsequent advance.[88]

Despite the success of British forces, the casualty list remained high overall during the final months. David Bilton's history of the Hull Pals draws attention to the issue of the manpower shortage in the British Army generally and its impact upon the quality and quantity of available replacements for the units of the 31st Division. He refers to 'the extreme youth of the replacements' and that 'many men of less than perfect health were being sent to the front line'.[89] The latter group of reinforcements were initially sent to France as garrison troops (designated Category B1) in order to release existing troops for the front line. However, as referred to earlier, the demand for replacements could and did lead to their B1 status and 'garrison' designation being removed, and their deployment in the front line.

The practical consequences are illustrated by reference to the history of the 10th Battalion (Hull Pals), East Yorkshire Regiment (10/East Yorkshires):

> On the 13th [August 1918] we were unexpectedly relieved by the 15th KOYLI so that we could move to the left to replace some B1 men of the 8th Royal Irish Regiment… They had only done four days trench duty altogether, while their signallers had had but six weeks training, and the whole battalion had but six weeks training, and the whole battalion seemed amazed to find themselves actually in the fighting area.[90]

This example was not untypical for British forces including Second Army at that time. On 2 August 1918 Major-General Nicholson of 34th Division had noted '… all Battalions were down

86 TNA WO95/2338, War Diary of 90 Infantry Brigade; the orders are included in 2nd Army O.B. 1851/A.

87 TNA WO95/2338, War Diary of 90 Infantry Brigade; TNA WO95/2340, War Diary of 2/14th Battalion, London Regiment; TNA WO95/2340, War Diary of 2/16th Battalion, London Regiment.

88 Captain H. Whalley-Kelly, *Ich Dien: The Prince of Wales's Volunteers (South Lancashire) 1914-1934* (Aldershot: Gale and Polden, 1935), pp. 61/2.

89 D. Bilton, *Hull Pals*, p. 156.

90 D. Bilton, *Hull Pals*, p. 156.

to an average strength of less than 250, short of officers and very tired… though quite willing to advance, I did not think the men were in a condition to go more than about 3 miles'.[91]

The 15/KOYLI was attached to 40th Division from June 1918. The battalion, initially designated as a Garrison battalion, was composed of mainly B1 and B2 classified soldiers, many transferred from Labour battalions. The first CO, Lieutenant-Colonel F C McCordick remarked with satisfaction that the men marched six miles from Watten to Buyscheure in full kit even though B2 men were technically certified as medically unfit to march more than five miles. I suspect that the view of the troops concerned may have been somewhat different on this breach of regulations.

By the time of the Final Advance it would have been very unusual for any battalion to be at full strength. The need to avoid unnecessary casualties was of increasing importance. On 6 September, 40th Division wrote to its units for the specific purpose of instructing officers to take additional care in this regard:

> 1 The situation as regards Reinforcements for the Division, particularly Infantry Reinforcements, is not, at the moment, entirely satisfactory. Hence it becomes more than ever necessary to conserve, as far as possible, Officers and men.
>
> The Divisional Commander looks to Unit Commanders for their whole hearted co-operation in this.
>
> He feels that much can be done in saving Officers and men unnecessary fatigue and exposure; in ensuring that they are well and regularly fed; in taking precautions about drinking water used, etc.
>
> 2 In the forward area there is not always sufficient attention paid to the avoidance of unnecessary movement, nor when movement is necessary is cover intelligently made use of.
>
> The necessity of wearing steel helmets and box respirators in the defined zones must be insisted on.
>
> 3 All matters of this sort which tend to prevent wastage must receive the attention of all Commanders.
>
> It is appreciated that much has been done already but it is felt that there is still more to do.[92]

The Operational Readiness of Second Army: Training and Deployment

As we have seen, training was of crucial importance given the number of reconstituted units within Second Army and the large number of new conscripts and re-designated men. The examples set out below represent Second Army's practical implementation of the processes outlined in the British Army's principal operational doctrine, *SS 135 The Training and Employment of Divisions* (issued in January 1918).

14th Division was one of the reconstituted divisions, put together during June 1918 before joining Second Army in July. There was therefore a very heavy emphasis upon training for the

91 IWM 01/14/1 Papers of Major-General Nicholson .
92 TNA WO95/2610, War Diary of 120 Infantry Brigade, 40th Division No. 23 (A), 6 September 1918.

officers and men making up the battalions and supporting arms. For the units in 41 Brigade, the training programme throughout that summer included such topics as:

- Gas drill
- Time on the firing range
- Small tactical schemes for platoons
- Company and patrol work
- Tanks
- 'Duties of the RAF and the difficulties' (a lecture attended by 200 soldiers)
- 'Fire discipline and fire control' (for officers and NCOs)
- Troop deployment: extended order, artillery formation.[93]

The range of the subject matter is very broad, from basic marksmanship through to co-operation with tanks and the RAF. What this list suggests is the ongoing need for the new formations, at all levels, to receive training in some of the more elementary aspects of their role. Having moved up into the front line on 28 August, the war diary conceded a few days later that 'Units [were] lacking in knowledge of elementary trench duties'.[94]

43 Brigade, also part of 14th Division, had been reconstituted in England, comprising 12th Suffolks, 20th (Shoreditch) Middlesex, and 10th Highland Light Infantry; both the latter two battalions had been rebuilt from cadre in June 1918. The brigade returned to France on 4-5 July 1918.[95] The war diary of 43 Brigade contains the details of a tactical exercise for training purposes carried out on specified days in the middle of July 1918, shortly after the units re-grouped. The memo also provides an insight into the tactical thinking at this point in the war. The new weapons systems had to be married to the priority of preparing relatively raw troops for the new offensive realities presented to allied forces on the Western Front:

43 Brigade July 1918 (1)
Tactical Exercise (extract)

43rd Bde G.S. 78.

[The circulation list includes the three constituent battalions, 14th Machine Gun Battalion, 43rd Trench Mortar Battery,43rd Division]

The Tactical Exercise to be carried out by the Brigade Group will be divided as follows:

1st day. 10th July. Tactical Exercise conducted by B.G.C.

C.O's and Adjutants of Battalions and C.O's T.M.Bty and Machine Gun Company will attend. Note books – pencils … and CALAIS maps will be brought. Officers will be mounted. Horse holders will be brought…

93 TNA WO95/1894/6, War Diary of 41 Infantry Brigade, entries for July and August 1918.
94 TNA WO95/1894/6, War Diary of 41 Infantry Brigade, 31 August 1918.
95 TNA WO95/1905, War Diary of 43 Infantry Brigade.

2nd day. 11th July.	Tactical Exercise (Battalions) without troops conducted by O.C. Battns. O.C. 43rd T.M. Bty. With 12th Suffolk Regt.	
3rd day. 12th July.	12th Suffolk Regt.) 20th Middx Regt.)	Tactical Exercise (Battalions) with troops O.C. T.M. Bty with 12th Suffolk Regt.
10th H.L.I. 13th July.	Tactical Exercise (Battalions) with troops.	
4th day. 15th July.	Brigade Exercise with troops.	

INSTRUCTIONS.

The object of the exercise is to practice the attack on a position by one Battalion.

The theoretical consolidation of it by that battalion and the passing through the first battalion and capture of a secondary position by another battalion.

The main points to be practiced on the Brigade day with troops being as follows:

43 Brigade July 1918 (2)
Tactical Exercise (extract)

a) The pushing forward of Lewis Guns, with boldness, so as to penetrate the enemy's defences, whenever a weak spot is found, in order to enfilade or turn any hostile troops that are holding out.
b) The pushing forward of the L.T.M. Bty in close support of the attacking Infantry, in order to deal with strong points and prepare the way for a further advance. The consideration of the supply of T.M. ammunition and carriage of the guns.
c) The support of the Infantry by the VICKERS M.G's with covering fire. The allotting to certain of these guns if definite tasks i.e. the scouring of a locality when captured, and the 'ear-marking' of certain guns of opportunity to deal with floating targets.

On the Battalion days with troops the following pints will receive attention:
a) Artillery formations.
b) Movement from Artillery formations into open order.
c) Preservation and maintenance of direction.
d) Use of ground and cover.
e) Mutual support, namely covering fire, no movement without fire.
f) Fire orders, control of fire, the giving of correct ranges, indication, description and recognition of targets, etc.

[Calais map reference]

GENERAL IDEA
The German advanced troops are holding a line as follows… the Battle has been in progress for three days and is of the semi-open warfare type.

SPECIAL IDEA
The 43rd Infantry Brigade has been ordered to carry out a minor operation with a view to capturing the high ground… troops on either flank are co-operating… the attacking troops are assembled… when orders for the attack are issued.

8th July 1918.

Captain, Brigade Major,
43rd Infantry Brigade.[96]

These manoeuvres demonstrate the adoption of a modern style of warfare based upon 'fire and movement', combining the effective use of infantry support weapons and the tactics of enfilade fire and flanking movement. These elements are demonstrated time and again in the planning and execution of Second Army operations at brigade and battalion levels.

The importance of learning lessons was widely recognised, with senior officers present to provide commentary and feedback. On 7 September a tactical exercise by 26 Brigade (9th Division) was viewed by the brigade and division commanders. The main points of the resulting feedback included:

- The importance of the prompt conveyance of orders from HQ to junior commanders
- Soldiers should be trained to use the Lewis Gun and rifles at long range, not waiting until the enemy is within 200-300 yards
- The best way to kill retreating Boche was not to bayonet individuals (however enjoyable that process may be) but to bring rapid and effective controlled fire to bear on them
- Unless the infantry are well supported by artillery, they will not advance as rapidly as they might do with the guns behind them – There was no reason why the Field Artillery should not always support the infantry as they were quite as mobile as if not more so than them
- A smoke screen is a valuable aid when attacking
- [A discussion on the relative merits of the 'snake' and other formations when attacking] … it was decided to adopt a more open formation than the 'snake' in future operations.[97]

The move away from emphasis upon cold steel (the bayonet) to the use of controlled fire indicates a major shift in doctrine. The comments on the field artillery, particularly with regard to expecting the guns to keep pace with the advancing infantry, would prove to be a challenge, particularly in the early stages of the campaign when the terrain was comprised of former battlefields, made worse by severe rain. The need for troops to deploy in open order when assaulting, adopting a looser formation than even that represented by the 'snake' profile, suggests a growing confidence in the initiative and ability of the individual soldiers; given that this would make it more difficult for NCOs and officers to maintain command and control during the attack. There

96 TNA WO95/1905, War Diary of 43 Infantry Brigade, memo: 43rd Bde G.S. 7S
97 TNA WO95/1765, War Diary of 7th Battalion, Seaforth Highlanders, 7 September 1918.

would be an implicit trust in the commitment of the troops to continue to manoeuvre forward, making maximum use of covering fire and available ground cover.

In a later exercise the same unit practised 'advancing over rough ground' with regard to the pace of the advance, to provide a useful guide when considering the timing for a creeping barrage, or plans for subsequent defensive fire. 'The average pace of advance was found to be 100 [yards] in 3 minutes and it was found impossible to maintain 'blob' formation'.[98] This latter view reinforces the need to allow troops to adopt a more open formation, although it would be crucial to maintain touch with a creeping barrage.

Having only been brought together in June 1918, with many men transferred from Labour Companies, 10/KOSB spent most of that month, July and the first half of August undergoing training; this included some time in support trenches (West Hazebrouck, 3-7 July 1918). The unit was finally put into front line positions in the third week in August; on 21 August it received orders to follow up a withdrawal by opposing enemy forces. Two days later the battalion attacked German positions and was met by machine gun fire and a defensive barrage; the attack was only 'partially successful' in consequence.[99]

Research of the war diaries of the battalions, with the original notes and diaries of the participants, illustrates that throughout the Final Advance, the units maintained regular army routines and procedures. Despite the speed of the advance and the problems created for communications, for example, the troops of 31st Division underwent a number of moves from front line duty to time out of the line in reserve or support occupations, or undertaking various forms of training. The latter was largely the responsibility of the battalion commander and could reflect his own priorities or be drawn from particular points arising from battle experience. During September 1918, 11/East Yorkshires spent time in reserve and received training sessions under the headings of 'NCOs', 'Lewis Gunners', 'Signalling', 'Observers', 'Scouts', and 'Stretcher Bearers'. On 21 September Captain C J Casey (Intelligence Corps) gave a lecture on 'The Work of the RAF and its use to infantry'.[100] This record is a very good reflection of the changed nature of the British Army by this stage of the war, and the developed nature of its fighting, weaponry and tactics. The influence of Lieutenant-General Ivor Maxse, in his new role with responsibility for training across the British Army, would now be in evidence. On 9 August 1918, senior officers from Second Army attended one of his lectures on 'The Training of Infantry'.[101]

On 23 and 24 September, 1/18th Battalion, Durham Light Infantry (1/18 DLI), perhaps reflecting optimism or prescience, ran a lecture on 'Education After the War'.[102]

The value of some of the training and lectures offered to troops was sometimes called into question. The following critical reviews were recorded in the war diary of 41 Brigade:

10 August	Lecture on 'Aeroplane Photography' by Second Army Photographic Officer [attended by over 100 soldiers] An interesting subject badly treated.

98 TNA WO95/1905, War Diary of 7th Battalion, Seaforth Highlanders, 18 September 1918.
99 TNA WO95/2611/4, War Diary of 10th Battalion, Kings Own Scottish Borderers.
100 War Diary of 11th Battalion, East Yorkshire Regiment.
101 TNA WO95/1894/6, War Diary of 41 Infantry Brigade.
102 TNA WO 95/2361, War Diary of 1/18th Battalion, Durham Light Infantry.

14 August	Lecture on 'Duties of Counter Batteries' A dull subject after a hard day's work.[103]

Units and troops also changed line responsibilities on a number of occasions, with time spent travelling (by rail, lorries, and on foot) between different points of the front. When out of the front line or support positions, units or contingents of soldiers could be involved in training, recreation or labouring. Senior command in Second Army looked to ensure that no group of soldiers endured an overlong period in the front line. The arrangement was designed to keep the fighting forces as fresh as possible, though success in this was to become a relative term given the subsequent pace of the advance, the problems of transport and supply, and the determined resistance by the enemy at particular defensive points.

During July 1918, the record of 5/Cameron Highlanders (26 Brigade, 9th Division) demonstrates the variety of deployments and activities which troops could expect to be engaged in. This breadth of experience differs markedly from the common perception today of the common soldier's daily routine amidst the trench warfare of the Western Front and the First World War. The following is a brief summary of the battalion's deployment over the course of the month:

1-4 July	Battalion stationed in the Reserve Line. Troops involved in work parties (One officer, 50 other ranks): for example, deployed as a 'carrying party' for the 3rd Canadian Tunnelling Company. Six other ranks spent time filling in shell holes under the supervision of the 64th Field Company RE. Some units also underwent training: for example, Reserve Company Lewis Gunners.
4-7 July	Battalion relieved 7/Seaforth Highlanders in the 'right front sub sector'. There is shelling by the enemy on a daily basis plus machine gun fire at night. Patrols are sent out each night: for example, four other ranks (no officer) from B Company ordered to search for the location of enemy machine gun posts.
7-12 July	Battalion based in Brigade Support. Training includes 'artillery formations and the attack', followed by a practice rehearsal which is watched by both Brigade and Division COs.
13-18 July	Battalion deployed back to the front line. During the relief there is an attack by a German raiding party on an advance post but this is repulsed. Regular periods of enemy shelling An enemy sniper is proving to be very active – the likely location is shelled by artillery and three hits observed. The Battalion HQ suffers heavy shelling and the Battalion Adjutant, Captain M.C. Muir, is wounded; Stoic Farm is evacuated as a consequence, this taking place during a 'violent thunderstorm' and heavy rain. On 18 July a raiding party of 20 other ranks led by Lieutenant A.L. Wilson attacked an enemy machine gun post; the action failed, due in part to the

103 TNA WO95/1894/6, War Diary of 41 Infantry Brigade.

covering smoke shells falling short, and the troops were beaten back by machine gun fire. Six soldiers were reported as missing, including Lieutenant Wilson.

The Battalion was informed that on 19 July it would take part in an attack on the village of Meteren, in conjunction with 8/Black Watch and units from the South African Brigade. The aim is to capture the village and prevent its use for observation purposes by the enemy.

19-24 July — Front line and support operations: attack on Meteren.
(This raid is described in more detail later in this book).

25-30 July — Battalion based in Corps Reserve.

31 July... — Battalion moved up into the Support Line (Meteren) and on the following day took over the Brigade's section of the front line. Two German carrier pigeons were shot down – more importantly, the messages being carried were retrieved.[104]

At the end of the first week in August, 35th Division, deployed in the Locre Sector, was relieved by 30th Division. Accordingly, 90 Brigade of 30th Division replaced 105 Brigade in line, with the latter moving back to billets in the area of Sylvestre Cappel.

Its war diary describes the subsequent training and work duties undertaken by the troops of 105 Brigade, much of the content in preparation for offensive action:

August 9th — One platoon from each Battalion, detailed for work in the forward area under No. 1. Foreways Company...

10th — The Units of the Brigade spent the day re-organizing and refitting.

12th — Orders were issued relating to a practice attack on the TERDEGHEM SWITCH by 15th. Sherwood Foresters and the 4th. North Staffordshire Regiment, to take place on Wednesday, 14th. August. Only Signallers on Brigade Headquarters and of each Unit to take part – assisted by a contact aeroplane of 53rd. Squadron R.A.F.
[An exercise demonstrating the crucial need for effective communications during an assault – and the importance of this within Second Army preparations.]
Battalions carried out training according to programme.
[15th Cheshires ordered to undertake] 4 days Range Practice.
[Brigadier-General Turner went on a short leave to England.]

13th — The 105th. Brigade Headquarters Staff... attended a Lecture... on 'Counter-Battery Work'. A closer co-operation between Infantry and Artillery was advocated, and facilities for more immediate action were promised.
[This could have been in part a response to the number of casualties being caused to the troops manning front line positions – and the concerns of their immediate commanders.]

104 TNA WO95/1767, War Diary of 5th Battalion, Cameron Highlanders.

14th	[Practice attack on the TERDEGHEM SWITCH by Signal troops carried out.] The object of the practice exercise was to improve the efficiency of Signal Personnel in the use of the 'T' POPHAM PANEL' and other means of communication (without cable). Communication between Headquarters of Assaulting Battalions and Headquarters of 105th. Infantry Brigade was satisfactorily established and maintained by means of (a) 'T' POPHAM PANEL', (b) Visual and (c) Runner.

On 15, 17, 20, 21, 23, 25, and 27 August, the diary refers to 'Training continued'.
Other elements of note include:

16th	Instructions (105th. Infantry Brigade G.1427) shewing 'Action of 105th. Infantry Brigade while in 10th Corps Reserve' issued.
19th	A short Brigade Tactical exercise (in which Officers only took part) was carried out during the evening.
22nd	Second Army Commander visited 15th. Cheshire Regiment and 15th. Sherwood Foresters and inspected them while training.[105] [Evidence of Plumer's interest in, and attention to, training for his men.]

These extracts show the range of activities in which units could be engaged during the period when they were withdrawn from the line. It supports a positive picture of Second Army's commitment to training, and its role as a learning organisation. There is very little reference to troops being used for work duties such as road repairs or similar; nor in this case is there any record of recreational activities such as inter-unit sports competitions. The emphasis appears to be very much on improving the skills of the soldiers while there is time and opportunity to do so. Reflecting the time spent behind the lines, the monthly casualties' report showed no soldiers killed or missing; two officers and 20 men were recorded as wounded.

Extracts from the war diary of 5/Cameron Highlanders, when out of the line during August and September 1918, provide a further snapshot of the range of activities which were arranged for the troops, recreational and educational:

12 August	Brigade Horse Show – the Battalion Transport won First Prize
13 August	Bathing parades
14 August	Gas Chamber
15 August	All officers tested in 'Playfair Cypher' Division Horse Show – the Battalion Transport won First Prize
2 September	Battalion Signallers, Officers and Officers from A, B, and D Companies attended a demonstration of message carrying rockets (no comments are recorded)
3 September	All officers attended a lecture on 'Tactical Deployment of Machine Guns'
9 September	Brigade Sports Day – 5/Camerons won First Prize:

105 TNA WO95/2486, War Diary of 105 Infantry Brigade.

The list of events, some of which reflect the Scottish origins of the troops, included:

Best Platoon	Tug O' War	Mile Race
½ Mile Race	Relay Race	High Jump
Hammer Throwing	Piping (Bagpipes I presume)	
Cross-Country	100 yards	200 yards
Hop, Skip & Jump	Putting the Shot	Long Jump
Dancing the Reel	Highland Fling	Sword Dance[106]

Maintaining the men in healthy condition was another important factor with regard to the organisation of a unit's routine of duties. The war diary of 7/Seaforth Highlanders notes on 8 July 1918 that, after a long spell of trench duties (33 days), the men had a bath and were issued with clean underclothing; the medical officer, following inspection and acknowledging the length of time spent in front and support positions, 'remarked on the clean condition [of the troops]'.[107]

In the circumstances of the trenches the risk of infection was ever-present; a later note from the same source records:

> The prevalence of diarrhoea was very marked during this tour and was attributed largely to the water supply. The MO should test all water supplies.[108]

Recreation was a regular feature of time out of the lines, officers making arrangements to promote sports competitions between units, with men taking part or as spectators. This was a means of ensuring healthy activity as well as providing entertainment for the troops. Appended to the war diary of 120 Brigade there is the programme, with cover page cartoon, for the brigade's Sports Day, 7 September 1918. There are a mix of events including athletic races, horse jumping, tug-of-war, sack race, mule race ('no saddlery, spurs or stick') and bicycle tortoise race ('last man in wins'). An entrance fee of 10 francs is to go to the General Fund.[109]

On 9 July 1918 the 7/Seaforth Highlanders held a battalion football tournament with inter-company matches; the following day its Division (9th) held a football match with a team from 31st Division (the result is not recorded – perhaps the officer writing up the diary was not a soccer fan).[110] Such activities were also used to bring allies together. On the evening of 17 September C Company of 7/Seaforth Highlanders played a football match against a Belgian team with the latter winning by two goals to one.[111]

There is other evidence of sport bringing together Belgian and British troops. 'Belgian Fete Day' is recorded as taking place on 21 July 1918 – at this event there were two sporting

106 TNA WO95/1767, War Diary of 5th Battalion, Cameron Highlanders.
107 TNA WO95/1765, War Diary of 7th Battalion, Seaforth Highlanders, 8 July 1918.
108 TNA WO95/1765, War Diary of 7th Battalion, Seaforth Highlanders, 10 August 1918.
109 TNA WO95/2610, War Diary of 120th Infantry Brigade, 120th Brigade Sports 7 September 1918.
110 TNA WO95/1765, War Diary of 7th Battalion, Seaforth Highlanders, 9 and 10 July 1918.
111 TNA WO95/1765, War Diary of 7th Battalion, Seaforth Highlanders; the Battalion belonged to 9th (Scottish) Division, the northernmost of the Second Army divisions, and deployed next to the Belgian Army.

competitions for teams from the Belgian Army and British Second Army, with prizes provided by Princess Philippa of Caraman-Chimay. The briefing note from 29th Division continues:

> The CARAMAN-CHIMAY CUP, to be competed [for] annually, and 11 medals, for the winning Divisional Association Football Team, from the two Armies.
>
> 8 Medals for a Cross Country Run of 10 kilometres. Open to 8 runners from each of the [Belgian and British Second] Armies. Further information is being asked for, as to whether this is a team or individual event…
>
> It is thought that the best way of selecting a Divisional Team, as time is so short, will be to find out the best Battalion or other Unit team by an eliminating tournament and then give that Unit the choice of playing in the Corps tournament with the team as then constituted, or of selecting one or more men from any other Unit for inclusion in their team…
>
> Brigades and Divisional Artillery will select 8 men and all other Divisional Units… 4 men to represent them in a race to be arranged by Divisional H.Qrs over a 10 Kilometre course. The first 8 men in will represent the Division …[112]

On 3 July, 36th Division held its Horse Show at Proven, with Belgian guests of demonstrable ability:

> Upon this the officers of the neighbouring Belgian Cavalry Division, including an Olympic competitor, descended like wolves on the fold, giving a remarkable display of skill and horsemanship, and taking practically all the prizes for jumping events.[113]

As late as 10 September, just two weeks before the Battle of Ypres began, a football match took place between British and Belgian teams, from 18/York & Lancaster and 2nd Belgian Grenadier Regiment; the latter winning by two goals to one, 'the Belgians being slightly the better team'.[114]

Gas

A striking feature of the war diaries from Second Army formations is the commonplace reference to the use of gas as one of the components of both sides' weaponry. This should not be a surprise, given that more than half of the recorded use of gas occurred during the final year of the war, and around half of the fatalities resulting from exposure to gas on the Western Front occurred in 1918.[115]

It was in operations in Flanders, in the Ypres Salient in the spring of 1915, that the Germans had been the first to make use of chemical warfare. However the British then also adopted gas as a weapon, becoming the leaders in gas warfare, such that 'the Germans never regained

112 TNA WO95/2299, War Diary of 86 Infantry Brigade, Administrative Order, 29th Division, No. 160/136, 1 July, 1918.

113 C. Falls, *A History of the 36th (Ulster) Division* (London: Constable, 1996; first published Belfast: McCraw, Stevenson, 1922).

114 TNA WO95/1894/6, War Diary of 41 Infantry Brigade.

115 Stevenson, *Backs to the Wall*, p. 200; the section pp. 200-205 gives a useful summary of poison gas usage by both sides during 1918.

their early advantage'.[116] In his chapter on the application of chemical warfare from his book on the impact of chemistry on the war,[117] Michael Freemantle discusses the development of the weapon and its effectiveness. He quotes the conclusion of Albert Palazzo that 'gas [became] 'the most effective method' of neutralising the enemy's guns and achieving fire supremacy. It also lowered the morale of the enemy and reduced their ability to resist.[118]

Lloyd describes how the deployment of gas as a weapon had become commonplace by this final year of the war:

> The allied armies had to operate in a terrible and dangerous chemical environment... gas evoked a fear that was unlike any other weapon and had a significant effect on how the war was fought ... By 1918 all sides had incorporated gas into their battle tactics, with both front and rear sectors regularly being deluged with gas, which poisoned the ground and caused a constant trickle of casualties.[119]

Gas was a constant feature of the fighting in Ypres and Flanders. It had become part and parcel of the front line soldier's daily experience. In a lecture to troops in September 1918, a Divisional Gas Officer is recorded as '... reminding his audience that the YPRES Sector has always been the enemy's gas experimental ground'.[120]

Peter Hart, writing on the warfare in 1918, summarises the gases and gas shells used by the German Army:

> The Germans were using a mixture of gases including Blue Cross, Green Cross and Yellow Cross. The Blue Cross was... a truly deadly weapon – if it had worked properly. It contained an arsenic-based compound that acted as a powerful [irritant on] the nasal and repertory passages to cause coughing, sneezing and sometimes vomiting... When the... victim tore off his mask in an effort to breathe he would then be exposed to the deadly Green Cross shells that contained phosgene, a lung irritant sixteen times more lethal than the chlorine gas used in 1915... [but] the German Blue Cross shells were one of the biggest failures of the war as the detonation of the shell on landing proved inadequate to properly disperse the powder ...Far more dangerous was the menace of the Yellow Cross mustard gas. Exposure to this unpleasant substance severely burnt the skin and had a terrible effect on the eyes... [It] took some time to disperse and thereby rendered areas virtually impassable for long periods.[121]

116 G. Corrigan, *Mud, Blood and Poppycock: Britain and the First World War* (London: Cassell, 2003), p. 173.
117 M. Freemantle, *Gas! Gas! Quick Boys! How Chemistry Changed the First World War* (Gloucestershire: The History Press, Spellmount, 2012), Chapter 6, pp. 115-120.
118 A. Palazzo, *Seeking Victory on the Western Front: The British Army and Chemical Warfare in World War I* (Lincoln, Nebraska: University of Nebraska Press, 2000), p. 2; quoted in Freemantle, *Gas!*, p. 120.
119 Lloyd, *Hundred Days*, p. 102.
120 TNA WO95/1905, War Diary of 7th Battalion, Seaforth Highlanders, 17 September 1918.
121 P. Hart, *1918: A Very British Victory* (London: Wiedenfeld & Nicolson, 2008), pp. 68-9.

Lloyd observed that:

> Mustard gas… was used in increasing amounts by the German artillery. As the retreat [by the German forces] gathered momentum, German gunners fired thousands of these shells at their pursuers, using it as an area denial weapon, through which the Allies could not advance, or at least not without difficulty.[122]

He quotes the findings of Tim Cook:

> German gunners simply blocked out map grids and fired shells to saturate the whole sector, thereby eliminating that area from the front.[123]

Despite the dangers from gas, the references within the war diaries of Second Army units indicate that it was dealt with as part of the normal routine of the troops. In spite of the relative inexperience of many units making up Second Army, from their first time in the front line men had to be able to cope with the gas shells delivered as part of enemy bombardments. On 17 August 1918 (on the first morning of only the second spell for the battalion on front line duty), the war diary of 11th Cameron Highlanders records that 'In the early morning Lt. G.S. Young and four men were gassed and two men wounded'.[124] On 24 September, 104 Brigade records that 'Gas, especially Blue Cross, being used very extensively by the enemy'.[125]

Within the war diaries of Second Army units there are constant references to the use of gas shells by the German artillery. This could affect both front and support lines. There is no particular importance attached to these references – it was obviously viewed as par for the course during front line duty and the routine harassment from the enemy's guns:

> [5/Cameron Highlanders]
> 18 August Meteren Heavy gas concentration put down over our whole front line.
> 22 August Meteren Enemy threw over a few Gas shells during Night.[126]

The use of gas shells in enemy artillery fire was a commonplace feature for the men on duty in the front line trenches. The following extracts are from the war diary of 120 Brigade while on a tour of duty at the front during August 1918:

22/23 Aug	[Enemy artillery carried out] continuous shelling of sector with H.E. mixed with gas shells ('Mustard').
23/24 Aug	Some heavy-calibre gas shells fell near VERT RUE, also 6 or 8 fell [nearby].
25/26 Aug	Between 2 a.m. and 6 a.m. [the enemy fired] over 100 rds. 10.5 c.m. phosgene gas … [other areas nearby] also received a few rounds of gas …

122 Lloyd, *Hundred Days*, p. 102.
123 T. Cook, *No Place To Run: The Canadian Corps and Gas Warfare in the First World War* (Vancouver: UBC Press, 1999), p. 200; quoted in Lloyd, *Hundred Days*, p. 102.
124 TNA WO95/2611/4, War Diary of 11th Battalion, Cameron Highlanders.
125 TNA WO95/2483, War Diary of 104 Infantry Brigade, 24 September 1918.
126 TNA WO95/1767, War Diary of 5th Battalion, Cameron Highlanders.

26/27 Aug During the night a few gas shells were mixed with H.E...
28/29 Aug Our patrols of the Right Company were successful in gaining an entrance into BOWERY COTTAGES... but due to a heavy enemy barrage mixed with gas... they were unable to advance.[127]

There are later references which give more details of the types of gas used; for example:

18/19 Sept ... heavily shelled with sneezing gas and Yellow Cross shells...
6 October ... a heavy barrage of mustard gas mixed with H.E. was put down on our support lines...
10/11 Oct ... Lachrymatory Gas... Mustard Gas mixed with H.E...[128]

Precautions were also necessary when men came into subsequent contact with everyday materials which had been present during a gas attack. In July 1918, 120 Brigade's war diary makes reference to gas being introduced into a dugout through the use of sandbags which had previously been in an area fired on by the German artillery, the barrage including gas shells.[129] Men's clothing could also be contaminated by gas. The following is from 120 Brigade's instructions issued in August 1918:

> Gassed Clothing Such men as have been affected with Yellow Cross gas will be sent to the Divisional Main Dressing Station with a certificate signed by an officer stating that their clothing has been affected, when fresh clothing will be issued.[130]

Hence contact with other soldiers who had themselves been subject to a gas attack, carried with it the threat of contamination. This and other concerns were addressed in guidance issued to the units of 40th Division in September 1918; the aim was to ensure all possible steps were taken to minimise the risk of injury through exposure to the after-effects of gas shelling, and to put in place suitable arrangements for disinfection:

1 As a result of recent experiments it has been found that Chlorine gas destroys Yellow Cross and its use as an external disinfectant has given very satisfactory results in treating clothing and equipment contaminated with this gas, thus saving 'gas' casualties among men who have not actually been in contact with the gas itself, but who came into contact later with men who have.
In an Army on our right many 'gas' casualties have been saved in this way.
2 A small chlorine gas chamber will therefore be established and maintained at the Advanced Dressing Station... under arrangements to be made between the A.D.M.S. and 40th Division Gas Officer: all personnel who have been in contact with Yellow Cross gas and are therefore likely to be contaminated with it, will be despatched as

127 TNA WO95/2610, War Diary of 120 Infantry Brigade, Intelligence Summaries.
128 TNA WO95/2610, War Diary of 120 Infantry Brigade.
129 TNA WO95/2610, War Diary of 120 Infantry Brigade.
130 TNA WO95/2610, War Diary of 120 Infantry Brigade, Administrative Instructions No. 215, 23 August 1918.

soon as possible to the A.D.S. and there passed through the chamber: this treatment should be carried out, if possible, before the men are allowed to congregate in any contained space. A period of 10 minutes in a concentration of about 1:1000 is sufficient.

3 When their condition permits of it, wounded men who are contaminated, and Yellow Cross gas casualties should also be passed through the chamber.

4 It has also been found that shell holes and inhabited localities such as dugouts, huts, gun positions, etc. that are contaminated with Yellow Cross Gas can be disinfected by being sprayed with Chlorine Gas: 40th Division Gas Officer will therefore arrange as soon as possible for the Gas N.C.O.'s of all units to receive instruction in this and they are in possession of the necessary equipment to carry out this disinfection process as soon as possible in any locality which may have become contaminated ...[131]

By this time in the war the British Army was also making regular use of gas as part of its artillery fire plans; arguably outpacing its enemy:

> Chemical warfare developed from a novelty in 1915 to an approved component of the British method of waging war by 1916 ... it made a significant contribution to the eventual British victory in 1918.[132]

Army and corps HQ had the position of Chemical Adviser on their staff; information on the use of gas by British forces and its effects on the enemy's troops and operations was an important part of intelligence gathering. Prisoner interviews were the most common source, with questions designed to assess the impact of British gas shells and gas operations on its enemy. Air photographs could show areas of bleached or contaminated ground.[133]

There are various routine references within the unit records of Second Army to the use of gas by British forces. This applied during periods of relative inactivity, as well as in support of offensive operations. The following order is recorded in the war diary of 121 Brigade:

> 121 Brigade: Order No. 30
>
> 600 gas bombs will be fired by 'L' Special Company, R. E. on the night of the 30th/31st July, or the first subsequent night when favourable weather conditions admit, from projectors [target details follow]...
> Code words: SNIP — Conditions favourable for gas discharge
> REMNANT — Conditions unfavourable, operation postponed 24 hours
> Troops to be clear of designated areas... box respirators to be worn.
> 31st Division artillery will co-operate.
> 31st Battalion Machine Gun Corps will fire some bursts of fire after the gas discharge.[134]

131 TNA WO95/2610, War Diary of 120 Infantry Brigade, 40th Div. No. 10/61 (G), 18/9/18.
132 Palazzo, *Seeking Victory*, p. 2.
133 For examples see TNA WO158/294, (Second Army) Effects of our Gas and Gas Shells, 11 October 1915-17 October 1918.
134 TNA WO95/2614, War Diary of 121 Infantry Brigade, 5 August 1918.

As described, gas operations by Second Army had become a normal feature of a soldier's daily routine. Where actions involving the use of gas were recorded in unit war diaries they were rarely noteworthy of particular comment. They were afforded no more comment than the regular exchanges of artillery fire, as this example from 42 Brigade shows:

> [9th September 1918]
> 280 Gas cylinders were discharged on Halfway House. Railway Wood and Dormy House. No Retaliation.
>
> [11th September 1918]
> 200 Gas Cylinders were successfully discharged on MILL COTS. and THE STABLES.[135]

The Army's use of gas as an offensive weapon also meant that British troops needed guidance regarding their approach to ground which had been subject to a gas bombardment by their own artillery; although much of the general advice and training provided on anti-gas measures was equally applicable. This example is from instructions issued by XV Corps in October 1918:

> <u>OUR OWN GAS SHELL BOMBARDMENTS</u>
>
> In an advance following our own gas shell bombardments Divisions will issue suitable instructions to the troops to prevent gas casualties while passing over the late target. While the length of time during which such an area is dangerous, unless respirators are worn, depends to a great extent on the weather conditions, the following figures are issued for guidance:

Gas.	Ground dangerous for	Remarks
With C.G.	½-2 hours	No under surface persistency
With N.C.	½-15 hours	Digging may not be possible for 24 Hours
With H.E.	48-60 hours	Under surface may remain dangerous for weeks

> NOTE
> The persistence of the liquid of [in] the ground is diminished by heavy rain, by sunshine or strong wind. During frosty and dull weather the persistency is increased.[136]

Despite its fearsome reputation, particularly in modern perception, gas was not the deadly killer of men that perhaps the general public might believe. It was the ability of gas to spread confusion and disorder, to distract the soldier through his having to concentrate on anti-gas measures, wherein its main practical value lay. A man having to struggle with his protective gear while choking or with eyes streaming, was less of a threat to the enemy. Freemantle has described how

135 TNA WO95/1899, War Diary of 42 Infantry Brigade.
136 TNA WO95/2610, War Diary of 120th Infantry Brigade, XV Corps No. 89/145 G. 28 October 1918.

he considers the prime value of the gas weapon lay in its psychological impact; it was more likely to cause soldiers to leave the field of battle, or be far less effective on it, than to be killed by it.[137]

It was therefore important for British troops to take appropriate steps in order to issue warnings as early as possible of a forthcoming gas attack and to take steps to protect themselves. Soldiers needed to be able to carry out anti-gas measures with little forethought, as a routine activity. At the beginning of August, 121 Brigade was issued with three closely typed pages of 'Anti-Gas Instructions', which also referred the reader to SS534 (March, 1918) where 'full details of Gas Defence' could be found.[138] The key elements of the 'Anti-Gas Instructions' included:

2. In the LA MOTTE Divisional Sector the Gas Zones are as follows:
   ALERT ZONE – East of the Hazebrouck-Morebecgue Railway.
   READY ZONE – East of a line joining BELLINGHEM & BLARINGHEK
3. A supply of Strombos Horns, Rattles, Gongs, and Fans may be obtained on application to Brigade…
4. All Formations and Units within the ALERT ZONE will prepare at their Headquarters and at such other places as Commanding Officers may find necessary 'WIND DANGEROUS' Boards, and will make arrangements for displaying them at appropriate times.
   'WIND SAFE' Boards will not be used, and any such boards now in existence will be destroyed.
5. The following points should be brought frequently to the notice of all ranks:
   Gas will often hang for a long time in woods, valleys, and villages, and may be dangerous after several days have elapsed.
   It is not safe to rely on the degree of detonation as a means of recognising gas shell, because H.E. shell often contains Gas.
6. The following is a précis of the various forms of gas attack, the warnings given in each case, and the duties of various Headquarters and Units on receiving the warning…
   a) GAS CLOUD ATTACK
   b) HEAVY GAS SHELLING OR GAS PROJECTOR SHOOTS
   c) LIGHT GAS SHELLING
   [Under each heading the arrangements in place and the action to be taken are detailed].[139]

On 14 August, while out of the line, the troops of 5/Cameron Highlanders had experience in the 'Gas Chamber' – an arrangement designed to provide soldiers with first-hand experience of being gassed. The intention of the Army was for all units to spend a session in the chamber,

137 Freemantle, *Gas!*, p. 120 – quoting from T. A. Ryan, C. Ryan, E. A. Seddon and K. R. Seddon, *Phosgene and Related Carbonyl Halides* (Amsterdam: Elsevier, 1996), p. 40.
138 TNA WO95/2614, War Diary of 121 Infantry Brigade, Centre Sector Defence Orders, Appendix III.
139 TNA WO95/2614, War Diary of 121 Infantry Brigade, Centre Sector Defence Orders, Appendix III.

helping to condition them to the prospect of gas operations, as part of their training and preparation for front line operations.[140]

Despite such measures, there remained concern at the number of casualties resulting from enemy gas attacks. Second Army wrote to its corps commanders at the start of September 1918 to place its concerns on record. At this time the Army had been active in advancing its line to take advantage of German withdrawals and a policy of probing attacks and harassment of the enemy:

> The gas casualties during the past month have been unusually high. In order to combat these excessive casualties the Army Commander wishes Corps Commanders to go thoroughly into this question and to ensure that the responsibilities of the General Staff of formations and of all Commanders for successful anti-gas measures is fully realised. C.O.s should be constantly reminded that they are responsible for casualties occurring in their units which prove to be the result of lack of training in defensive gas measures in accordance with the orders which have been issued on the subject from time to time.[141]

Given the range of precautionary measures which could be taken in preparation for a gas attack, unit leaders were being held directly accountable for their effective implementation.

In its response, on 11 September XV Corps referred the instruction to its divisions:

> Forwarded.
> Attention has been drawn frequently to the importance of this subject.
> Arrangements will be made to have further 1 day courses for C.Os and Second-in-Command.
> The question is, however, largely one of discipline; the strictest gas discipline is always to be enforced.[142]

40th Division then looked to emphasise the practical measures which units should have in place, to be supported and enforced through the Divisional Gas Officer:

> The G.O.C. is confident that the most careful attention will be given to this matter by all concerned and the strictest supervision exercised in the anti-gas training of all units, both in the knowledge of all anti-gas precautions and in the care and upkeep of anti-gas equipment. In order to assist formations and units in this connection, the Divisional Gas Officer will make the following arrangements:

140 TNA WO95/1767, War Diary of 5th Battalion, Cameron Highlanders.
141 TNA WO95/2610, War Diary of 120th Infantry Brigade, Second Army G.T. 420, 9th September 1918.
142 TNA WO95/2610, War Diary of 120th Infantry Brigade, XV Corps No. 89/137 G. 11 September 1918.

a) In the case of the Infantry Brigade in rest:
   i. To inspect all box respirators and anti-gas equipment at least once during the period the Brigade is out.
   ii. To hold a short refresher course for all Battn and Coy Gas N.C.Os during the period of rest, to ensure their being up to date and efficient in anti-gas measures.

   He will make similar arrangements regarding the resting company of the 39th M.G.Bn. taking each Coy. in turn as it comes into Reserve.
b) In the case of other units he will arrange direct with the units concerned, to carry out similar inspections and refresher courses for the Gas N.C.Os so that each unit will receive periodically his assistance and attention.
c) On the completion of his inspection of each unit, he will render to Div. Hd. Qrs. a report on the state of the anti-gas training and equipment in that unit.[143]

The incentive for units is to avoid the prospect of a critical report being passed to division HQ. What these instructions imply is the scale of the ongoing threat posed by the German use of gas on a regular basis, and the resulting concern of Second Army commanders to manage the consequences of this. There is a clear concern to minimise the resulting number of casualties by attaching a very high importance to the range of anti-gas measures available to units.

One week later, XV Corps issued some amendments to its Anti-Gas Instructions, reflecting particular concerns at that time. In part it is possible to detect a casual reaction by troops to gas shelling, perhaps a result of the frequency of this type of artillery fire, or the reaction of 'old hands' believing in their own ability to decide how to respond following a gas attack. Troops also intensely disliked wearing the respirators which were uncomfortable and restricted the visibility, and therefore the movement, of the wearer:

1 Gas casualties are frequently caused by neglect of proper precautions being taken after a gas shell bombardment. Mustard Gas will persist for long periods after a bombardment and respirators must be worn and protective clothing and gloves put on where available, by all troops in the affected area, as long as the smell of gas, no matter how faint, can be detected.

2 As the persistency of the mustard Gas may extend under suitable conditions over several days, units in the forward area will select alternative positions to which, in the event of a gas bombardment, they can move if the tactical situation permits.

   The exchange of positions, either to the alternative or back to the original position, should not be made until a Gas N.C.O. has reported the area which is to be occupied is free from gas.

3 Enemy gas bombardments should invariably be reported, and it is important that any new gas or projectile should be investigated at once.

4 All ranks should be warned that the recognition of gas shell by degree of detonation is not to be relied upon.[144]

143 TNA WO95/2610, War Diary of 120th Infantry Brigade, 40th Div. No. 10/56 G. 13-9-18.
144 TNA WO95/2610, War Diary of 120th Infantry Brigade, XV Corps No. 89/141 G. 21-9-18.

A new danger would be that of gas contained in booby traps left behind by the German soldiers as they withdrew. XV Corps instructions stated:

> <u>TRAPS</u>
> 1 The enemy has on several occasions, before retreating, infected cellars, dugouts, etc., with Mustard Gas, and therefore such places lately vacated by him should be entered with caution. His usual method is either to scatter the liquid gas about or else to open a shell, thereby allowing the contents to leak into the ground.
> 2 Water from shell holes must on no consideration be used either for washing, cooking, or drinking purposes.
> Wood must not be handled or burnt if there are any signs of gas shelling or gas in the vicinity.[145]

Gas – in spite of its routine use by both sides – remained an important concern for the Second Army leadership throughout the Hundred Days. In instructions issued after the Battle of Courtrai, the command of XV Corps stated that it was considered probable that the Germans would 'make considerable use of gas' during the retreat. Cloud gas attacks were considered unlikely and the main threat would be from gas shells delivered using HE. It was acknowledged that with the ongoing advance causing 'frequent changes of positions' then units would not be able to receive the same amount of supervision from senior anti-gas personnel and would have to rely principally upon their soldiers being suitably trained and experienced. Frequent inspections of respirators were to be carried out together with the maintenance of anti-gas appliances such as respirators, containers and rattles.[146]

The War in the Air

The final year of the war saw a further increase in the importance of air power – and the corresponding need to defend against it. The impact of this development on the British military can be illustrated by the creation of the post of Anti-Aircraft Defence Commander on the Army General Staff. The relative rank and status of the officer, Lieutenant-Colonel, reflected both the newness of the role and that the available technology meant the full potential of air power was yet to be realised. Nevertheless, ground troops could expect to be observed and, of greater immediate concern to them, to be attacked by enemy aircraft. Air bombing raids upon troops and key strategic points were increasingly common.

While it was in reconnaissance that the aeroplane continued to make its most important contribution, the commander of Second Army had come to recognise the broader contribution that air power could make as part of the combined arms approach to warfare. Referring to the battles of April 1918, Sir John Slessor, a future Marshal of the Royal Air Force, wrote that Plumer 'pressed urgently for concentrated bombing of vital points of the German supply system to help slow down the enemy advance… [he] was emphatic that an essential condition of

145 TNA WO95/2610, War Diary of 120th Infantry Brigade, XV Corps No. 89/145 G. 28 October 1918.
146 TNA WO95/2610, War Diary of 120th Infantry Brigade, XV Corps No. 89/145 G. 28 October 1918.

success was the concentration of all available aircraft continuously on the minimum number of points where the greatest dislocation could be produced'.[147] By the final phase of the war, with the allied aircraft outnumbering their German counterparts, such an approach was a feasible prospect.

Even during quieter periods, the war in the air was a common feature of the daily routine for the soldiers at the front, and for the aircrews involved:

> One enemy aeroplane dropped a few light bombs on our front line doing little damage. Considerable aerial activity on part of the enemy. Two of our planes brought down by enemy squadron behind our lines.[148]

The control of the air space above the opposing forces was an important factor in the allied advance. The RAF, together with its French and Belgian counterparts, enjoyed a numerical superiority during the campaign; the success that this led to is shown by the high number of enemy aircraft destroyed in this period. This control of the skies – when the weather permitted – gave a significant advantage to coalition troops. It allowed effective reconnaissance of German troop activity and positions, including artillery, plus the crucial details of the new terrain over which the troops would be advancing. French and RAF planes also carried out regular bombing of enemy communications, headquarters and transport, thereby disrupting German command and movement. A further feature of air operations was the most dangerous task of direct attacks at low level upon enemy troops.

The much smaller Belgian Air Corps, around 150 craft, played its part; primarily in observation and reconnaissance, but also via its fighter squadrons, which had been reorganised at the start of the year.[149] On 17 October pilots of the Groupe de Chasse Jacquet (Fighter Group Jacquet) landed in Oostende to become the first members of the Belgian armed forces to enter the town after German occupation.

The table below shows a summary of RAF activity during the final weeks of the war in Flanders:

Summary of RAF activity during the Final Advance in Flanders

Week commencing	21 Sept	28 Sept	5 Oct	12 Oct	19 Oct	26 Oct	2/9 Nov	Total
Enemy aircraft destroyed	13	51	36		2	52	38	642
RAF machines lost to enemy	10	30	12	Severe weather	10	18	10	90
Enemy balloons burnt	1	8	2		0	8	5	24
RAF balloons burnt	0	1	1		0	1	0	3

147 Sir J. Slessor, *The Great Deterrent* (London: Constable, 1957), pp. 51-2.

148 TNA WO95/1765, War Diary of 7th Battalion, Seaforth Highlanders, *2nd July 1918, Stoic Farm, nr. Fletre (Meteren Sector).*

149 This paragraph is based upon information from the website <www.wwiaviation/ww1_belgium1918>

Week commencing		**21 Sept**	**28 Sept**	**5 Oct**	**12 Oct**	**19 Oct**	**26 Oct**	**2/9 Nov**	**Total**
Bombing Summary									
Bombs dropped	Other	31	54	27	20	9	0	0	113
	112lbs	272	534	240	152	113	84	117	1,512
	25lbs	2,071	6,365	2,820	1,825	581	2,256	1,403	17,321
	Total	2,374	6,953	3,087	1,997	703	2,340	1,520	
SAA rounds fired at ground targets		–	42,068	6,500+	1,670	–	–	–	–
Photos taken		1848	–	–	300	–	–	578	

Compiled from weekly operations reports produced by Second Army HQ
Source: TNA WO158/218

Communications with aircraft by advancing troops relied almost entirely upon visual aids. The normal practice was an agreed system of coloured flares. For example, during an action by advance platoons of 31st Division on 18 September 1918 (described in an earlier chapter),[150] a 'Contact Aeroplane' was identified to 'co-operate with the attack'. Troops carried SOS flares: red smoke by day, green over green over red by night; plus white Very lights: three to be fired when a platoon reached its objective.

The deployment of the RAF was a regular feature in the operational planning of Second Army. Attack orders issued by 89 Brigade in August 1918 included reference to the RAF dropping supplies to forward troops:

> RAF: ammunition and stores as follows will be dropped by aeroplane at [map reference] …
> 20 Boxes SAA
> 2 SAA Boxes filled with VERY Lights
> 1 SAA Box filled with Special S.O.S. Signal
> 30 coils of barbed wire
>
> 2nd Battalion S Lancs Regt. will detail a party under a N.C.O. to collect these stores as they are dropped and issue them as required to troops of 89th and 90th Infantry Brigades. This party will mark the dropping ground by two white letters 'N'.[151]

An attack on 19 July to capture the village of Meteren, by 26 Brigade and the South African Brigade (9th Division), was given cover by the RAF:

150 TNA WO95/2361, War Diary of 15/17th Battalion, West Yorkshire Regiment, Narrative of Operations 13-18 September 1918.

151 TNA WO95/2332, War Diary of 89 Infantry Brigade, 89th Infantry Brigade Order No. 180, 18 August 1918.

> Six of our planes hovered over our front from dawn to ZERO, and denied aeroplane observation to the enemy.[152]

The preparations for the forthcoming Battle of Ypres give a good example of requirements for the various units of the RAF to undertake specific missions in support of the attacking infantry. The priority, through the use of 'contact aeroplanes', was to track the progress of the attack in order to inform HQ:

> CONTACT AEROPLANES
>
> a) The most forward troops will carry RED FLARES, American Cloth on Box Respirators, and Vigilant periscopes for the purpose of signalling to Contact Aeroplanes.
> b) These, and every other means of signalling their position, will be used by the attacking troops at:
> ZERO plus 2 hours 15 minutes
> and at
> ZERO plus 4 hours
> and at such other times as called for by the Contact Aeroplane.
> c) Contact Aeroplanes will call for Signals from the attacking troops by sounding the Klaxon Horn and dropping WHITE Lights.
> d) Contact Aeroplanes will be marked with two BLACK RECTANGULAR FLAGS (2 feet by 1 foot 6 inches) attached to and projecting from the lower plane on each side of the fuselage. Each contact plane will also have a TRAILING STREAMER.
> All troops will be warned how to recognise contact aeroplanes.[153]

Another important role was that of the 'counter attack aeroplane', used to identify possible counter-attacks by the enemy and to signal for a defensive barrage by artillery. The following extract from operational orders describes the general role:

> COUNTER ATTACK AEROPLANE
>
> A counter attack aeroplane will be in the air on II Corps Front [west of Ypres] from Zero plus one hour onwards for the purpose of giving warning of an impending hostile attack.
>
> On perceiving hostile infantry moving to attack the counter attack aeroplane will call for annihilating artillery fire by Wireless and will also signal the fact that a hostile attack is impending by dropping a RED SMOKE PARACHUTE VERY LIGHT.[154]

152 TNA WO95/1767, War Diary of 5th Battalion, Cameron Highlanders.
153 TNA WO95/2300, War Diary of 1st Battalion, Lancashire Fusiliers, Operation Instruction No: 2, 24/25.9.1918, 2. CONTACT AEROPLANES.
154 TNA WO95/2300, War Diary of 1st Battalion, Lancashire Fusiliers, Operation Instruction No: 2, 24/25.9.1918, 3. COUNTER ATTACK AEROPLANE.

The reference to 'wireless' would most likely be through a code signal; for example, the arrangements for 88 Brigade refer to an 'LL' or 'GF' call.[155] These arrangements also illustrate the increasing importance of wireless communications; while the existing equipment was too heavy and bulky for advancing units to utilise, it could be fitted to an aircraft with suitable adaptations. Hence this further example from 88 Brigade:

> Aeroplane fitted with Wireless Telephone
>
> From time to time an aeroplane fitted with a wireless telephone will patrol the II Corps Front. Receiving Stations to take down messages from this aeroplane are being arranged for at YPRES, and GOLDFISH Chateau
>
> It is to be remembered, however, that all messages sent by this machine can be intercepted by receiving stations and on no account whatever will any messages referring to the positions of our troops be sent 'in clear' by this means.[156]

The main HQ of corps, division, and increasingly brigade, would have access to wireless receivers. It was crucial for the forward infantry to be able to indicate that an objective has been taken and, as required, to signal for the necessary materiél or other forms of support in order to protect the gains made; reconnaissance aircraft made an important contribution to the various means of communication employed by advance formations. However there was concern at the ability of the enemy to access wireless communications.

The initial planning for the Battle of Ypres, arranged at divisional and brigade levels, also included what at the time was the relatively novel proposal to use aircraft to deliver supplies, principally ammunition, to forward troops. The system depended upon the ability of the advance troops to display the required layout of strips of white cloth, along with the firing of a white flare. Parachutes (to be collected and returned to division) were employed to prevent the weighty packages from just falling directly to the ground (which would have increased the likelihood of damaging the contents – as well as creating a physical threat to those troops in the vicinity).

The following instructions are typical of the arrangements made:

> DROPPING OF AMMUNITION FROM AEROPLANES
>
> a) Arrangements have been made with the R.A.F. to drop ammunition from aeroplanes, if required.
>
> b) Two kinds of ammunition will be dropped:
>
> a. bundle packed S.A.A.
>
> b. M.G. Ammunition packed in belts (4 belts per box)
>
> The ammunition prepared for dropping will be in the proportion of two of bundle packed ammunition to one of M.G. Ammunition in belts.
>
> c) Infantry will signal that ammunition is wanted as follows:
>
> ['N' shaped layout] Machine Gun Post requiring M.G. Ammunition.

155 TNA WO95/2307/4, War Diary of 88 Infantry Brigade, 88th Infantry Brigade Operation Instructions No. 3, Contact and Counter- Attack Patrols, 25 September 1918.

156 TNA WO95/2307/4, War Diary of 88 Infantry Brigade, 88th Infantry Brigade Operation Instructions No. 3, Contact and Counter- Attack Patrols, 25 September 1918.

['triangle' layout] Bundle packed ammunition required.
Each signal will be made up of strips of white cloth 12 feet by 1 foot and in each case attention will be called to the signal by the firing of a white flare from the ground. Two strips per Battalion and one per Machine Gun Co. will be carried. The Brigade Signalling Officer will make arrangements for supplying them.

d) The aeroplanes will be ready to drop ammunition from ZERO plus two hours onwards and will continue to do so as long as the ground signals are displayed.
Once the signals are removed no more ammunition will be sent by aeroplane unless a report is received from a contact machine that more is required.

e) It is probable that each ammunition dropping aeroplane will be able to drop about two boxes of ammunition per hour and possibly at the outside three machines can be made available for the purpose on the Divisional Front.
It will not be practicable that these aeroplanes will continue dropping ammunition for a longer period than about four hours and during the day it is calculated that the maximum number of boxes which can be dropped will be 9 boxes of mg Ammunition and 16 boxes of bundle packed ammunition.

f) It is of very great importance, therefore, that ammunition should not be called for except when really required. Platoon and Company Commanders will make every endeavour to collect enemy rifles, machine guns and ammunition and bring them into use against the enemy.

g) As many parachutes as practicable must be recovered and returned to Division.[157]

Here the prime objective of these preparations for the forthcoming Battle of Ypres was to deliver additional supplies of ammunition. However, a few weeks later, by the time of the planning for the Battle of Courtrai, the scope and ambition of such operations had been extended. The dropping of supplies now included food and rations, as well as small arms and machine gun ammunition. Those supplies could also include a number of pigeons to be used for communication purposes. The planning also provided for different arrangements of ground sheets by which advance units could indicate the type of supplies required. The attention of the contact aeroplane would be attracted by the firing of a white very light or the lighting of a white flare.[158]

All units were now required to take the necessary steps to protect themselves from attack from the air, normally co-ordinated at brigade level. In the front line the main emphasis was upon the deployment of Lewis guns. In August 1918 the following divisional orders were issued to units in 121 Brigade (40th Division):

Anti-Aircraft Defence

All units are responsible for their own protection against attacks from the air, and should ensure that they are complete in A.A. small arms, sights and mountings, according to establishment.

157 TNA WO95/2300, War Diary of 1st Battalion, Lancashire Fusiliers, Operation Instruction No: 2, 24/25.9.1918, 4. DROPPING OF AMMUNITION FROM AEROPLANES.
158 For an example see TNA WO95/2307/4, War Diary of 88 Infantry Brigade, 88th Infantry Brigade Operation Instructions No. 2, 12 October 1918.

[Chief considerations for the defence of the area include]:

a) Fire will be opened on low flying aeroplanes by rifles and Lewis Guns, but in every case the sentry in front line posts will continue to watch the front.
b) Lewis Guns told off for anti-aircraft purposes in the line should not be placed at greater intervals than 500 yds. Positions may be changed, but changes should be reported to Brigade Headquarters so that anti-aircraft defence may be co-ordinated.
c) Most implicit orders are necessary to ensure that no Lewis Gun or rifle is to fire unless the 'CROSS' on the hostile plane can be clearly seen with the naked eye. It is useless to fire at a range greater than 1,300 yards. This is to be made clear to every Lewis Gunner, and steps will be taken to deal with those who fire wildly at aeroplanes obviously out of range.
d) Anti-aircraft Lewis Guns will, as far as possible, be placed in groups of 4, or in pairs. If in groups of 4, they will be under an officer, or if in pairs, under N.C.O.'s to be supervised by an officer.

Fire at night will not be opened unless:

i. The hostile aircraft can be seen against the sky.
ii. The struts of the planes can be distinguished in the beams of a searchlight.[159]

Subsequently the orders were added to:

An order board is to be provided at every post. Units will also arrange that the 'Letter and Colours of the Day' (particularly the latter) are communicated to each of their posts and understood by them.

The Letters and Colours change daily at 12 noon and are to be communicated daily to A.A. Lewis Guns as if they were passwords.

An additional reason for the restriction of A.A. Lewis Gun fire at night, particularly in back areas, is that the A.A. defences depend largely on listening for the location of hostile aeroplanes and that this is made more difficult if Lewis Guns fire unnecessarily…

… copies of a paper of orders for A.A. Lewis Gunners have been forwarded for distribution to each gun… This paper should be pasted to a board of [or] piece of tin and tied to the mounting or some part of the emplacement of the gun.[160]

By 1918 defence against attack from the air had become an important component of operations, offensive and defensive. In November 1918, British Second Army had five anti-aircraft batteries and two sections of 13-pdr guns for anti-aircraft defence. In total this provided the firepower of twelve 3-inch anti-aircraft guns, plus forty-two 13-pdr guns dedicated to ground defence against enemy air attack and reconnaissance.[161]

159 TNA WO95/2614, War Diary of 121 Infantry Brigade, Centre Sector Defence Orders, Appendix II.
160 TNA WO95/2610, War Diary of 120 Infantry Brigade, N. 120/415, 120th, Defence Orders.
161 A. F. Becke, *Official Orders of Battle: Part 4: The Army Council, GHQs, Armies and Corps 1914-1918* (London: HMSO, 1945).

3

Breakthrough: The Battle of Ypres 1918, The First Day – 28 September 1918

> The Western Front was crumbling. Ludendorff might be able to hold the centre, but he could not hold the flanks. On… 28 September, the Allies attacked at Ypres, and finally, this time, they broke through.[1]

In his book on the First Battle of Ypres, Ian Beckett makes reference to the concept of the 'immortal salient', thrusting defiantly eastwards from the Belgian city of Ypres into the German line. Here the British Army demonstrated its stubborn commitment to retaining a last remaining hold on Belgian territory – a daily reminder to the enemy that it had failed in its attempt to dominate Western Europe. As became clear over the progress of the war, 'they shall not pass' was a phrase that could have been invented to describe the long term defiance presented by British soldiers.

Beckett coined this term in tribute to the defence of the city by the original BEF in the autumn of 1914, together with the subsequent battles in 1915 and 1917 which added 'yet more British blood to the salient'.[2] He has pointed out the important part played by the French and Belgian forces in the battles of 1914. This has added resonance when considering that the liberation offensive in 1918 would be waged by a new coalition formed from the armies of these three countries – this time co-operating under the single banner of the *Groupe d'Armées des Flandres*.

During September 1918 Second Army had concentrated on occupying ground conceded by the enemy as the latter carried out a planned withdrawal. This pulling back allowed the Germans to shorten their lines thereby maximising the use of their manpower to improve their defensive capabilities. Increasingly, as the month progressed, Plumer's attention was focused on the forthcoming major offensive. There were regular efforts by Second Army to disrupt the German withdrawal through a combination of artillery shoots, frequent probing advances and small raids to capture and consolidate small pieces of ground. The seizing of enemy prisoners was also encouraged; for instance, on 17 September a forward patrol of 17/Cheshires (105 Brigade, 35th Division) captured an NCO of the 40th Saxon Division, who provided valuable information on the nature and quality of the opposing German troops.

1 Lloyd, *Hundred Days*, pp. 175-6.
2 I.F.W. Beckett, *Ypres: The First Battle, 1914*, (Harlow: Pearson Education Limited, 2004), pp. 5-6.

Training remained a high priority for Second Army, particularly for those units more recently reconstituted. The Flanders' weather continued to cause problems however. During September, 41 Brigade (14th Division) prioritised close order drill and patrol formations, but rain hampered a number of the exercises and forced cancellation of outdoor training on at least one occasion.[3]

The RAF was active, recording a weekly outscoring of the enemy. During 10-30 August, 75 German aircraft were destroyed for the loss of 14 RAF planes. The next four weeks prior to the Battle of Ypres saw an increase in enemy air activity, anticipating the pending attack, with poor weather 7-13 September preventing either side from flying.[4] Overall for the period 31 August – 27 September, the RAF lost 32 aircraft for 53 German planes destroyed; nine of the RAF planes were lost over the British First Army front. As well as attacking enemy planes the RAF were engaged in bombing German targets such as aerodromes, roads, railway lines and bridges. The Second Army operations report for the week 21 – 27 September lists RAF raids on stations, (ammunition) dumps, aerodromes and docks, with 2,374 bombs dropped.[5] However, high winds and low levels of cloud had restricted the RAF work on counter-battery observation, although 232 'flashes' were located. The report also notes that German air activity was 'above normal'.

In the week prior to the attack, both sides' artillery maintained their regular duelling. British Second Army artillery fired 93 HE (high explosive) concentrations, 9 gas concentrations and 535 'neutralisations'. In addition to the use of gas shells there were two recorded releases of gas: 10/11 September, from 379 projectors in the Ypres sector; 23 September, from 197 projectors in the Ploegsteert sector. In response, the Germans continued their harassing fire, including neutralising fire directed at field and forward siege batteries. The British line was advanced via minor operations in the sectors of Steenwerek, Wulverghem, Vierstraat and Ypres, in readiness for the pending attack.[6] These local successes included the captures listed in the table below:

British Second Army Captures 1-27 September 1918

Officers	7
Other Ranks	671
Machine Guns	87
Trench Mortars	31
Guns	9

Source: J. Edmonds, *Official History Vol. V.*

This was a style of warfare – a war of fire and movement – very different from the trench-bound experience of many of the troops. On 21 September, Sergeant Miles of 15/KOYLI noted '… Jerry's blown the bridges up. As soon as the Engineers have repaired the bridge we move

3 TNA WO95/1894/6, War Diary of 41 Infantry Brigade, entries for September 1918.
4 Information compiled from TNA WO158/218, Second Army, Weekly Operations Reports .
5 Information compiled from TNA WO158/218, Second Army, Weekly Operations Report 21-27 September.
6 TNA WO158/218, Second Army, Weekly Operations Reports.

forward again... He comes over bombing at night... trying to get our supply columns. On the move at last...'[7]

Commanders were becoming aware of the need to ensure their units could operate effectively in this new environment of advance and manoeuvre. For example, at the end of August, Major-General Nicholson commanding 34th Division, II Corps, became aware that his troops had not been '... up to standard required for a war of movement and manoeuvring'.[8] Accordingly he issued orders to all soldiers in the division reminding them of the need to be able to operate as 'a mobile formation, not ... one whose raison d'etre is to settle down in a trench system'.[9] To address these shortcomings he concentrated on training designed to equip the troops for mobile warfare; alongside a revised organisation for supporting advancing units (including the removal of 'surplus baggage'), and a new 'mobile system' for ammunition supply. To help ensure that senior commanders could deliver effective command and control, he made arrangements for an advanced divisional HQ with different 'echelons' of support to allow for speedy communication between the front line and HQ staff.

Evidence of the inexperience of many of the British infantry is illustrated by the nature of the orders being issued. For instance, preparatory instructions provided by 41 Brigade prior to the launch of the offensive included such elementary points as:

> The attack will not be carried out in a series of rigid extended lines but platoons and sections will be kept under the control of their Commanders for as long as possible, in small column and group formations.
>
> Various roads and light railways lend themselves to the maintenance of direction, but in addition each Company will be given its direction by at least one compass. Troops will be warned that the majority of our field gun barrage will be shrapnel, and that though the shells will burst just over their heads they are not directed at them, and are not short, but that the bullets will strike the ground in front of them. Troops will similarly be warned that our machine guns will be firing over their heads, which may be disconcerting unless accustomed to it.[10]

Troops were also reminded by brigade of such essential points as distinguishing and communicating with RAF contact aeroplanes, sending back regular messages with times and locations clearly marked (my emphasis), and the potential for enemy dugouts to contain mines or traps.

Signs of nervousness can be detected as the deadline for the attack grew nearer. A joint operation had been ordered between 41 Brigade and its neighbouring Belgian Regiment, to seize a number of small farms on the night of 15-16 September, in order to improve observation lines.

7 IWM, 83/6/1, E. Miles, Sergeant and Company QM, 15th Battalion Kings Own Yorkshire Light Infantry, 40th Division.
8 IWM, 01/14/1, From the papers of Major-General Sir Cecil Lothian Nicholson KGB CMG, 34th Division July 1916-March 1919.
9 IWM, 01/14/1, From the papers of Major-General Sir Cecil Lothian Nicholson KGB CMG, 34th Division July 1916-March 1919.
10 TNA WO95/1894/6, War Diary of 41 Infantry Brigade, Instruction No. 1, 23/9/18.

Although the planning for the operation led to it being subsequently much reduced in scope, it was then directed to be cancelled 'owing to pressure from a senior authority'.[11]

The launch of the allies' grand offensive was to follow the timetable agreed by Haig and Foch:

26 September	American First Army French Fourth Army	To attack between the Meuse and To attack Reims, towards Mezieres
27 September	British First Army British Third Army	To attack in the Cambrai area" —"—
28 September	GAF	To gain a line from the Ypres-Comines Canal to Clerken (10 miles north of Ypres)
29 September	British Fourth Army French First Army	To assault main Hindenburg —"—

Map 1 shows the overall disposition of the allied armies as of July 1918.

The starting positions of the GAF prior to the attack were as follows:

British Second Army (4 corps of 10 divisions)	Responsible for a front of 14 miles Armentières–Ypres
Belgian Army 13 divisions And 1 Cavalry Division	Responsible for a front of 23 miles Ypres to the coast
French forces VII Corps (three divisions) XXXIV Corps (three divisions) II Cavalry Corps (three divisions)	Echeloned as a reserve

The table below shows the disposition of the four corps of Second Army, north-to-south:

II Corps	9th Division
	29th Division
	36th Division
XIX Corps	14th Division
	35th Division
	41st Division
X Corps	30th Division
	34th Division
XV Corps	31st Division
	40th Division

Map 3 denotes the progress of the British and Belgian forces through the initial fighting in the Liberation of Flanders offensive.

11 TNA WO95/1894/6, War Diary of 41 Infantry Brigade, entries 14-16 September 1918; Order No. 15, 14 September 1918.

For the Belgian Army, Chief of Staff Gillain had issued his principal orders on 12 September 1918 followed by certain modifications one week later.[12] Preliminary operations were necessary in order to establish the base for the attack and to provide for the forward placement of artillery. These included the capture of two key enemy positions (at Hwaebeek and Kloostermolen); expansion of the bridgehead on the east of the Steenbeek (area of Wiedendreft); and securing strong sight lines across the Steenbeek in the St Julien area, such that temporary crossings for infantry could be erected immediately prior to the attack.

The plan for the offensive comprised two phases:

1 Securing an operational base for the advance through the capture of the strategic points of Clercken, Stadenberg, Passchendaele, Zonnebeke, Veldhoek, and Verbrandemolen.
2 Attacks towards the initial objectives of Bruges and the Bruges – Ghent railway line, designed to cut the German's communications to the coast.

The operations would involve securing the right of the Lys, from Comines towards Ghent, in order to cover the advance towards Bruges and to resist enemy counter-attacks from the south. The securing of key bridges and crossing points was emphasised.

> Secrecy, surprise, speed of execution are [the] essential elements of success.[13]

The orders made clear that the nine Belgian divisions, organised in two *groupements d'attaque*, were to act in co-operation with the two divisions of British Second Army on their right. Gillain's initial written instructions ran across fifteen pages with a three-page appendix of detailed artillery tables and the associated deployment arrangements for the guns (British and Belgian). The role of each infantry division was set out in detail for both the initial attack and the subsequent advance.

Recognising the tactical importance of the limited high ground, the opening assault was designed to capture the ridge between Zonnebeck and Clercken; five divisions in the first line, three in the second line. The neighbouring Houthulst forest was not to be attacked at this stage – probably because of the potential for troops to be tied down in lengthy operations clearing enemy defenders – but to be surrounded in order to initially secure the position.

The second phase of the attack would be through the use of attacking patrols reinforced by engineers in order to make the initial break into the enemy's defences. Once the initial breaches were achieved, reserve forces would move up to secure the position. The need for ongoing support from artillery fire was stressed, particularly to create gaps in wired defences. The orders recognised that there would be a need to relocate some of the guns forward as the attack proceeded and – reflecting the general problems presented by the geography of

12 Main Headquarters, Belgian Army: Order No. 255/6, 12 September 1918, from General Gillain to all commanders, OPERATIONAL ORDERS FOR AN OVERALL OFFENSIVE IN FLANDERS; Order No. 255/6, 19th September 1918, from General Gillain to all commanders, MODIFICATIONS [TO OPERATIONAL ORDERS No. 255/6] FOR AN OVERALL OFFENSIVE IN FLANDERS; both these sets of orders were located within 29th Division records: TNA WO95/2285, War Diary of 29th Division. The orders were issued in French – all quotes are from an English translation.

13 Belgian Army: Order No. 255/6, 12 September 1918, p. 1

Flanders – that 'given the state of the terrain and the road network, this will present the most difficult problem to resolve'. Accordingly all artillery was to be positioned as far forward as possible when the attack commenced. The fire plans included the use of 'special' – i.e. gas – shells, specifically for counter-battery work.

Second Army artillery was to co-operate with supporting fire south of the line Janshoek-Patte Dreef, Staden. While operating under the orders of British command, cooperative arrangements were in place such that the guns would react to requests for support from designated Belgian forces. At this stage of the assault it was intended to move into Houthulst forest, to capture the enemy gun batteries placed there. Gillain's orders also included the arrangements for a second attack – centred upon Dixmuide and Woumen – the timing of which would be decided at the time and in the light of the progress achieved by the first assault. Again there would be an initial preparation by artillery, including British guns.

Throughout there is a heavy emphasis upon the role of the artillery, both in terms of the initial bombardment and the rolling barrage in front of the assaulting infantry. An essential requirement was for as many guns as possible to be moved forward once the attacks went in; ongoing fire support for the infantry was obviously considered crucial in order to maintain the momentum of the advance.

The need for secrecy in the planning and attack preparations was stressed:

> … the utmost precautions must be taken to ensure that reconnaissance is carried out with the necessary discretion; officers must at all costs avoid being seen checking out positions with maps in hand, or groups of officers being seen with binoculars…
>
> The munitions sited near to their positions planned for the attacks must be taken there at night at the last possible moment, or make the most of existing works and covers to hide them; these depots must be camouflaged with care.[14]

Measures were outlined to try and minimise the additional traffic on the approach roads in the days immediately preceding the offensive; and only the most essential preparatory works were to be carried out for artillery emplacements. The importance of logistics – particularly supplies and communications – to sustain the pace of the advance was recognised. The plans made reference to the need to put in place as soon as possible road links between the Belgian and German positions, capable of providing for horse-drawn and light motor vehicles initially; heavier vehicles once 'sufficient progress' had been made.

The planning provided for all attack divisions to have the assistance of an air reconnaissance squadron. Air support was also available to provide reconnaissance for the artillery, together with specific squadrons for bombing and ground attack roles. The supporting Second Army artillery would have its own reconnaissance support from the RAF.

The GAF received its first set of orders from the King of the Belgians on 19 September, signed 'au nom du roi' by General Degoutte as chief of staff. This was followed by further orders on 21 September which provided for exploitation of the attack by the French and Belgian cavalry, plus sought to clarify the key responsibilities of Second Army. These were to provide flanking cover to the Belgian forces to the north, and to establish a bridgehead south of the River Lys.

14 Belgian Army: Order No. 255/6, 12 September 1918, pp. 10-11

Plumer had issued his main operations order at 0900 on 19 September, before receipt of Degoutte's instructions, in line with the GHQ briefing he had received three days previously. The GAF was to attack between Dixmude and St Eloi, to break through the enemy's lines and then use these as the base for further exploitation. The implication in the *Official History* is that the thoughts and actions of Degoutte did not impress Plumer or the writer of the History. For example, Edmonds writes '…going dead against the expressed opinion of General Plumer, it was laid down [by Degoutte] that 'it is not necessary in the first instance to attack the Wytschaete-Messines area…". Later he concludes that 'General Degoutte made no attempt to co-ordinate action at the junction of the Belgian and British Second Armies, and it was discovered by General Plumer that several points of difference required adjustment'.[15]

Harris and Barr draw the conclusion that:

> Plumer and his staff seem, however, to have regarded Degoutte as officious and inefficient and to have thought that he did little to co-ordinate planning between themselves and the Belgians.[16]

Powell, in his biography of Plumer, comments:

> It now fell to Plumer to remedy faulty staff work in the GAF and to carry out much of the essential co-ordination necessary between his own Army and the Belgians, especially the scope and details of the artillery programme.[17]

As the time of the attack approached, Plumer and his staff worked flat out to ensure that there was full cooperation between the British and Belgian armies and their plans for the opening of the offensive were carefully linked:

> From the 18th to 23rd [September] constant modifications of the [plan of attack], of the rate of barrage, pauses in the barrage in order to suit the Belgians, etc. were made and the date of the attack was altered on the 22nd September to the 27th and then to the 28th.[18]

Plumer saw no need to amend the main components of his original orders to Second Army. These took into account information collated at Army HQ which suggested that the Germans were making ready to undertake a planned withdrawal in order to shorten their line. It was considered that this could create a degree of disruption to enemy defences, offering some advantage to the attackers.

On the northern sector of the British line, II Corps (9th and 29th Divisions, with 36th in reserve) and XIX Corps (14th and 35th Divisions, with 41st in reserve) would attack at Zero hour. To the south, X Corps and XV Corps were to await the initial outcomes of the assault and

15 Edmonds, *Official History, Vol. V*, p. 58, p. 60.
16 Harris with Barr, *Amiens*.
17 Powell, *Plumer*.
18 TNA WO95/2470/1, War Diary of 35th Division Headquarters General Staff: Narrative of Operations from 28 September to end of October, 1918.

to advance should opportunity permit – to '…watch their opportunity and take every advantage of the enemy weakening on their front to press their advantage'.[19]

In accordance with Second Army's reputation for thorough preparation, a large-scale model of the positions to be attacked was constructed at Army HQ. Officers from each attacking division were brought in to be briefed on the overall attack and their place within it. This recorded experience of 35th Division was typical:

> On the 25th and 26th September the G.O.C. [of 35th Division] took large parties of Officers, about 60 each day, to CASSEL and with the help of Major General PERCY (M.G.G.S. Second Army), and Captain HEYWOOD (G.3) explained the ground they were going to attack over on the large scale model at Second Army Headquarters, pointing out the marshy places, cuttings, land marks, dug-outs, etc., which all three Officers knew intimately from previous experiences. Afterwards the various Commanders of Battalions and Companies discussed their mutual co-operation and practically played a war-game of their portion of the attack. It is certain that this was responsible in a great degree for the smoothness with which the operations were subsequently carried out.[20]

On 24 September a joint conference took place between leaders of the Belgian Army and British Second Army in order to agree the practical arrangements for the attack. In particular the discussion focused on the deployment of the artillery support, with the British favouring a surprise attack without a preliminary bombardment. In contrast, the Belgians were concerned at the ability of their forces to breach the German defences without an initial bombardment. Thus it was agreed that the Belgian artillery would commence a barrage three hours before Z-hour. Both forces were to apply a creeping barrage to cover the attacking troops but with lifts of 100 *metres* for the Belgians and 100 *yards* for the British – preserving the integrity of the British Imperial unit!

That same day, Plumer issued a summary set of orders to his four corps commanders which show the initial caution in his interpretation of the directions being issued by the GAF. He was conscious of the army's foremost responsibility for securing the right flank of the Belgian Army. The Second Army commander makes clear that corps will make no attempt to 'exploit' or take any further action once the initial agreed objectives have been achieved; and this will happen only once further orders have been given by him. As well as demonstrating his 'grip' of the situation, Plumer does however show his appreciation of the potential for Second Army to make a strategic breakthrough by outlining how each corps could contribute to a broadening of the offensive:

> If the first phase of the operation is carried out as planned the Second Army will have as their next task the capture of the ground west of the YPRES – COMINES CANAL and west of the [RIVER] LYS north of ARMENTIÈRES.

19 Second Army Order No 35, 19 September 1918, signed by Major-General J Percy, CGS of Second Army – from J. Edmonds, *Official History Vol. V.*

20 TNA WO95/2470/1, War Diary of 35th Division.

> … II Corps will have to keep touch with the Belgian Army on its left and the XIX Corps on its right and to prepare for a further advance eastward.
> The XIX Corps will have to move along the CANAL to HOUTHEM and COMINES.
> The XV Corps will have to secure the crossings over the LYS and move on COMINES.
> The X Corps will have to move forward via WYTSCHAETE and MESSINES to join up with the XV and XIX Corps.[21]

This prediction of how operations could proceed would be reflected in the development of the campaign and Second Army's advance.

Second Army orders below Army HQ and corps levels were being shared with the allied forces within the GAF. Copies of divisional orders were provided to the 'French Mission' and the 'Belgian Mission'. The evidence for this comes from 29th Division, part of II Corps, the latter with the responsibility of maintaining touch with the Belgian Army during the battle.[22]

Some units of Second Army were already used to co-operating with their Belgian allies at tactical and operational levels, having spent time alongside each other at the boundary of the two armies. For example, during the latter part of August, 41 Brigade had spent time deployed on the extreme left flank of Second Army. Its orders give specific details on the practical arrangements for liaison by its battalions with the adjacent Belgian formation:[23]

> The 2nd Belgian Grenadier Regt. is on the left of this Brigade front. Officers and O.Rs. for liaison are required as follows:
> 1 1 Senior Officer and 2 runners for duty with H.Qs., 2nd Belgian Grenadier Regt. will be found by 33rd London Regt …
> 2 1 Officer and 2 runners for duty with H.Qs. Right Battn., 2nd Belgian Grenadier Regt. will be found by 29th D.L.I …
> 3 *To H.Qs., 103rd Inf. Bde. [the* 2 runners for duty with Right Front Coy., Belgians, will be found by 18th Y. & L.
> 4 2 runners for duty with Support Battn. H.Qs., 2nd Belgian Regt., to be detailed by 29th D.L.I.
>
> [The above personnel will report *Brigade being relieved*].

The detail of these arrangements was repeated in the orders for those brigades subsequently deployed as relief for 41 Brigade along the boundary of the two armies.[24]

The precise details of the arrangements for the support of the attacking infantry from the gunners were becoming clearer. Infantry barrages would be put down without prior registration. Both smoke and gas barrages would be included in the overall artillery barrage, in order to neutralise defensive positions and reduce the defenders' visibility, giving some further protection

21 These orders, G452, 24 September 1918, are located within TNA WO95/2285, War Diary of 29th Division.
22 TNA WO95/2303, War Diary of 87 Infantry Brigade (29th Division).
23 TNA WO95/1894/6, War Diary of 41 Infantry Brigade, Order No. 10, 26 August, 1918; Amendments & addenda to… Order No. 10, 27 July [27th August] 1918.
24 TNA WO95/1894/6, War Diary of 41 Infantry Brigade, Order No. 11, 3 September, 1918; Order No. 13, 11 September, 1918.

for the advancing troops. In addition to the field artillery creeping barrage, a proportion of the heavy artillery would fire a rolling barrage ahead of the 'creeper'. This would help to prevent the defenders in the front-line from carrying out an orderly withdrawal and also discourage the bringing up of reserves. The rest of the heavy artillery would engage in counter-battery fire and bombardment of specified targets. Certain batteries were to select and camouflage forward positions to which they could move once the infantry advanced, thus allowing them to extend the time and distance over which they could offer support to the advancing troops. Time limits were set for the indirect barrage fire, after which this would cease west of certain pre-determined lines The exception was observed direct fire from field guns affiliated to units of the attacking infantry. These arrangements would allow ground troops to exploit any successes without being hindered by gunfire from their own side.

The barrage would also involve heavy machine guns which would:

> ... [support] the creeping barrage in conjunction with the Artillery and also to fire concentrations on selected points. Certain guns were detailed to work forward with the infantry to act as a Battery of opportunity.[25]

Troops of the assaulting units would wear 'fighting order' of 170 rounds SAA, two bombs and two flares per soldier, plus smoke bombs for 'dealing with hostile Machine Guns and Dug-outs'.[26] Units moving up in reserve would bring five sandbags per soldier plus a variety of picks and shovels.[27]

Typical of the wide range of materiél issued to support the attacking infantry is that listed in the orders for 2/15 London Regiment (90 Brigade, 30th Division):

> 1 AMMUNITION:
> a) 1 extra bandolier will be carried by each rifleman...
> b) 16 Lewis Gun magazines per Lewis Gun will be carried forward...
> c) Bombs – Each rifleman will carry 2 Mills Grenades No. 23
> d) Rifle Grenades – 5 Mills Grenades No. 23 will be issued
> e) Smoke Bombs will be issued to rifle grenadiers on the same scale as (d)
>
> 2 WIRE CUTTERS: All available wire cutters will be carried...
>
> 3 AEROPLANE FLARES: 1 tin containing 2 flares will be carried by every other man
>
> 4 AEROPLANE DISCS: All ranks must be in possession of aeroplane Discs
>
> 5 VERY LIGHT PISTOLS: All officers and each Lewis Gun Section will carry Very Pistols and 6 Very lights

25 TNA WO95/1876, War Diary of 14th Division: General Staff, Report on Operations, 28 September 1918.
26 TNA WO95/2486, War Diary of 105 Infantry Brigade, Order No. 267, 24 September 1918.
27 TNA WO95/2486, War Diary of 105 Infantry Brigade, Order No. 267, 24 September 1918.

6 SPECIAL SIGNALS: Special signals will be carried by A & C Coys – 3 will be issued to each platoon & 3 to Coy HQ – 24 will be kept at Battn HQ
Special signals will be – Signals / White / White / White
– Red smoke bombs
– Blue smoke bombs

7 MESSAGE ROCKETS: 4 Message Rockets will be issued to A & C Coys

8 PICKS & SHOVELS: Support & Reserve Coys will each carry 24 picks & 48 shovels

9 RATIONS: 2 days rations will be issued tonight – Each man will carry unexpended portion of day's ration plus 2 days rations plus Iron Ration

10 WATER: Water will be brought up in Petrol Tins tonight & each man must have a full water bottle at ZERO hour…

11 DUMPS: All packs will be dumped at Coy HQ by midnight 27th inst – Men proceeding on leave tomorrow will remain in charge of these dumps – The QM will detail 4 men per Coy from Rear HQ to move these dumps on to WULVERGHEM-MESSINES RD

12 CARRYING PARTIES: D Coy will provide 2 parties of 1 Sgt & 25 men each to be at [designated map reference] at 9 pm tonight, 27th inst, to carry stores as per attached schedule to A & C Coys – Each Coy will provide its own ration party – A & C Coys will arrange for guides to be at [designated map reference] at 9 pm

13 RAP: The RAP will be situated at [map reference].[28]

Reading these and many other of the preparatory documents leading up to the Battle of Ypres, the level of detail and organisation described suggests that there was an inner confidence building up within Second Army and its troops. I do not think this is just the benefit of hindsight, from knowing now of the successes achieved in the initial attack. There is an overwhelming sense of men who had begun to believe that their time had come – they were finally going to make that breakthrough which had for so long eluded them. There is a confidence running throughout the text – confidence in the range of materiél available, in the capabilities of the troops, in the success of training and recent small actions and raids, in the reduced state of the opposition, in their leaders, in their own abilities – which builds up to a conviction that success awaits.

For an example of the final operational planning, the brief for 35th Division (attacking on the left flank of XIX Corps in the direction of Zandvoorde) included references to:

- A creeping barrage at the rate of 100 yards in three minutes

28 TNA WO95/2340, War Diary of 2/15th Battalion, London Regiment, Admin Instructions to Order LXVI. The typed orders also included handwritten annotations.

- Double pauses in the barrage at 500, 1000 and 1500 yards
- (Following fine-tuning of the attack plans) After 1500 yards the rate of lift to slow to 100 yards in five minutes
- Designated 'special points' to be 'dealt with by Field Howitzers'
- Other 'special points further forward' to be dealt with by corps heavy artillery
- As the advance proceeded beyond the line of the first objective then the two forward brigades would each have access to one battery of 18 pounder field guns and one section of 4.5" howitzers, under the direction of the brigadier-general
- The division would also have two additional brigades of field artillery available.[29]

The plan also included orders for the immediate repair of certain roads once the attack commenced – reflecting the concerns of commanders regarding their ability to supply and support those troops at the front of the advance over the battle scarred and weather worn Flanders terrain.

The extent of the forward planning and the cooperation between service arms is also demonstrated by arrangements to provide extra supplies of ammunition to advance guards. The orders for units of 14th Division included details on communications and operational support:

> SUPPLY OF AMMUNITION
> S.A.A. can be delivered by aeroplane.
>
> In the case of Ammunition being required in a place not previously arranged the letter 'V' will be put out and will be reported by the Contact Machine to the O.C. 10 Squadron R.A.F. who will arrange to drop 6 boxes at the place marked.[30]

(It is ironic that, following these arrangements for this innovative operation, another side of the Army is reflected in the instruction, 'The parachute on which the S.A.A. is suspended must be returned to Brigade H.Qs. at once'. (My emphasis). I suspect this was not the first priority for the men on the ground.)

Further evidence of the careful preparations being undertaken is the mapping of current and proposed supply arrangements. The orders of 29th Division included map overlays to show roads ready, or to be opened up now or later, for field artillery; plus tramlines and mule tracks.[31]

The 14th Division orders prior to the attack stressed the importance of capturing and holding the key objectives (in this case craters designated 'The Bluff' and 'Saint Eloi'), and for these to be recaptured by counter-attack if necessary. The prior instructions stated:

> It must be impressed on all ranks that not only have they to take their various objectives but they must hold them, and this may prove to be the most difficult task…

29 TNA WO95/2470/1, War Diary of 35th Division.
30 TNA WO95/1899, War Diary of 42 Infantry Brigade, 42nd Inf Bde Instructions for the Offensive No.4.
31 TNA WO95/2285, War Diary of 29th Division, CGS 67/123, Operations Instructions No. 4.

> The objectives given are those that must be taken and held but this does not mean that the Infantry are not to take every advantage of exploiting their success either by following up the enemy or sending out strong patrols to test the strength of the enemy...[32]

These requirements make clear that while strong defence was expected from the Germans, every opportunity to maximise the penetration of the advance should be explored. There was a firm emphasis on driving home the assault:

> The general principle guiding the attack is that it is to be pushed most at the points where resistance is least and is consequently most successful. Portions of the line held up are to be relieved by the flanks being pushed forward and enveloping the enemy centre of resistance.
>
> Reserves will be used to accentuate success and not to reinforce portions of the line in difficulties.[33]

Despite the strong belief that the Germans were on the defensive and the attack was being made at an opportune time, Second Army could not anticipate a clear breakthrough. The orders issued by 14th Division include instructions for consolidating the capture of enemy positions and for units to be prepared as soon as possible to repel any counter-attack:

> All ranks must realise that not only is the position to be captured but in addition it must be consolidated.
>
> CONSOLIDATION in depth is essential.
> The defensive zone will consist of ground East of the ST. ELOI craters.
> As a general principle not less than two defensive lines will be established in front of the Craters.
> The C.R.E. is arranging that the following stores are brought up by pack transport:
> 85 Coils of barbed wire.
> 100 Medium screw pickets.
> 1000 Sandbags.[34]

One week before the battle, 5/Cameron Highlanders (26 Brigade, 9th Division) spent a period of time in reserve, at 'P.Camp'. The activities included drill, training, physical exercise, parades and medical inspections. Seven days later 'the day was spent on inspections and packing up prior to going into the line to take part in operations on 'J' day'.[35]

32 TNA WO95/1894/6, War Diary of 41 Infantry Brigade, Instruction No. 1, 23/9/18.
33 TNA WO95/1894/6, War Diary of 41 Infantry Brigade, Instruction No. 1, 23/9/18.
34 TNA WO95/1899, War Diary of 42 Infantry Brigade, Instructions for the Offensive No. 2, 24 September 1918.
35 TNA WO95/1767, War Diary of 5th Battalion, Cameron Highlanders, entries for 20 and 27 September 1918.

The war diary of 104 Brigade Evidence contains typical evidence of the attention to detail within the advance planning: a map showing the dispositions of the German defence, with information on the regiments in the line and support formations.[36]

The Belgian right wing would receive creeping barrage support from the adjacent II Corps heavy artillery. The Belgian forces had also been allocated air support from the eight squadrons of the 5th Group RAF. During the battle, '200 hostile artillery positions were kept under fire during the operations and very little hostile shelling was reported'.[37]

The ground over which the attacks would be launched had been the battlefields of autumn 1917, Third Ypres, popularly known as 'Passchendaele':

> These attacks were to take place over a battlefield of bitter memories. In 1917, it had taken the British Army four and a half months to reach Passchendaele, meanwhile suffering grievous casualties in appalling conditions... Now the same ground had to be crossed again.[38]

During the build-up, on 25 September, the commander of 28 Brigade (9th Division) wrote in his diary:

> How familiar the place-names of today were 14 months ago: the Menin and Lille gates, Bellewaarde and Westhoek ridges, Zonnebeke Redoubt. We shall presently assault the identical positions then attacked by the 8th Division, containing the 2/West Yorks under my command. The bones of most of my officers and many of the other ranks lie between here and Zonnebeke. I hope the 28th Brigade will have better luck ...
>
> All is ready for the battle; we can think of nothing left to chance ...[39]

The line of the first objective was the crest of a ridge overlooking Ypres from the east. South of this lay the Wytschaete-Messines ridge which the British had gained in 1917 but been forced to retire from during the April 1918 German offensive. The British line extended south to Ploegsteert Wood and Armentières; between 30 August and 6 September, the Germans had withdrawn from the area west of this in order to shorten their lines.

Various steps had been taken to ensure that the British units were in the most advantageous positions from which to mount the forthcoming attack. For example at 2223 hours on 15 September, 103 and 104 Brigades (35th Division):

> ... carried out a minor operation and established a line of posts 500 to 200 yards in front of [the 35th Division] line on the whole front of 4,000 yards and captured 49 prisoners and 4 machine guns. Two more prisoners and 2 of the enemy killed were accounted for next day... total casualties [for the two brigades] were 3 killed and 8 wounded.
>
> The objects of the operation were:

36 TNA WO95/2483, War Diary of 104 Infantry Brigade, appended to record for September 1918.
37 TNA WO 158/218, Operations Reports.
38 J. H. Johnson, *1918: The Unexpected Victory* (London: Cassell & Co, 2000 edition), p. 141.
39 Terraine, *General Jack's Diary*, p. 269; the 28 Brigade, with Brigadier-General J. L. Jack as its commander, was only reformed at the start of September 1918 .

1 To give more room for deployment of Left and Centre Brigades in the attack near ZILLEBEKE.
2 To enable machine guns to be brought within effective range for barrage purposes.
3 To shorten the distance of attack by 14th Division on the Bluff and ST. ELOI.[40]

The importance of such operations for the Army's preparations, and reflecting his individual style of leadership, saw General Plumer first wiring congratulations on the success of the raid, and then visiting the division personally on the following day.[41]

As zero hour approached, final preparations were made. The war diary of 7/Seaforth Highlanders (26 Brigade, 9th Division, on the left of the Second Army front) recorded:

26th September	All officers took the opportunity today of studying the ground in view of the impending active operations.
27th September	Various conferences held during the day for the purpose of settling details [for tomorrow's active operations].[42]

Unlike the other British armies, Second Army had no tanks of its own; in practice, for certain operations with coalition forces, its troops did receive some support from tanks or armoured cars operated by Belgian or French units.[43] Second Army also had no cavalry formation but as will be seen there were examples of co-operation with mounted units of the French army. The attacks by Second Army would require the successful application of the combined arms available to its formations.[44]

Second Army deployed around 400 heavy guns and howitzers (equating to one gun per 70 yards of front), and 20 brigades of field artillery (about 480 field guns, giving one gun per 60 yards of front). In addition there were the sixteen squadrons of the RAF's II Brigade available to secure air superiority. Despite rain and low cloud on the night of 27/28 September, the RAF flew reconnaissance missions and bombing raids were carried out on supply dumps and the principal road, water and railway communications used by the enemy. During the next week 28 September – 4 October, British aircraft would drop almost 7,000 bombs on German sectors, including over 50 heavy (230 pound) bombs. Increased German efforts led to the downing of 30 RAF aircraft; in response the RAF recorded 51 enemy aircraft destroyed.[45]

Final arrangements were focused on adopting a confident approach to a German army that was now very clearly on the defensive. On 20 September a member of an enemy (Bavarian)

40 TNA WO95/2470/1, War Diary of 35th Division Headquarters General Staff: Narrative of Operations from 28 September to end of October, 1918.
41 TNA WO95/2470/1, War Diary of 35th Division.
42 TNA WO95/1765, War Diary of 7th Battalion, Seaforth Highlanders.
43 The French deployed 181 tanks in Flanders during October 1918: Stevenson, *Backs to the Wall*, p. 218.
44 Jonathan Boff has observed: ‘By this stage of the war [September 1918], the British army had, in addition to infantry, six arms available: artillery; ...gas; cavalry; medium machine guns; aeroplanes; and tanks’ (J. Boff, ‘Combined Arms During the Hundred Days Campaign, August-November 1918’, *War in History*, 2010, 17(4), pp. 459-477, online at <http://wih.sagepub.com/content/17/4/459>
45 TNA WO158/218, Operations Reports.

patrol had entered British lines and promptly given himself up.[46] This single incident was just a snap-shot of increasing evidence of a change in the enemy's mind set:

> Information has been obtained pointing to the probability of the enemy withdrawing in the near future from his present front to positions beyond the MESSINES-WYTSCHAETE ridge or still further back. It is possible that a bold & aggressive approach on our part may bring about this withdrawal … The Battalion will be prepared to advance on J Day [28 September] in conjunction with troops on either flanks and press the enemy if signs of hostile withdrawal are observed. It is the intention of the Commanding Officer to press close on *the tails of the retreating enemy but avoiding casualties as far as possible.*[47]

The final reference to 'avoiding casualties as far as possible' is indicative of the ongoing concerns, within and beyond Second Army, regarding troop numbers and available replacements; plus a shared commitment to reassure all soldiers that no casualties would be caused unnecessarily. A note from 86 Brigade, reporting on operations in which the brigade had taken part on 4-5 September, emphasised the essential need for covering artillery fire to support an attack by the infantry:

> [Point 2.] ARTILLERY BARRAGE
>
> Owing to circumstances a barrage was not possible on the whole front of the Brigade, owing to the number of Light Machine Guns now used by the enemy, the front of the attack not supported by barrage fire was held up and heavy casualties occurred, whereas the front supported by artillery fire suffered comparatively slight losses.[48]

One of the practical steps taken by infantry commanders to support this commitment to keeping casualty numbers to a minimum was the deployment, at the head of the advance and on the flanks, of 'fighting patrols'. These were designed to probe the enemy lines; with the knowledge gained then used to inform decisions on the bringing forward and deployment of supporting units.[49]

Though it was one year later, the physical consequences of the earlier conflicts on the ground in front of Second Army were all too real. British troops would have to advance across a barren landscape scarred by warfare:

46 TNA WO95/1766, War Diary of 8th Battalion, The Black Watch.

47 TNA WO95/2340, War Diary of 2/15th Battalion, London Regiment, Order No. LXVI by Major A.C.H. Banks (commanding) 2/15 London Regiment, p. 1.

48 TNA WO95/2299, War Diary of 86 Infantry Brigade, Notes On Minor Operations 4 and 5 September, 7/9/18.

49 TNA WO95/2340, War Diary of 2/15th Battalion, London Regiment, Order No. LXVI by Major A.C.H. Banks (commanding) 2/15 London Regiment, pp. 1-3.

> The fearsome artillery bombardments of 1917 had destroyed the fragile drainage system and left a wilderness of water-filled shell craters, decaying trenches, rusting wire entanglements and all the debris of a war that had passed by.[50]

The cratered ground would subsequently prevent the hoped-for deployment of the GAF cavalry reserve, which had been intended to exploit the anticipated early gains by the infantry in the forthcoming battle.

The ten divisions of the British Army were confronted by an initial six divisions of the German Fourth Army: a mix of experienced and new troops, some rested and others recovering from recent fighting. Second Army Intelligence reported on 28 September that most of the enemy divisions were '... of good quality having had from 3-4 weeks rest after heavy fighting'.[51] Appendix I includes the Order of Battle of the German forces involved in the Battle of Ypres, as assessed by Army intelligence staff.

The defenders were largely deployed well-forward, utilising prepared defences of dug-outs, wire and pillboxes; their reduced numbers precluded the adoption of the strength-in-depth arrangements used in 1917. The German positions offered excellent observation of the slippery, shell-marked and generally open ground over which the British troops would be advancing. Map 13 shows the disposition of the German forces, and the assessment by Second Army Intelligence of their combat readiness, at the start of the battle.

An attack had been anticipated by the enemy, and counter-preparation bombardments aimed at the British lines and support positions had been fired at dawn for several mornings leading up to and including 28 September. The disruption caused for the attacking forces had however been minimal.

As part of the preparations Second Army Intelligence had developed a series of maps which showed the location of the German defensive lines and the disposition of the supporting supply lines and assets immediately prior to the battle. Map 11 shows the interconnecting series of German defensive lines, with support and communication trenches, as mapped by Second Army Intelligence, facing the British forces.[52]

Map 12 illustrates Second Army's assessment of the German supply system and assets immediately prior to the battle.[53] In terms of communication, the Germans still retained the defender's benefit of operating on interior lines – as shown by the series of railway tracks which were available to support the movement of men or materials.

Despite the problems created by the condition of the ground for communications, transport and supply, the outcomes of the attack were to be very different from previous allied attempts to relieve the Ypres salient. The offensive on 28 September would produce a total advance by the attacking corps of Second Army of between four and six miles. Casualties were reported as light although the RAF lost 26 aircraft during low-level ground attacks on enemy defences, believed to be due mainly to poor visibility. British troops established a new line beyond the

50 Johnson, *Unexpected Victory*, p. 141.
51 TNA WO157/128, Second Army Intelligence Summary, 28 September 1918.
52 TNA WO157/128 Second Army Intelligence Summaries: September 1918.
53 TNA WO153/508 Second Army: Enemy Organisation 1918.

Ypres ridge. The Belgians captured Houthulst and Zonnebeke, and reached Passchendaele; the British retook Wytschaete.[54]

The disposition of Second Army units, and the progress achieved on the first day of the attack – relative to the objectives set, are shown in Map 4. The first objectives for the British were listed as: Molenaarelsthoek – Stirling Castle – Observatory Ridge – Hill 60 – 'The Bluff'.[55] These were to be regarded as a line from which a further advance would be launched. In the event the overall attack was a success although the resolution of the defenders increased as the day wore on and progress subsequently slowed. The outcome was an overachievement by the British, save for the blunting of the attack at Ploegsteert Wood.

II Corps

II Corps was positioned on the right of the Belgian Army. The Belgians were to attack in the direction of Passchendaele and to secure the ridge overlooking the area.

On the first day of the battle, II Corps committed two divisions to open the assault, 9th (left) and 29th (right), with 36th Division in support. Each attacking company had two attached machine guns; supporting companies each had one Stokes mortar attached. The signals officer of each battalion was to accompany the support companies and be responsible for the establishment of a 'visual and message station' at appropriate stages of the attack. In addition he was to set up a temporary station at a previously specified point on the line of advance; plus a more permanent station once the first objective was achieved. Troops were advised to remain 'alert' at all times given 'the broken nature of the ground and the long grass'. It was made explicit to all that sustaining the momentum of the attack was paramount:

> In the event of a unit on either flank of the [29th] Division or within the Division being held up, adjoining units will not check their advance but will carry on and if necessary detail a party to watch their exposed flank.[56]

The 9th Division, which occupied the extreme left of Second Army along the boundary with the Belgian Army, had the crucial task of maintaining touch with its allies. It was essential that the assault by the division was successful in order that the right flank of the Belgians was held securely; and to provide the Belgian troops and commanders with the confidence to drive home their assault. Plumer continued to remain fully mindful that providing this reassurance had been the primary aim of Foch and Haig in putting Second Army under the authority of King Albert.

The 26 Brigade was on the left of 9th Division, operating in co-operation with Belgian forces. 8/Black Watch was deployed on the left flank of 26 Brigade and therefore held the immediate responsibility for liaison with the advance troops of the Belgians; the war diary for 28 September notes:

54 TNA WO157/128, Second Army Intelligence Summary, 29 September 1918.
55 TNA WO158/218, Operations Reports: 28 September to 13 October 1918.
56 TNA WO95/2300, War Diary of 1st Battalion, Lancashire Fusiliers, Operation Instruction No: 1, 24/25.9.1918.

> Conferences with Commanders of Battalions of 17th Belgian Regiment on left and Liaison assured. Lieut. H.F. Calder and 4 runners with Belgian Bn HQ. Lieut. B.M. Laing in charge of International Platoon to attack along the International Boundary…
> [0800-0900] Liaison established on left and right with Belgians and 7th Seaforth Hrs. respectively.[57]

The nature of the ground was 'soft, boggy and pitted with shell holes'.[58]

> The enemy appeared to have been completely surprised by our attack making no show of resistance, surrendered freely.[59]

Acknowledging the problems of command and control once an assault was underway, 7/ Seaforth Highlanders emphasised the importance of soldiers maintaining contact with their immediate leaders as the attack progressed and casualties resulted. Expressing concern at men becoming separated from their NCOs and officers, the war diary noted that '…all men should be thoroughly trained to follow their section commander or, if he becomes a casualty, his understudy.'[60]

A crucial question on that early morning of 28 September was whether, once the fighting started, would the 'fog of war' impede the effective co-operation on the ground between the forces of the two different nations, British and Belgian. The outcome was a positive one, reflecting the efforts put into the planning of the offensive, as confirmed by the war diaries of those battalions most closely involved:

> [The] Belgian Army co-operated with the 2nd British Army in the operation, which was completely successful.[61]
>
> [0900]
> Advance resumed – The Belgians had some difficulty with MOORSELEDE and to assist them, 26th Brigade was ordered to bear slightly N of line of advance.
>
> [1000-1500]
> … 5th Camerons [26 Brigade] coming into line between Belgians and 28th Bde. 8th Black Watch and 7th Seaforths continuing in support.[62]

These conclusions demonstrate the important manner in which Second Army was treating its responsibility to link with and provide support to the Belgian Army. This commitment was now being demonstrated in practice by the troops on the ground.

57 TNA WO95/1766, War Diary of 8th Battalion, The Black Watch.
58 TNA WO95/1765, War Diary of 7th Battalion, Seaforth Highlanders.
59 TNA WO95/1765, War Diary of 7th Battalion, Seaforth Highlanders.
60 TNA WO95/1765, War Diary of 7th Battalion, Seaforth Highlanders.
61 TNA WO95/1765, War Diary of 7th Battalion, Seaforth Highlanders.
62 TNA WO95/1766, War Diary of 8th Battalion, The Black Watch.

The first objective of the Freiberg[63] Ridge was gained by 26 Brigade with limited resistance. The only particular problem was the weather, the troops having to contend with heavy rain and mist. 5/Cameron Highlanders then moved through its partner battalions (8/Black Watch and 7/Seaforth Highlanders) following a creeping barrage, over Anzac Ridge where an enemy strong point was taken out,. The next obstacle was the Glasgow Spur which required a flanking movement in order to take out a defended pill box. The southern stretch of the Passchendaele Ridge was also 'carried without much trouble' whereupon the line achieved was consolidated and touch confirmed with the Belgian forces to the left. 'Battle patrols' were sent out at regular intervals to check for the presence of the enemy.[64] 27 Brigade, in divisional reserve, was charged with exploiting the breakthrough towards Becelaere and then to Terhand. In recognition of the responsibility for supporting of the Belgian Army, the brigade was also tasked to move northwards if it became necessary to reinforce its allies' attack on Passchendaele. The brigade began its advance at 1500 hours and two hours later the troops of the 11/ and 12/Royal Scots were involved in 'heavy fighting' to capture Becelaere; by dusk the village was taken. Enemy reinforcements east of the village were driven back by small arms fire. The flanks of the advance troops were unsecured for a time but the locations of the Belgians and to the right, 29th Division, were known and touch was re-established in due course.[65]

For 29th Division, 86 and 87 Brigades took the lead, with 88 Brigade in support; initial objectives included Hooge and Chateau Wood on the left, down to Sanctuary Wood. In common with similar preparations across the Second Army front:

> Every effort was made to get the attacking troops into their Concentration Areas as soon after dark as possible, so that directly after a hot meal was served, as much rest as possible could be obtained before the Assembly ...[66]

The brigades adopted the now orthodox arrangement of leading initially with one battalion and then, once the first objective was achieved, the supporting battalion passed through and moved towards the second objective. Each battalion would attack on a two company front with two companies in support. In this case, for 86 Brigade, the plan proceeded with 1/Lancashire Fusiliers as the leading Battalion; 1/Royal Dublin Fusiliers in support, passing through the Lancashire Fusiliers when the latter was on the line of the first objective, to maintain the attack and exploit the first success; 2/Royal Fusiliers, initially in reserve, moving up and subsequently through the Dublin Fusiliers, to make the final push towards the target line of Polderhoek Spur and Cameron House. At the appointed time, subject to the progress of the attack, 88 Brigade would move through the two forward brigades to continue the advance.[67]

63 This is spelt as 'Frezenberg' on the Official History map for 28 September.
64 TNA WO95/1767, War Diary of 5th Battalion, Cameron Highlanders.
65 TNA WO95/1771/4, War Diary of 27 Infantry Brigade, diary entries; Preliminary Instructions 23 September 1918; Narrative of Operations 28 September-28 October 1918.
66 TNA WO95/2299, War Diary of 86 Infantry Brigade, Report On Operations by 86th Infantry Brigade from 28 September to 2 October 1918.
67 TNA WO95/2299, War Diary of 86 Infantry Brigade, Report On Operations by 86th Infantry Brigade from 28 September to 2 October 1918.

The attack went in under a creeping barrage of smoke and HE shells, and corps artillery was retained to provide covering fire up to the final target line. Reflecting the fresh composition of many of Second Army's units, the report of 86 Brigade points out that 'Troops of this Brigade had never previously advanced under an H.E. barrage and owing to the intense enthusiasm of all ranks and the fact that one battery fired very short throughout the barrage – the greater number of casualties suffered throughout the day was caused by our own barrage'. The diary records that those casualties very nearly included the brigade commander and his deputy. On the division's front there was limited defence from the Germans in the face of the infantry's attack, 'but wherever the enemy offered any opposition he was immediately killed'. The GOC, 86 Brigade, is recorded as having brought down an enemy aircraft (these had been active during the afternoon) with rifle fire.[68]

Resistance from the enemy was not sustained and the advance by 29th Division proceeded as planned, with initial objectives secured by 0900 hours; the reserve battalions of each brigade (2/Royal Fusiliers for 86 Brigade, 1/KOSB for 87 Brigade) moved through to exploit the gains.[69] Within the hour, 88 Brigade began its move up and through the front troops, to maintain the momentum of the attack. Rain during the morning had cleared away and the weather proved to be fine for the afternoon and evening. 1100 hours saw the capture of Gheluvelt and 88 Brigade, its flanks secured by troops of 86 and 87 Brigades, advanced up high ground above the Menin Road until checked by machine gun and artillery fire in the vicinity of Kruissecke.[70] Reference is made in the battalion's records of using ('driving forward') prisoners to identify enemy strong-points and pill-boxes.[71] By dusk the advance troops were well to the east of Gheluvelt and close to the Kruiseecke-Cabaret cross-roads; here the attacking units halted, facing considerable defensive fire from enemy machine guns.[72] The leading troops were also attacked at 1700 hours by four enemy aircraft; these were met by Lewis gun and rifle fire, resulting in the downing of one plane, at which point its companions withdrew.[73] During the evening, 36th Division moved up in readiness to move on Terhand the next day.

XIX Corps

The two attacking divisions of XIX Corps, 14th and 35th, had the objective of capturing and holding the general line: St Eloi Mound – The Bluff – Zandvoorde – Alaska Houses – Kruiseecke – Gheluvelt; operating along an east then south-east axis, in conjunction with

68 TNA WO95/2299, War Diary of 86 Infantry Brigade, Report On Operations by 86th Infantry Brigade from 28 September to 2 October 1918.
69 TNA WO95/2285, War Diary of 29th Division, Report on Ypres Operations, Period 28 September 1918-4 October 1918.
70 TNA WO95/2285, War Diary of 29th Division, Report on Ypres Operations, Period 28 September 1918-4 October 1918.
71 TNA WO95/2300, War Diary of 1st Battalion, Lancashire Fusiliers, Narrative of Battle 28 September 1918-1 October 1918.
72 TNA WO95/2299, War Diary of 86 Infantry Brigade, Report On Operations by 86th Infantry Brigade from 28 September to 2 October 1918.
73 TNA WO95/2285, War Diary of 29th Division, Report on Ypres Operations, Period 28 September 1918-4 October 1918.

29th Division (II Corps) on the left.[74] 41st Division stood in reserve, ready to exploit the hoped for breakthrough.

On the left of XIX Corps was 35th Division which, with 14th Division, had transferred from II Corps, on 12 and 20 September respectively; these arrangements were linked to the plans for the forthcoming offensive. Following subsequent planning and discussions between senior officers, that also involved General Plumer and Corps commanders, the scheme for the attack was determined.

35th Division had proposed that all three of its brigades take part in the attack (rather than the more common arrangement of two attacking brigades with one in reserve), due to the frontage of the advance expanding from 1700 yards at the jumping off point to 3800 yards at the line of the third objective. Given the logic of the argument, Army command had agreed to the arrangement. The right and centre brigades, 105 and 104 respectively, each had two battalions in line and one in reserve; the attack battalions to move into the assault through troops from a partner unit. Machine gun sections were deployed to be ready to move forward as soon as their involvement was called for. 106 Brigade on the left launched its attack with one battalion (12/Highland Light Infantry) through a company of another battalion. 18/Highland Light Infantry, in support for the first objective, had an attached platoon from 19th Cyclists Corps to assist in the advance to the second objective.[75]

The attack commenced at 0530 hours.[76] The plan provided for a creeping barrage at a rate of 100 yards per three minutes, with a first lift four minutes after zero. In the event, after 1500 yards, the rate changed to 100 yards per five minutes. An initial 'Line of Pause' was identified, during which time the artillery would 'search backwards and forwards';[77] after which four companies held in reserve (two per attacking battalion) would resume the advance. The priority was to seize and hold 'at all costs' the first objective around the Triangular Bluff and Buff's Bank – the line to be arranged for defence as quickly as possible. This action was necessary to make secure the flank of the corps and the corps boundary, and thus provide a firm base from which to take forward the next stage of the attack. 105 Brigade, supported by 35th Division Machine Gun Corps, was responsible for holding this line, acting at that point as division reserve; available to pursue a retreating enemy or to make a flank attack should the Germans attempt a counter-attack through Zandvoorde.[78] 104 Brigade noted that the field artillery had experienced '... great difficulty in getting their guns forward owing to the extremely bad state of the ground'.[79] This delay meant that the German machine guns were able to mount a considerable resistance to the attack. Pack transport was used to bring rations, water and ammunition up to the advance troops.[80]

For 106 Brigade, 12/Highland Light Infantry achieved the first objective within two hours and pushed on for a further 500 yards, subsequently capturing a section of German field guns which had been firing on the supporting advance by 18/Highland Infantry. Further progress

74 TNA WO95/2486, War Diary of 105 Infantry Brigade, Order No. 267, 24 September 1918.
75 TNA WO95/2489, War Diary of 106 Infantry Brigade, Report to 35th Division on Operations 28September-2 October, 4 October 1918.
76 TNA WO95/2470/1, War Diary of 35th Division.
77 TNA WO95/2486, War Diary of 105 Infantry Brigade, Order No. 267, 24 September 1918.
78 TNA WO95/2486, War Diary of 105 Infantry Brigade, Order No. 267, 24 September 1918.
79 TNA WO95/2483, War Diary of 104 Infantry Brigade.
80 TNA WO95/2483, War Diary of 104 Infantry Brigade.

was generally steady during the day despite ongoing problems in bringing forward the field guns designated to provide fire support ('the road was extremely bad and mined'); it was evening before these could be brought into action, sited in the region of Hedge Trench Tunnels. The problems with the ground conditions also held up the cyclists' section. The brigade secured and made good its final objective Alaska Houses by around 1230 hours. Communication was established with 29th Division on the left.[81]

41st Division was deployed in the centre of XIX Corps; it would advance in support of the two other divisions in the corps at the opening of the battle, initially on a one brigade front via 124 Brigade. The division moved forward at 1430 hours, with its right flank against the east bank of the Comines canal, experiencing limited enemy resistance. (Note: *Map 4*, Second Army: 28th September 1918, based on the map from the *Official History*, does not show 41st Division/124 Brigade as part of the attacking force, which is an omission; *Map 5* shows the division and the brigade, represented at the front line on 29 September; and the division's subsequent advance during the attack). The brigade was deployed in order to exploit the enemy's retreat from Zandvoorde towards Wervicq, following the success of 35th Division; pushing forward through Kortewilde to the canal bridge. A holding line was set up on a ridge north of the village of Houthem, securing crossings over the Ypres-Comines canal. The intended attack to seize the bridge at Houthem was deferred until dawn the following day.[82]

14th Division, operating under XIX Corps, would attack in cooperation with 34th Division (X Corps, to its right) and 41st and 35th Divisions (to its left). 42 Brigade would lead on the right with the objective of the St Eloi Craters; 43 Brigade on the left, with the objective of The Bluff; 41 Brigade was to start as reserve. The crucial significance of the pending battle – for the troops involved to prove their worth and for Second Army to demonstrate its support for its coalition partners – was demonstrated by the detailed plans, and back-up arrangements, for communications within the division and its subsidiary units, and with corps HQ. As orders put it:

> These objectives will be gained and held at all costs.[83]

The subsequent report on the operation stated:

> 6. COMMUNICATIONS. All the usual wire routes were established between the Brigades and the Divl. H.Q. D.R. routes were reconnoitred and laid down.
>
> Brigade forward centres were provided with Trench wireless sets and loop sets only to be used in case telephonic communications broke down.
>
> Pigeon, dog and rocket communication was also arranged.

81 TNA WO95/2489, War Diary of 106 Infantry Brigade, Report to 35th Division on Operations 28 September-2 October, 4 October 1918.

82 TNA WO95/2618, War Diary of 41st Division; TNA WO95/2642, War Diary of 124 Infantry Brigade, Report On Operations Commencing 28 September 1918.

83 TNA WO95/1899, War Diary of 42 Infantry Brigade, 14th Divisional Artillery Operation Order No.162. 24 September 1918.

> Diagrams of buried cable routes in the area immediately in front of the present line, which were used by us in before the enemy advance in April of this year were in possession of all Brigade Signal Officers and instructions were issued for their use in the case of an advance.
>
> In addition to the above, 5 mounted orderlies were attached to each Brigade in the line and 5 to Divl. H.Q.
>
> Further the Despatch riders of XIX Corps Cyclist Battalion with [Corps HQ] were available for use by the Division if required.
>
> It was also arranged for Contact Aeroplanes to drop messages and dispositions obtained by flares, at Divl. H.Q. and an aeroplane fitted with wireless telephone to patrol the Corps front from time to time.[84]

The attack started successfully with a limited reply from the German artillery to the opening British barrage (as already described, there was no preliminary bombardment). The first objective was achieved on schedule despite the troops having to advance 'over very rough ground, pitted with shell-holes and covered with debris',[85] with large numbers of prisoners reported. For example, 35th Division had processed 750 German prisoners through the divisional 'cage' by 1200 hours. More prisoners and a large amount of materiél (guns, trench mortars and machine guns) continued to be captured throughout the day. The first objective (the Triangular Bluff and Buff's Bank) together with the adjacent railway embankment, was secured with little opposition.[86] A German counter-attack against Zandvoorde at 1830 hours was easily beaten off, resulting in a further haul of prisoners. Pioneers and Royal engineers were employed immediately following the start of the attack in carrying out repairs to roads; this allowed artillery to move forward in support of the advance in spite of the poor terrain.

At 1605 hours the division issued orders for brigades to secure the ground gained, to establish outposts and push forward patrols. All steps were to be taken to bring forward attached artillery and machine guns, supplies and ammunition; with a view to being in a position to resume the attack at short notice. Pack trains were used to deliver rations and ammunition, a means of supply which the division noted 'worked admirably during this and succeeding days'.[87] Such arrangements were reflected across the Army front.

43 Brigade advanced along the Ypres-Comines Canal; 12/Suffolks on the northern bank, 20/Middlesex on the southern bank (with 10/Highland Light Infantry as reserve). The canal divide proved troublesome for communications between the two battalions. A further problem was the condition of the ground, pitted with shell holes and amounts of broken wire. The brigade's report on the day's action notes that all the men's helmets, brasses and bayonets had been dulled to assist in keeping assembly preparations secret from the enemy (successfully so). Attacking troops formed 'worms' i.e. section columns in single file.

As well as the waterway, the most notable terrain feature was high ground on the north side of the canal described as 'The Bluff', with an approach containing a large amount of marshy ground. On the south side the ground rose gradually up to the 'White Chateau', essentially a

84 TNA WO95/1876 War Diary of 14th Division: General Staff.
85 TNA WO95/2470/1, War Diary of 35th Division.
86 TNA WO95/2486, War Diary of 105 Infantry Brigade.
87 TNA WO95/2470/1, War Diary of 35th Division.

large mound offering clear views of the surrounding area. The report describes the attacking battalions as 'weak' and made up of men who 'belonged almost entirely to 'B' category', but their attack proved successful. The Bluff was captured by 12/Suffolks through a flanking move allied to a frontal attack that 'pinned' the defenders. The capture of this key point prevented the Germans from being in a position to enfilade fire on the attacks north of the canal by 35th Division. 20/Middlesex captured the White Chateau and were able to use that feature in order to secure the right flank of the advance. Special mention is made of 184th Tunnelling Company which supported the attack: the unit cleared fourteen tunnels and dugouts, of which at least four had been mined.[88]

On the left, 42 Brigade concentrated on capturing the St. Eloi Craters. The objectives were achieved in the face of limited opposition, and the front battalions were consolidating the line within two hours of the start of the attack. In fact the advance units went beyond the final objective, eventually reaching the line of the Dammstrasse; unfortunately, due to the prearranged artillery fire plan, the troops had to pull back to the consolidated line. The following day saw the brigade 'pinched' out of the line by 34th Division extending across its front in the direction of the Ypres-Comines Canal; as a consequence 42 Brigade moved into reserve.[89]

X Corps

For the opening day of the battle, with the main attacks being conducted by II and XIX Corps, it was X Corps and its southern neighbour XV Corps, which had the role of ensuring that Second Army's and thus the GAF's right flank was securely held; and demonstrating sufficient action such that the opposing Germans would not transfer any units north.

On 23 September the command of 34th Division and the line it held, had been transferred from XIX Corps to X Corps; the division was then engaged in the preparations for the forthcoming battle.[90] On the first day of the battle the division, with 101 and 103 Brigades in the lead, was successful in capturing the Wytschaete Ridge.[91] Its commander had subsequently relied upon the successes of Second Army to its north in order to make good the assault:

> As we had very little artillery [the capture of Wytschaete Ridge] was impracticable until at least the Northern flank had been turned by the capture of the line of the Ypres-Comines canal ...[92]

General Nicholson subsequently concluded that 'On the whole it was not a brilliant performance, progress being much too slow and information very bad'.[93]

88 TNA WO95/1905, War Diary of 43 Infantry Brigade, Brigadier-General, 43 Brigade, Report on Operations 28 September 1918.
89 TNA WO95/1899, War Diary of 42 Infantry Brigade.
90 TNA WO95/2437, War Diary of 34th Division.
91 TNA WO95/2437, War Diary of 34th Division; TNA WO95/2456, War Diary of 101 Infantry Brigade.
92 Nicholson, *34th Division.*
93 Nicholson, *34th Division.*

The immediate objective for 30th Division was Messines and from there to advance in the direction of Houthem on the Ypres-Comines Canal. For the opening day of the battle the main priority was to conduct a 'strong reconnaissance' linked to and in support of the principal operations further north under XIX and II Corps. The division's task was to widen the overall frontage of the Second Army's assault and be prepared to take advantage of any favourable circumstances, such as a withdrawal by the enemy, in response to the larger operations further north.[94] For 30th Division, its machine gun battalion supported the attacks on Messines Ridge, subsequently being involved in consolidating the forward slopes; eight teams moved forward to provide cover across the Douve Valley.[95] Over the next two days the division would be called on to show that, despite its relatively recent genesis, its performance could keep pace with its Second Army comrades.

XV Corps

31st and 40th Divisions formed the right (southern) flank of Second Army, the latter division at the junction with British Fifth Army. The immediate prospect facing 31st Division was Ploegsteert Wood. The planning by the division for the early stages of the battle was linked to the results from the principal attack by the northern forces of Second Army.

> It was expected that this attack, if successful, would compel the enemy to withdraw from the MESSINES RIDGE and also from our front.
>
> In the event of definite information being received that the enemy was retiring on our front, an attack was to be launched against his rearguards, and his retreat north of the WARNAVE Stream pressed.
>
> The role of [31st] Division was:
>
> a) To cover the Right Flank of the advance.
> b) To press the enemy's retreat towards WARNETON [a village lying north-east of Ploegsteert Wood].[96]

The division's plan called for an attack by 92 Brigade on Ploegsteert Wood from the north, aiming to gain and consolidate a line on the eastern side of the wood, based on the River Warnave. 93 Brigade would then move through and maintain the pursuit of the Germans; initially towards the River Lys south of Warneton, then north along the line of the River Warnave (in the direction of Warneton). On 27 September 18/Durham Light Infantry was transferred temporarily to 92 Brigade, and took over the right of that brigade's line in place of 11/East Yorkshires.[97]

94 TNA WO95/2338, War Diary of 90 Infantry Brigade.
95 TNA WO95/2323, War Diary of 30th Battalion, Machine Gun Corps.
96 TNA WO95/2360, War Diary of 93 Infantry Brigade, Narrative of Operations 26 September-1 October 1918.
97 TNA WO95/2360, War Diary of 93 Infantry Brigade, Narrative of Operations 26 September-1 October 1918.

The attack by 92 Brigade began at 1500 hours, with the advance troops approaching the wood from the north, then looking to work their way southwards. Despite heavy enemy shellfire the attack made good progress initially, with the high ground being:

> ... defiladed from the Wood and screened from Messines Hill by smoke barrage. But the going is appallingly bad – a tangle of old shell holes, wire, trench systems and concrete emplacements.[98]

The intensity of the enemy's defensive fire is shown by the killing of the British artillery observation officer based on Hill 63. The brigade was also concerned that 30th Division to the left had still not cleared Petite Douve Farm and Donnington Hall. The day saw fierce fighting to try and push the enemy out of its positions in the Wood, including the beating back of a counter-attack at 1746 hours. Overnight the brigade held the northern part of the wood, although it considered its position to be precarious due to a gap between the positions held by 11/East Lancs and 10/East Yorkshires.[99]

The successful progress to the north, specifically the capture of Zandvoorde by II Corps forces and their subsequent drive towards Houthem, led to changes in the initial plans of XV Corps. Having awaited instructions to commence action for most of the day, at 1700 hours 93 Brigade was told that its original orders were cancelled and it was to advance as quickly as possible towards objectives north-west of Comines (thereby trapping any German troops remaining on the Messines Ridge). By the time the new arrangements had been made it was dark, and the two battalions leading for the brigade were only south of Neuve Eglise at 2230 hours. Enemy shell fire caused the advance to pause for an hour in extended order around Hill 63. 11/East Yorkshires (92 Brigade) was now attached to 93 Brigade, as 18/Durham Light Infantry was already committed in line with 92 Brigade, and the East Yorkshires took on the role of advance guard. Enemy machine guns were encountered at Ash Crater, and although the defenders were being pushed back by the attacking troops, the advance became slowed. The brigade halted on Tilleul Farm, with 15/West Yorkshires now taking on the front position.

The circumstances were not ideal as touch had been lost with neighbouring British forces; both of the brigade's flanks were in the air. Lewis gun teams were placed around the position; the priority now was to be able to beat off any counter-attack from north or south. Losses overall had been low, most of these the result of the shelling around Hill 63.[100]

It is worth reminding ourselves that 40th Division had been originally re-formed as 'semi-mobile' and deployed to 'hold a quiet sector of the line'. During September, 121 Brigade had operated as its advance guard, moving forward in the wake of enemy withdrawals; over the space of 23-24 September, 23/Cheshires established four advance posts north of the village of Nieppe and along the River Lys. The division was now charged with securing the right flank of Second Army, focusing on the line of the River Lys, running west and north of the town of Armentières. 121 Brigade occupied the junction with Fifth Army, 119 Brigade on its left. On

98 TNA WO95/2356/5, War Diary of 92 Infantry Brigade, Report of Operations... 27 September to 4 October 1918.
99 TNA WO95/2356/5, War Diary of 92 Infantry Brigade, Report of Operations... 27 September to 4 October 1918.
100 TNA WO95/2360, War Diary of 93 Infantry Brigade, Narrative of Operations 26 September-1 October 1918.

27 September, having taken over the front line from the Cheshires, 23/Lancashire Fusiliers attacked in the direction of the Lys.[101] The instructions for the assault give a valuable insight into the main considerations for operational planning within Second Army during the battle, at brigade and battalion levels; particularly for these reconstituted units. That the action failed to achieve its objectives at this first attempt illustrates the scale of the potential challenges facing Second Army, and the steep learning curve that its rebuilt formations were having to undertake, during these early stages of the campaign.

The initial plan for 121 Brigade, 'a minor operation … to clear the West Bank of the Lys…', was issued on 23 September.[102] The main elements included:

- 23/Lancashire Fusiliers to carry out the attack; two companies to lead the assault, two companies to support with mopping up activities
- Posts to be established on the line of the River Lys
- The attack to be supported by:
  - A field artillery creeping barrage: sixteen 18-pounder batteries, to move forward at a rate of 100 yards per three minutes; to fire one final round of smoke, to make the infantry aware that the final barrage line (and the objective) had been reached
  - A smoke screen to be fired by the Trench Mortar Battery to protect the right flank of the attack; two mortars to be placed under the command of 23/Cheshires[103] in order 'to assist the advance and cover the consolidation'
  - Heavy artillery co-operation, initially firing on specified areas (buildings) in the direction of Armentières; then to target hostile batteries
  - A machine gun creeping barrage: to move forward at a rate of 100 yards per five minutes, keeping 200 yards ahead of the field artillery barrage
- A contact aeroplane to call for flares over the objective, to be lit by the most advanced troops, three hours after the commencement of the attack.

There were subsequent minor changes and corrections to these arrangements – illustrative of the care being taken with planning for the attack – the most important being:

- Six (not sixteen) 18-pounder batteries to fire the creeping barrage
- An additional smoke screen to be fired by a group of 4.5 inch howitzers
- The machine gun creeping barrage will move forward at the same rate as the field gun barrage i.e. a rate of 100 yards per three minutes
- Once the initial targets have been fired on, the heavy artillery will target a specified road section (intended to restrict enemy fire on the advancing troops).[104]

101 TNA WO95/2614, War Diary of 121 Infantry Brigade.
102 TNA WO95/2614, War Diary of 121 Infantry Brigade, 121st Infantry Brigade Order No. 54.
103 This was an error – the orders were subsequently corrected so that the mortars were correctly placed under the command of 23rd Lancashire Fusiliers who were leading the attack: TNA WO95/2614, War Diary of 121 Infantry Brigade, Amendments and Addendum to 121st Infantry Brigade Order No. 57 dated 25 September 1918.
104 TNA WO95/2614, War Diary of 121 Infantry Brigade, Amendments and Addendum to 121st Infantry Brigade Order No. 57 dated 25th September 1918.

In the event the Lancashire Fusiliers made limited progress, eventually establishing a small number of advance posts to the east of Pont de Nieppe. The preliminary report on the operation, which curiously did not include a report from the battalion commander of 23/Lancashire Fusiliers, described how the two supporting companies had come under heavy enemy fire: the company on the left fell back to the line of the River Warnave; the right company became split with some men retreating to the start line and others becoming mixed up with troops in the assaulting company. In the circumstances it was not considered possible to secure the original objectives. The reasons presented for this setback were:

- The strength of the German forces, including a number of fresh troops
- The effectiveness of the German enfilade fire into the supporting companies
- The consequent loss of contact between the support and advance companies on the left of the attack
- The 'thin' nature of the supporting barrage (though the smoke screen was considered to be effective, smoke having been launched at the pre-agreed timings of 0525-0730, 0930-1130, and 1400-1700 hours).[105]

The original orders had been set for Z day i.e. 28 September; this initial attack actually took place on 27 September, no doubt intended to strengthen the hold on Second Army's right flank. On the evening of 27 September 23/Lancashire Fusiliers were relieved by 23/Cheshires, who would in due course move forward to maintain contact with a retreating enemy – a consequence of the pending actions by 31st Division. The following day had a party of 10/KOSB deployed with 'L' Special Company RE, the latter to launch timed smoke screens as cover for advancing troops.[106]

28 September saw Second Army capture over 2,000 prisoners, plus considerable arms and materials. In what might be termed a return to the battle tactics of a previous century, 'Field batteries moved forward with the advance and engaged enemy troops and machine gun nests over open sights'.[107]

The successful achievements of the day can be attributed to a number of factors:

- Overall the artillery fire-plan proved successful with a limited response from German artillery, believed to be due at least in part to effective counter-battery fire:

  > The creeping barrage was good and the indirect [machine gun] barrage was excellent.[108]

  The effectiveness of the weight and direction of the different fire-plans on particular areas of the front did vary; the resistance met by 121 Brigade in an initial operation on

105 TNA WO95/2614, War Diary of 121 Infantry Brigade, Preliminary Report on Operations 27 September, 1918.
106 TNA WO95/2594, War Diary of 40th Division.
107 TNA WO158/218, *Operations Reports.*
108 42 Brigade, Summary of Attack on September 28th 1918 (from TNA WO95/1876, War Diary of 14th Division: General Staff).

27 September (described earlier) was attributed in part to there being a 'thin' barrage in support of the attacking battalion[109]

- The resistance of the German defenders was found to be weak overall although defence stiffened in pockets as attackers moved further forward
- The early morning mist combined with the use of smoke and gas from artillery shells, allowed 'machine-gun nests and pill-boxes [to be] isolated and overcome with less difficulty than had been expected';[110] however there were alternative views:

  The smoke made it extremely difficult to keep direction but undoubtedly saved a considerable number of casualties.[111]
- The bringing forward of covering artillery provided support for further advances and the exploitation of early gains
- Air support had been available in the form of ground attacks
- The maximum use was made of covering artillery and machine gun fire to support attacking forces
- Troops were deployed flexibly, making good use of advance squads, and carrying out encircling attacks
- Immediate fire support was available from the Lewis light machine gun teams within advancing units
- The troops involved, contrary to fears that many would not be of the right quality or have received sufficient training, proved fully capable of undertaking offensive operations.

The commander of 43 Brigade assessed his troops as follows:

> Although battalions were very weak and the men belonged almost entirely to 'B' category, yet they were filled with keenness and confident of success. They moved across the ground with energy keeping close to the barrage…
>
> … they showed all the energy, keenness and fighting spirit of 'A' men, and though they may not be physically capable of undergoing the same hardships for a long strain, I feel the utmost confidence in them…[112]

The successful breakthrough of the enemy lines is illustrated by the view from the air, via the reports of the RAF planes undertaking reconnaissance of the front on the following day. The HQ of 11th Wing, RAF, had telephoned orders through to 206 Squadron, requiring a special low-level reconnaissance mission in order to determine the positions of the advance troops.[113] The squadron consisted of DH9 bombers. Second Lieutenant John Blandford took part in the mission and his written memoirs present a vivid snapshot of the conflict:

109 TNA WO95/2614, War Diary of 121 Infantry Brigade, Preliminary Report on Operations 27 September 1918.
110 Edmonds, *Official History Vol. V.*
111 42 Brigade, Summary of Attack on 28 September 1918.
112 Brigadier-General, 43 Brigade, Report on Operations 28 September 1918 (from TNA WO95/1876 War Diary of 14th Division: General Staff).
113 P. Hart, *Aces Falling: War Above the Trenches 1918* (London: Weidenfeld & Nicolson, 2007), pp. 321-2.

> There was a thin ground mist covering all the low-lying devastated area between Ypres and Passchendaele, which was a morass of water-filled shell craters. We could see a good many shell bursts popping through the mist, German as it proved, for beyond the misty area we could see our infantry patrols and some tanks probing forward and in action against the German rearguards in open country, all along the front. We knew then that the Second Army had broken clean through all the German defences, and that here was open warfare again after four long years! A great moment believe me.[114]

At 1900 General Plumer issued further orders to continue operations on the following day. These included important strategic objectives which were essential for maintaining the progress of the offensive. The key elements were for II Corps to continue its flanking role for the Belgians; XIX Corps to secure Ypres-Comines canal crossings and support X Corps, once the latter had gained the Wytschaete – Messines ridge, in clearing the area west of the canal; XV Corps to move north-east and seize crossings over the River Lys.

Once again, further orders were received from Degoutte, around 1930, after Plumer had determined the next day's actions. Degoutte stated that resistance had been weaker opposite the British Second Army and the Belgian right flank. Accordingly, he concluded that it was here the attack must be pressed without pause. He also included instructions for the use of the French Cavalry Corps and VII Corps – though neither were to come into action subsequently.

The *Official History* dryly concludes that 'General Plumer saw no reason to modify the orders he had already given'.[115]

114 IWM documents , J. S. Blandford, Second Lieutenant, 206 Squadron, typed manuscript, *Sans Escort*, p. 16.

115 Edmonds, *Official History Vol. V.*

4

Advance to Contact: The Battle of Ypres 1918, 29 September-3 October 1918

> Company have dug themselves in in shell holes out in open country. Pouring with rain. Troops fed up.[1]

---

29 September

As the second day of battle opened the increasingly poor weather, allied to the deteriorating ground conditions, was already beginning to disrupt transport and supply lines. There was heavy rain on the night of 28-29 September, causing troops to be impeded in reaching attack jumping-off points. Mist caused troops to lose direction. Many attacks on the 29th were delayed as a consequence. Artillery support would be limited as guns were restricted in their ability to move to forward positions, even where preparations for this had already commenced. The day also saw an increase in German resistance and there was hard fighting in a number of areas, particularly east of the Ypres-Comines canal. Army intelligence had anticipated that the enemy would bring forward any available bodies of men to reinforce defences. Subsequently it was found that four divisions held in reserve had been added to the line.[2] The Germans were forced of necessity to make use of any men available in order to help restore defences. This meant increasingly that the capture by the British of a prisoner or prisoners from a particular unit, would not necessarily indicate that the full regiment or division was deployed at the front. For further details of the German Order of Battle, please refer to Appendix I.

II Corps

The 28 Brigade took the lead for the 9th Division, moving forward to take the Keiberg Ridge. The British troops and the neighbouring Belgian forces were then forced to pause in front of Waterdamhoek due to enemy fire. Additional units were moved up to strengthen the attack; 5/Cameron Highlanders (26 Brigade) moved into the junction between the Belgians and 28 Brigade. The renewed assault proved too strong for the Germans and the village was captured, with the advance troops continuing east, and over the Waterdamhoek Ridge. At this point,

1 Private H.T. Pope, 2/15th London Regiment, 30th Division, 30 September 1918, from his diary of the war, Imperial War Museum 78/42/1.
2 TNA WO157/128, Second Army Intelligence Summaries, 29-30 September 1918.

owing to casualties and some loss of direction, contact between British and Belgian forces was lost briefly; the gap was filled by companies of the Black Watch. Heavy machine gun fire and wired defences led to a line being consolidated in front of Slypskappelle, facing Slypswood.[3] During the afternoon the Belgians were reported to have moved through the village of Moorslede; meanwhile 36th Division had finally succeeded in capturing Terhand. For 27 Brigade, 11/Royal Scots and 6/King's Own Scottish Borderers (KOSB) had initially provided cover for the right flank of 28 Brigade, which had been exposed by the delay in driving the German defenders from Terhand. Subsequently 11/Royal Scots moved east of Dadizeele following 'hard fighting' to take Kanterhoek Farm. The brigade secured a line along Richmond Crossroads. The pace of the advance reported in the diary is further ahead than that recorded on the map from the *Official History* (which indicates that Richmond Crossroads was reached by 2 October).[4]

The advance of 29th Division continued, largely in a south-easterly direction, with Gheluwe the objective; maintaining touch with 36th Division on the left and 35th Division (XIX Corps) on the right. Progress was limited, mainly owing to increased machine gun fire and, as the day continued, artillery fire from German reserve batteries; a counter-attack directed at 86 Brigade at 1200 hours was repulsed by Vickers and Lewis gun fire. French cavalry provided valuable support through maintaining liaison between the advance units of 29th Division and 36th Division to its left, although touch was lost with 35th Division around midday, when the latter was unable to advance east of Zandvoorde. Artillery support was limited by 'the state and scarcity of roads'.[5]

While having no covering artillery fire 'owing to the shocking state of the roads',[6] 36th Division managed to push forward in the face of enemy machine gun positions. These were making use of available hedges and isolated buildings for cover, as the British advance was now moving beyond the damaged terrain of the former battlefield. The village of Terhand was taken in late afternoon together with the hamlet of Vijfwegen two hours later. This lay one mile south of the village of Dadizeele, which had been finally captured by 9th Division at 1600 hours.[7] The report of 1/Lancashire Fusiliers, on the left of 29th Division, states that contact was lost with the right flank of 36th Division during the afternoon; as per orders the advance was continued, with contact re-established later in the evening. Heavy rain began falling from 1800 hours.[8]

3 TNA WO95/1767, War Diary of 5th Battalion, Cameron Highlanders.
4 TNA WO95/1771/4/5, War Diary of 27 Infantry Brigade, Narrative of Operations 28 September-28 October 1918.
5 TNA WO95/2285, War Diary of 29th Division, Report on Ypres Operations, Period 28 September 1918-4 October 1918.
6 C. Falls, *A History of the 36th (Ulster) Division* (London: Constable, 1996; first published Belfast: McCraw, Stevenson, 1922), p. 264.
7 TNA WO95/2489, War Diary of 106 Infantry Brigade, Report to 35th Division on Operations 28September-2 October, 4 October 1918; WO95/2299, War Diary of 86 Infantry Brigade, Report On Operations by 86th Infantry Brigade from 28 September to 2 October 1918; Falls, 36th (Ulster) Division, pp. 263-5.
8 TNA WO95/2300, War Diary of 1st Battalion, Lancashire Fusiliers, Narrative of Battle 28 September to 1 October 1918.

XIX Corps

For XIX Corps, 14th Division was withdrawn from the line into reserve.[9] 35th Division was directed to attack in a south-easterly direction towards Tenbrielen and Werwicq. The advance units were held up near Zandvoorde, largely the result of the mist causing 105 Brigade to attack from the south-east when the original plan had been for an assault from the north. 104 Brigade had successfully taken the western side of the village including the western spur, but the Germans still retained the eastern spur, from where they continued their defence from fortified pill-boxes and entrenched machine gun positions. This was despite initial reports which had indicated that British forces held the whole village. The resulting delay would have consequences for 41st Division on its right, particularly for 123 Brigade, during the course of the afternoon.

Following the preliminary manoeuvring, at 1230 hours 105 Brigade began its advance on Zandvoorde, immediately becoming the target of shellfire. General Pollard of 106 Brigade was ordered to push through the troops of 105 towards Tenbrielen and Blagnaert Farm or to support the east/south advance on Zandvoorde. To accomplish this he was to assume command of all advance troops – creating a combined battlegroup made up of troops from 105 and 106 Brigades. Initially, Pollard put 17/Royal Scots on the left flank of 105 Brigade (4/North Staffs) through Zandvoorde. An artillery barrage targeted on Tenbrielen was arranged. In the afternoon 105 Brigade was able to breakthrough south-east of Zandvoorde and advance on Tenbrielen. Under Pollard's command the result by nightfall was that 106 Brigade, with 4/North Staffs of 105 Brigade, held the line Tenbrielen – Blagnaert Farm, with the remaining units of 105 Brigade in support.

While it had been possible to bring forward field artillery and machine gun units, both 'Cyclists and T.M.B. [Trench Mortar Battalion] had to be left behind'.[10] Active patrols were put in place in front of the secured ground; Pollard issued orders for the attack to be resumed, by the six battalions now under his command, at 0615 hours the following day.[11]

41st Division maintained the advance on the right of XIX Corps, with 124 Brigade initially halted on a ridge overlooking the village of Houthem. At 0700 hours the brigade attacked the village and its bridge, with 123 Brigade in support; the capture of the village was reported by1000 hours.[12] Under the covering fire of trench mortars, 123 Brigade moved quickly through the village; the troops' progress was 'exceedingly rapid, prisoners being freely taken, and opposition slight'.[13] At this stage, German machine guns continued to fire from the opposite west bank of the Comines canal, causing some casualties. Accordingly, once clear of the village, a platoon was dispatched across the canal to take out the enemy positions; this raid was successful with 36 prisoners and three machine guns being captured. 123 Brigade continued its advance, taking

9 TNA WO95/1880, War Diary of 14th Division, Administration Section.
10 TNA WO95/2489, War Diary of 106 Infantry Brigade, Report to 35th Division on Operations 28 September-2 October, 4 October 1918.
11 TNA WO95/2470/1, War Diary of 35th Division; WO95/2486, War Diary of 105 Infantry Brigade; WO95/2489, War Diary of 106 Infantry Brigade, Report to 35th Division on Operations 28 September-2 October, 4 October 1918.
12 TNA WO95/2642, War Diary of 124 Infantry Brigade, Report On Operations Commencing 28 September 1918.
13 TNA WO95/2639/3, War Diary of 23rd Battalion, Middlesex Regiment, Report on Operation carried Out On 29 September 1918.

up positions along the railway line which offered good sight lines from which its troops could direct rifle and Lewis gun fire upon enemy targets. However by 12 noon the attack had stalled; the Germans were clearly intent on holding their current positions and enemy machine gun fire had intensified, in front of the advance companies and also from across the canal. Attempts to outflank the defenders were unsuccessful and 'a good many casualties' resulted.[14]

During the course of the afternoon the outcome hung in the balance with the brigade's left flank remaining exposed; 35th Division was not at this stage in touch with the brigade.[15] There was evidence that the Germans were attempting to manoeuvre machine guns forward so as to be able to enfilade the forward companies, in preparation for a possible counter-attack. An enemy aeroplane dropped lights to support the targeting of artillery fire. As a consequence of the heavy fighting so far there were concerns that ammunition levels were becoming very low, and the casualty rate was increasing. Making effective use of their own machine guns to cover the action, the front companies aligned their positions in order to stabilise the line by the railway. S.O.S. rockets were fired and pigeons released in order to call for artillery support and for more ammunition. With the circumstances of 35th Division unclear, 122 Brigade was ordered to move along the Tenbrielen line and establish contact with the right of the division.[16]

The situation was saved in the late afternoon through the successful advance by units of 30th Division on the west bank of the canal, to the right of 41st Division. Contact was made between the respective advance forces such that enfilade fire from 30th Division troops was brought to bear on the enemy across the front of 123 Brigade's line. Also, at 1600 hours, the requested artillery support commenced, with fire directed onto the German positions. The result was to allow 123 Brigade to secure its front along a line about 1,000 yards to the east of Houthem.[17] In accordance with orders received, the brigade established a line of outposts for the night. The problem of low ammunition supply was alleviated by the dropping of three boxes of SAA by aeroplane, in response to the brigade's signal.[18]

X Corps

Following its capture on the first day of the Wytschaete Ridge, 34th Division proceeded to advance to the Ypres – Comines Canal.[19]

30th Division was tasked with clearing the area to its front between Messines Ridge and the Ypres-Comines Canal (target: Houthem).[20] The neighbouring 31st Division (XV Corps) was reported to be held up 1500 yards in front of Warneton (south-east of Messines) so 90 Brigade,

14 TNA WO95/2639/3, War Diary of 23rd Battalion, Middlesex Regiment, Report on Operation carried Out On 29/9/18.
15 TNA WO95/2642, War Diary of 124 Infantry Brigade, Report on Operations Commencing 28 September 1918.
16 TNA WO95/2618, War Diary of 41st Division.
17 TNA WO95/2642, War Diary of 124 Infantry Brigade, Report on Operations Commencing 28 September 1918.
18 TNA WO95/2639/3, War Diary of 23rd Battalion, Middlesex Regiment, Report on Operation carried out on 29 September 1918.
19 TNA WO95/2456, War Diary of 101 Infantry Brigade: 2/Loyal North Lancs occupied Wytschaete.
20 TNA WO95/2323, War Diary of 30th Battalion, Machine Gun Corps, Order No. 5, 28 September 1918.

on the right of 30th Division, was ordered to adjust its direction in a south-easterly direction to threaten to outflank the Germans in the village. The advance by the brigade was moving forward quickly; the pace was such that the OC 2/15 London Regiment 'reported that he was 1 mile [east] of MESSINES and his Bn. advancing so fast that he could not catch them up'.[21]

The attack had been successful, so that by mid-afternoon 2/15 and 2/16 London Regiments of 90 Brigade 'were well on their way' to the Ypres-Comines canal,[22] to the point where they were now out of communication from brigade HQ. The speed of the advance and the distance covered left the troops 'somewhat exhausted and disorganised' as noted in a handwritten addition to the original typed diary. The reserve battalion, 2/14 London Regiment, was ordered to secure the line of the advance, based on Warneton-Comines railway. A written addendum to the brigade's war diary points out that support was available 'at [the Brigade's] disposal on this front from 2 RFA Brigades and 1 MG Company'.[23]

XV Corps

During the day 92 Brigade, led by 10/East Yorkshires and the attached 18/Durham Light Infantry, 'began to penetrate [Ploegsteert] Wood from N. and E.'; by mid-afternoon the wood was held with posts established to the east and south. 12/Royal Scots Fusiliers (94 Brigade) was now attached temporarily to the brigade.[24] The immediate priority for 31st Division was to reach and then cross the River Douve, west of Warneton; despite some resistance from enemy machine guns reasonable progress was made. Later that day the division reinstated the original target of the River Lys south of Warneton – to be attacked by 93 and 94 Brigades:

> Owing to the extreme fatigue of the men, and the difficulty of assembling for a further attack in daylight, it was decided to defer the attack till 06.00 the following day.[25]

Overnight, 119 Brigade, on the left of 40th Division, had made bridges across the Warnave, ready to take advantage of any enemy withdrawal.[26]

The second day of the battle had seen significant further advances. A notable feature was co-operation on the adjoining flanks between British 9th Division (II Corps) and Belgian forces. This joint offensive had achieved a breakthrough of the prepared German defensive position, *Flanders Line I*; by late afternoon, all formations/units were in place in front of *Flanders Line II*. The Belgians had regained Passchendaele, plus Zarren and Dixmude to the north.[27]

Plumer issued two sets of orders during the day. At mid-day he once again confirmed the key role of Second Army in acting as flank guard for the Belgians, emphasising the aim of covering and securing the crossing points of the Lys. That evening, taking account of the day's progress,

21 TNA WO95/2338, War Diary of 90 Infantry Brigade.
22 TNA WO95/2338, War Diary of 90 Infantry Brigade.
23 TNA WO95/2338, War Diary of 90 Infantry Brigade.
24 TNA WO95/2356/5, War Diary of 92 Infantry Brigade, Report of Operations… 27 September to 4 October 1918.
25 TNA WO95/2360, War Diary of 93 Infantry Brigade, Narrative of Operations, 26 September-1 October 1918.
26 TNA WO95/2594, War Diary of 40th Division.
27 TNA WO157/128, Second Army Intelligence Summary, 29 September 1918.

he set out the objectives for each corps for the following day, in accordance with the Army's responsibilities to its ally.

The progress on 29 September had however been disappointing in comparison with the significant gains on the first day. There were advances on the left but inconsistent results elsewhere, although large numbers of prisoners and war material had been taken. The *Operations* record for the first two days of the battle records the capture of an estimated '3,660 prisoners, about 100 guns, and large numbers of T.M.s [trench mortars] and M.G.s [machine guns]. 17 E.A. [enemy aircraft] were destroyed, and 5 balloons burnt, at a cost of 3 of our machines missing.'[28] The *Official History* puts this down to 'the inexperience of the staffs in open warfare… [and] weather preventing the RAF from giving the usual assistance, and to the difficulties of the war-torn ground'.[29] The Germans had brought forward advance troops from a further four divisions, either to reinforce the line or in consideration of a possible counter-attack.

There was some action possible by the RAF that day, this in response to the German forward movement of reserves. Hart writes of 206 Squadron undertaking a bombing raid on Menin railway station in response to reports from RAF fighters of enemy reinforcements detraining.[30] Each bomber dropped twelve 25 lb bombs as well as strafing the station ('… which was full of rolling stock with German troops all over the place unloading and forming up')[31] with machine gun fire:

> We learned next day that we had so disrupted the detrainment and deployment of the German division that the expected counterattack never materialised … and the 206 Squadron raid was generally considered to have had a real impact on the course of the battle.[32]

There had been one bonus from the physical progress that had been made. The extent of the advance meant that most of the country which had been scarred by previous battles now lay to the rear of the forces leading the offensive. The prospect was now open of advancing across virgin territory, with troops able to relieve towns and villages which had been under German occupation since 1914. The Germans would no longer have the benefit of defending amidst the detritus of previous battles. On the downside however the new terrain would be unfamiliar to the attackers, requiring quality maps to aid planning and manoeuvre, together with the support of air reconnaissance.

General Degoutte was still anxious for exploitation of the gains he anticipated. He drew up plans for a 'groupement d'exploitation' comprising French infantry, cavalry and artillery, together with two Belgian divisions. However, no directions were issued for their deployment and circumstances did not bring about their involvement.

British orders issued that evening for the following day included 105 and 106 Brigades of 35th Division, under General Pollard, to attack the northern outskirts of Wervicq, and to establish a bridgehead overlooking the town. All available artillery was to carry out a barrage

28 TNA WO158/218, Operations on the Second Army Front: 28 September to 13 October 1918.
29 Edmonds, *Official History Vol. V.*
30 Hart, *Aces Falling*, p. 322.
31 Blandford, *Sans Escort*, pp. 16-17.
32 Blandford, *Sans Escort*, pp. 16-17.

of Wervicq from 0550 to 0650 hours. This operation would be carried out in co-operation with an attack by 41st Division on Comines. Later that night these orders were modified, with 35th Division ordered to continue its advance through to the railway north of Vervicq; its right wing to co-operate with the left wing of 41st Division in the direction of Les Casernes.[33]

30 September

The ground in front of Second Army was now unfamiliar and the terrain was not immediately helpful for the attacking forces. It was generally flat and under cultivation. The continuing bad weather, in particular the torrential rainfall on the night of 29-30 September, and heavy rain throughout the following day ('The weather was bad, with heavy rain and strong wind')[34] prevented the badly-needed air reconnaissance, as well as disrupting supply traffic. With the limited number of decent roads, delivery of ammunition and rations to advancing troops was becoming near impossible. At the same time the resistance of the enemy was stiffening. The German defenders had withdrawn behind the Lys and were determined to retain some hold for as long as possible on *Flanders Positions 1* and *II*. Plumer directed that artillery operations focus on disrupting those enemy forces crossing the Lys, together with ongoing counter-battery and general harassing fire.

II Corps

The importance of continuing to maintain the link with the Belgian forces, and hold secure the right flank of the Belgian Army, remained a prime concern for the 9th Division. The war diary of 8/Black Watch (26 Brigade) recorded:

> [Brigade HQ] pointed out that the Belgians on the left were not to attack till 11a.m. and reply received that this was understood and that arrangements had been made to secure our [i.e. 9th Division's and therefore Second Army's] left flank.[35]

An attempt to outflank Slypswood was called off due to casualties.[36] 27 Brigade consolidated the positions in and around Dadizeele which had been taken during the previous day; during the evening, orders were received for the brigade to attack Ledeghem.[37]

36th Division was engaged in a series of hard fights to capture and secure Hill 41, a key feature south of Dadizeele offering clear views of the surrounding area, and populated with farms and outbuildings that provided excellent cover for its defenders. Artillery support was still awaited and the initial attacks by British units were rebuffed. Arrangements were subsequently

33 TNA WO95/2470/1, War Diary of 35th Division.
34 TNA WO95/2489, War Diary of 106 Infantry Brigade, Report to 35th Division on Operations 28 September-2 October, 4 October 1918; TNA WO95/1771/4/5, War Diary of 27 Infantry Brigade, Narrative of Operations 28 September-28 October 1918.
35 TNA WO95/1766, War Diary of 8th Battalion, Black Watch.
36 TNA WO95/1767, War Diary of 5th Battalion, Cameron Highlanders.
37 TNA WO95/1771/4/5, War Diary of 27 Infantry Brigade, Narrative of Operations 28 September-28 October 1918.

made for 12/Royal Irish Rifles to mount a further attack at 1630 hours under the cover of a smoke and high explosive barrage from 50th Brigade, RFA of 9th Division; the initial success of this operation proved to be brief as a heavy enemy counter-attack that evening recaptured the position.[38]

The 29th Division was now engaged in heavy fighting for Gheluwe, from where it was intended to take up positions to threaten Menin. To its left, snipers from 1/Lancashire Fusiliers were protecting the flank; the fusiliers were also charged with maintaining touch with 36th Division. Efforts were made to link up with reserve elements of 35th Division (XIX Corps) on the right of 29th Division in order to give effect to this manoeuvre. Advance troops, with covering fire from the attached Vickers guns, met heavy machine gun fire from enemy positions in Gheluwe, and from houses and strongpoints on its northern edge.[39] This plan was then further offset by a strong counter-attack from fresh enemy troops during the late morning, which pushed back the units of 88 Brigade within Gheluwe:

> [T]he enemy was holding an organised and strongly wired line in considerable strength … Owing to the exhaustion of the troops and the lack of artillery support no further advance could be made …[40]

By the close of the day, 1/Lancashire Fusiliers had managed to push forward to within a few hundred yards of the Dadizeele-Gheluwe Road.[41] I believe there may be an error in the report as it states that the line reached was the Dadizeele-Gheluvelt road, but the report by 29th Division and the OH map would suggest that the road is actually Dadizeele-Gheluwe, which is the description I have used. Gheluwe lies some 4-5 miles south east of Gheluvelt.

At 1800 hours, the battalion used the covering fire from machine guns plus the support of attached field artillery to succeed in taking a farm held as a strong point by the enemy, which had been frustrating its advance.[42] The artillery was commanded by the Battalion R.S.M. who was unfortunately killed during the attack. Next, a pill-box was rushed and captured using Lewis guns to provide covering fire; then a further farm was taken. At that point the advance stalled in the face of continuing machine gun fire, primarily from the right of the battalion.[43] At 2110 hours, II Corps issued orders for the advance to continue with the objectives of Ledeghem (9th Division), Hill 41 (36th Division) and Menin (29th Division in cooperation with XIX Corps).[44]

38 TNA WO95/1771/4, War Diary of 27 Infantry Brigade, from reports noted to Brigade HQ; Falls, 36th (Ulster) Division, pp. 265-7.
39 TNA WO95/2300, War Diary of 1st Battalion, Lancashire Fusiliers, Narrative of Battle September 28th to October 1st 1918.
40 TNA WO95/2285, War Diary of 29th Division, Report on Ypres Operations, Period 28 September 1918-4 October 1918.
41 TNA WO95/2299, War Diary of 86 Infantry Brigade, Report On Minor Operations by 86th Infantry Brigade from 28 September to 2 October 1918.
42 TNA WO95/2300, War Diary of 1st Battalion, Lancashire Fusiliers, Narrative of Battle September 28th to October 1st 1918.
43 TNA WO95/2300, War Diary of 1st Battalion, Lancashire Fusiliers, Narrative of Battle September 28th to October 1st 1918.
44 TNA WO95/2285, War Diary of 29th Division, Report on Ypres Operations, Period 28 September 1918-4 October 1918.

XIX Corps

During the course of the morning units of 35th Division moved forward to approach Wervicq from the north and west, supported by 159 Brigade, RFA, advancing from Tenbrielen. Troops from the battlegroup comprising the six battalions of 106 and 105 Brigades, aiming to complete the capture of Wervicq and making good the line of the canal, were now engaged in heavy fighting in front of the town. At 0615 hours 12/Highland Light Infantry (right) and 18/Highland Light Infantry (left) had led the attack, with 15/The Cheshires and 17/Royal Scots in support, 15/Sherwood Foresters and 4/North Staffords in reserve.[45]

At 0905 hours General Pollard reported the claims of a prisoner that German forces had moved back overnight to positions five kilometres east of the Comines canal. The enemy had retreated in the direction of Wervicq and were now operating from prepared positions, including trenches and pill-boxes, north of the railway line. General Pollard reported that heavy casualties had considerably weakened his forces, and that he would need artillery support in order to progress; it would not therefore prove possible for him to extend his line to the left to Reeke. Arrangements were put in place for a bombardment of the enemy positions by heavy artillery from 1600 to 1630 hours; the bombardment would also take in the bridges in Wervicq across the River Lys. To support the troops on the ground, 157 and 159 Artillery Brigades were each placed under the direct command of 104 and 106 Brigades (General Pollard was still at this stage in command of the battlegroup of 105 and 106 Brigades) respectively. However no effective artillery support was actually in a position from which to cover a new attack that day. It had also not been possible to obtain touch with flanking units; the advance line was maintained overnight, albeit with no further progress made. Machine guns were sited to the north of the position, to provide enfilade fire should it prove necessary.[46]

The strength of the German resistance around Wervicq is demonstrated by the uncertain nature of the British positions at the end of the day's fighting. 104 Brigade, under General Sandilands, had been unable to establish the clear link required with units of 29th Division on its left; its forward units could extend as far as 1000 yards west of the village of Coucou, and the brigade requested that 29th Division look to join up at that point. Overnight the left flank of 104 Brigade remained in the air. The bad weather had restricted the ability of the artillery to get forward but positions were eventually established near Tenbrielen and Blaegneart Farm. Delivery of rations and evacuation of the wounded had presented serious problems due to the muddy ground.[47]

45 TNA WO95/2489, War Diary of 106 Infantry Brigade, Report to 35th Division on Operations 28 September-2 October, 4 October 1918.

46 TNA WO95/2470/1, War Diary of 35th Division – from the report of General Pollard; TNA WO95/2486, War Diary of 105 Infantry Brigade; TNA WO95/2489, War Diary of 106 Infantry Brigade, Report to 35th Division on Operations 28 September-2 October, 4 October 1918.

47 TNA WO95/2470/1, War Diary of 35th Division – from the report of General Pollard.

For 41st Division, 124 Brigade attacked successfully in the direction of the Wervicq-Comines railway, capturing signal stores, machine guns and a lorry. The speed of the subsequent advance meant that the brigade was for a time in front of neighbouring units and its flanks were exposed, though no problems resulted from this. It consolidated on a line to the north west of Comines and patrols were pushed forward into the town which appeared to have been evacuated.[48]

XIX Corps orders issued at 1300 hours, anticipating the position on the following day, 1 October, were as follows:

a) 30th Division (X Corps) to relieve 35th Division along the line from Les Casernes to Wervicq
b) 35th Division to hold the line Wervicq to Menin
c) 34th Division (X Corps) to move to Zandvoorde area (lying north of Tenbrielen, west of Gheluwe); then to relieve 104 Brigade (35th Division) on 2 October, along the line Wervicq – Menin
d) On 2 October, 41st Division to move behind 35th Division, to take over the line Menin, east to Wevelghem.[49]

X Corps

On 30 September 34th Division was withdrawn into corps reserve, with 30th Division taking full responsibility for the corps' front and the gains made by the troops so far. The morning found the division's units unclear as to the position on the flanks of the advance:

> We were now in a somewhat unsatisfactory position as situation of troops both on right (31st Div.) and left (41st Div.) was obscure.[50]

Advance parties from 2/14 London Regiment moved through to the River Lys; pack animals were used to carry mobile guns for the support of the forward troops. They found all possible river crossings in the division's area to be destroyed; the Germans had taken up positions on the south side of the river, apparently intent on holding this line.[51]

XV Corps

The attack by 31st Division to reach the Lys was launched at 0600 hours, with 93 and 94 Brigades leading. Enemy resistance, principally from machine guns, increased as the advance troops moved ever nearer to the river. Due to heavy casualties, the attacking forces paused on the high ground overlooking the Lys, before renewing their efforts during the course of the afternoon. Progress then became easier, the defenders' machine gun fire eased (presumably due to the Germans' withdrawal across the Lys) and 'by night all objectives had been reached on the

48 TNA WO95/2642, War Diary of 124 Infantry Brigade, Report On Operations Commencing 28 September 1918.
49 TNA WO95/2470/1, War Diary of 35th Division.
50 TNA WO95/2338, War Diary of 90 Infantry Brigade.
51 TNA WO95/2338, War Diary of 90 Infantry Brigade.

whole front'.[52] For 92 Brigade, 10/East Yorkshires advanced to the Warnave River; 18/Durham Light Infantry and 12/Royal Scots Fusiliers (attached from 93 and 94 Brigades respectively) continued to push towards the Lys.[53]

The 93 Brigade suffered a number of senior casualties during operations, evidence of the commitment of commanders at brigade and battalion levels to maintaining close touch with their advancing troops. Lieutenant-Colonel Wauhope of 13/York & Lancaster was wounded (with Major Goodburn assuming command of the battalion); Brigadier-General Taylor was wounded (with Lieutenant-Colonel Hickman of 11/East Lancs assuming command of the brigade); and the Acting Brigade Major, Captain Watts, was killed. The 40th Division 'continued to drive in the enemy's covering screen', seeking to push forward to the west bank of the Lys.[54]

The 'Operations' record describes enemy activity as a 'minor consideration as compared with the problem of communications':

> We continued to make progress [on 30 September] on the whole Battle front in spite of unfavourable ground, considerable opposition and incessant rain.[55]

Over much of the reclaimed land, the roads were almost non-existent and the ground had been churned over through the combined effects of shellfire and the rain. To try and deal with these circumstances, Second Army had improvised via 'corduroy' roads (using wooden boards) and through the extension of existing railway lines. This was a notable priority for Plumer – he required his air reconnaissance to continually report back on the state and location of the railway lines in front of his advancing forces, so that advance planning could take place to link up with these as soon as possible. This was crucial for aiding the provision of supplies – and artillery support – for advancing troops. As an example of these preparations, by day three the German railway system east of Ypres had been linked up to the Passchendaele railway station. However the Belgian Army had no experience of dealing with such conditions while at the same time it had to learn the lessons of this new war of movement. Second Army now found it necessary to slow its advance in order to maintain military coherence with its ally.

What was the view of the ordinary soldier at this crucial stage of the battle? The reader will note the quote featured at the start of this chapter – and its adoption to provide the title for this book:

> Company have dug themselves in in shell holes out in open country. Pouring with rain. Troops fed up.

52 TNA WO95/2360, War Diary of 93 Infantry Brigade, Narrative of Operations 26 September-1 October 1918.
53 TNA WO95/2356/5, War Diary of 92 Infantry Brigade, Report of Operations… 27 September to 4 October 1918.
54 TNA WO95/2594, War Diary of 40th Division.
55 TNA WO158/218, Operations on the Second Army Front: 28 September to 13 October 1918 and WO157/129, Second Army Intelligence Summary, 1 October 1918.

This entry, dated 30 September 1918, is taken from the very brief papers, held in the Imperial War Museum, of Private H T Pope, 2/15 London Regiment, 30th Division.[56] For me it neatly encapsulates the view the public likes to have of the British Tommy – practical, never happier than when complaining, while also getting to grips with the job in hand. Pope’s comments probably give a pretty good summary of the common soldiers’ feelings towards Flanders and its weather (and the British do like to talk about the weather). You do not need a picture to conjure up the scene his remarks describe. In their sparseness they sum up the likely views of the Second Army troops as well as any chapter in a history book.

An increasing feature of the warfare these troops were encountering could be described as ‘street-fighting’ – an unpleasant necessity in order to capture and make secure a town, village, street or farm, as the advancing troops encountered each in turn. In some cases, control of a village could change hands more than once during a single day. On 1 October a brigade of 9th Division approaching the village of Ledeghem from the east was attacked. The fighting moved into the village itself and the Germans were eventually pushed back. However they in turn subsequently put in a further counter-attack during the afternoon which successfully recaptured the village. A latter example, on 11 October, is of 36th Division which captured Mansard Farm near Ledeghem. The enemy launched a successful counter-attack during the evening and the farm was to change hands three times during the night, before finally remaining in British possession in the morning.

1 October

Second Army was striving to maintain the tempo of its operations to date. This was in the face of increasingly stubborn resistance from the Germans whose defence had been bolstered in places through pushing forward those reserves which could be made available. It was now the turn of the notorious Flanders’ weather to intervene – to the increasing frustration of the attackers.

II Corps

The strength of the enemy was growing: an operations report of 36th Division at 0830 hours stated that there were reports from prisoners of three fresh divisions being brought up.[57] 107 Brigade had attacked at 0615 hours, with the objectives set as Heule, Bisseghem and Courtrai. The action was not successful, the troops being ‘held up by enemy machine guns’.[58]

Improved weather on 1 October allowed the RAF to resume low-level attacks on German forces. Ten enemy aeroplanes were destroyed and 24 tons of bombs were dropped. During late morning, reports from the RAF reached 36th Division, referring to enemy troops heading south towards Menin; No. 7 Squadron RAF reported that it had silenced two enemy machine guns by fire from the air.[59] However the rains were to return on the next day, worsening the poor state of the available approach roads and increasing the existing chaos behind the forward lines, thus restricting further advances.

56 From his diary of the war: Imperial War Museum 78/42/1.
57 TNA WO95/2492, War Diary 36th Division: Summary Record of October Operations.
58 TNA WO95/2502/1, War Diary, 107 Infantry Brigade.
59 TNA WO95/2492, War Diary of 36th Division: Summary Record of October Operations.

In the II Corps area on the left wing of the British advance, the 9th Division, attacking at the junction with the Belgian Army, was seeking to exploit the breakthrough, requesting support from all available troops including the reserve cavalry brigade. 27 Brigade noted at 0825 hours that 'French Cavalry Patrols do useful work on the flanks'.[60] The Belgians were reported to have moved up to be in line with II Corps by late morning, though facing 'heavy opposition'.[61] At the same time however, German counter-attacks were being reported. These were particularly prolonged around Hill 41, which lay directly to the front of the eastward advance by the divisions of II Corps; enemy attacks being recorded at 1600 and 1840 hours.[62]

This was to be a day of problems for the attacking units of 9th Division, as the Germans sought to reinforce their lines and attempted to limit the extent of the breakthrough by the British forces. 26 Brigade had attack orders for 0600 hours but with the Belgians delaying their attack until noon, the morning saw a gap on the left of the British line. A machine gun company had been designated to fill this breach but due to the distance it needed to cover, was unable to do so in time. 8/Black Watch on the far left 'was counter-attacked as it passed the Menin-Roulers Railway'. This led to a short withdrawal of the British line and 'if the BOSCHE had been really in strength [the Black Watch] would have been cut off'. Units from 5/Cameron Highlanders moved forward to secure the gap and it was a relief that the Germans did not press further. The front was consolidated along the railway line.[63]

7/Seaforth Highlanders, 26 Brigade mounted an attack on the Menin-Roulers railway, north of Ledeghem, with the aim of then capturing the village. The troops met strong resistance, with the enemy seeking to hold onto its pillboxes and strongpoints for as long as possible; machine gun and rifle fire was very 'hostile' and 'snipers [were] particularly active':

> In view of our losses… [21 men killed, 2 died of wounds, 73 wounded including the Brigade commander, 4 missing] … the whole Battalion was formed into one composite [Company] in the line.[64]

27 Brigade had been ordered to capture Ledeghem. To assist this, one company of 11/Royal Scots was tasked with securing Telford farm on high ground to the north west of the village, which it did with assistance from a field gun placed to the west, 'firing point blank'.[65] 6/KOSB, attacking from the south, met heavy enemy fire as it moved forward; it only achieved its objective after experiencing heavy casualties, such that all the remaining troops were deployed to set in place a firm defensive line. Meanwhile, 12/Royal Scots were able to push into the village and advance to the railway about 1,000 yards to its east.[66] What happened next is succinctly described in the subsequent report by 27 Brigade:

60 TNA WO95/1771/5, War Diary of 27 Infantry Brigade.
61 TNA WO95/1771/5, War Diary of 27 Infantry Brigade.
62 TNA WO95/2492, War Diary of 36th Division: Summary Record of October Operations.
63 TNA WO95/1767, War Diary of 5th Battalion, Cameron Highlanders.
64 TNA WO95/1765, War Diary of 7th Battalion, Seaforth Highlanders, 1 October 1918.
65 TNA WO95/1771/5, War Diary of 27 Infantry Brigade.
66 TNA WO95/1771/4, War Diary of 27 Infantry Brigade, Narrative of Operations 28 September-28 October 1918.

> The enemy appear to have accurately gauged the predicament of the 9th Division. – both flanks in the air for he immediately counter-attacked on these flanks. As far as we were concerned the first counter-attack came from the South-East at 10.30a.m. and was wiped out by 4 Lewis guns firing from LEDEGHEM Cemetery. The enemy were in close column and were difficult to miss, their officers were mounted and behaved with great gallantry. The second attack came from the N.E. and S.E. at about 12.30 and forced the Brigade right back out of LEDEGHEM. The position was partially restored by the 11th Royal Scots and the station building and about 200 yards of the town were reoccupied, the 6th K.O.S.B. restoring their line under cover of a gallant attack by the 1st Inniskilling Fusiliers [109 Brigade, 36th Division] which, though costly to them, came just at the right moment… Had the attack been general there is little doubt that a partial failure would have been turned into a complete success… it was largely due to the unflinching support of the gunners [50 Brigade, RFA] that we were able to hold what had been won at great cost.[67]

At 1810 hours the brigade's diary notes that '26 Brigade report in touch with Belgians who [were] 400 yards [east] of Menin' including a section of the railway.[68]

On the right wing of II Corps, at 0712 hours 29th Division reported that its troops were now in touch with 35th Division (104 Brigade) of XIX Corps. However it became clear later in the day that neither of these forces were as far forward as they believed, and attacks made during that day were unsuccessful. Subsequently it was determined that a fresh co-ordinated attack would be required.[69] 1/Lancashire Fusiliers (86 Brigade) succeeded in advancing its left flank through seizing two more farms and a pill-box, making good use of outflanking manoeuvres with supporting fire from machine guns and Lewis guns. The 86 Brigade war diary, in its summary of operations, makes no reference to this attack by the Lancashire Fusiliers, stating that:

> During [1-2 October] little progress was made, owing to the very strong opposition offered by enemy machine gunners from the line of numerous pill-boxes opposite our front. It was considered that further advance without many losses was impossible, without effective artillery support, which at that time was not available.[70]

This may be a reflection of the reserve role which the brigade carried out during 1-2 October, and its relief on 3 October, because units of 29th Division were engaged in attacks through until the 3rd (see below). In its *Operations Report*, 29th Division concluded that despite attempts to advance 'no headway could be made owing to very strong opposition'.[71] By the close of the day's

67 TNA WO95/1771/4, War Diary of 27 Infantry Brigade, Narrative of Operations 28 September-28 October 1918.
68 TNA WO95/1771/5, War Diary of 27 Infantry Brigade.
69 TNA WO95/2470/1, War Diary of 35th Division.
70 TNA WO95/2299, War Diary of 86 Infantry Brigade, Report On Operations by 86th Infantry Brigade from 28 September to 2 October 1918.
71 TNA WO95/2285, War Diary of 29th Division, Report on Ypres Operations, Period 28 September 1918-4 October 1918.

fighting the Germans were still in control of Gheluwe and their machine gun fire from positions in the town frustrated further progress.

That evening II Corps received orders for the following day with operations to commence at 0700 hours. The aim was to clear the enemy from the area Ledeghem – Gheluwe – Menin. From there, 36th Division would be in a position from which to push on towards Courtrai.[72]

XIX Corps

Much of the day was taken up with a re-grouping of British forces, in line with the orders issued previously. 41st Division moved through 35th Division to establish a position on the latter's left, with orders to advance on Menin 'without delay'.[73] 30th Division (X Corps) moved up to be available to relieve General Pollard's troops on the right of 35th Division. The Germans appeared to take little interest in this intensity of movement at the rear of the British positions, and continued to concentrate artillery fire on the forward troops. Thus for example, when 122 and 123 Brigades (41st Division) moved east in daylight to a position north of Menin, they were heavily shelled.[74]

The emphasis from high command was that all efforts were to be concentrated on driving in the direction of Menin, hence the realignment of units in order to concentrate forces for this attack. The advance troops of 41st Division should push forwards south of Gheluwe, while on its right 35th Division should do everything possible to maintain touch. The overall situation was frustrating: attacks by 104 Brigade from the north of Wervicq had been checked and co-ordination with 29th Division had been made difficult by the poor weather and muddy terrain. Troops from 35th and 41st Divisions were still in the process of re-arranging their positions. The casualties suffered by General Pollard's combined force (he reported that day that the approximate strength of 105 and 106 Brigades was 900 and 500 available troops respectively),[75] meant that it was not capable of mounting a further attack before its planned relief. The corps commander therefore arranged for a further shelling of Wervicq between 1600 and 1700 hours; once it was dark, advance patrols should then be sent into the village to establish whether the enemy was withdrawing (as per intelligence reports passed down by Army HQ). Strong patrols found the village remained strongly held and covered by artillery.[76]

General Pollard, in his summary report on the operations, gave particular praise to the signals officer of 106 Brigade, for maintaining:

> [C]ommunication throughout between the Brigade and Division without any break worth mention. In addition to his own Brigade he also provided a line for 105th Infantry Brigade,

72 TNA WO95/2492, War Diary of 36th Division: Summary Record of October Operations.
73 TNA WO95/2618, War Diary of 41st Division.
74 TNA WO95/2642, War Diary of 124 Infantry Brigade, Report On Operations Commencing 28 September 1918.
75 TNA WO95/2470/1, War Diary of 35th Division – taken from General Pollard's report.
76 TNA WO95/2470/1, War Diary of 35th Division.

> and as far as I understand, for others as well... [he] not only enabled me to be in close touch with events in front, but ensured Division and the R.A., being also freely informed.[77]

Despite the bad weather and poor approach roads, and the severity of some of the fighting, Pollard was also able to conclude that, due to the work of transport officers '... troops were provided daily with water and rations by, or soon after, nightfall, and an adequate supply of ammunition maintained'.[78]

For Plumer, capture of the Wervicq – Menin line was as an immediate priority. At the Army conference held that day orders were prepared for a joint attack on 2 October by 35th Division (104 Brigade), 41st Division and 29th Division; the opening bombardment to commence at 0630 hours with the attack going in at 0700 hours.

At 1930 hours the relief of 105 and 106 Brigades by 30th Division (21 Brigade) commenced. 'On relief they withdrew to near KRUISEBEECKE cross-roads where transport and cookers met them'.[79] Behind the lines teams of pioneers and engineers were struggling to make good the road between Klein Zillebeke and Zandvoorde, to link up with the road heading east. The evacuation of casualties was speeded up by operating an alternative route, north-west out of Tenbrielen. As an example of the problems for transport and communications being experienced behind the front line positions, it took a Corps staff officer six and a half hours to deliver written orders from Corps HQ to the command post of 104 Brigade.[80]

X Corps

In support of 30th Division units, its machine gun battalion moved up to the eastern side of the Ypres-Comines Canal.[81] The war diary of 90 Brigade notes that 'A continued stream of traffic of all kinds circulated on the main roads [drawing] hostile fire'. By now, civilians were a substantial proportion of that traffic, looking to return to former homes or trying to avoid the new battlefields.[82]

XV Corps

31st Division continued to push towards and consolidate its positions along the River Lys; temporary attached battalions were returned to their host brigades.[83] 40th Division now advanced across the ground north of Armentières; from Pont de Nieppe, units pressed on overnight to continue 'the envelopment of LE BIZET', establishing a number of ouposts.[84]

77 TNA WO95/2489, War Diary of 106 Infantry Brigade, Report to 35th Division on Operations 28 September-2 October, 4 October 1918.
78 TNA WO95/2489, War Diary of 106 Infantry Brigade, Report to 35th Division on Operations 28 September-2 October, 4 October 1918.
79 TNA WO95/2470/1, War Diary of 35th Division.
80 TNA WO95/2470/1, War Diary of 35th Division.
81 TNA WO95/2323, War Diary of 30th Battalion, Machine Gun Corps.
82 TNA WO95/2338, War Diary of 90 Infantry Brigade.
83 TNA WO95/2356/5, War Diary of 92 Infantry Brigade, Report of Operations... 27 September to 4 October 1918.
84 TNA WO95/2594, War Diary of 40th Division.

Enemy resistance had 'stiffened considerably' to the north and west of Menin. In its centre, Second Army held the western side of Ledeghem; the left flank was secure west of Gheluwe. The Belgians continued to advance, capturing Vierschaar, Kruisstraat (north of Staden) and Hazewinde.[85] Army orders directed XV and X Corps to extend their lines north eastwards, assuming responsibility for Armentières-Comines and Comines-Wervicq respectively. XIX Corps was to 'clear up the situation towards Menin' and then, as X Corps extended its line, drive east alongside II Corps. This corps was to clear the ground south of Ledeghem, before resuming the advance eastwards.[86]

2 October

2 October saw the advance units of Belgian and Allied troops cut off from supplies and without food. To avoid these having to pull back, eighty aircraft were deployed to air-drop 15,000 rations to them; an overall load of thirteen tons. Small sacks were used, each with five or ten packs, and padded with earth to absorb the shock of hitting the ground after being thrown out of the aeroplane. The war diary of 107 Brigade (36th Division) records the event as follows:

> The supply of S.A.A. [small arms ammunition] and rifle grenades, Nos. 36 and 37, was difficult; this was met by the Royal Air Force who dropped in two days 36,000 rounds of S.A.A. including some boxes of bombs in the Brigade Sector.[87]

Every effort was being made to build and repair roadways behind the advance, to improve the flow of arms and supplies to the front line troops. Teams from the pioneer battalions directed by Royal Engineers were ordered to remove debris and put new surfaces in place which could support the heavy transport and guns. From the opening day of the battle, 6/South Wales Borderers (Pioneers) had worked on repairing roads in the Wytschaete-Oostaverne-Houthem area, attached to 21 Brigade (30th Division).[88]

II Corps

For the 9th Division, 26 Brigade held the line established on the previous day. The war diary of 7/Seaforth Highlanders noted that an infantry attack had initially made small gains which were 'however nullified almost immediately by counter-attack'.[89] The Germans also attempted to break through the line held by 27 Brigade and units of 6/KOSB and 12/Royal Scots were ordered forward in response. At 2045 hours the situation was recorded as quiet and no breakthrough had been made. The following night saw 27 Brigade moved up to take over the new line and relieve the existing troops who had been in action since the opening day of the battle.[90]

85 TNA WO157/129, Second Army Intelligence Summary, 2 October 1918.
86 TNA WO158/212, Second Army Operations, 1 October 1918 – 20 January 1919, Order No. 39, 1 October 1918.
87 TNA WO95/2502/1, War Diary, 107 Infantry Brigade.
88 TNA WO95/2323, War Diary of 6th Battalion, South Wales Borderers (Pioneers).
89 TNA WO95/1765, War Diary of 7th Battalion, Seaforth Highlanders; TNA WO95/1767, War Diary of 5th Battalion, Cameron Highlanders.
90 TNA WO95/1771/5, War Diary of 27 Infantry Brigade; TNA WO95/1767, War Diary of 5th Battalion, Cameron Highlanders.

The 107 Brigade had taken over the advance role for 36th Division from 1 October. Despite the reverses initially experienced it made a further attempt to push forward on 2 October but little progress was made.[91] The 109 Brigade repulsed an enemy counter-attack on Twig Farm.[92]

For 29th Division, 2/Hampshires (88 Brigade) fought their way into Gheluwe but were subsequently 'compelled to withdraw'.[93] A new prepared attack with artillery support would be required.

XIX Corps

The planned attack by all its three divisions, with 35th and 41st assaulting defences towards Menin, went in as directed at 0700 hours; the aim was to capture the Terhand Line of the enemy. By 0830 hours it was reported that patrols of 122 Brigade were clearing Gheluwe and along the railway line, in the face of continual rifle and machine gun fire. However a strong counter-attack in the evening would force a slight withdrawal to a line along the Wervicq – Gheluwe road.[94] Overall the assault on Wervicq failed although some progress was made in a few places. The enemy defence line, the Gheluwe Switch, was proving to be too strongly held for the weakened British forces; the evidence from prisoners was that the Germans were under firm orders to hold this line for the present.

General Sandilands reported that morning that his 104 Brigade, attacking the high ground west of Reeke (north of Wervicq), had sustained 'heavy casualties' and that 'High ground even if taken would be impossible to hold as it is machine gunned from three sides including houses in Wervicq ... Enemy artillery and [machine guns] increasing'.[95] 122 Brigade (41st Division) attacked with 18/King's Royal Rifle Corps (KRRC) and 15/Hampshires; the battalions were themselves counter-attacked and forced to withdraw slightly and consolidate.[96] Due to these circumstances, 124 Brigade moved up during the evening as support for 41st Division but was not called upon.[97]

Intelligence from corps HQ stated that a large number of enemy troops had been seen moving on roads west and north-west of Menin; between 0800 and 1200 hours 16 trains were recorded as entering the town. This evidence of the commitment by the Germans to hold their lines led British commanders to conclude that 'a heavy bombardment and organised attack would be necessary before the [Gheluwe] Switch could be carried'.[98] With further evidence suggesting that a possible counter-attack from the direction of Menin was planned, XIX Corps secured the commitment of support from X Corps should such a situation materialise. Arrangements now

91 The War Diary of the 107 Brigade states that the advance halted at Dibsland Farm (TNA WO95/2502/1).
92 TNA WO95/2509, War Diary of 109 Infantry Brigade.
93 TNA WO95/2285, War Diary of 29th Division, Report on Ypres Operations, Period 28 September 1918-4 October 1918.
94 TNA WO95/2618, War Diary of 41st Division.
95 TNA WO95/2470/1, War Diary of 35th Division; TNA WO95/2483, War Diary of 104 Infantry Brigade.
96 TNA WO95/2365, War Diary of 18th Battalion, Kings Royal Rifle Corps.
97 TNA WO95/2642, War Diary of 124 Infantry Brigade, Report On Operations Commencing 28 September 1918.
98 TNA WO95/2470/1, War Diary of 35th Division.

proceeded for the relief of 35th and 41st Divisions by 34th Division (X Corps); 41st Division took over the Gheluwe sector from 29th Division.[99] Over the course of the battle, 35th Division, involved in some of the fiercest of the fighting, had sustained 1748 casualties (264 killed, 1366 wounded, 118 missing), distributed across all its constituent brigades and battalions.[100]

14th Division had 41 Brigade send forward advance patrols to reconnoitre the bridges over the River Lys – there was concern that 90 Brigade (30th Division) did not have full control of the river banks.[101]

X Corps

The first priority for 30th Division was to secure the line of the River Lys to its front. From this the aim was to advance this line north east through Wervicq, taking advantage of the operations under XIX Corps to the north and east.[102] In support of these and other operations there had been as much work as possible carried out on building and repairing roads to allow supplies and artillery to be moved forward.

XV Corps

The previous day, 14th Division had transferred to the command of XV Corps from XIX Corps; its 41 Brigade now took over the line from 30th Division (X Corps) on the left.[103] 92 Brigade (31st Division) advanced its line to the Armentières-Ploegsteert Railway, and set up posts on the eastern side.[104]

For 40th Division, 2 October saw 10/KOSB across the Lys at Erquinghem with its 120 Brigade reserve, 11/Cameron Highlanders, deployed in support.[105] The following day, following an evacuation by the Germans, the division was able to surround Armentières; it found 'All chimneys, towers and churches blown up by enemy, who has also fired many villages E. of LYS'. By 4 October, Warneton was secure and 31st and 40th Divisions were established in positions on the west of the Lys, with footbridges in place to commence further crossings.[106] The primary task of 40th Division, to maintain touch with 59th Division on the flank of Second Army, had been achieved.

Day five of the Battle had seen 'obstinate resistance' from the Germans, particularly around Gheluwe and Ledeghem. The Belgians had captured Hazewind but a strong enemy counter-attack had pushed their advance troops out of Roulers. A combined attack by French and Belgian forces the following day, supported by tanks, made gains west of the city.[107]

99 TNA WO95/2618, War Diary of 41st Division.
100 TNA WO95/2470/1, War Diary of 35th Division.
101 TNA WO95/1894/6, War Diary of 41 Infantry Brigade.
102 TNA WO95/2323, War Diary of 30th Battalion, Machine Gun Corps.
103 TNA WO95/1880, War Diary of 14th Division, Administration Section.
104 TNA WO95/2356/5, War Diary of 92 Infantry Brigade, Report of Operations … 27 September to 4 October 1918.
105 TNA WO95/2611/4, War Diary of 11th Battalion, Cameron Highlanders.
106 TNA WO95/2356/5, War Diary of 92 Infantry Brigade, Report of Operations, 27 September to 4 October 1918; TNA WO95/2594, War Diary of 40th Division.
107 TNA WO157/129, Second Army Intelligence Summaries, 3-4 October 1918.

The impact of Flanders' mud upon military operations should not be underestimated. Griffith, in reference to the operations twelve months previously, has provided a concise and clear description of the resulting problems for weaponry:

> HE shells became buried and smothered in [the mud]. If they could fly at all, aircraft could not tell friend from foe since the uniforms of both had been equally discoloured by it. Mortar base plates sank into it every time a bomb was fired... Small arms became hopelessly clogged by it within an hour of opening fire ...[108]

The report of 29th Division concluded:

> The nature of the country, over which the advance was made, was indescribable, waterlogged and absolutely destroyed after 4 years of incessant shelling ... After the first day, the weather broke and there was 36 hours of continuous heavy rain ... The almost complete absence of shelter... made the conditions very trying for the troops.[109]

In the face of such conditions, the scale of the advance achieved and the continued deliveries of arms and materials to the troops, illustrates the high levels of motivation and morale held by the men involved both at the front line and in support. The report of 29th Division makes the point that 'despite the difficulties of communication, ration and ammunition supply ... at no time was there any failure of supplies'.

Recognition of the worsening problems for transport and supply, as well as the extreme demands upon the advancing troops caused by the wet weather and the deteriorating ground conditions, is reflected in the orders from II Corps:

> Divisions will consolidate and hold whatever line is held on the evening of to-day 2nd October... until such time as it is practicable to move forward heavy artillery and launch forward another properly organised attack with artillery support ... so soon as practicable as many troops as possible will be withdrawn into reserve.[110]

Falls has described the problems for transport as early as 30 September, given the need to both bring forward artillery and also to establish a relay system for supplies:

> The roads were choked. The only tolerable among them ... were the Menin and Zonnebeke Roads. Upon each was a solid mass of transport, which often for hours at a time remained immobile.[111]

A summary by 107 Brigade (36th Division, II Corps) of its experiences during the recent fighting gives a valuable insight into the views and experiences of the front line troops. The

108 Griffith, *Battle Tactics*, pp. 88-89.
109 TNA WO95/2285, War Diary of 29th Division, Report on Ypres Operations, Period 28 September 1918-4 October 1918.
110 TNA WO95/2492, War Diary of 36th Division: Summary Record of October Operations.
111 Falls, *36th (Ulster) Division*, p. 269.

passage illustrates the problems caused by the extent of the advance achieved when also faced with severe weather conditions, poor road links, and difficult terrain. This effort was in the face of an enemy which had the advantage of operating on interior lines, thereby closer to its supplies and supporting artillery. This same enemy had brought up its reserves and was increasingly determined to hold its ground:

> The Brigade came into the attack [from 30 September to 2 October] when the enemy defence was thickening and becoming organized. Owing to the bad weather and extensive crater area from YPRES to BECELAERE it had not been possible to bring up more than, at first, 18-pdrs. The supply of artillery ammunition was very limited owing to the difficulty of carriage by pack on long and almost impassable roads. The limited roads that existed were blocked with transport and troops (including a French Cavalry Division) for long periods. Certain wagons of Brigade Headquarters took 36 hours to get from WHITE CHATEAU, YPRES TO TERHAND [the location of the Brigade HQ]. Opposite the Brigade Sector was 172nd [Infantry Regiment], 1st Bavarian Division. From evidence of prisoners their Battalion strength was only 100, but they had nine light machine guns per Company, with these well-ensconced in concrete pill-boxes. The Infantry, unsupported by Tanks and with very little artillery support – practically no smoke shells being available – could make very little progress without suffering considerable losses ... While it was important to push towards COURTRAI, and further, out-flank the enemy defensive lines protecting LILLE, the losses suffered by troops (in good spirits though tired) decided in favour of a policy of waiting until our guns and supplies came up, before undertaking an advance again on a big scale. The enemy was well supplied with artillery which he used freely. He relied on his artillery and machine guns to defend the sector. Without this support it/is doubtful whether his Infantry would have put up any fight.[112]

With the worsening transport and supply problems, together with German reserves strengthening the defensive lines of the Flanders defences, the battle ceased. The Belgians were glad to halt in order to re-group following the fighting of the past five days. Stevenson describes how 'an inexperienced army operating in difficult circumstances (and unfamiliar with open warfare) ran ahead of its supplies'.[113]

The British were now two miles short of Menin – which had been an original objective in the autumn of 1914. The subsequent report of 29th Division on the battle suggested that had cavalry been available to exploit the gains of the first day, then the important line of the Menin – Roulers railway might have been captured at that time.[114]

General Plumer recognised that heavy artillery and planned preparations would be necessary to achieve the next breakthrough and create the circumstances for a full breakout. He issued orders for attacks to cease for the present, the ground currently held to be consolidated, artillery to be manoeuvred forward, and communications improved. Order no.40 stated:

112 TNA WO95/2502/1, War Diary of 107 Infantry Brigade.
113 Stevenson, *Backs to the Wall*, p. 136.
114 TNA WO95/2285, War Diary of 29th Division, Report on Ypres Operations, Period 28 September 1918-4 October 1918.

1 The attack carried out on the Army front today made little progress owing to the determined resistance offered by the enemy, both with Artillery and machine gun fire.
2 Corps will consolidate the ground they now hold and no further attacks will be made until further orders.
3 Every effort will be made to improve communications and push forward Artillery as rapidly as possible.[115]

Reports from civilians and prisoners indicated that the morale of the German troops was fragile, that of Bavarian units particularly poor, and of concern to their officers. Depots were being evacuated and materiél moved back to reserve positions.[116]

Many of the post battle operations reports made reference to the importance of artillery support for the infantry to be able to overcome determined enemy defences and entrenched machine gun posts. The comments of 86 Brigade were typical:

> Very great credit is due to the supporting artillery. Many guns only took up position on Y/Z night and fired their barrage as a Map Shoot. The barrage, though ragged, was excellent…[117]

Reports also related positive observations about the direct support to infantry units by attached and supporting machine gun and trench mortar sections:

> Machine Guns advanced with Battalion Headquarters under the immediate control of Battalion Commanders. Section Officers, however, were encouraged to seize every opportunity of using their own initiative, and, by their untiring efforts, skill and boldness in handling their weapons, the Machine Gunners assisted very considerably throughout the operation.[118] Stokes Mortars proved invaluable in overcoming hostile points of resistance.[119]

Map 5 depicts the relative steps making up the advance by Second Army, after the first day of the Battle through to the decision by Plumer to break off the attack on 3 October.

The more flexible tactics adopted by the advancing infantry units of Second Army, which varied in precise detail between brigades and divisions, generally received positive comments. The tactics involved the men and their officers in exercising far more initiative when moving forward, making decisions on the use of terrain and cover, and the deployment and direction of supporting firepower.

115 TNA WO158/212, Second Army Operations, 1 October 1918 – 20 January 1919.
116 TNA WO157/129, Second Army Intelligence Summary, 3 October 1918.
117 TNA WO95/2299, War Diary of 86 Infantry Brigade, Report On Operations by 86th Infantry Brigade from 28 September to 2 October 1918.
118 TNA WO95/2299, War Diary of 86 Infantry Brigade, Report On Operations by 86th Infantry Brigade from 28 September to 2 October 1918.
119 TNA WO95/2299, War Diary of 86 Infantry Brigade, Report On Operations by 86th Infantry Brigade from 28 September to 2 October 1918.

> Very few casualties were suffered from hostile fire. I attribute this largely to the fact that all ranks had been trained to 'dribble' forward and under cover of trench mortars, Lewis Guns, Rifle Grenades and rifle fire, outflank centres of resistance.[120]

Writing to the commander of 29th Division, Lieutenant-General C.W. Jacob (II Corps) pointed out that the division had been 'specially selected' for a key task on the opening day of the battle, the taking the Broodseinde Ridge, which it had achieved and more in the first 24 hours of the attack. He also congratulated the division on its subsequent capture of Gheluvelt on 28 September and, after very heavy fighting, the village of Gheluwe, on 3 October.[121] These gains were important in terms of maintaining the momentum of the army's initial breakthrough.

Second Army Order 41 directed all corps to maintain harassing actions by infantry and artillery, intended to persuade the Germans that a new attack was imminent. The aim was to prevent the enemy from moving troops north where the Belgians, with French support, intended to exploit Second Army's breakthrough.[122] Although Degoutte wished for a new general advance to commence on 7/8 October, King Albert subsequently set the date as 14 October. The high number of Belgian casualties so far was an important factor in this decision to allow more time for preparation of the next phase.

The Battle of Ypres saw overall British Second Army casualties of 303 officers and 4,392 other ranks. For the Belgians, around 2,000 soldiers had been killed and 10,000 were sick or wounded; their total net loss was 4,500 including 50 per cent of the officers.

Second Army had captured 4,672 prisoners and about 100 guns. Overall, the GAF had taken over 10,000 German prisoners, 300 guns, 100 trench mortars, and 600 machine guns. As well as all this, and the physical extent of the advance, perhaps the most significant achievement of Second Army was a symbolic one. The breakthrough of the German defences and the pushing back of the enemy brought an end to an iconic set-piece of the war. As Brice has so eloquently expressed it:

> The long guard was over, and the shattered tower of Ypres still stood, the pointing witness of an inviolated charge. The curving belt of fire and steel – so often strained near to breaking-point, so often pierced but never broken – had spread wide, had gone forward. There was no Salient.[123]

120 TNA WO95/2299, War Diary of 86 Infantry Brigade, Report On Operations by 86th Infantry Brigade from 28 September to 2 October 1918.

121 TNA WO95/2300, War Diary of 1st Battalion, Lancashire Fusiliers, Letter, 3rd October 1918, Headquarters, II Corps, from Lieutenant-General C.W. Jacob, forwarded as 29th Division No. C.G.S. 51/39.

122 TNA WO158/212, Second Army Operations, 1 October 1918 – 20 January 1919, Order No. 41, 3 October 1918.

123 Brice, *The Battle Book of Ypres*, p. 52.

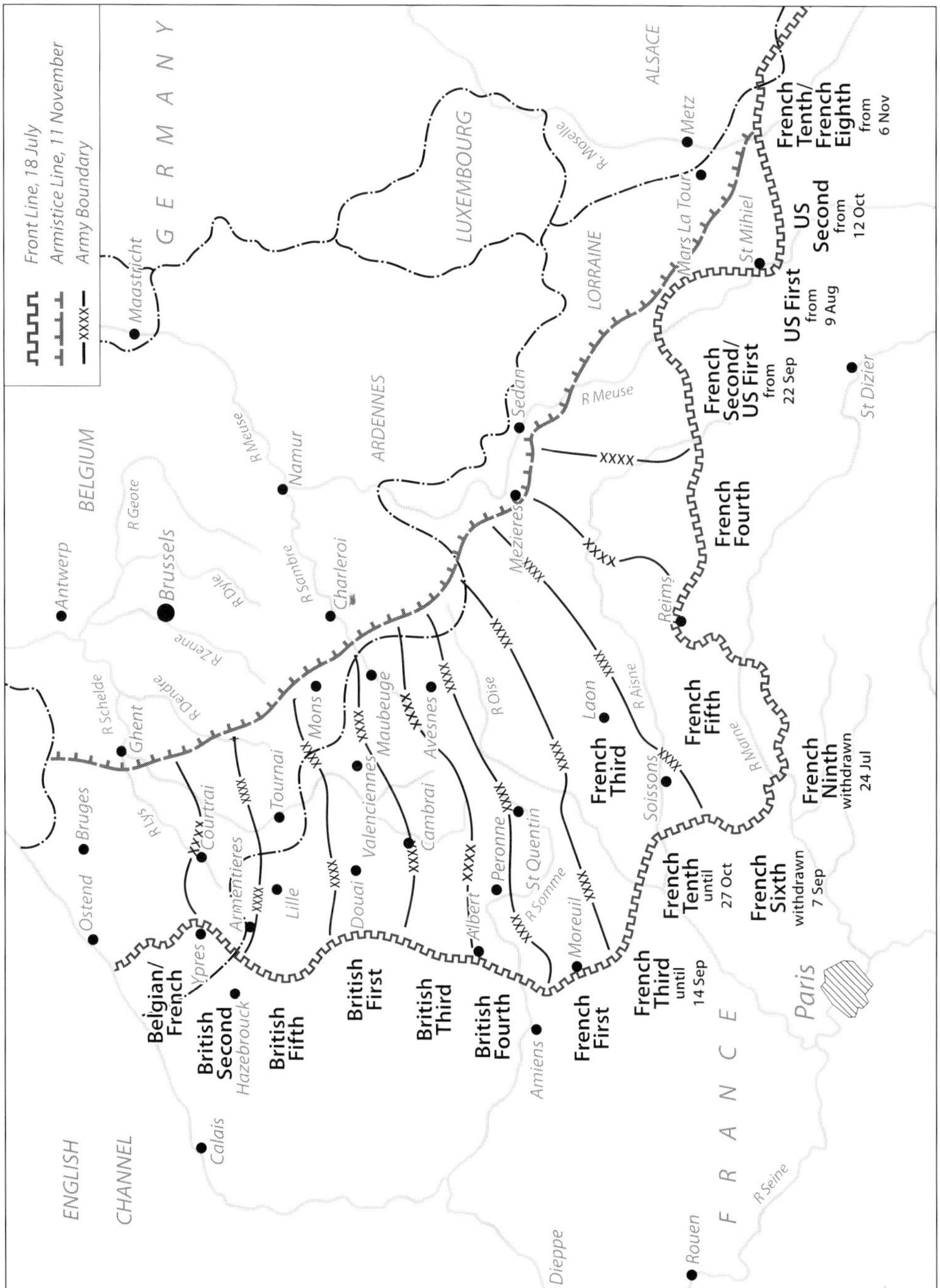

Map 1 The Allied Advance, 1918.

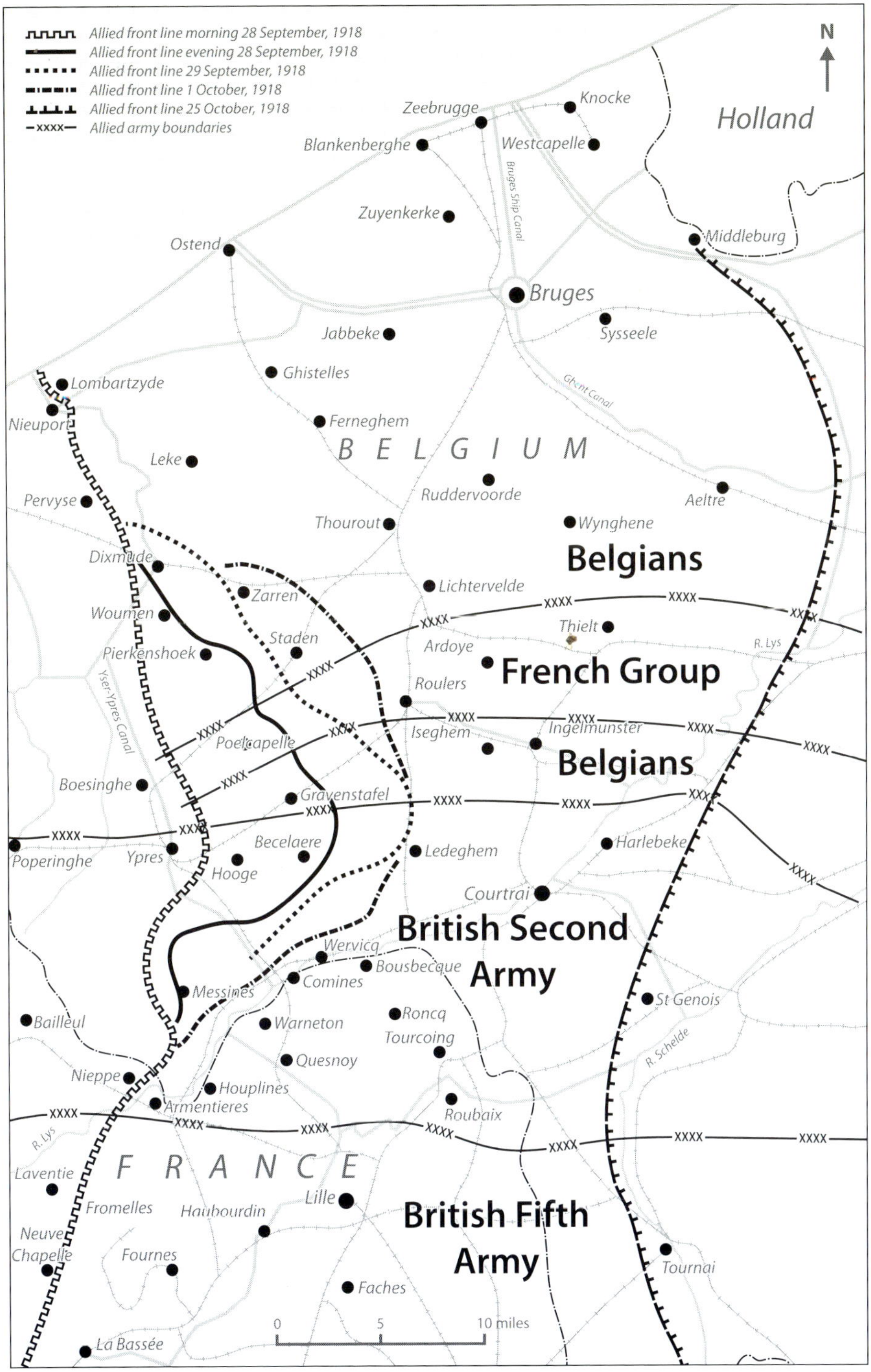

Map 2 The Liberation of the Belgian Coast, 28 September to 25 October 1918.

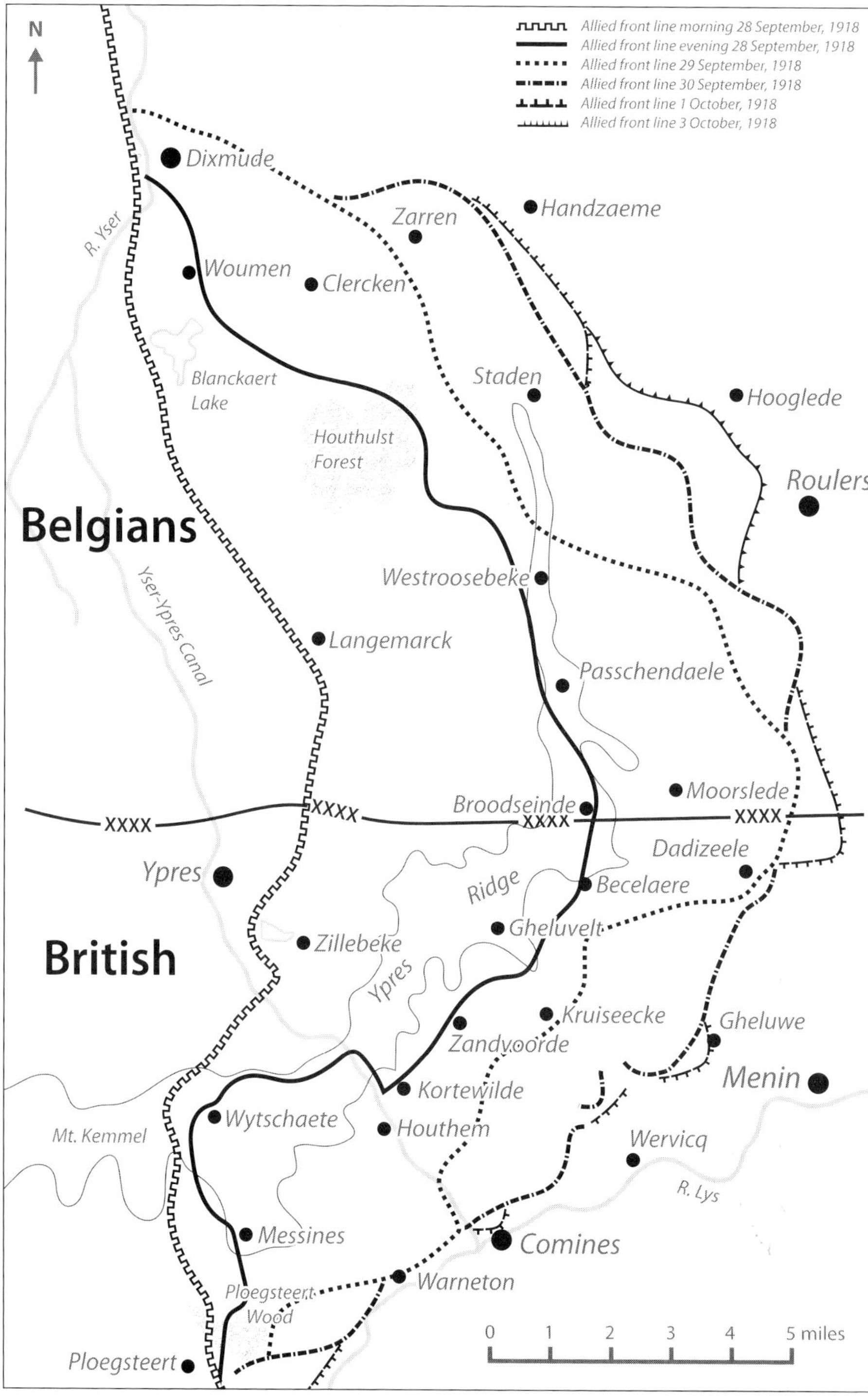

Map 3 The GAF Offensive in Flanders, 28 September to 2 October 1918.

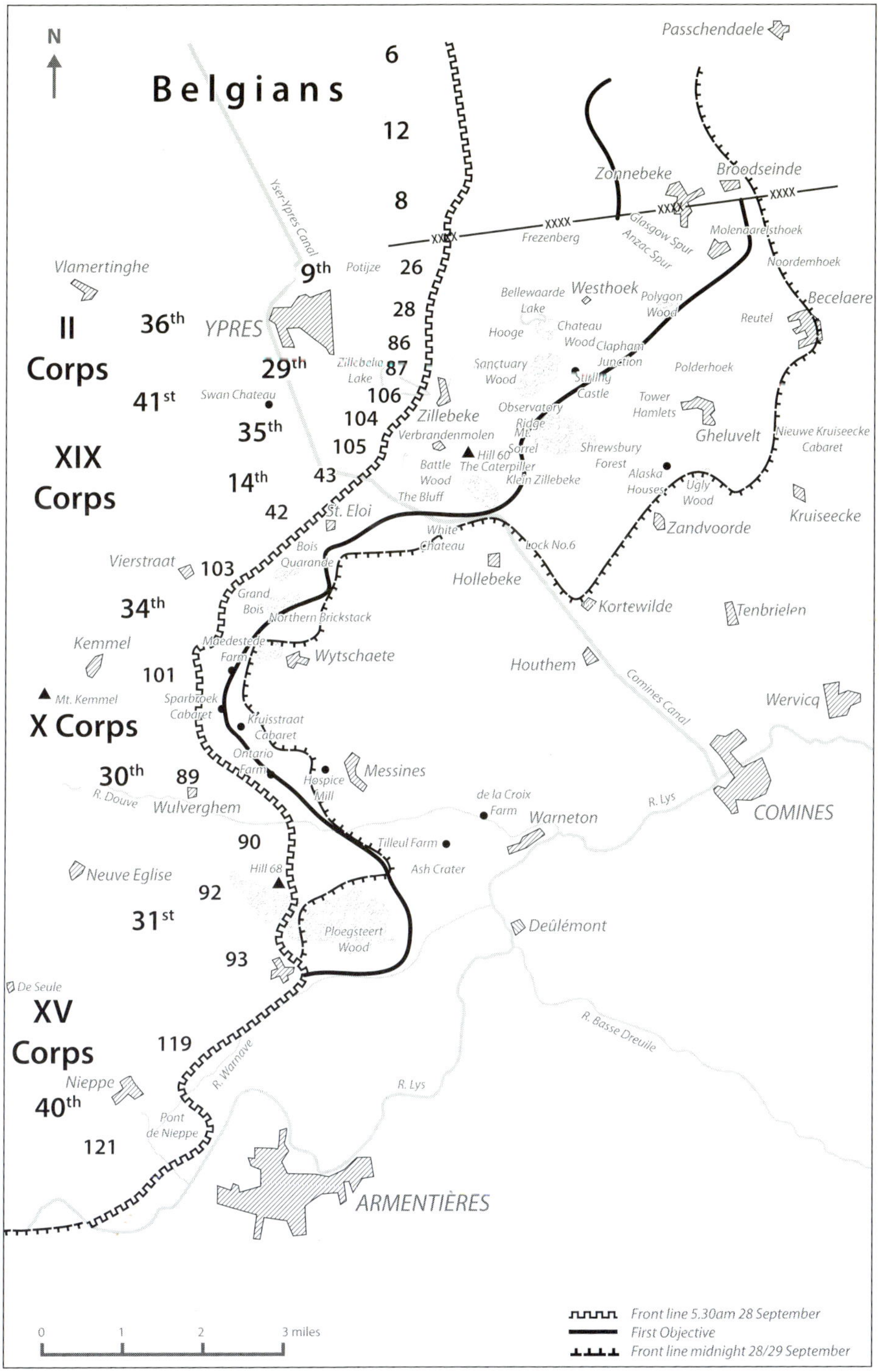

Map 4 British Second Army: The Battle of Ypres, 28 September 1918.

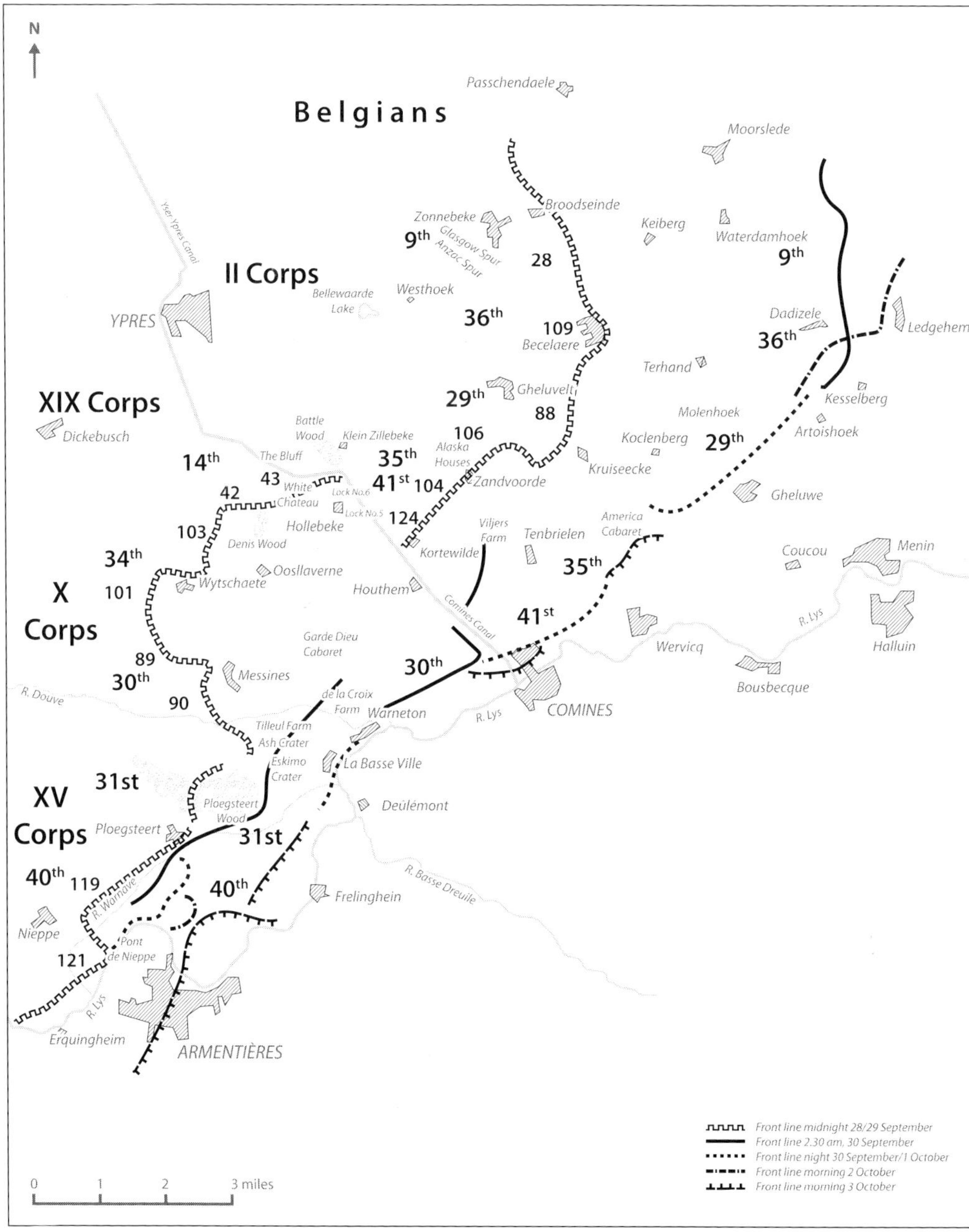

Map 5 British Second Army: The Battle of Ypres, 29 September to 3 October 1918.

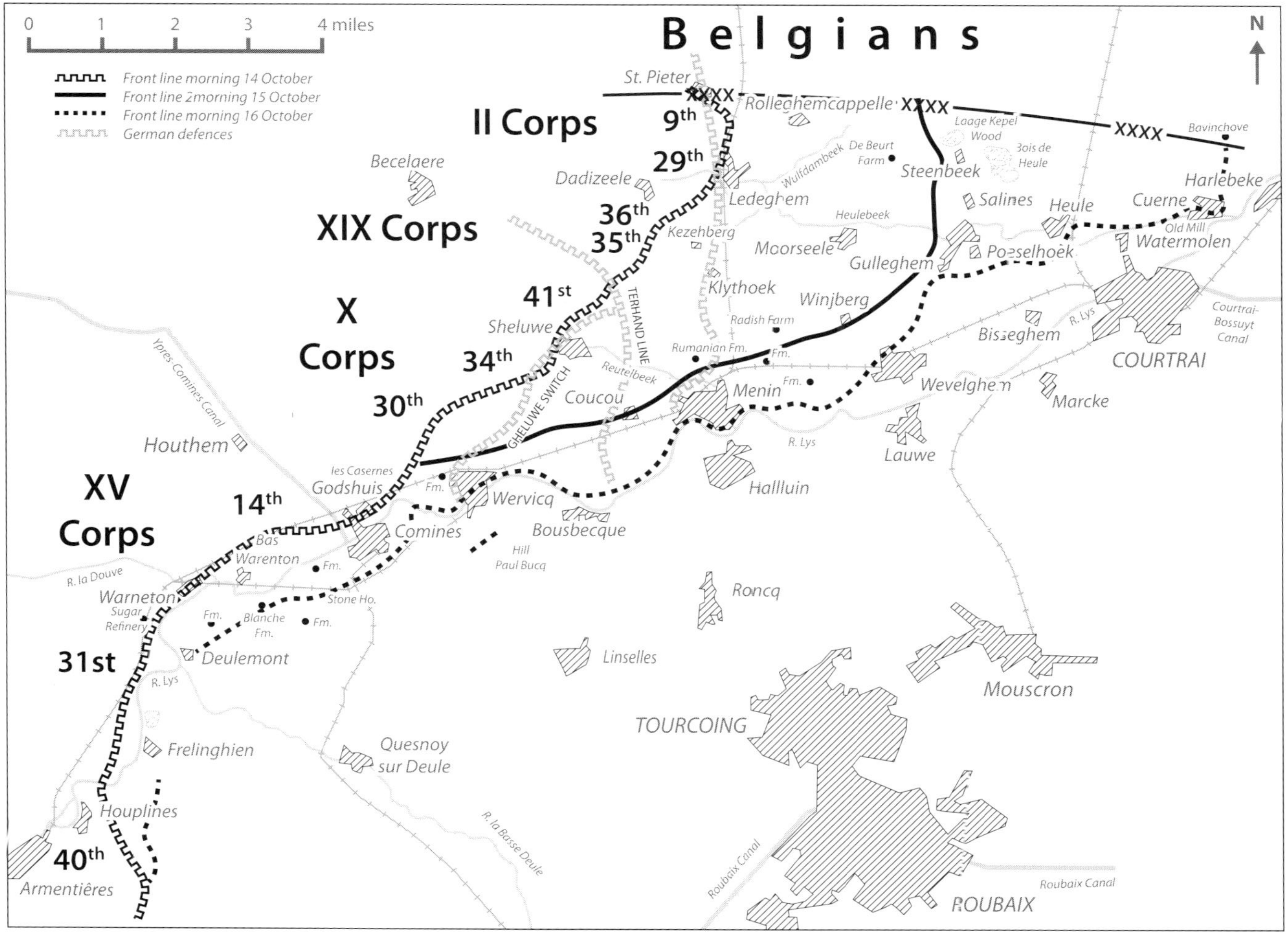

Map 6 British Second Army: The Battle of Courtrai, 14-16 October 1918.

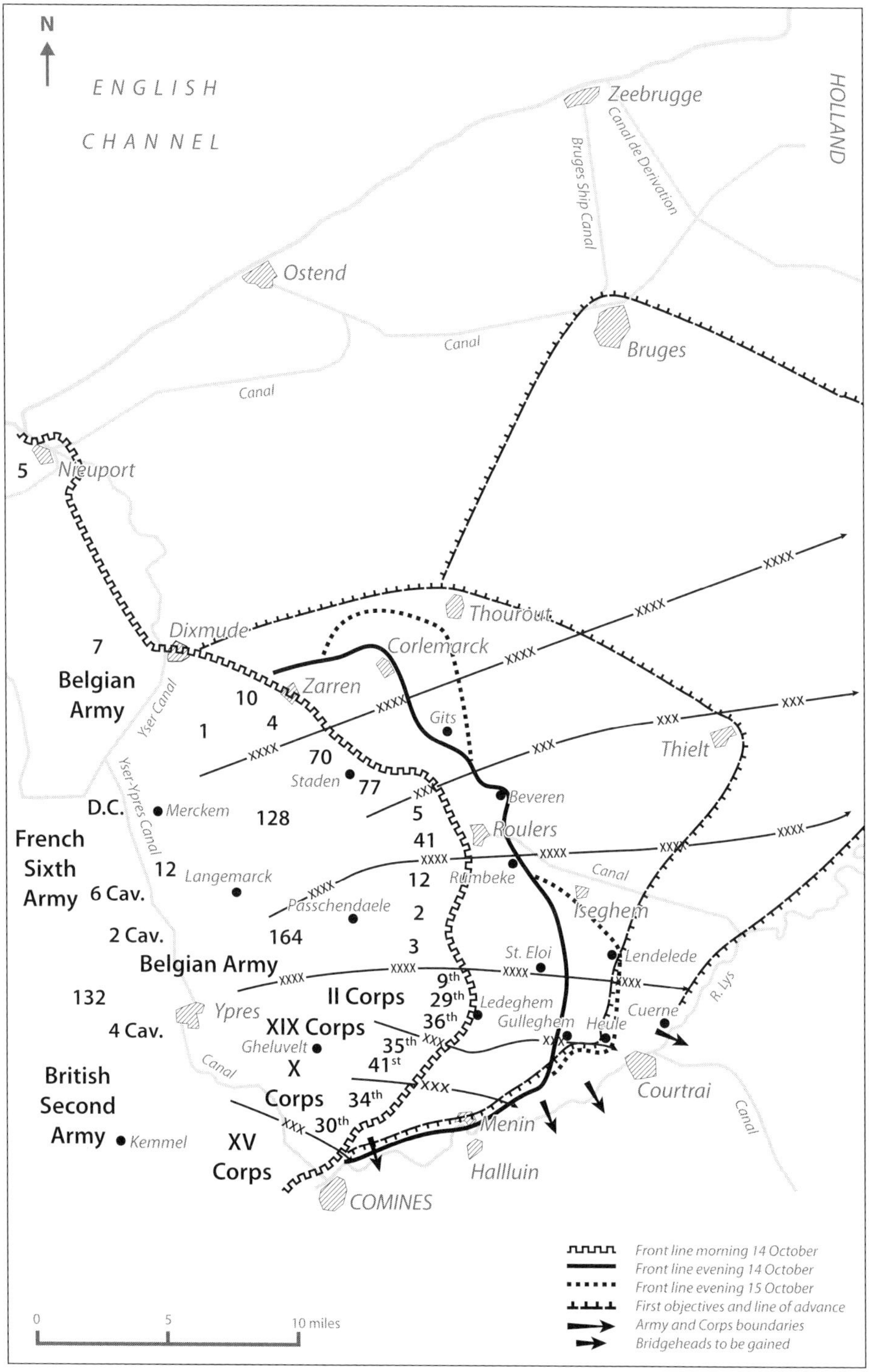

Map 6a The Battle of Courtrai, 14-15 October 1918.

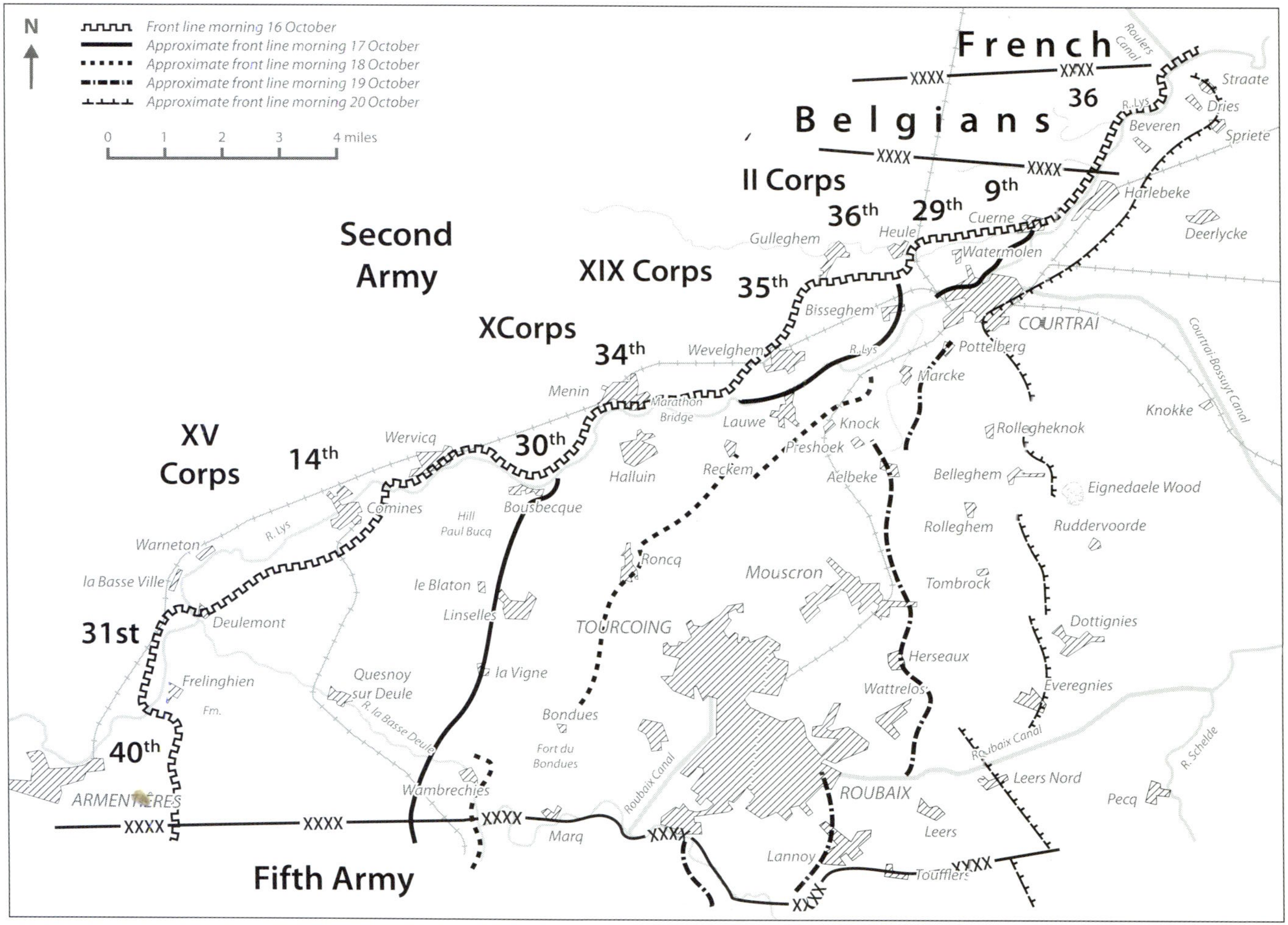

Map 7 British Second Army: The Battle of Courtrai, 16-19 October 1918.

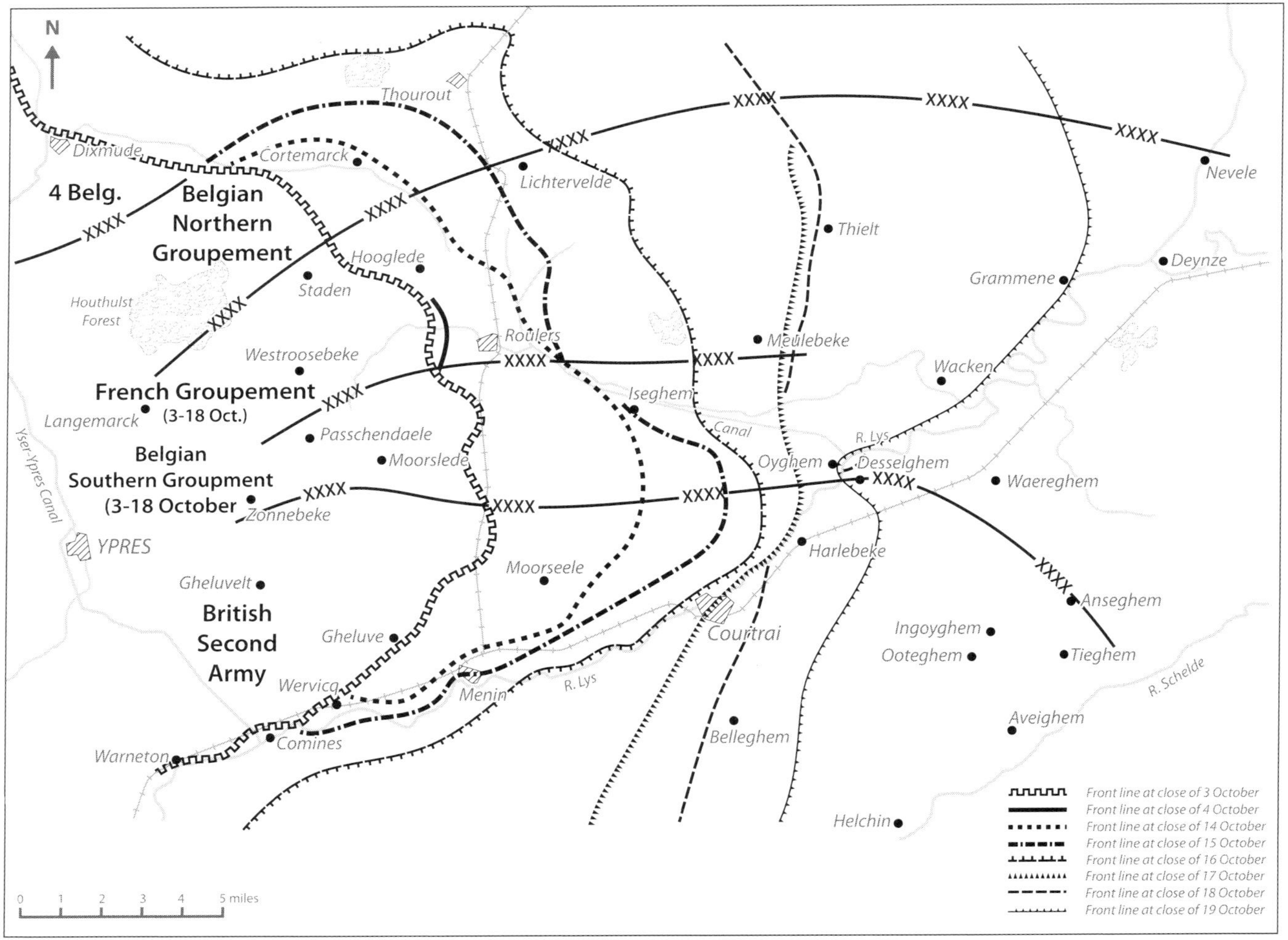

Map 8 The GAF Offensive in Flanders 1, 4-19 October 1918.

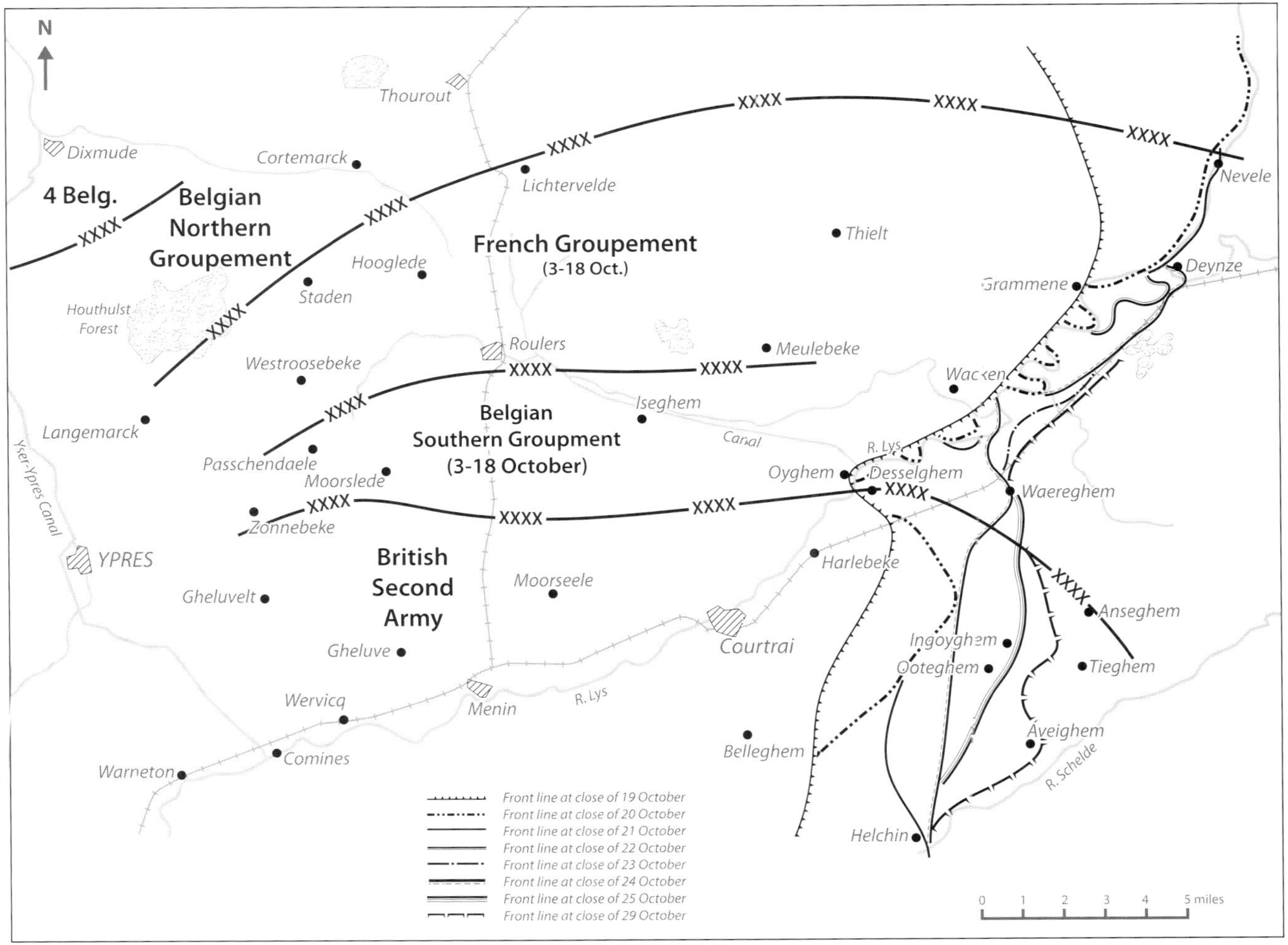

Map 8a The GAF Offensive in Flanders 2, 19-30 October 1918.

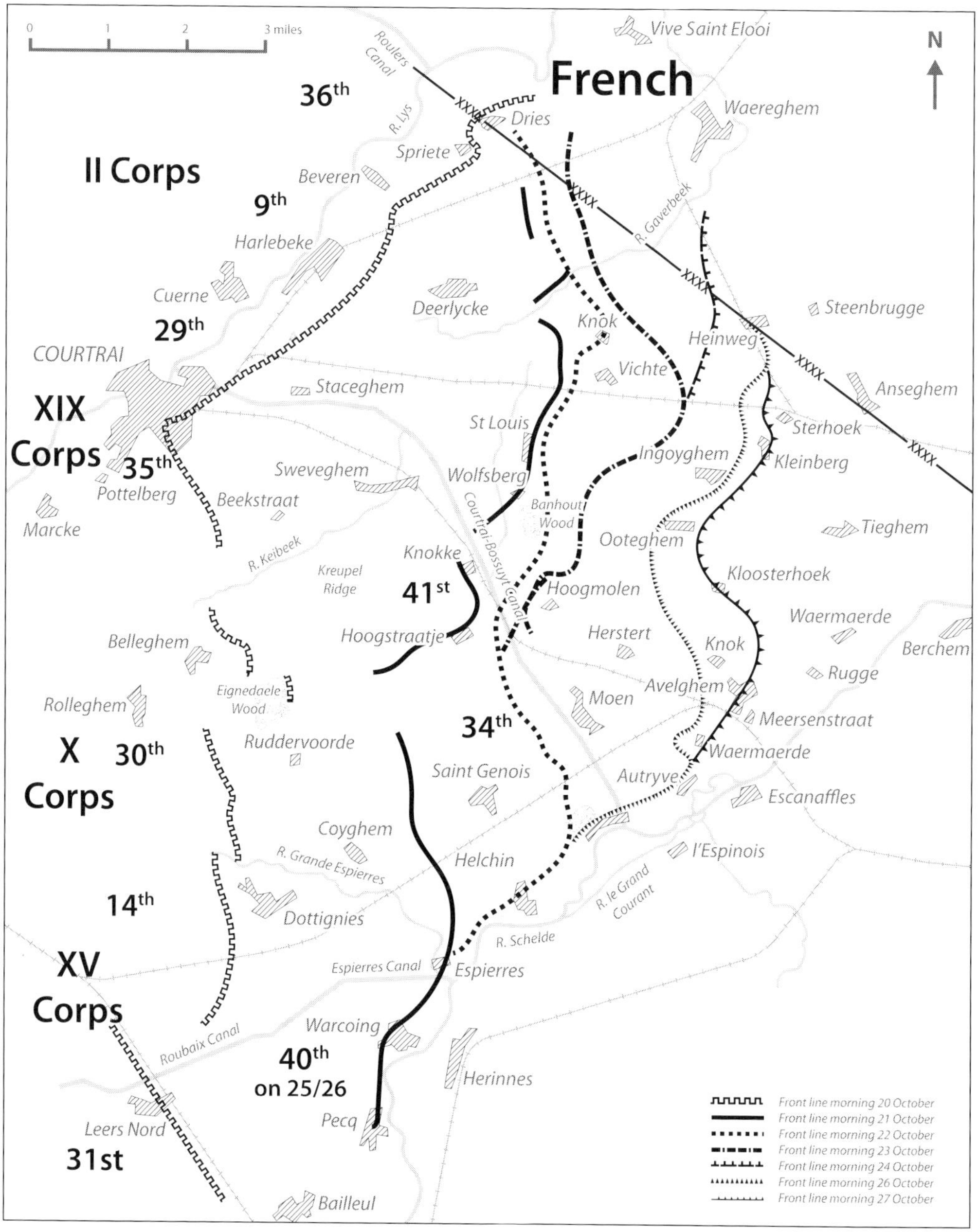

Map 9 British Second Army Operations, 20-27 October 1918.

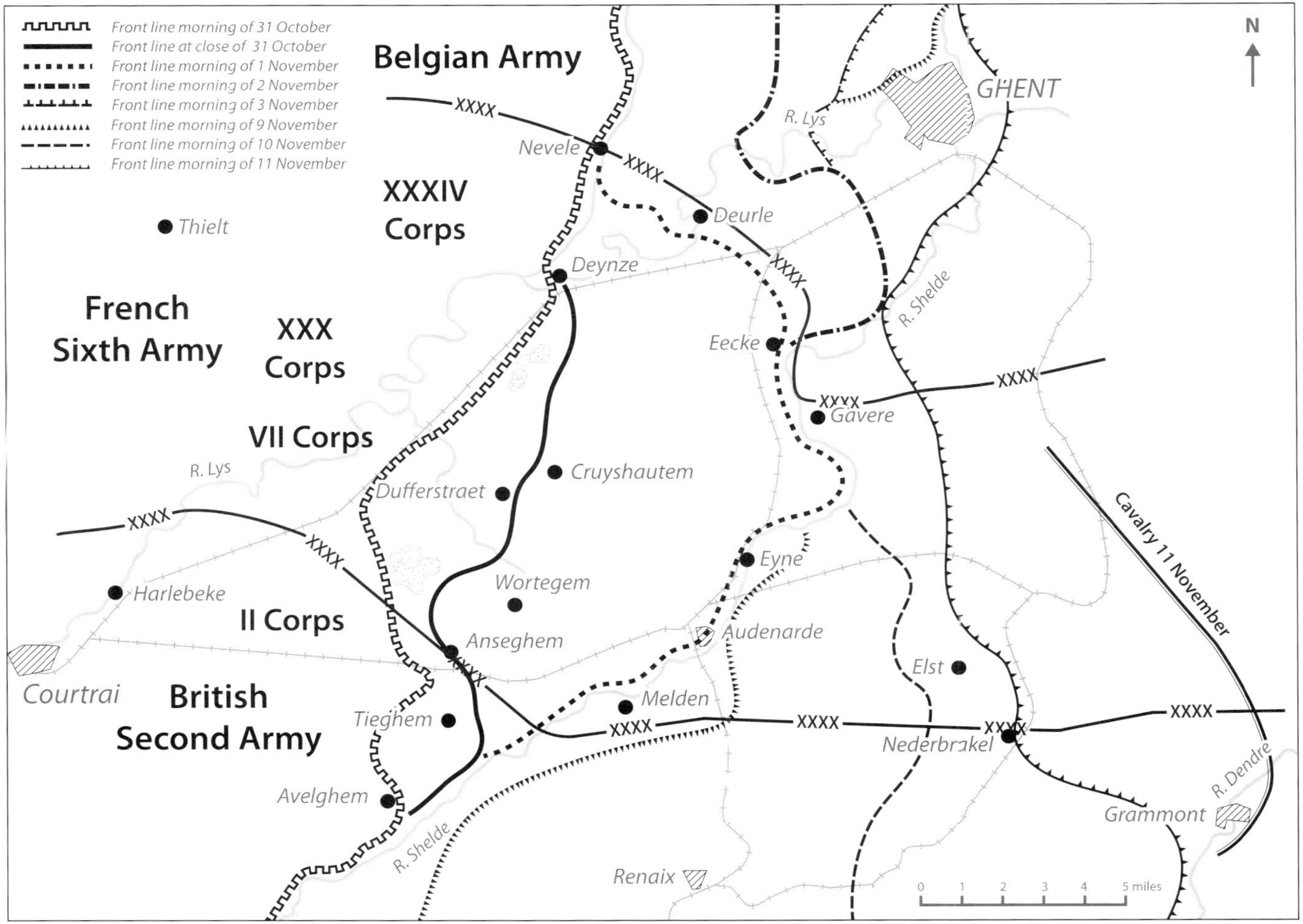

Map 10 The Offensive in Flanders: Allied Forces, 31 October to 11 November 1918.

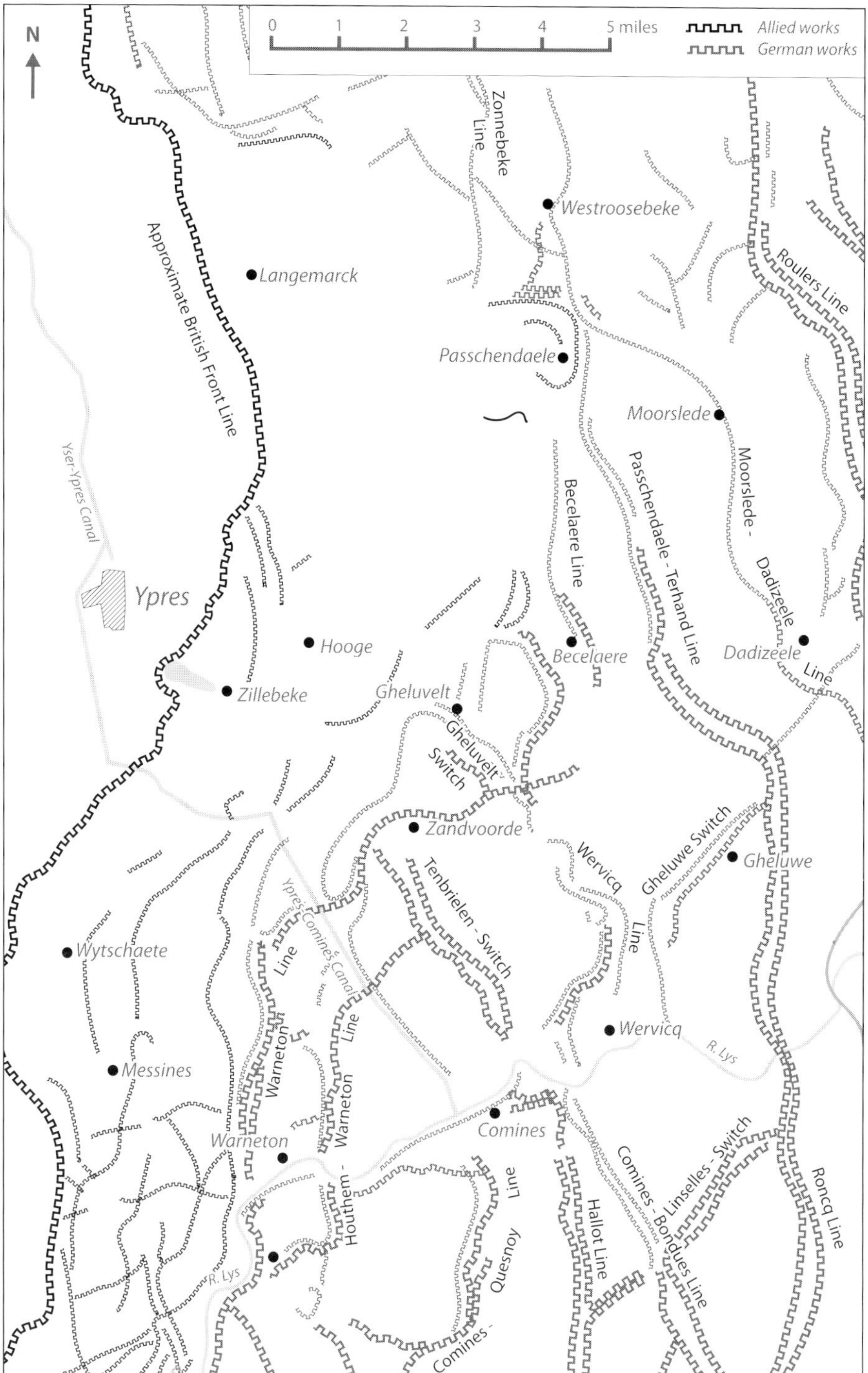

Map 11 German Defences in Flanders, 18 September 1918.

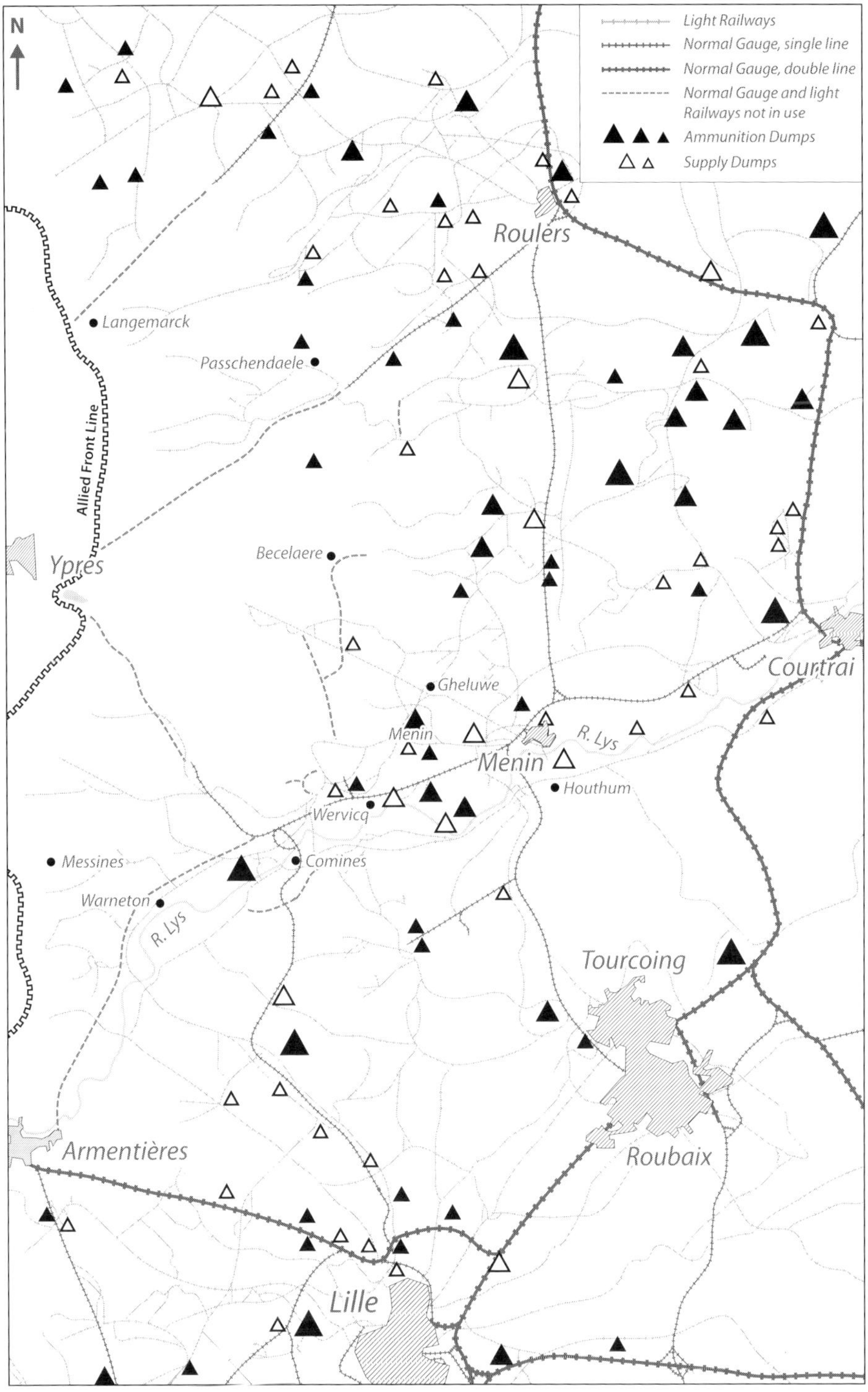

Map 12 German Supply System: British Second Army Front, 23 September 1918.

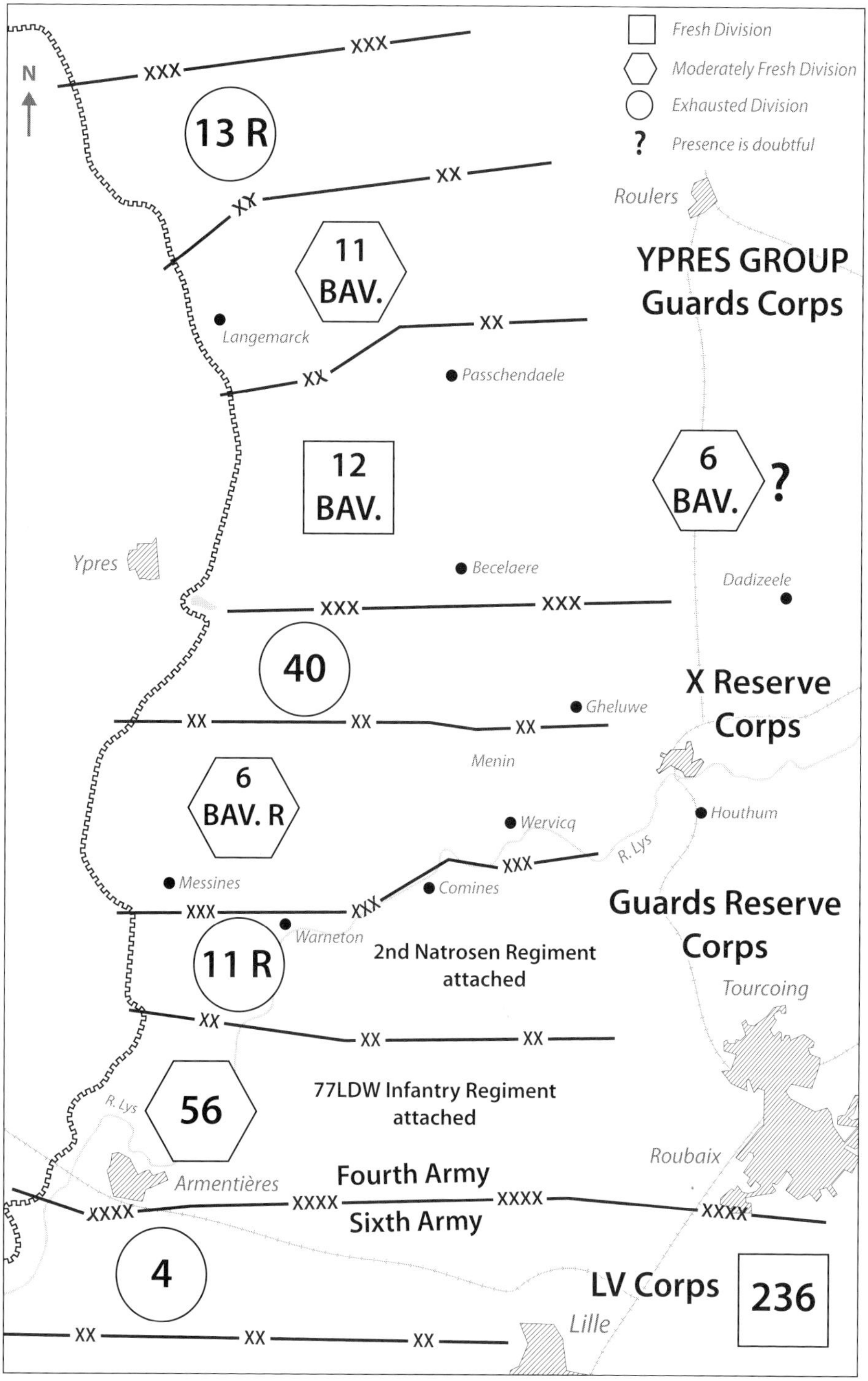

Map 13 German Order of Battle: British Second Army Front, 21 September 1918.

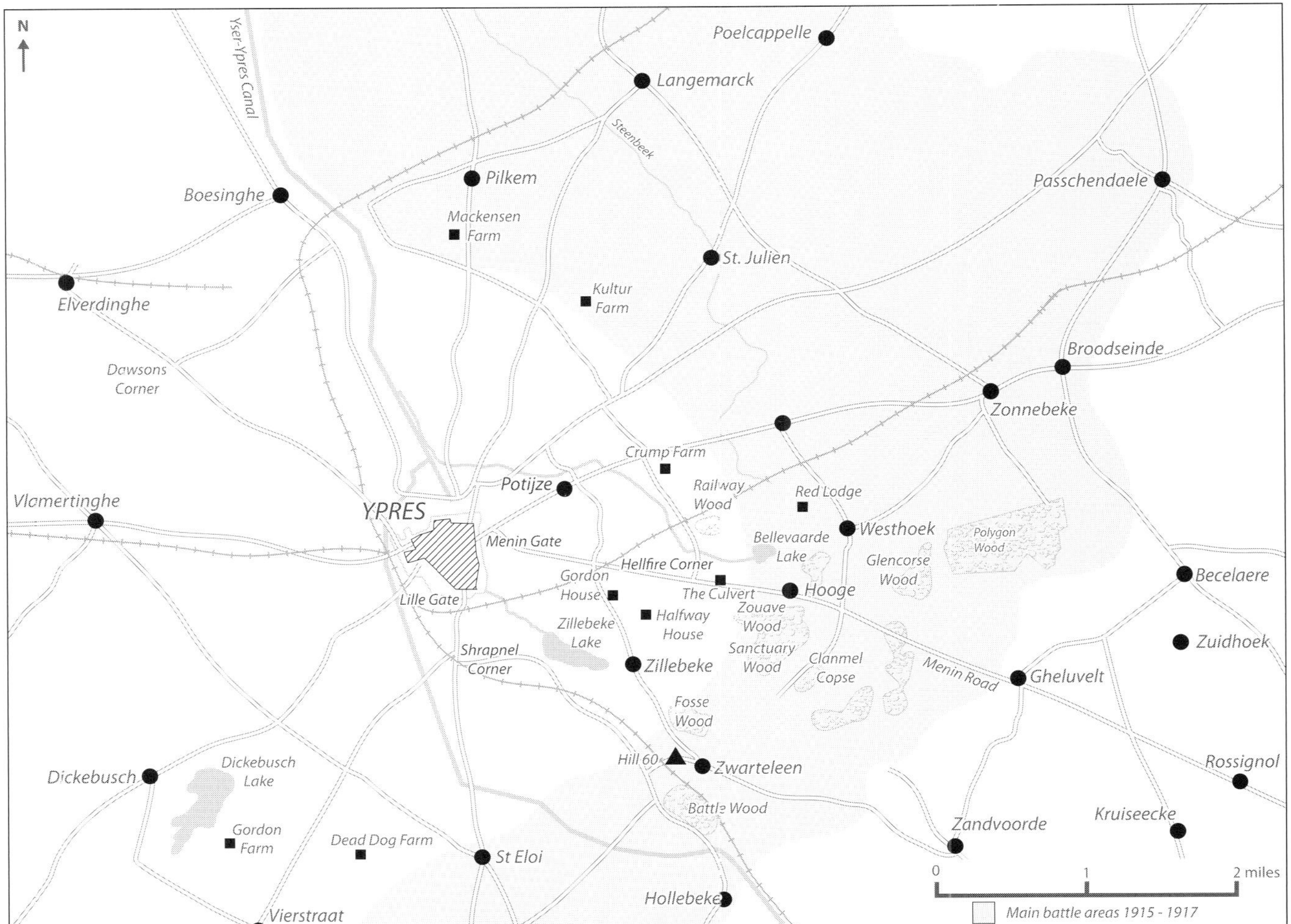

Map 14 The Ypres Salient and Principal Battlegrounds, 1915-1917.

5

Breakout: The Battle of Courtrai, 14-19 October 1918

> There are indications that the attention of officers and men is in danger of being diverted by insidious rumours from their single task of defeating the enemy... F.M.C.inC. [Haig] warns all ranks against the disturbing influence of such unfounded Peace talk and wishes it to be clearly understood that at no time has there been a greater need of relentless efforts or a fairer promise of greater results. The Army will concentrate in an entire energy of bringing operations in the field to a successful and decisive issue.[1]

In Flanders in 1302 the Battle of Courtrai was fought, with a result that confounded all known expectations. The workers of Bruges were in revolt and their Flemish infantry inflicted a major defeat on the flower of French knighthood – so many nobles were slain that royal commissioners were forced to, in the words of one author, 'scour the provinces for bourgeois and rich peasants prepared to pay for ennoblement'.[2] Just over six hundred years later a second Battle of Courtrai would be fought, and forces from an army once considered to be the most powerful in Europe would be defeated by a British Army largely made up of conscripts and transferees.

At zero hour of 0535 on 14 October 1918, British Second Army launched its opening assault.

The offensive took place against the background of the German High Command making efforts to pursue a negotiated armistice. The rumours regarding the prospects of an end to the war were now beginning to circulate amongst the British troops. It was in these circumstances that GHQ had acted to try and ensure that the focus of the British Army remained concentrated on defeating the German Army in the field. On 7 October 1918 Field Marshal Haig had issued an order making clear that nothing must be allowed to divert the attention of British forces away from the defeat of the German Army:

> The Army will concentrate in an entire energy of bringing operations in the field to a successful and decisive issue.[3]

1 Orders from Field Marshal Haig, 7 October 1918, as recorded in TNA WO95/2338, War Diary of 90th Infantry Brigade.
2 B. Tuchman, *A Distant Mirror: The Calamitous 14th Century* (London: Macmillan, 1979), pp. 76-77.
3 Orders from Field Marshal Haig, 7 October 1918, as recorded in TNA WO95/2338, War Diary of 90th Infantry Brigade.

Map 6 shows Second Army's disposition at the start of the battle, and the breakout achieved beyond the German defence lines after the first 48 hours of fighting.

For this battle the Army again deployed ten divisions, with 14th Division transferred from XIX to XV Corps.

The disposition north-to-south on 14 October was as follows:

II Corps	9th Division 29th Division 36th Division
XIX Corps	35th Division 41st Division
X Corps	30th Division 34th Division
XV Corps	14th Division 31st Division 40th Division

The Germans held *Flanders Position II* and still held *Position I* south of Gheluwe. Since ceasing attacks on 3 October, which had seen the occupation of Armentières on the right of the line,[4] Second Army had maintained a daily programme of harassing artillery shoots (gas shells, hurricane bombardments and neutralising fire) and small arms fire, wire cutting, feint attacks and patrol work. This achieved its aim of persuading the enemy that an attack was constantly imminent, to the extent that the German artillery fired a counter-preparation bombardment every morning. Support services worked on re-making roads and laying new railway lines, allowing the artillery to be pushed forward. Much of the fighting during this period was for control of the various farmhouses and smallholdings that could serve as points of resistance. Despite bad weather that 'interfered considerably with flying' the RAF concentrated on important railway junctions, dropping over 3,000 bombs.[5] Overall the GAF deployed a total of 32 divisions (13 Belgian, 10 British and 9 French) (See Appendix I Orders of Battle), facing 24 Divisions of German Fourth Army.

In conjunction with the Belgian and French forces to its left, Second Army launched the new offensive on 14 October. Its role was to again protect the right flank of the GAF. The recently inserted French XXXIV and VII Corps were to act as the main strike force with immediate flanking support from Belgian divisions on either side. The aim was for the Belgian forces to seize Roulers and from there advance to Thielt and Ghent. XX, XIX, and II Corps of Second Army received initial orders to advance in the direction of the River Lys, thereby linking with XV Corps (holding the right flank) along the north-east / south-west line of the waterway. 'All that was required of the Second Army was a wheel to the right up to the Lys'.[6]

However, Plumer was apparently mindful of the potential for his Army to do rather more than securing a flank. This perhaps reflected agreement on his part with Haig's opinion that

4 TNA WO157/129, Second Army Intelligence summary, 4 October 1918.
5 TNA WO158/218, Operations Reports – From which much of the supporting information in this paragraph is also taken.
6 Edmonds, *Official History 1918 Vol. V.*

the British armies were providing the cutting edge for the allies' offensive operations.[7] However as far as Second Army was concerned Haig still urged Plumer to concentrate on the flank role as originally assigned: his formations were not to mount an assault across the River Lys unless there were clear signs of a German withdrawal. At the same time Haig was anxious for Second Army to cross the river to the east of Courtrai so that it could link up with the BEF near Tournai.[8] It is also probable that Plumer was influenced by other factors, not least his continuing lack of confidence in GAF Chief of Staff, Degoutte. The strong performance of the British troops during the opening battle would have given Plumer renewed belief in their strength and abilities. There was increasing evidence that the defence put up by the German forces was weakening and that their commanders were making preparations for a further withdrawal.

On 11 October, Plumer issued a modification to his earlier orders, changes which implied that a far more aggressive assault should be launched. At the same time he was anxious to ensure that Second Army continued to conform to its original orders to secure the right flank of the Belgian Army. However the delays in the advance of the Belgian forces were impeding the coordination of artillery fire support for the forthcoming attack. Therefore Army Order 43 directed II Corps to detail a detachment of infantry and machine guns on the left flank, to 'move in touch with and at the same rate as' the Belgians. Meanwhile each nation's army would 'move at its own pace', with the inevitable consequence that 'Second Army will gradually become echeloned forward'.[9]

It was considered that the threat of Second Army crossing the Lys (together with the associated pressure to the south from British Fourth, Third and First Armies) might hasten German evacuation from the industrial cities of Lille, Roubaix and Tourcoing. Therefore corps commanders should be prepared to use forward advanced guards to establish bridgeheads south of the river, targeting sites such as Wervicq, Lauwe and Marcke.

This line of reasoning was supported by GHQ Intelligence, which reported on 14 October that the enemy was evacuating material from the Belgian coast and showing little interest in constructing further defences in the area. The conclusion drawn was that the Germans would not fight indefinitely to retain the region and were likely to look to withdraw south of Lille and then to a line based on the River Schelde.

Various conferences and meetings took place as preparations proceeded. On 12 October, 26 Brigade held a conference at its headquarters to discuss the 'forthcoming operations'.[10] North of Second Army, French forces had been moving forward in preparation for this next phase of the campaign. On 4 October, the Diary of 27 Brigade (9th Division) recorded that 'French 7th Corps reported advancing towards ROULERS'.[11] There were also some minor adjustments between the adjoining British (9th Division) and Belgian units; on 5 October, '6th Belgian Regiment relieved 12th Royal Scots on the left'.[12]

7 See references in Haig's Diary for October 1918 (TNA WO158/244); these views are also referred to in various secondary assessments of Haig's views e.g. Harris with Barr, *Amiens*.
8 Powell, *Plumer*, p. 276.
9 TNA WO158/212, Second Army Operations, 1 October 1918 – 20 January 1919, Order No. 43, 11 October 1918.
10 TNA WO95/1765, War Diary of 7th Battalion, Seaforth Highlanders.
11 TNA WO95/1771/5, War Diary of 27 Infantry Brigade.
12 TNA WO95/1771/5, War Diary of 27 Infantry Brigade.

Since the successes of Ypres, Second Army had continued to maintain training and preparations for the next major battle of the offensive. The war diary for October 1918 of 15/West Yorkshires, who would be in reserve during the Courtrai fighting, shows a pattern of training incorporating practical skills and tactical considerations. Between 9 -12 October, training sessions included 'musketry', 'firing field practices', and 'Lewis-Gun training'. On 14/15 October training focused on 'platoon schemes' and '... section and platoon commanders [were] particularly exercised'. Later that month, the three days 29-31 October were spent undertaking 'tactical exercises'. Prior to the Ypres battle the battalion commander had been concerned about the use of grenades – less experienced or newly-trained soldiers were felt to be safer, more effective and less profligate when grenades were delivered by rifle. As a consequence 'rifle grenades' was a priority for training exercises held on 9 and 27 September.[13]

By way of contrast, 42 Brigade (14th Division), having moved into reserve after the opening of the Battle of Ypres, spent most of the period 4-12 October undertaking 'work on roads' under the supervision of Royal Engineers.[14]

There was still evidence of enemy resistance. One unit in 9th Division recorded that on 4 October there had been a night attack by German aircraft, bombing roads around the battalion camp behind the village of Waterdamhoek.[15] At the same time, in 40th Division, 120 Brigade recorded that its infantry continued to make advances in the face of heavy shelling, machine gun and trench mortar fire by the enemy.

There was also fighting above the battlefield:

> At 1400 four E.A.s [enemy aircraft] crossed our lines bringing down one of our O.B.s [observation balloons] in flames... Strong formations [of RAF planes] were observed to cross the enemy lines meeting with heavy A.A. fire... Repeated attempts were made [by enemy aircraft] to cross our lines...[16]

On 7 October, Lieutenant-Colonel W A W Crellin, commanding 15/Sherwood Foresters (105 Brigade, 35th Division), was severely wounded by enemy shellfire and subsequently died of his wounds.[17]

British units were continuing to advance at regular intervals and at various points across the Second Army Front. On the right flank, the orders of 40th Division on 6 October established 120 Brigade as advanced guard, responsible for defences south of the Lys, with a brigade RFA, a machine gun company and a half company of cyclists attached.[18] 119 Brigade assumed responsibility for the north bank. The subsequent instructions of 120 Brigade on 7 October illustrate the arrangements made to address the operational challenges of this war of movement. There are references to 'the wide frontage' and the consequent 'large gaps between posts' which required advance patrols and scouting sections to take special precautions. All patrols were to be deployed as 'strong fighting patrols capable of dealing with any small parties of the enemy encountered'.

13 From the War Diary of 15th WestYorkshire Regiment.
14 TNA WO95/1899, War Diary of 42 Infantry Brigade.
15 TNA WO95/1765, War Diary of 7th Battalion, Seaforth Highlanders.
16 TNA WO95/2610, War Diary of 120 Infantry Brigade, Intelligence Report 3-4 October 1918.
17 TNA WO95/2486, War Diary of 105 Infantry Brigade.
18 TNA WO95/2594, War Diary of 40th Division.

There was also emphasis on guarding and covering any bridgeheads achieved, taking account of the various streams and rivers which lay across the general line of advance by the Army.[19]

On 9 October, units from 9/Irish Fusiliers (108 Brigade, 36th Division) captured Goldflake Farm, a fortified position on the south facing the slope of Hill 41. A strong counter-attack by the Germans not only retook the Farm but also pushed back the troops holding Twigg and Mansard farms on the crest of the hill. The importance of these last two positions for the forthcoming operations led to British counter-attacks in turn; Twigg Farm was secured after an immediate attack and Mansard Farm was retaken following an assault just before dawn.[20]

In 14th Division, 41 Brigade recorded the regular harassment experienced as a consequence of enemy artillery fire, as well as trench mortars and machine guns. There was some frustration with the response of the British guns, given the perceived advantage enjoyed of well-positioned observation points held by the German defenders. On 10 October the brigade welcomed the artillery 'crashes' on selected enemy positions, noting:

> The silly sentiment of not wanting to shell COMINES and WERVICQ Churches certainly helped to increase [our] casualties, which would not have happened had the enemy been deprived of such excellent observation.[21]

That same day the brigade observed fires in Wervicq which, together with the 'enemy's wild harassing fire, indicates a possible withdrawal soon'.

For the new attack it was again decided to dispense with a preliminary bombardment and to fire a creeping barrage in support of the infantry assault. This would commence three minutes before zero hour and proceed at the rate of 100 yards every two minutes, with a pause of 15 minutes every 1,500 yards. This rate of advance would have been unthinkable twelve months previously and probably reflected the confidence of the attackers, the changed nature of the terrain over which they were to advance, and the perceived weaknesses of the defenders.

On the evening before the assault the British artillery conducted targeted shelling of enemy lines:

> At 1900 our Artillery heavily gas shelled hostile positions with the new BB (Mustard Gas) shell.[22]

There was a notable German casualty caused by the use of mustard gas shells in the British bombardment:

> [T]he British opened an attack with gas on the front south of Ypres... They used the yellow gas whose effect was unknown to us, at least from personal experience. I was destined to experience it that very night... We were subjected for several hours to a heavy bombardment with gas bombs, which continued throughout the night with more or less intensity...

19 TNA WO95/2610, War Diary of 120 Infantry Brigade, Instructions No. 2, 7 October 1918.
20 C. Falls, *A History of the 36th (Ulster) Division* (London: Constable, 1996; first published Belfast: McCraw, Stevenson, 1922), p. 272.
21 TNA WO95/1894/6, War Diary of 41 Infantry Brigade.
22 TNA WO95/2338, War Diary of 90 Infantry Brigade .

> About midnight a number of us were put out of action, some forever. Towards morning I also began to feel pain. It increased with every quarter of an hour; and about seven o'clock my eyes were scorching as I staggered back and delivered the last despatch I was destined to carry in this war.[23]

Corporal Adolf Hitler, serving with the Bavarian Reserve Regiment Nr. 16, was virtually blinded; his eyes described as 'glowing coals' upon his return to HQ.[24] The gas has been assumed to be mustard but could have been British 'White Star' gas – a mixture of chlorine and phosgene; in the event it was considered that the blindness was due to hysteria rather than the physical effects of the gas.[25]

RAF aerial support was delayed; the weather was dry but a ground mist prevented air operations until after 1100.

II Corps

The 9th Division still operated on the left of II Corps and Second Army, with the 9th Regiment of the Belgian Army on its left; for the initial attack, 26 Brigade was deployed on the left of the division with 28 Brigade on its right, and 27 Brigade in reserve. The immediate objective was the Winkel-St-Eloi – Drie Masten Road, and then to drive for the Courtrai-Lenlade Railway. Once this was achieved the division was expected to undertake a crossing of the River Lys and the capture of the town of Harlebeke.

On the immediate boundary of the two armies, to assist in the coordination of operations, liaison platoons were established drawn from neighbouring units. Each liaison platoon comprised one officer and twelve men of each nationality:

> 8/Black Watch (26 Brigade) – 28 Brigade – 2nd Battalion, 9th Belgian Regiment
> 5/Cameron Highlanders – 1st Battalion, 9th Belgian Regiment
> 7/Seaforth Highlanders – 3rd Battalion, 9th Belgian Regiment.[26]

There had also been arrangements agreed for a series of light signals which the Belgian forces would use to report on progress or call for support as they advanced.[27]

With no preliminary bombardment, the 18 pounder barrage of HE and smoke would begin three minutes before Z hour, then moving forward in 50 yard lifts per minute. The RAF was involved in monitoring the progress of the attack, including a 'Counter Attack Aeroplane… for the purpose of giving warning of hostile attack' – the warning would be via the dropping of a red parachute light. The changed nature of the warfare by this point is illustrated in the order

23 A. Hitler, *Mein Kampf*, translated by J. Murphy (London: Hurst & Blackett, 1939), p. 162.
24 Quoted in S. Jones, *World War I Gas Warfare Tactics and Equipment* (London: Osprey, 2007), p. 54.
25 Freemantle, *Gas!*, p. 116; the author also points out that 'It is interesting to note that Hitler did not use chemical weapons during the Second World War'.
26 TNA WO95/1765, War Diary of 7th Battalion, Seaforth Highlanders, Order No. 36, 13/10/18.
27 TNA WO95/1771/5, War Diary of 27 Infantry Brigade, 27th (Lowland) Brigade Order No. 276, 12/10/1918, Appendix B: Light Signals to be used by the Belgian Army.

stating that company commanders 'will ensure that no men leave their units to go in search of souvenirs'.[28]

With zero hour set at 0535 hours, the immediate objective for 29th Division was Ledeghem, and the cutting of the railway between Courtrai and Ghent. The day's attack began under the cover of 'an intense artillery barrage' with a twenty minute defensive barrage planned once intermediate objectives were reached. Unfortunately the early morning mist combined with the smoke of the barrage created visibility problems for the attackers, causing infantry to lose touch with the barrage or, in some cases, to lose direction entirely. However the fog proved to be of overall assistance to the assaulting troops 'who were able under its cover to get close to and surround hostile posts without encountering any aimed fire'.[29] There was some initial street fighting but the capture of the village was largely achieved by 0700 hours, with large numbers of the enemy surrendering. 1/Lancashire Fusiliers, starting as 86 Brigade reserve, was responsible for 'mopping up'.

The approach used by 86 Brigade was typical of the battle plan adopted by II Corps formations. The attack was made on a one battalion front, with support and reserve battalions moving up and through the front battalion as each objective line was reached. In this way the pressure of being the lead unit rotated across each of the battalions as objectives were taken. Maximum use was made of supporting gun fire as the men moved forward. The advance on the first objective was covered by a field artillery barrage; the next advance received a covering barrage from heavy artillery. Subsequent covering fire included trench mortars. In due course, touch was restored between the attacking battalions, both within the 29th Division and with the right flank of 9th Division. Progress was steady despite opposition from enemy machine guns and light artillery fire.[30] Importantly, during the evening all supporting field artillery and much of the heavy artillery was able to move up into position to support the next day's attack.[31]

88 Brigade was tasked with supporting the arrangements to cross the Heulebeek Stream, as its battle orders show:

> 30 Bridges will be in RAYMOND FARM on Y/Z night ready to be taken forward to bridge the HEULEBEEK, and will be allotted as follows:
> 2nd Leinster Regt – 16 Bridges
> 4th Worcester Regt – 14 Bridges
>
> The 2nd Hampshire Regt will carry these forward and place them in position across the Stream… 35 Pioneers of the 1/2nd Monmouthshire Regt [will assist]…[32]

28 TNA WO95/1765, War Diary of 7th Battalion, Seaforth Highlanders, Order No. 36, 13/10/18.
29 TNA WO95/2285, War Diary of 29th Division, Report on Operations, Period October 14th 1918 – October 22nd 1918.
30 TNA WO95/2300, War Diary of 1st Battalion, Lancashire Fusiliers, Narrative of Operations 13-15th October 1918; Report on Operations by 86th Infantry Brigade on 14 October 1918; TNA WO95/2307/4, War Diary of 88 Infantry Brigade, Operation Instructions No. 1, 12th October 1918.
31 TNA WO95/2285, War Diary of 29th Division, Report on Operations, Period October 14th 1918 – October 22nd 1918.
32 TNA WO95/2307/4, War Diary of 88 Infantry Brigade, Operation Order No. 212, 12th October 1918.

By 1730 hours, the Hampshires were 'going for Salines' and had reached the Driemaasten-Gulleghem Road, from where they attracted enemy machine gun fire from the direction of Gulleghem; it seemed that reports that 36th Division had captured the village appeared to be premature (which was correct). 9th Division was held up by defensive fire from the Bois de Heule Wood.[33]

The results from RAF reconnaissance as recorded at 36th Division HQ reportedly showed that the artillery preparations had been successful in shutting down the initial defensive fire from enemy batteries:

> [1000 hours] Aeroplanes report our neutralisation effective, as hostile arty. activity almost nil after 0600.[34]

This was not necessarily the experience of 36th Division's units on the ground. 107 Brigade recorded that at H Hour as the attack commenced there was a 'fairly heavy enemy reply to our barrage', but by 0600 hours 'enemy artillery quieter'.[35] Reports from German prisoners that the attack had not been anticipated showed the value of the decision to commence the assault with a creeping barrage at Z-3 minutes, and dispense with a preliminary bombardment.[36]

The division made good progress, entering Moorseele (1033 hours) and then looking to outflank Gulleghem from the north and south (1325 hours). Heavy machine gun fire from the latter was reported and the attack stalled here. Plans by 107 Brigade to deploy a motor machine gun battery supported by a platoon of II Corps cyclists were changed as these units were ordered to pull back into divisional reserve during the evening. A line 300 yards west of Gulleghem was consolidated and plans made to make a fresh assault in the morning.[37]

The liberation of occupied towns and villages meant there were new considerations amidst the fighting, as civilians were overtaken by the advancing allied forces. A report on the progress of 35th Division (XIX Corps) on the right flank of II Corps stated that the division was advancing towards the Lys via 'Woelvelghem which [the] enemy [is] shelling… Civilians released'.[38] 107 Brigade recorded that 'A number of civilians were found in Moorseele and the outskirts of Gulleghem and evacuated to the rear'.[39] The unexpected pace of the advance was illustrated by an unconfirmed report that the 6th Cavalry Division had reached Gulleghem.[40]

By the close of the day, the advance on the II Corps front had progressed around three miles, on a two mile frontage.

> [Message from II Corps HQ] The Army Commander wishes me to convey to you and all commanders and troops engaged to-day his congratulations on the successful results achieved on what has been a long and arduous day.[41]

33 TNA WO95/2307/4, War Diary of 88 Infantry Brigade.
34 TNA WO95/2492, War Diary of 36th Division.
35 TNA WO95/2502/1,War Diary of 107 Infantry Brigade.
36 Falls, 36th Division, pp. 272-3.
37 TNA WO95/2502/1, War Diary of 107 Infantry Brigade; Falls, 36th Division, pp. 274-5.
38 TNA WO95/2492, War Diary of 36th Division, 1200 hours.
39 TNA WO95/2502/1, War Diary of 107 Infantry Brigade.
40 TNA WO95/2492, War Diary of 36th Division, 1245 hours.
41 TNA WO95/2502/1, War Diary of 107 Infantry Brigade.

A line running north-south was established on the west side of Gulleghem, one and a half miles west of Heule (which was situated astride the rail line out of Courtrai), with units deployed for 'defence in depth' i.e. troops placed on the front line and in support positions, with machine gun posts dispersed throughout.[42] Gas shelling by the Germans of Moorseele was recorded on a number of occasions that evening and the following day, no doubt designed to disrupt the build-up of British forces for the anticipated further attacks.[43]

XIX Corps

At 0535 hours, 104 and 105 Brigades led the attack by 35th Division, under a creeping barrage; 106 Brigade in support. The advance was towards the River Lys, in a direction to the south of Courtrai and the village of Marcke. The immediate task was to capture and secure high ground south of the village of Gulleghem, overlooking the River Lys.[44] Troops found welcome benefits from moving over ground unaffected by the fighting in previous battles:

> It is interesting to note that the advance and arrangements for the accommodation of troops were much facilitated on account of the fact that we were now operating in open Country untouched by heavy shelling and free from concrete pill-boxes. The good roads and level ground made possible the quick advance of the Field Artillery and Infantry and the existing farms, houses etc., which were not destroyed by shell fire were used for the accommodation of Support and Reserve Troops.[45]

At the close of the day the division was held up on a line just west of the hamlet of Kloefhoek (Klythoek).

At the synchronised Z hour of 0535 hours, 122 Brigade moved forward to begin the attack by 41st Division, with 124 Brigade (plus 23/Middlesex from 123 Brigade) in support; following a creeping barrage of 100 yards every two minutes. In front lay the 'Terhand Switch' – the Terhand line of prepared trench works and defensive positions assembled by the Germans. Early morning mist combined with the smoke within the enemy's defensive barrage to create difficulties for the assaulting troops. Direction was hard to discern and those in command faced problems in exercising control of their men, as an addendum to the subsequent operations report described:

> [A]ll supervision of units larger than a section or half platoon [was rendered] impossible. Officers and N.C.Os, however, took command of the nearest body of men and collected stragglers of all units ...[46]

42 TNA WO95/2300, War Diary of 1st Lancashire Fusiliers, Narrative of Operations 13-15 October 1918.
43 TNA WO95/2502/1, War Diary of 107 Infantry Brigade.
44 TNA WO95/2483, War Diary of 104 Infantry Brigade.
45 TNA WO95/2486, War Diary of 105 Infantry Brigade.
46 TNA WO95/2642, War Diary of 124 Infantry Brigade, Report on Operations commencing 13 October 1918.

As the advance progressed the fighting became more intense; the area contained a number of small farms which provided cover for defenders. The attacking troops were confronted by the expected machine gun fire and also by 'enemy light field guns firing over open sights at point blank range'.[47] The latter were engaged by the British 18 pounder guns attached to each of the attacking battalions. The success of this action once the fog began to disperse, combined with outflanking manoeuvres to take out in turn each farm and its defenders, saw progress resumed over the course of the morning. The first day's objective, a line running south-west to north-east through the hamlet of Wijnberg, was achieved by around noon. Enemy resistance persisted throughout the day and the Germans also attempted counter-attacks on the junction between 41st and 35th Divisions, though these were repulsed without reported difficulty. At 1600 hours the division's advance troops had consolidated the ground won.[48]

X Corps

With Menin as its objective, 34th Division launched its attack through 102 and 103 Brigades, operating in liaison with 41st Division on its left and 30th Division (also under X Corps) on its right.[49] The troops began from the starting line of the Gheluwe Switch, facing the village of Gheluwe. Two days previously a raiding party from 4/Royal Sussex had captured a German soldier, their prisoner providing some valuable information for the attackers. The division's subsequent summary report provides a concise account of the resulting advance:

> The 103rd Infantry Brigade on the left of the Divisional front enveloped GHELUWE from the North and South capturing all the enemy garrison located there. They were hung up temporarily in the TERHAND SWITCH by enemy field guns shooting over open sights from RUMANIAN FARM. The 5th K.O.S.B. [King's Own Scottish Borderers] and 8th Scottish Rifles, however, succeeded in capturing two and one of these guns respectively, and established themselves on their final objective on the N.E. outskirts of MENIN. The 102nd Infantry Brigade on the right came under heavy machine gun and artillery fire when they commenced to advance. They overcame all resistance, however, and established themselves in the TERHAND SWITCH by nightfall, being all along their final objectives on the Western outskirts of MENIN.[50]

The 34th Division commander, Major-General Nicholson, recorded that 'the barrage at 100 yards in two minutes ... was much too fast... communications were bad and information inaccurate'. He also subsequently heard stories from troops that '...putting the barrage down 300 yards ahead of the infantry line was too far and the cause of heavy casualties from machine guns which were not touched by the barrage'. Despite this, his division had played its part in

47 TNA WO95/2642, War Diary of 124 Infantry Brigade, Report on Operations commencing 13 October 1918
48 TNA WO95/2642, War Diary of 124 Infantry Brigade, Report on Operations commencing 13 October 1918
49 TNA WO95/2456, War Diary of 101 Infantry Brigade.
50 TNA WO95/2437, War Diary of 34th Division, Summary of War Diary for October 1918.

the successful capture of Gheluwe village which had been 'smashed and shelled with Thermite shells'. 'The Hun surrendered freely, only machine-gunners fighting'.[51]

For 30th Division, 21 Brigade (right flank) and 90 Brigade (left flank) led off the attack. Support included the division's 30th Battalion, Machine Gun Corps, and also one company from 14th Battalion, Machine Gun Corps (its host division, 14th, would be attacking on the right of 30th Division). The barrage would provide cover for the attack on the railway line, the village of Reeke and the road junction there.[52] 7/Royal Irish (21 Brigade) launched its assault under the cover of an artillery barrage of smoke and HE, together with Stokes mortars. The advance pushed on into Wervicq despite resistance in the village from enemy snipers and machine guns. With further support from artillery and mortars, the troops then moved on Hoogemotte.[53]

The use of machine guns as part of the artillery barrage to cover infantry assaults had become a regular feature of the British Army's plan of attack from the latter part of 1917 onwards. The 'Machine Gun Barrage', with sections of heavy machine guns providing indirect fire onto enemy positions, was designed to pin down defenders while the attacking infantry advanced. The other crucial task of the heavy machine gunners was to then take forward their guns in order to deploy in defensive or covering positions, consolidating the ground won by the infantry. A clear system for command and control was required as the battle developed and units advanced. The orders to 30th Battalion, Machine Gun Corps, for the attack on 14 October, reflected both of these roles, as the following extracts show:

> The attack will be supported by the 30th Bn. M.G. Corps and by one company of the 14th Bn. M.G. Corps. The 30th Bn. M.G. Corps will be divided into two groups …
>
> Right Group … Headquarters with 21st Inf. Bde …
> … 'B', 'C', & 'D' Coys, 30th Bn. M.G.C.
> Left Group … Headquarters with H.Q's 2/14 London Regt …
> … 'A' Coy, 30th Bn. M.G.C.
> The Company of the 14th Bn. M.G. Corps will form a separate group…
>
> The Right Group and the Group of the 14th Bn. M.G. Corps, will fire a barrage as laid down in Barrage Organisation Scheme…
>
> 'D' Company, 30th Bn. M.G. Corps will also, on the capture of the objective by the 21st Inf. Bde., consolidate the captured area by pushing forward one section to each of the [marked areas]…
>
> The O.C. 'D' Company will push forward a patrol at H plus 45 minutes to discover whether the Infantry Objective has been gained, and as soon as he receives information that the ground has been taken, will forthwith move his Sections to their positions of consolidation without any further orders. He will report to the Group Commander immediately these positions have been consolidated.

51 Nicholson, *34th Division*.
52 TNA WO95/2323, War Diary of 30th Battalion, Machine Gun Corps.
53 TNA WO95/2330, War Diary of 7th Battalion, Royal Irish Regiment.

> As soon as the 90th Infantry Brigade have captured their objective, the Left Group Commander will consolidate the captured area by pushing forward his Sections ... He will obtain information as to the capture of the objective from the Os' C. the two attacking Infantry Battalions... [and] immediately report to 90th Inf. Bde. and through 90th Bde. to Bn. H.Q.'s. that the Machine Gun consolidation has taken place.[54]

These arrangements show how important it was to have machine gun teams in situ in order to defend captured ground. As well as providing the additional firepower to resist a counter-attack by the enemy, the newly arrived teams allowed the infantry the space and time to regroup and to move onto the next objective, as required.

The detail in the orders to the machine gunners regarding timing, and the relay and receipt of information, is indicative of the 'modern' style of warfare being waged during this final period of the war – yet without the benefit of a mobile system of wireless communication. In these circumstances, much was dependent on the carefully worked out plans drawn up in advance of the operations, with timings based on such factors as distance and terrain. Alongside this preparation, there was then the need for commanders to assess the situation for themselves as the assault developed.

The covering barrage began at 0531 hours with the synchronised attack beginning four minutes later. The line of the River Lys was 'held by the enemy in fair strength' with the main points of resistance being fortified pill boxes.[55] For 30th Division, 1/6 Cheshires (21 Brigade) had begun to cross the Lys during the afternoon.[56] The smoke barrage helped the attackers to take the enemy by surprise in the drive for the Lys, engineers commencing bridging works as soon as possible.[57]

XV Corps

14th Division had been transferred to the command of XV Corps, while maintaining its position along the Ypres-Comines Canal and continuing to face the village of Comines. Its role in the attack was to take advantage of any withdrawal by enemy forces as a consequence of the attacks by X Corps forces on its left. In such a scenario the division was to establish a bridgehead across the Lys, covering the village; linking with 30th Division on its left, with whose progress it was to keep pace.[58]

At 0750 hours, with 30th Division reported to have reached Wervicq, 41 Brigade pushed forward patrols to the river. The neighbouring farms, Blanche and Lamlash, were found to be strongly defended, and there was heavy machine gun fire from Comines (probably using the church tower as an observation post). Artillery fire was brought to bear on the town, the barrage including smoke. From 1215 hours the RE began putting pontoon crossings over the river at four specific points identified in the original attack orders, as well as making temporary repairs

54 TNA WO95/2323, War Diary of 30th Battalion, Machine Gun Corps, Order No. 43. 11 October 1918.
55 TNA WO95/2338, War Diary of 90 Infantry Brigade.
56 TNA WO95/2328, War Diary of 21 Infantry Brigade.
57 TNA WO95/2330, War Diary of 2/23rd Battalion, London Regiment.
58 TNA WO95/1905, War Diary of 43 Infantry Brigade; TNA WO95/1899, War Diary of 42 Infantry Brigade, Order No. 23, 13 October 1918.

to a damaged bridge. The attacking battalions, 33/London and 29/Durham Light Infantry, were each allocated two bridges. By mid-afternoon, infantry began to cross the river and orders were issued for a bridgehead to be established and for reserve units to move forward in support. However this initial success could not be sustained. In the face of heavy enemy shelling, the 'Advanced posts East of River... were blown out of position',[59] and the bridgehead was withdrawn. Orders from division were for a crossing to be forced the following morning, with artillery support.

The early fighting in the battle shows the continuing effective use of flexible tactics by Second Army forces:

- Smoke and gas shells were again used in specific circumstances to screen the attackers
- There are several instances of the successful use of Lewis guns in support of infantry units; for example, the capture by 107th Brigade, 36th Division, of a length of the *Flanders Position II* plus the railway and Moorseele behind it
- 36th Division also successfully employed cyclists and motor machine guns to outflank enemy machine gun positions west of the village of Gulleghem
- 28th Brigade of 29th Division, crossed the Wulfdambeek river using eight portable bridges; each battalion had 18-pounder field guns and 6-inch mortars deployed alongside the attacking troops
- 29th Division's report praised the quick thinking of 'Junior Commanders' who 'took prompt steps... to overcome opposition... when the line was checked'[60]
- Some divisions brought selected gun batteries forward as soon as the initial advance commenced, in order that a second advance could receive artillery support; for example, 36th Division made a planned halt at 0747 in order for guns to move forward in support of the attack on the next objective.

The 1/Royal Irish Rifles attacked Gulleghem but without artillery support, the attack becoming held up by the density of the defensive wire and machine gun fire. A second attack took place at 1700 with an outflanking operation but there was a gain of only 200 yards. The war diary notes however, that a group of troops brought down a German reconnaissance plane and captured its crew.[61]

The close of the day saw the GAF capturing over 6,000 prisoners, of whom the British share was more than 3,500. The Belgian Army, with the French XXXIV Corps operating between its Northern and Southern *Groupements*, had reached Rumbeke, Roulers and Gitsberg. Second Army took Gheluwe and Moorselle, and was positioned to strike for Menin.[62] With the significant amount of ground gained, the operations were a convincing success and overall the resistance by the enemy had proved to be limited. Private Pope (2/15th London Regiment) recalled that his unit 'stopped by a pill box to collect prisoners [who gave] no resistance... we lighted

59 TNA WO95/1894/6, War Diary of 41 Infantry Brigade.
60 TNA WO95/2285, War Diary of 29th Division, Report on Operations, Period 14 October 1918-22 October 1918.
61 TNA WO95/2502/3 War Diary of 1st Battalion, Royal Irish Rifles.
62 TNA WO157/129, Second Army Intelligence Summary, 14 October 1918.

cigarettes as we went forward … [encountering] stranded Germans who gave themselves up after being threatened'.[63]

The scale and scope of the advance delivered broader strategic gains:

> The capture of German lateral communications on the line Roulers-Thourout-Courtrai forced a general German retirement in Flanders.[64]

The Second Army commander was rightly pleased with the outcome from the first day of the battle:

> Please accept my congratulations and convey them to all commanders and troops engaged today on the very successful results on what had been a long and arduous day.[65]

15 October

This progress was repeated on 15 October. Plumer's orders urged units to consolidate the gains of the previous day, while at the same time forward patrols were to be pushed forward for the purpose of establishing bridgeheads across the Lys. Map 6A shows the priorities for the British in terms of objectives. The caveat from Plumer was that such action should only be pursued if possible to achieve 'without undue loss.'

On the right XV Corps, employing the cover of artillery and machine guns, put temporary bridges across the Lys and established a firm bridgehead. This was a crucial move as it allowed enemy defences on the right (southern) bank of the Lys to be outflanked. To the north, II Corps in conjunction with the Belgian right wing made good progress despite encountering considerable resistance in the initial stages of the attack.

The Germans were estimated to now have twelve divisions facing the GAF with between seven and nine divisions available as reserves. Second Army intelligence assessed two of the divisions as 'fresh', two-three as 'moderately fresh', with three-four considered to be 'tired'.[66] The enemy continued to make full use of snipers and machine gun posts well dug-in behind fortified positions, including abandoned farmhouses. Enemy artillery continued to resist as the British troops advanced. 'Jerry was shelling the bridge [over the Lys] with heavy stuff … He shelled every road and street…'[67]

II Corps

On the left of Second Army, the Belgians attacked at 0900 hours, with a preliminary barrage opening ten minutes earlier.[68] Initial covering fire for the British advance made effective use of

63 Private Pope, personal diary.
64 W. J. Philpott, *Anglo-French Relations and Strategy on the Western Front 1914-18 (*London: Palgrave Macmillan, 1996), p. 159.
65 The message is recorded in WO95/2330, War Diary of 7th Battalion, Royal Irish Regiment.
66 TNA WO157/129, Second Army Intelligence Summary, 14 October 1918.
67 Private Pope, personal diary.
68 TNA WO95/1771/5, War Diary of 27 Infantry Brigade.

machine gun attachments as well as battalion Lewis guns.[69] The principal objective for II Corps was the village of Heule.

For 9th Division, 27 Brigade now took the lead, with the objectives of Hill 40 and the village of Steenbeck. 11/Royal Scots attacked the Hill but were hit by surprise fire from the direction of Laaga-Kepel Wood (north of the Steenbeck) which had been reported to have been cleared of the enemy. This led to the battalion having to carry out a mopping up exercise in the vicinity of the wood before resuming its assault. Despite encountering heavy wire defences the Hill was subsequently 'successfully stormed', its capture recorded at 1010 hours. Thereafter the battalion was forced to outflank Heetje in order to progress, whereupon it became pinned by the enemy's defence, concentrated around a windmill which dominated the surrounding ground. As the evening approached the German defenders appeared to recognise the danger of being trapped in what had become a small salient and the position was evacuated. Belgian troops were now entering the area and some were persuaded to consider moving on Heetje.[70]

Meanwhile, 12/Royal Scots had moved up behind its sister battalion and proceeded to attack and capture Steenbeck, under the cover of an artillery and machine gun barrage. 9th Division was initially checked west of Heule Wood but an outflanking action by 2/South Wales Borderers (87 Brigade, 29th Division) captured the wood and allowed the advance to continue.[71] At this point 27 Brigade paused to ensure contact with the Belgian and 29th Division units on its flanks. It was now looking to drive towards Harlebeke but became concerned to learn that the Belgians had been checked by a counter-attack in the vicinity of the railway line, and that 29th Division had at that time no further orders to progress; 'an obvious opportunity for the Battalion Commander to use his initiative' in the opinion of 27 Brigade. GOC 9th Division subsequently authorised the resumption of the advance, ordering the brigade to 'press on whether the others followed or not'. The cyclists and motor machine guns proved to be very effective in maintaining the pace of the advance, driving towards the river and preventing the defenders from getting the opportunity to reorganise. The machine guns were able to cause severe casualties to the enemy troops retreating via the main road and the adjoining railway.[72]

By late evening, the Belgian forces had taken and held Heetje and Bavichove, despite a heavy counter-attack by the Germans. Opposite the British forces, the enemy had dug itself in to retain a small bridgehead west of the Harlebeke-Courtrai road. Civilians gave warnings that roads leading to the Lys in the vicinity of Courtrai had been mined.[73]

The 87 Brigade took the lead for 29th Division, 88 Brigade in support. The infantry kept close touch with the barrage and made good early progress. 87 Brigade was at the outskirts of Heule by 1330 hours, whereupon it was decided to consolidate the ground gained and await the capture of the village itself by 36th Division; thus avoiding the risk of a counter-attack from that

69 TNA WO95/2300, War Diary of 1st Battalion, Lancashire Fusiliers, Narrative of Operations 13-15 October 1918.
70 TNA WO95/1771/4/5, War Diary of 27 Infantry Brigade, Narrative of Operations 28 September-28 October 1918.
71 TNA WO95/2285, War Diary of 29th Division, Report on Operations, Period 14 October 1918-22 October 1918.
72 TNA WO95/1771/4/5, War Diary of 27 Infantry Brigade, Narrative of Operations 28 September-28 October 1918.
73 TNA WO95/1771/5, War Diary of 27 Infantry Brigade.

direction when the advance resumed. At 1800 hours, crossings over the Heulebeek were secured at Watermolen and Old Mill. Orders were received to drive for the Lys on the 16th.[74]

Within the 36th Division there were morning reports that Gulleghem was believed to be taken except for some remaining enemy machine gun positions. As ordered, 1/Royal Irish Rifles had made a further attack at 0900 hours on Gulleghem which this time, aided by a creeping barrage in front of the attacking infantry, was successful. An advance was made to a point 1000 yards east of the village. The attack had not been without problems, heavy wire causing the troops to lose touch with the barrage after a time.[75] The village was targeted by enemy artillery fire later that day, mostly with gas shells.[76] This allowed 2/Royal Irish Rifles (from the same 107 Brigade) to pass through and advance in the direction of the II Corps objective of Heule.[77] This village, less than a mile from the outskirts of Courtrai, was captured by units from 109 Brigade (reported to 36th Division HQ at 1515 hours).[78] Numerous prisoners were reported, from 2nd and 3rd Battalions, 181st Infantry Regiment (40th Saxon Division) and 9th Uhlan Regiment (6th Cavalry Division). Troops were now through Heule and advancing easterly towards the Courtrai-Ingelmunster railway. That evening a defensive flank was formed and any further operations were deferred until the following day.[79]

However, overnight 107 Brigade was ordered to try and find out whether the enemy intended to make a stand on the west bank; 2/Royal Irish Rifles sent forward a patrol into Courtrai, the troops finding that the bridges across the Lys had been destroyed. In delaying its return to report its findings the patrol appears to have acted contrary to the orders from division. This was no doubt on the initiative of Lieutenant Adams, the patrol's leader, who may have had some particular motives of his own as he was 'a native of Courtrai' according to the war diary record. The group 'failed to send back reports of its whereabouts' and 'remained in Courtrai until involved in our own barrage, returning later with five prisoners'.[80] Falls, in his history of 36th Division, refers to the choice of Lieutenant Adams not being 'altogether an advantage, for he made an investigation so thorough that he was not back till the following morning'.[81]

During the evening II Corps issued orders that 36th and 29th Divisions, acting in co-operation with 35th Division (XIX Corps) on their right, were to continue the attack towards the River Lys, it being a priority to seize and hold river crossings.[82]

74 TNA WO95/2285, War Diary of 29th Division, Report on Operations, Period 14 October 1918-22 October 1918; TNA WO95/2307/4, War Diary of 88 Infantry Brigade.
75 TNA WO95/2502/1, War Diary of 107 Infantry Brigade.
76 TNA WO95/2492, War Diary of 36th Division, 1930 hours (the shelling was reported to have taken place around 1730 hours).
77 TNA WO95/2502/3, War Diary 1st Battalion, Royal Irish Rifles.
78 TNA WO95/2492, War Diary of 36th Division.
79 TNA WO95/2502/1, War Diary of 107 Infantry Brigade; Falls, 36th Division, pp. 275-6.
80 TNA WO95/2502/1, War Diary of 107 Infantry Brigade; WO95/2502/4, War Diary 2nd Royal Irish Rifles.
81 Falls, 36th Division, p. 277
82 TNA WO95/2492, War Diary of 36th Division, 1930 hours.

XIX Corps

For 35th Division, 105 Brigade attacked at 0900 hours, between Kloefhoek and Kappelhoek. Despite enemy machine gun fire from houses on the outskirts of Wevelghem, the units moved forward; shortly after 1000 hours posts were established on a line Wlinberg – Kloefhoek Cross Roads – Kappelhoek. During the afternoon 4/North Staffs leading for the brigade worked its way forward; operating in conjunction with 104 Brigade on its left, and troops from 41st Division on its right, protecting the southern flank of the advance. Posts were then set up east of the Wevelghem – Gulleghem Road. Under cover of darkness a patrol of 15/Sherwood Foresters reached Wevelghem Church, encountering no enemy soldiers. On report of this to HQ a second patrol of 4/North Staffs was sent forward; this group made its way through Wevelghem and reached the north bank of the Lys, just above the village of Lauwe.[83]

The 106 Brigade received orders to pass through 104 and 105 Brigades, then to attack and secure the 'high ground commanding the Bridge head crossing the Lys opposite the village of Marcke'. A conference of the unit commanders together with their opposite numbers from the artillery was held later that evening, and zero hour set for 0530 hours the following morning.[84]

The initial attack by 41st Division was also impeded by machine gun fire from Wevelghem, striking the left flank of the British troops. The pace of the advance was maintained nonetheless and the west bank of the Lys was duly reached. A line was consolidated from there, through the northern outskirts of Wevelghem, and along the Wevelghem-Gulleghem road. That night the division was relieved by troops of 101 Brigade (34th Division, X Corps) and its units moved north, taking up positions west of Courtrai.[85]

X Corps

After the successes on day one, the troops of 34th Division completed the occupation of Menin. Their orders were then to strike for a line from Le Malplaquet, south and east of Halluin, to Le Cornet. Subsequently, in the face of strong resistance, patrols fought their way across the Marathon and Mongrel bridges over the River Lys and managed to create two bridgeheads. Both of these positions were under threat but the soldiers 'managed to hang on' until relief forces from 30th Division arrived.[86]

On the left flank of the division, as mentioned above, 101 Brigade had moved north to take over positions previously held by 124 Brigade of 41st Division, on the line of the River Lys at Ruddy Farm.[87] During these manoeuvres the brigade also carried out the clearing of the village of Wevelghem, establishing jumping off points from which to make a crossing of the Lys on the following day.[88]

83 TNA WO95/2486, War Diary of 105 Infantry Brigade.
84 TNA WO95/2489, War Diary of 106 Infantry Brigade.
85 TNA WO95/2642, War Diary of 124 Infantry Brigade, Report on Operations commencing 13 October 1918.
86 TNA WO95/2437, War Diary of 34th Division, Summary of War Diary for October 1918; TNA WO95/2323, War Diary of 30th Battalion, Machine Gun Corps, Order No. 46. 15 October, 1918.
87 TNA WO95/2456, War Diary of 101 Infantry Brigade.
88 TNA WO95/2437, War Diary of 34th Division, Summary of War Diary for October 1918.

The 202 Field Company, Royal Engineers (30th Division), was ordered to reconnoitre and repair the bridges over the canal section of the River Lys between Wervicq and Comines, and to put two foot bridges in place for the infantry.[89] The orders for 30th Division were emphatic: 'The enemy are retreating. The 30th Division will advance and maintain touch with the enemy'.[90]

The 21 Brigade led by 7/Royal Irish continued to press forward. By the morning the battalion had established positions along the northern bank of the Lys.[91] Later that day, south of Wervicq, 1/6 Cheshires managed to force a passage across,[92] aided by the success of 14th Division on its right which had secured a crossing to the south west. Approaching midnight, the engineers succeeded in putting a pontoon bridge in place despite regular shelling by the enemy.[93]

90 Brigade was ordered to cross the River Lys between Bousbecque (where the bridges were reported to be burning) and (Le) Malplaquet. Advancing to the high ground above, fighting patrols were then to push forward and maintain close contact with the enemy. 'A' Company of 30th Battalion, Machine Gun Corps would provide support as required.[94] 2/15 London Regiment was initially ordered to cross at Bousbecque. In practice, 'A' Company crossed via Wervicq and established a bridgehead which was subsequently reinforced by 'C' Company.[95]

XV Corps

14th Division forced a crossing of the River Lys south west of Wervicq. 41 Brigade had launched a further assault at dawn and met little opposition. The first troops across successfully were then able to outflank the remaining German defenders on the facing east bank. More worrying was the loss of touch with neighbouring units on both flanks, which were yet to cross. It was 1600 hours before contact was re-established and the line running along the Wervicq-Comines road, and the railway line south of Comines, secured. 'The mopping up of Comines was completed' the brigade's war diary concluded.[96] 42 Brigade moved up into line at Comines, with 41 Brigade withdrawn into reserve.[97]

On the Army's right, 40th Division operated with orders for 'further objectives for the pursuit and harassing of the enemy in the event of his withdrawal', whilst maintaining touch on its right with 59th Division at the junction of the two British Armies.[98]

As the battle progressed, the main weight of the fighting fell to the units on the northern left wing of the Second Army line, in and around Courtrai. To the south, the main task for XV Corps was to continue to sustain its advance eastwards across the Lys and towards Tourcoing and Roubaix. The intention was to wheel the right wing of the Army into a north-south alignment

89 TNA WO95/2323, War Diary of 202 Field Company, Royal Engineers (30th Division).
90 TNA WO95/2323, War Diary of 30th Battalion, Machine Gun Corps, Order No. 46. 15 October, 1918.
91 TNA WO95/2330, War Diary of 7th Battalion, Royal Irish Regiment.
92 TNA WO95/2330, War Diary of 1/6th Battalion, Cheshire Regiment.
93 TNA WO95/2338, War Diary of 90 Infantry Brigade.
94 TNA WO95/2323, War Diary of 30th Battalion, Machine Gun Corps, Order No. 46. 15 October, 1918.
95 TNA WO95/2340, War Diary of 2/15th London Regiment.
96 TNA WO95/1894/6, War Diary of 41 Infantry Brigade.
97 TNA WO95/1899, War Diary of 42 Infantry Brigade.
98 TNA WO95/2594, War Diary of 40th Division.

with its left wing and the coalition forces to the north. There was the opportunity to try and take advantage of the pressure on the enemy further north, such that the movement forward by the British could be effected with limited casualties.

The sequence of daily orders issued by 92 Brigade (31st Division) during the battle, from which the following extracts are taken, illustrate the nature of the drive towards and across the Roubaix canal:

92ND INFANTRY BRIGADE ORDER 302 12.10.18.

On the night October 13/14, the method of holding the Brigade front will be changed...
... the front posts being chosen so as to command to the best advantage the approaches to the river crossings at WARNETON, PONT ROUGE, and FRELINGHIEN...

92ND INF. BDE. ORDER NO. 303 15.10.18.

1 Tonight October 15/16 and tomorrow October 16, the line will be advanced...
2 11 E.Lan.Regt. [11/East Lancs] will endeavour to push a strong patrol across the river LYS... and to establish themselves on the Eastern bank, forming a bridgehead and patrolling in advance of the post established. This crossing will not be pressed if considerable casualties are likely to be incurred. 1 Battery 165 Bde. R.F.A. [will provide fire support]...
3 10. E.York.R. will push forward strong patrols this afternoon over the River LYS by a bridge existing in the area of 41st. Inf. Bde [14th Division], & this evening by reinforcing and advancing the lodging already obtained on the East bank...
This advance will be carried out by patrols & will not be pressed if severe casualties are likely to be incurred.
Covering fire by Field Arty. Is being given by 170 Bde. R.F.A. plus 3 Batteries of 165 Bde. R.F.A... & is taking the form of harassing fire.
Machine Gun and T.M. co-operation has been arranged.
4 11 E.York.R. will... relieve the troops of 10 E.York.R. East of the River with 2 companies, which will patrol to their flanks so as to aim at occupying... the Road north of the DEULE River – through DOULEMONT – ...with patrols towards Ferme WAUSTINE...
5 Arrangements for twenty 15 ft. infantry bridges and for the launching of the cork bridge have been made... [plus] other raft and bridge arrangements

92nd INF. BDE. ORDER NO. 304 15.10.18.

1 The XV Corps is continuing their advance today Oct. 15th.
2 The Corps objective for today is [line] WERVICQ... – QUESNOY-SUR-DEULE...
3 The 11 E.York.R. will carry out this advance N. of the DEULE River. 11 E.Lanc.R. S. of river DEULE...

92ND INF. BDE. ORDER NO. 305 16.10.18.

1 On night 16/17 Oct. and tomorrow 17th Oct, XV Corps is continuing to advance.
2 XV Corps objectives will be : BOUSBECQUE – LINSELLES (incl) – LA VIGNE incl) – DESPAING – WAMBRECHIES.
4 11 E.York.R. on gaining objectives… will push patrols forward and hold the line as detailed in para. 2 above…

92ND INF. BDE. ORDER NO. 306 17.10.18.

1 11 E.York.R. are now on the line LINSELLES – LA VIGNE.
2 At 0830 10 E.Y.R. will advance from present location through 11 E.Y.R.
3 Objective of 10 E.Y.R. is the RONCQ – CROIX BLANCHE RD.
Patrols will be sent forward of this line…
4 After passing through 11 E.York.R. the 10th E.York.R. will form the vanguard…

92ND INF. BDE. ORDER NO. 307 17.10.18.

1 The 15th Corps is continuing its advance tonight and tomorrow morning.
2 The objective allocated to the 31st Division is from FORT [DE] BONDUES…
3 The 10th E.York.R. will carry out this advance tonight; objective to be gained before dawn tomorrow morning.
Corps Cyclists Battalion is co-operating as an independent force and is establishing standing patrols at [key] cross roads…
6 A Contact aeroplane will call for flares each night and each morning… from front line troops.
7 10 E.York.R. on gaining the above objective will push forward patrols, but no patrols will enter either the towns of TURCOING or ROUBAIX.

92ND INF. BDE. ORDER NO. 308 16.10.18.

1 XV Corps is continuing their advance tomorrow 18th inst.
[Objectives are listed for 31st, 14th and 40th Divisions].[99]

The subsequent orders for the following days continue in this format, putting in place the arrangements for maintaining the direction and pace of the advance. Units were regularly rotated in turn to act as the front line or vanguard of the brigade or division as appropriate. The logistics of sustaining the advance would have placed a heavy workload upon staff and support services. These faced the daily challenge of ensuring that the necessary arrangements

99 The orders referred to are attached as appendices to TNA WO95/2356/5, War Diary of 92 Infantry Brigade, October 1918.

for transporting and supplying the advancing troops, and the resources to underpin this, were in place. There would also be a need for new billeting arrangements for those troops placed in support or reserve roles as the advance rolled forwards; and the position of advance guard was rotated between the different battalions and brigades.

While 9th Division on the far left of the Army was forcing its way through a couple of miles of German defences, the units of 40th Division were about to begin an advance of over 15 miles to bring the front of Second Army into line. Moving across more open country, these forces had to remain vigilant in the face of the perpetual prospect of encountering a point of enemy resistance. Second Army was across the Lys near Comines, though the latter was yet to be taken. Wervicq and Kloethock ridge had been captured; Menin was poised to fall. Reports suggested that the enemy intended to evacuate Lille – all civilians would be left behind except males of military age.[100]

The *Official History* quotes a German history of the war in reporting that on 15 October, the German Army Group commander Crown Prince Rupprecht ordered a general retirement to prepared positions east of Thourout-Roulers and south to Menin.[101] This ground was in fact already held by the allies, illustrating the significant progress achieved so far. The same source attributes this success to the overwhelming numbers of the attackers (not strictly correct) and to the use of tanks (not correct at all for British forces in Flanders).

The progress made by French forces in the north was considerably less. Their advance of only four kilometres fell considerably short of the ten kilometres achieved by the neighbouring Belgian Southern Groupement and II Corps. In his 1922 account of the war,[102] G.A.B. Dewar made reference to a new term in British military language, to 'Deb': this was based on the supposed actions of the French General Debeney on the right of British Fourth Army during the Battle of Amiens. Dewar defines the term whereby its subject intended 'to remain quiescent for a while, till advance on his front had been made easier by the progress of his neighbours'. Dewar uses this term to describe the actions of the French during the Battle of Courtrai; the implication is that the French forces interposed between the Belgian Army on British Second Army's left, were content to 'Deb' during the fighting. Dewar explains this lack of initiative by the French as prompted by the desire to 'preserve a powerful French Army to give weight to French counsels in the peace negotiations', which was justified by 'the incomparable exertions and sacrifices of the French Army and nation in the early years of the war'.

Foch however proved to be unhappy with this situation – to the extent that he subsequently arranged for a regrouping of French forces. The outcome was the creation of the French Sixth Army under General de Boissoudy. On 19 October this formation took over the line held by the Belgian Southern Groupement and adjoining II Corps of Second Army.

In his book on the final year of the war, Stevenson summarises the position at this stage in the Battle of Courtrai, by 15 October, as follows:

100 TNA WO157/129, Second Army Intelligence Summary, 15 October 1918.

101 M. Schwarte (ed.), *Der Deutsche Landkrieg* (Leipzig: Barth, 1923), described by the *Official History* as 'A well-known and reliable general history of the War'.

102 Dewar, *Haig's Command Vol. II*, p. 332.

[The GAF forces] were advancing faster than expected and threatening the Germans on the Flanders coast, who had the greatest distance to retreat if the Western Front became untenable. The local commanders feared being cut off and for two weeks Ludendorff had rejected their requests to pull back, but now their position became critical and on the 15th [October, 1918] the OHL authorised a general withdrawal.[103]

16 October

The third day of the battle saw the aspirations of Plumer's modified orders from 11 October begin to be realised through operations on the ground. II, X and XIX Corps were to cross the Lys and establish bridgeheads on the south side. XV Corps was already across and so the Army's left pivoted on Bousbecque to allow the right wing to swing around and undertake an advance of over five miles. By the close of the day the four divisions on the right of Second Army (40th, 31st, and 14th of XV Corps and 30th of X Corps) held a line across the Lys up to Bousbecque. The remainder of the army rested on the north bank of the river.

II Corps

From 16 October onwards the heavy howitzers and long-range guns of II Corps engaged targets south of the Lys. Harassing fire and bombardment of targets selected by the infantry was conducted. The artillery of the other corps moved forward as conditions permitted, crossing the Lys as soon as appropriate bridging was in place. Overnight, 29th Division had consolidated a line in the centre of II Corps, holding Cuerne and Watermolen.[104]

9th Division continued to keep pace with the Belgians on the left of the Army, with arrangements in hand to cross the Lys. By lunchtime, the division was reporting that patrols had crossed the river at Menin, Wervicq and Comines. The Belgians were now in possession of the southern side of the Roulers-Lys Canal. By early evening their forces were reporting the retirement of enemy artillery from Harlebeke in the direction of Deerlyck and Vichte.[105] In front of 27 Brigade, during the night a team of Royal Engineers had put two bridges across the Lys, but being placed very close together a German shell destroyed both. Despite this, three companies of 6/King's Own Scottish Borderers made a crossing that evening and attacked the Courtrai Road. The operation was successful but a subsequent attempt to work round Harlebeke was rebuffed. Accordingly a bridgehead was formed on the road with its flanks secured on the loop of the river. The enemy made a limited attempt to take out the position but was easily beaten off.[106]

Advance units of 29th Division kept pace with neighbouring forces to reach the Lys; otherwise the day was focused upon crossings preparations. In response to a request from 9th Division for support in holding the initial bridgehead, that night 88 Brigade sent two platoons of 2/

103 Stevenson, *Backs to the Wall*, p. 165.
104 TNA WO95/1771/5, War Diary of 27 Infantry Brigade.
105 TNA WO95/1771/5, War Diary of 27 Infantry Brigade.
106 TNA WO95/1771/4/5, War Diary of 27 Infantry Brigade, Narrative of Operations 28 September-28 October 1918.

Hampshires across the river; a further bridging attempt was made to provide an alternative line of retreat but stopped by heavy enemy machine gun fire.[107]

By early morning the advance troops of 36th Division had reached Courtrai and the west bank of the Lys, finding many civilians still living there. The divisional historian summarised the result:

> There were scenes of great enthusiasm among the citizens, who came forth from their cellars to greet the troops.

However this had been no easy victory and his account continues:

> But the Germans were not far off. As the first British troops appeared on the quays of the Lys, here eighty feet wide, heavy machine-gun fire burst out all across the opposite bank.[108]

Bridges across the river were found to have been destroyed by the retreating enemy and so arrangements proceeded for the putting down of pontoon crossings, under the cover of a smoke screen. The objective remained that of clearing Courtrai of the enemy and establishing bridgeheads across the Lys, beyond the town. That afternoon, 60 men of 108 Brigade were reported to have established an initial position on the east bank but their bridge was subsequently destroyed by enemy artillery fire; fierce enemy counter-attacks led to them subsequently being withdrawn by ferry.[109] There was another reason for the withdrawal: rather than a direct assault on Courtrai, the city would be outflanked to the north and a drive made to the Scheldt – thereby making it untenable for the Germans to continue to hold the industrial cities to the south. In these circumstances there was no value in fighting to retain a bridgehead without a bridge.[110]

XIX Corps

At 0530 hours 106 Brigade moved through its companion brigades in 35th Division and attacked the enemy to the front. The Germans were overrun and the brigade advanced down to the River Lys, east of Wevelghem. Units from 104 and 105 Brigades were pulled back to secure the area west of the Menin-Roulers railway. 41st Division was involved in the relief of 36th Division.[111]

X Corps

After the capture and clearing of Wevelghem, 101 Brigade of 34th Division crossed the Lys between Halluin and Marcke, successfully establishing advance posts.[112] For 30th Division, in the early hours ‘A’ Company of 2/15 London Regiment (90 Brigade) crossed the Lys via

107 TNA WO95/2307/4, War Diary of 88 Infantry Brigade; TNA WO95/2285, War Diary of 29th Division, Report on Operations, Period 14 October 1918-22 October 1918.
108 Falls, *36th Division*, pp. 277-9.
109 TNA WO95/2492, War Diary of 36th Division.
110 Falls, *36th Division*, p. 278.
111 TNA WO95/2470/1, War Diary of 35th Division.
112 TNA WO95/2456, War Diary of 101 Infantry Brigade.

a destroyed bridge and moved into Bousbecque. In response the Germans shelled the village including gas shells.

Later in the day, 30th Division was ordered to adjust its line northwards during the evening, to take over a portion of line from 34th Division.[113]

Arrangements were already underway to improve the transport infrastructure in support of the advance. For the next few days the pioneer battalion 6/South Wales Borderers worked on repairing firstly the approaches to Menin before moving onto the neighbouring bridges.[114]

XV Corps

The emphasis was on crossing the Lys to maximise pressure on the German defenders:

> All indications point to the enemy carrying out an early withdrawal in front of 40th Division ... The 40th Division will be ready to advance... and will vigorously press the retreating enemy.[115]

Information from prisoners together with observed evidence, suggested that the enemy were looking to undertake a planned withdrawal to the Schelde. Though advancing British forces encountered strong covering detachments of artillery, machine guns and small arms, they were able to execute pursuit of the retreating enemy. German Fourth Army had been instructed to retire on the prepared *Hermann Position* (running from Ghent, through Tournai and Conde, east of Le Cateau). However, this line would itself be broken on the following day, by the British Fourth Army operating south of Flanders.

The day had brought the clearing of the north bank of the Lys up to Halebeke. Intelligence assessments concluded that the enemy had brought up seven divisions from its reserves to reinforce the Flanders battlefront, giving a total of 17 German divisions engaged since the battle began. It was believed that five divisions were still held in reserve in the Courtrai and Lille areas; but north of Courtrai, all enemy divisions had now been committed.[116]

On 16 October, reflecting his own unhappiness with the limited progress of the French forces, King Albert prepared orders which would alter with immediate effect the responsibilities of Second Army within the Army Group at this stage of the battle; the orders were received by Plumer on 17 October. Stevenson concludes that '... the French in Flanders in October did little more than shadow the retreating enemy, leaving the fighting to their allies'.[117]

Albert's action meant that the British force would no longer retain its original designation as the flank guard – not that Plumer had shown himself restricted to that role. XV and X Corps were to push eastwards, south of the Lys; XIX and II Corps were to consolidate their positions and then to clear the enemy from the vicinity of the Lys and Coutrai. The *Official History* states

113 TNA WO95/2323, War Diary of 30th Battalion, Machine Gun Corps, Order No. 46. 15 October, 1918.
114 TNA WO95/2323, War Diary of 6th Battalion, South Wales Borderers (Pioneers).
115 TNA WO95/2610, War Diary of 120 Infantry Brigade, Warning Order No. 229.
116 TNA WO157/129, Second Army Intelligence Summary, 16 October 1918.
117 Stevenson, *Backs to the Wall*, p. 274, reference Edmonds, *Official History 1918 Vol. IV*, pp. 114-5 and *Vol. V*, pp. 281, 584.

that 'General Plumer again ignored the orders of the GAF… [directing] XV and X Corps to advance to the Tournai-Courtrai railway… XIX and II Corps to make all preparations to cross the Lys when the situation demanded'.[118]

17 October

The Second Army Intelligence Summary reported that naval forces had landed at Ostend and occupied the town. British Fifth Army was entering Lille. Reports indicated that the Germans were attempting a planned withdrawal to the Scheldt, including delaying positions along the Lys and the Courtrai-Bossuyt Canal. It was estimated that up to 19 enemy divisions in total had now been deployed against Second Army and its allies in the GAF.[119]

II Corps

II Corps and XIX Corps were ordered to consolidate positions and to make preparations for river crossings.[120] Overnight there was fierce fighting as 9th Division struggled to retain its hold on the bridgehead across the Lys, just south-east of the village of Cuerne.[121] In the early hours, troops from 2/Hampshires (88 Brigade, 29th Division) had crossed the river to secure the right flank of 27 Brigade. British advance forces faced strong enemy shelling followed by a determined counter-attack at 0510 hours which caused some initial withdrawal; however a bayonet charge managed to recover the ground. During the early morning there were concerns regarding supplies for the troops on the east bank; the damaged bridges were preventing the delivery of fresh ammunition across the river. At 0830 hours arrangements were made to carry out a planned supply drop for the advance troops from the air. Aeroplanes of the RAF subsequently dropped ammunition and rations in order to ensure that the bridgeheads were suitably resupplied. While there were at that time no engineers available to repair the bridges, infantry continued to manage to cross the river by making use of the remaining wreckage.

On the right, 29th Division succeeded in clearing the enemy from a farm which had been holding up the advance. However at 1630 hours, the advance troops of the division holding the bridgehead had faced a strong enemy counter-attack supported by an artillery bombardment. Though the attack was repulsed it was decided to withdraw the troops given that no reliable or uninterrupted support could be delivered until secure bridges were in place. During the course of the evening the division's engineers successfully constructed six bridges.[122]

36th Division was ordered to transfer north and to relieve the 3rd Belgian Division in the front line, thereby taking on responsibility for the left flank of Second Army. The division would therefore take the lead in the drive by the Army to cross the Lys, while acting in conjunction

118 Edmonds, *Official History 1918 Vol. V.*
119 TNA WO157/129, Second Army Intelligence Summary, 17 October 1918.
120 TNA WO158/212, Second Army Operations, 1 October 1918-20 January 1919, Order No. 44, 17 October 1918.
121 TNA WO95/2492, War Diary of 36th Division.
122 TNA WO95/1771/4/5, War Diary of 27 Infantry Brigade, Narrative of Operations 28 September-28 October 1918; TNA WO95/2285, War Diary of 29th Division, Report on Operations, Period October 14th 1918 – October 22nd 1918.

with French forces to its left. The Belgian Army would then concentrate on clearing the coast as far as the Dutch border. II Corps orders were for efforts to establish bridgeheads to be put on hold pending the identification of suitable crossing points and the putting down of appropriate bridging materials.[123]

XIX Corps

The 41st Division was ordered to consolidate its position, clearing any remaining enemy from the vicinity of the River Lys and Courtrai. While preparations were to be made for bridging the river, no attempt should be made to cross while opposition was in situ.[124]

X Corps

Army Order No. 44 instructed XV Corps to maintain the drive eastwards, supported by X Corps.[125] For 34th Division, 102 and 103 Brigades (who had led the attack on the opening day of the battle) were withdrawn into reserve and support respectively.[126] The 101 Brigade maintained the division's advance eastwards, troops of 2/Loyal North Lancs crossing the Lys at Ruddy farm. The brigade subsequently proceeded to capture a series of villages between 16-19 October: Lauwe, Knocke, Rolleghem and Belleghem.[127]

30th Division now made a radical response to the tactical demands of the current fighting. The different arms within the division were reformed into what were described as 'Brigade Groups', and named for the Brigade commander:

89 Brigade	Currie's Group
90 Brigade	Stevens' Group
21 Brigade	Goodman's Group.[128]

These formations brought together the infantry brigade with units from other specialist services under one unified command structure. In what can be termed as a 'battlegroup' formation, this bringing together of combined arms in response to battlefield requirements gives a foretaste of a more common practice in a later world war.

In common with its companions, the order of battle for the Stevens' Group comprised:

Brigade HQ

1 × Infantry Battalion	(2/14 London Regiment)
1 × Infantry Battalion	(2/15 London Regiment)
1 × Infantry Battalion	(2/16 London Regiment)

123 TNA WO95/2492, War Diary of 36th Division.
124 TNA W095/2618, War Diary of 41st Division.
125 TNA WO158/212, Second Army Operations, 1 October 1918-20 January 1919, Order No. 44, 17 October 1918.
126 TNA WO95/2437, War Diary of 34th Division, Summary of War Diary for October 1918.
127 TNA WO95/2456, War Diary of 101 Infantry Brigade.
128 TNA WO95/2332, War Diary of 89 Infantry Brigade.

1 × Light Trench Mortar Battery
1 × Brigade, Royal Field Artillery (with 1 × Section, Divisional Ammunition Column; 1 × Trench Mortar Battery)
2 × Companies, 30th Machine Gun Battalion
1 × Section, Royal Engineers
1 × Cable laying Signal Section, Royal Engineers
1 × Field Ambulance Unit
1 × Company, 30th Divisional Train ASC
1 × Section, Cyclists[129]

This arrangement was intended to provide for a more direct and immediate approach to the tactical challenges of command and control. The reorganisation was a calculated response to the particular circumstances on the battlefield at this point in time – demanding of a rapid advance in pursuit of a retreating enemy.

The 'Brigade Groups' allowed the infantry brigade commander to have immediate operational control of specialist weapons and support services, able to issue orders and to direct their deployment. The aim was to both encourage and provide the means for a flexible approach to the various potential challenges posed by the different forms of enemy resistance. A related factor would have been the changing nature of the terrain and the level of advantage, or otherwise, which it offered the defender.

This formal restructuring was in contrast to the other examples of the combined arms arrangements which Second Army formations had been and were adopting, examples of which have been regularly described in this and earlier chapters. In these cases, the most common approach has been to have one or more support units attached to an infantry formation for the purposes of a particular attack or operation. The attack orders have then specified the respective responsibilities of the infantry commanders and the commanders of the support units, and how these commands would relate to each other as the operation progressed. There is no doubt that there had been significant success through the attachment of, for example, machine gun or field gun sections to infantry units. However most of these examples involved only the addition of usually one or two specialist arms whereas the battlegroup formation introduced by 30th Division represented a radical overhaul of the arrangements for the infantry and the various specialist arms normally held at division level.

The commander of 30th Division, Major-General W Williams, would appear to have been looking for an improvement in the pace of the advance, believing that his troops were slow in adapting to the mobile warfare now taking place. This is demonstrated by his subsequent message to the troops. An entry on 20 October in the war diary of 90 Brigade records:

> The Div. Commander considered that hitherto our advances had been too slow. This appeared to be due to the excess of caution exercised by Battalions in advancing, a relic of trench warfare. Also artillery and M.G. support was not made use of to the best advantage, in order to overcome quickly such resistance as we experienced.[130]

129 TNA WO95/2338, War Diary of 90 Infantry Brigade, listed in entry for 19 October 1918, 'The Brigade Group now consisted of …'
130 TNA WO95/2338, War Diary of 90 Infantry Brigade.

These remarks show that Major-General Williams was looking for the more effective use of fire support units in suppressing or taking out defensive positions.

There was evidence reported in the early hours of the enemy retreating and efforts to cross the Lys were increased. Some troops of 90 Brigade/Stevens' Group used rafts made from duckboards, able to carry two or three men, in order to ferry themselves across the water. 2/15 London Regiment crossed at Bousbecque, 2/16 London Regiment at Menin, using pontoon bridges. As the day progressed units encountered civilians from neighbouring villages that the enemy had evacuated, such as Tourcoing and Roncq. As the advance brigade group for the division, the troops held the line Roncq-Mont D'Halluin-Reckem (with 34th Division on the left and 31st Division on the right).[131]

XV Corps

Having moved up into line two days previously, 42 Brigade now led the advance by 14th Division. Units of 40th Division moved forward across the Quesnoy railway line with patrols entering Wambrechies; it was necessary to erect a footbridge as 'All bridges across [the Canal] between Quesnoy and Wambrechies had been destroyed by the enemy'.[132]

Between 16-19 October (as shown in Map 7), units along the Second Army line crossed the Lys in the face of resistance by the German covering forces. Considerable use was made of deploying field guns in advanced positions in order to neutralise or take out enemy machine gun positions. Where daylight crossings were deemed too dangerous then an offensive was launched by night. The variations in the depth and breadth of the Lys meant that a variety of bridging arrangements were used including rafts, a barrel bridge, and pontoon bridges. X Corps crossed on 17 October, thereby clearing the southern bank from Bousbecque up to Lauwe.

The 202 Field Company, Royal Engineers (30th Division) was deployed to construct a bridge across the Lys at Halluin. Later in the day, once the enemy had been cleared from the opposite bank, a barrel tier bridge (for infantry crossing in single file) was constructed.[133]

18 October

II Corps

26 Brigade (9th Division) ordered 7/Seaforth Highlanders to reconnoitre the Lys Canal to ascertain the most suitable places for bridging as well as the best positions from which to deliver covering fire for a crossing. The battalion was also to try and identify enemy strong points which would require attention from the artillery.[134] At dusk, 5/Cameron Highlanders (26 Brigade) moved into the line at Bavichove, relieving 3 Battalion, 9th Belgian Regiment.[135]

131 TNA WO95/2338, War Diary of 90 Infantry Brigade; WO95/2340, War Diary of 2/14th Battalion, London Regiment.
132 TNA W095/2614, War Diary of 121 Brigade; TNA WO95/2594, War Diary of 40th Division.
133 TNA WO95/2323, War Diary of 202 Field Company, Royal Engineers (30th Division).
134 TNA WO95/1765, War Diary of 7th Battalion, Seaforth Highlanders.
135 TNA WO95/1767, War Diary of 5th Battalion, Cameron Highlanders.

Overnight, 88 Brigade (29th Division) looked to put a patrol of 2/Hampshires across the river to probe for enemy defences. Signs of enemy retirement would be the signal for further units to cross the river. In the event, heavy machine gun fire from the enemy was considered to make the use of pontoons no longer possible and the action was postponed.

36th Division completed its relief of the 11th Belgian Infantry Regiment (3rd Belgian Division), east of Hulste.[136] The intention now was to put bridges across the Lys on the following day. The French would not be ready to cross until 20 October at the earliest, but the importance of driving beyond the river was considered paramount by Second Army.[137]

XIX Corps

As news filtered through of military successes elsewhere on the GAF Front, the war diary of 105 Brigade recorded:

> Troops much elated by the news of the capture of LILLE and BRUGES and the landing at OSTEND.[138]

Such reports on successes achieved elsewhere by allied armies gave a valuable boost to morale. Sharing such information was an important means by which to encourage the men to keep up the pressure on the enemy.

That same day, preparations were in hand to renew the advance, with 35th Division HQ in conference with unit commanders to plan an attack to capture Marcke, south of Courtrai. For 41st Division, the planned crossing of the Lys was postponed for 24 hours; 123 Brigade was to push patrols across the river if an opportunity arose. The division's diary records heavy enemy shelling, including gas, of Courtrai, Heule and surrounding roads.[139]

X Corps

101 Brigade (34th Division) continued its successful progress eastwards, liberating the village of Knocke. The brigade's CO, Brigadier-General Woodstock, took part in a successful victory parade into Lauwe, meeting an 'enthusiastic reception by liberated civilians'.[140]

XV Corps

43 Brigade (14th Division) had successfully moved through 42 Brigade to take the lead for the continuation of the advance. With 10/Highland Light Infantry as the lead battalion, it successfully attacked the railway at Mouscron and pushed on through the village.[141] Advance guards of 31st Division were moving beyond the line Roncq – Croix Blanche.[142]

136 TNA WO95/2509, War Diary of 109 Infantry Brigade.
137 Falls, *36th Division*, p. 281.
138 TNA WO95/2486, War Diary of 105 Infantry Brigade.
139 TNA W095/2618, War Diary of 41st Division.
140 TNA WO95/2456, War Diary of 101 Infantry Brigade.
141 TNA WO95/1905, War Diary of 43 Infantry Brigade.
142 TNA WO95/2356/5, War Diary of 92 Infantry Brigade.

40th Division continued to press the retreating German forces, and issued orders to this effect:

> Enemy withdrawing Eastwards through ROUBAIX and TOURCOING. 40th Division is to continue to advance. 120th Infantry Brigade will be about WAMBRECHIES by 12.00 hours 18th inst.[143]

Later that day its diary recorded that 'Roubaix was evacuated by the enemy and entered by our troops'.[144]

18 October saw Second Army extend its left flank northwards, relieving part of the Belgian line. The leftwards wheel of Second Army continued, bringing British forces to the south of Courtrai. Advance guards went forward, probing the defences and making use of cycles for transport where appropriate. On 19 October Courtrai was taken. In fact it was 'regained' as an advance unit of the 9/Royal Inniskilling Fusiliers (36th Division) had entered the town two days previously but been forced to retire due to enemy gun-fire. That night II Corps finally forced a crossing of the Lys and by the first light of 20 October, the whole of Second Army was across the river, or moving forward in support.

The various challenges relating to communications have featured regularly in the accounts of the fighting in Flanders. The pace and extent of the advance placed a heavy responsibility upon signals teams to ensure that some form of contact was maintained between unit headquarters and the forward troops; to allow progress to be monitored and for appropriate support to be provided. In addition to disruption from the enemy there remained the potential for the weather and the terrain to cause significant problems. Formations continued to adopt a wide range of methods of communication, no doubt working on a 'belt and braces' approach – at least one of the methods tried at any particular time would make the necessary connection. Reviewing its operations and the arrangements for communication employed during the battle, one divisional signals company concluded:

> TELEPHONIC AND TELEGRAPHIC
> Communication was at all times well maintained. During the whole period of operations communication was never lost to the Brigades, but great difficulty was experienced in maintaining the lines, which were very frequently cut. It was necessary at times to have as many as six lines to ensure communication at all.
>
> WIRELESS
> Wireless was used with success. Over 100 messages were sent during operations. This method of communication proved good.

143 TNA WO95/2610, War Diary of 120 Infantry Brigade.
144 TNA WO95/2594, War Diary of 40th Division.

> PIGEONS
> Pigeons were again used with great success. As on previous occasions, the first message to arrive from the front line after the attack had been launched was by Carrier Pigeon.
>
> VISUAL
> Four stations comprising the visual system were manned during the whole period of operations, but were never used.
>
> RUNNERS
> The usual system of 'runners' was employed, and was satisfactory. The state of the trenches, however, such as they were, made great delay in this service.
>
> DESPATCH RIDERS
> The roads were entirely impassable for motor cyclists, and Horse Despatch Riders had invariably to be used for work forward of FRICOURT.[145]

The advantages of wireless in comparison with wire communications (telephone and telegraph) in terms of reliability is notable, but the size of the necessary equipment and its related lack of mobility meant it could only be used for contact between the major headquarters at brigade level and above. Although there is concern at the amount of work involved in maintaining telephone links, there is a more positive view taken at brigade level. The war diary of 90 Brigade recorded that 'the new practice' of the laying of phone lines from battalions to brigade as the advance proceeded had been a success.[146]

Given the problems of enemy shelling and poor road connections, the most successful methods identified were those which had been used on battlefields over centuries: the carrier pigeon and the horse mounted despatch rider. This is a very vivid demonstration of how the attempts to come to terms with the immense changes in firepower and the technology of warfare by 1918, were constantly frustrated by the lack of an effective, secure and mobile form of battlefield communications. Given all the circumstances, perhaps we should express some admiration at the amount of communication that did actually take place, whilst recognising the limitations placed on offensive operations by the urgent need for an improved technology.

Much effort was focused on putting effective transport arrangements into place and to move resources and supplies forward in support of the front line troops. The pace of the advance allied to the poor roads and shelled terrain was causing problems. 41 Brigade noted:

> Owing to congestion of roads and bad traffic control over bridges transport of units seriously delayed.[147]

145 TNA WO95/2323, War Diary of 30th Divisional Signals Company … notes on operations during the period 11-21 [October].
146 TNA WO95/2338, War Diary of 90 Infantry Brigade, 20 October 1918.
147 TNA WO95/1894/6, War Diary of 41 Infantry Brigade.

As a consequence of further German withdrawals to the north, the French and Belgians were able to accelerate their advance. On 17 October the Belgians had entered Ostend. Two days later they were in Zeebrugge and Bruges.

19 October

II Corps

Original orders called for advance units to force a crossing of the River Lys during the night of 19/20 October. Towards midnight troops crossed the Lys via the pontoon bridges ('barrel raft' and 'barrel pier' constructions), with very light casualties overall. 5/Cameron Highlanders (26 Brigade, 9th Division) crossed at 2300 hours, establishing an initial bridgehead extending 250 yards east of the river; then moving 500 yards east of Harlebeke.[148] For 29th Division, 88 Brigade began ferrying men across the river from 1800 hours, via rafts and pontoons. Once a crossing of the river was forced then the division was to aim for the village of St. Louis and ultimately for the River Escaut. By 0130 hours, 2/Hampshires had successfully secured the Harlebeke-Courtrai Road east of the river, which was to be used as the assembly position pending a new attack.[149]

At 2330 hours, 36th Division HQ recorded that two of its battalions from 109 Brigade were now across the Lys. 9/Royal Inniskilling Fusiliers plus a unit of three machine guns was the first, working its way beyond the river and halting in front of Beveren (held by German machine gun teams), 400 yards east of the Courtrai-Ghent road. 1/Royal Inniskilling Fusiliers then crossed to its left, securing the left flank and, with the aid of covering artillery fire, pushed north-east. In turn the troops attacked the four small villages of Desselghem, Spriete, Straete and Dries, capturing the first three before consolidating on the western edge of the latter. In the divisional history the success of what was a difficult operation in terms of coordination and deployment, was put down to 'good staff work, intelligent local leadership, and the dash of the private soldier…'[150]

XIX Corps

35th Division delivered its planned attack across the Lys, capturing Marcke, with over 1,000 civilians 'released' as a consequence of the advance.[151] Around midday, two companies from 123 Brigade (41st Division) crossed the river, seeking to maintain touch with 35th Division, and subsequently reaching Courtrai Railway Station; during the rest of the day the brigade deployed in strength along the railway line and the canal.

148 TNA WO95/1765, War Diary of 7th Battalion, Seaforth Highlanders.
149 TNA WO95/2300, War Diary of 1st Battalion, Lancashire Fusiliers, 86th Infantry Brigade Order No. 280, October 19th 1918; TNA WO95/2307/4, War Diary of 88 Infantry Brigade; TNA WO95/2285, War Diary of 29th Division, Report on Operations, Period 14 October 1918-22 October 1918.
150 TNA WO95/2492, War Diary of 36th Division; TNA WO95/2509, War Diary of 109 Infantry Brigade; Falls, *36th Division*, pp. 281-4.
151 TNA WO95/2483, War Diary of 104 Infantry Brigade.

That afternoon further planning took place to prepare for a new operation on the following day, attacking in the direction of Sweveghem (three miles east of Courtrai). XIX Corps set final objectives as the River Scheldt between Bossuyt and Avelghem.

X Corps

There was fierce fighting for Belleghem as 101 Brigade struggled to secure the village in the face of determined resistance. The turning point was the capture by two companies from 2/ Loyal North Lancs of a farm on the northern edge; this threatened to outflank the Germans, whereupon the defence of the village ceased quickly; by 2300 hours, the battalion had cleared the village and reached the Courtrai road.[152] 34th Division was now ordered to withdraw into reserve positions.[153]

30th Division, its attacking formations continuing to be organised into brigade groups, maintained its drive for the line linking the hamlets of Belleghem and Ruddervoorde, although the opposing German forces 'appeared determined to hold up our advance' and enemy shellfire 'indicated that he intended to hold the line of L'ESCAUT RIVER'.[154] That night the brigade HQ issued orders for 2/14 London Regiment ('London Scottish') to continue to press forward on 20 October in order to reach the objective; the river would have to be attacked and taken by force.

> The London Scottish had now been fighting for some days, and were rather tired, but in excellent spirits. The Brigadier considered them fit to continue the advance.[155]

It had been decided to try replacing the field gun section attached to the forward battalion, with a mobile 4.5 inch howitzer. This was subsequently judged to have 'achieved good results'.[156]

The expectations of London Scottish were and remained high. At 1600 hours on 20 October the brigade's war diary states:

> The following message has been received from Div. tonight… [the] G.O.C. wishes to congratulate MAJOR WHYTE and all ranks of the London Scottish on the rapidity with which they reached their objective today and for the skilful way in which they fought forward … The Brigadier would also like to add his appreciation of the fine work done by the London Scottish during 10 days of hard fighting under the most difficult of conditions and wishes you all success in your advance to the final objective tonight… The Bde. has not yet failed to take all objectives allotted to it in this advance, and the Brigadier feels confident that the upholding of this reputation is safe in your keeping tonight.[157]

At just after midnight, the battalion made good the final objective of the L'Escaut River.

152 TNA WO95/2456, War Diary of 101 Infantry Brigade.
153 TNA WO95/2437, War Diary of 34th Division, Summary of War Diary for October 1918.
154 TNA WO95/2338, War Diary of 90 Infantry Brigade.
155 TNA WO95/2338, War Diary of 90 Infantry Brigade.
156 TNA WO95/2338, War Diary of 90 Infantry Brigade.
157 TNA WO95/2338, War Diary of 90 Infantry Brigade.

XV Corps

The advance troops of XV Corps were now in the vicinity of Heeseaux and Wattrelos, and the Canal east of Roubaix, seeking to push further east towards Dottignies and Leers Nord.[158] A realignment took place as 40th Division was withdrawn and 31st Division extended its line to the right to make touch with 59th Division.

19 October also saw a General Directive from Foch, instructing the GAF to advance in the general direction of Brussels. In response, Albert issued further orders for the GAF to move speedily to cross the Lys and the Deynze – Ecloo canal, thus denying the Germans the time to organise resistance. If resistance was encountered then 'the principal part in dislodging him would fall to the British Second Army'. This recognised that the success of the Army in already crossing the Lys put it in the position to rapidly exploit its gains and 'advance towards the Schelde'.[159] At the same time this would allow French and Belgian forces to make their way across the Lys and to move forward over the open ground ahead. The drive by the forces under XV Corps, able to take advantage of the hard fought gains by British troops to their north, saw an advance of around 15 miles between 16 and 19 October. The result brought Second Army formations into line on a north-south axis.

The outcome of the Battle of Courtrai had wider strategic implications, resulting from the consequent decision of the enemy to undertake a withdrawal from the coast. Allied forces were now able to drive for the border with Holland. This would bring control of the 'Bruges/Ostend/Zeebrugge triangle' incorporating the bases for the deadly U-boats and the last remaining threat that Germany could offer beyond its borders. The Germans had no choice but to recall this force or face the prospect of its capture – one of the prime objectives which Haig had sought when launching the battles of Third Ypres and Passchendaele twelve months earlier. In this way the success of the liberation offensive in Flanders removed a major plank from any hope the enemy had for continuing the war. The German withdrawal along its lines to the south also allowed the allies to outflank the manufacturing area formed by Lille, Roubaix and Tourcoing. Ludendorff had seen the retention of this region as an important bargaining chip in any negotiated peace – its loss meant a further weakening of any ability Germany retained to influence the war's outcome.[160] The Battle of Courtrai was now officially at an end – but not the drive by General Plumer and his Second Army to liberate Flanders.

158 TNA WO95/2356/5, War Diary of 92 Infantry Brigade.
159 Quoted from: Edmonds, *Official History 1918 Vol. V.*
160 Stevenson, *Backs to the Wall*, p. 165; reference Edmonds, *Official History 1918 Vol. V*, p. 293.

6

War of Movement: From the Lys to the Schelde, Second Army Operations 20 October-11 November

> [I]n 1918 the pressure was simply unrelenting. There was such a shortage of manpower that those units who could keep going were repeatedly used...
>
> Men were caught in an awful trap where they could see victory approaching but also knew that as things stood they might not live to see it, yet they fought on. This was self-sacrifice on a grand scale.[1]

The ground for what proved to be the final stage of the advance by British Second Army consisted largely of a ridge from which there were many spurs or smaller ridges. The land was predominantly agricultural and populated with numerous farms and cottages. The Bossuyt–Courtrai canal running south-east to north-west divided the area in two. Marshy land lay to the north but the whole area, due to heavy rainfall, was difficult going.

Second Army had learned many lessons from the fighting so far, not least the importance of having close artillery support available for the attacking infantry. 34th Division for example, made specific provision for this:

> A Brigade of Field Artillery [was] included in each Infantry Brigade Group... [in order to deliver] close and immediate Artillery support to our advancing infantry and to prevent checks'.[2]

The arrangements were also put in place for the divisional HQ to be informed of enemy gun positions so that heavy artillery fire could be called up. There were special instructions issued which reflected that 'the fighting of the last few days has become more mobile than has hitherto been the case and is now practically open warfare'.[3] While such steps were not as radical as the combined arms battlegroups created by 30th Division, the direct deployment of field guns

1 P. Hart, *1918: A Very British Victory*, (London: Wiedenfeld & Nicolson, 2008), p. 364.
2 Nicholson, 34th Division; the arrangements are described in Training Leaflet No 5: The Action of Artillery in Close Support of Assaulting Battalions .
3 Nicholson, 34th Division – culled from Field Service Regulations Part 1.

alongside the infantry could avoid the need for units to pause the advance while artillery support was requested.

Transport and supply remained an ongoing strain throughout the campaign. One example of the competing priorities is the Deputy Director Supply & Transport complaining on 30 October that the GOC Heavy Artillery had retained all the available lorries for siege guns only, concluding that 'this scheme is wrong in mobile warfare'.[4]

During this period there were further reports of German withdrawals. For example, given the situation in front of XV Corps, orders were issued which stressed the importance of advance units continuing to push forward and probe the enemy's defences. There is also reference to the potential deployment of mounted troops ahead of the infantry in order to reconnoitre enemy movement and dispositions.[5] Work continued along the Lys on the repair and construction of bridges. From 19-21 October, 202 Field Company, Royal Engineers (30th Division) concentrated on the construction of a 'super heavy pontoon bridge', capable of taking larger transport and artillery.[6]

The front line troops were increasingly weary from the exertions of the past month's fighting. On 20 October, the war diary of 7/Seaforth Highlanders (26 Brigade, 9th Division) makes reference to the 'tired condition of the troops' such that representations were made to delay a further push forward.[7] Some units had been in almost constant action for a sustained period. That same day, the war diary of 90 Brigade (30th Division) recorded:

> The Bde. had now been in action practically continuously since Aug. 15th, fighting almost the whole time and during that period had carried the 30th Division forward a distance of over 28 miles as the crow flies.[8]

The emergence of the flu pandemic was also beginning to be felt by the British forces. Two days later the same brigade noted that 'A considerable number of cases of the prevalent Influenza began to occur in the Brigade'. On a more positive note, on 24 October the war diary recorded that the three battalions 'all received drafts, the first for a very long time'.[9]

Peter Hart has summarised the fighting during the Hundred Days as 'some of the worst of the war ... what faced [British soldiers] was probably the hardest campaign ever fought by the British armed forces'.[10] He points out that, whereas in previous offensives such as the Somme and Third Ypres (Passchendaele) men had fought in the front line for a short number of days and then been withdrawn into support or reserve, there often proved to be no such break during the Hundred Days. He described the pressure as 'unrelenting' as the shortage of replacements meant that units had to spend longer periods in the front line. The pace and scale of the liberation offensive in Flanders also meant that it was more difficult to give troops time away from the front, although as we have seen, Second Army worked hard to rotate units between front

4 TNA WO95/292, Deputy Director Supply & Transport, Daily Visits and Inspections.
5 TNA WO95/1905, War Diary of 43 Infantry Brigade, Brigade Order No. 45.
6 TNA WO95/2323, War Diary of 202 Field Company, Royal Engineers (30th Division).
7 TNA WO95/1765, War Diary of 7th Battalion, Seaforth Highlanders.
8 TNA WO95/2338, War Diary of 90 Infantry Brigade.
9 TNA WO95/2338, War Diary of 90 Infantry Brigade.
10 Hart, *1918: A Very British Victory* , p. 364.

and reserve roles wherever possible. This form of pressure became more intense as the prospect of peace began to appear, and yet the men were having to continue to put their lives on the line.

In Second Army there is evidence of regular attempts to provide for the movement of units between front, support and reserve positions as the advance proceeded. Once the Army closed up to the Schelde – and the potential for an end to the war grew ever closer – whole divisions were starting to be withdrawn from the front line.

A snapshot of the roster of a battalion from 90 Brigade, 2/14 London Scottish, which had been heavily involved in the recent fighting as advance guard for the drive to the L'Escaut River, shows how much pressure there was on depleted troop resources in the front line. On 21 October 1918, the actual battalion strength was listed as:

41 Officers 764 Other Ranks.

These figures are below the full complement for a battalion, but still do not give the true picture. The actual 'fighting strength' was even lower:

25 Officers 539 Other Ranks (plus the Chaplain)

– due to the number of troops 'away'.

The table[11] below denotes where these 'missing' soldiers were:

Location	**Officers**	**Other Ranks**
Field Ambulance	6	92
Officer Rest Camp	1	1
Leave	5	70
Military Duty	–	13
F P Camp	–	1
Command	3	28
Courses	–	17
Detachment	1	3
TOTAL	16	225

As well as almost one hundred soldiers in receipt of medical treatment, of particular note is that 75 officers and men are on official leave, a high number given the ongoing demands on the battalion. It suggests that this remained a high priority despite the manpower problems and the pressure of the forward drive against the retreating German Army.

One week later, the problem of troop numbers was discussed at a conference of 120 Brigade (40th Division); the situation was considered to be so severe that a radical reorganisation was proposed:

11 TNA WO95/2340, War Diary of 2/14th Battalion, London Regiment.

> Owing to the under strength of Battalions it was decided to organise Companies on three platoon basis and, if necessary, subdivide platoons into three sections – 2 rifle and 1 Lewis Gun Section.[12]

This was a serious step, reducing the size of a company from four to three platoons. Crucially this reduction in boots on the ground was offset by increasing the reliance of the company upon the fire support from its Lewis guns.

II Corps was now advancing on a line from Hoogmolen (lying five miles east-south-east of Courtrai) then north-east through Ooteghem – Ingoyghem – Engelhoek. With the Army's left flank now positioned so as to cooperate with French forces, 36th Division was responsible for liaison. On 20 October, the 164th French Division reported that it was to send a brigade forward with the aim of crossing the Oyghem Bridge. During the afternoon the French line was advanced up to the junction of the Roulers canal and the River Lys, six miles north-east of Courtrai. An attack on the village of Leicant (Leikant) was initially successful but the Germans counter-attacked and the French were forced to retire.[13] The French were also reported to be unable to cross the Lys at that stage due to the absence of bridging materials, thereby delaying the advance of 36th Division.[14]

Having been at rest since 16 October, three days later at 2100 hours the units of 107 Brigade moved into assembly positions for taking over the lead position from 109 Brigade. A conference of battalion commanders at brigade HQ earlier that day had discussed the orders and arrangements for the crossing of the Lys and the subsequent attack. At 0200 hours on 20 October (a 'very wet night') the attack battalions (1/Royal Irish Rifles and 15/Royal Irish Rifles) moved forward. The enemy had continued to shell the Lys overnight and 'there was a direct hit on the bridge, a pontoon being damaged and a length of the superstructure destroyed'.[15] Engineers worked furiously to make good the repairs and the lead battalion crossed the river and assembled north-west of the Harlebeke – Vive St Eloi road; linking there with the forward units of 109 Brigade.

Following a creeping barrage, at 0600 hours the troops moved off, with some additional cover from an early morning mist. Beveren was soon captured but the attack then met heavy machine gun fire, and Lieutenant-Colonel B.J. Jones commanding 15/Royal Irish Rifles was amongst the casualties, subsequently confirmed as killed. Although the attack was checked on a number of occasions throughout the day – 'progress… was slow' – the main Courtrai-Ghent railway line was crossed before 0800 hours and the line was eventually halted west of the village of Knock, north-west of the River Gaverbeek. The village of Dries had been the one remaining position still held by the enemy, threatening the left flank of the advance, but was finally taken by 12/Royal Irish Rifles (108 Brigade) during the early hours of 21 October. In his history of 36th Division, Falls describes how it had been hoped that the advance by the French on the left of the division would support the pinching out of the Dries pocket. In the event the 133rd French

12 TNA WO95/2610, War Diary of 120 Infantry Brigade, 27 October 1918.
13 TNA WO95/2492, War Diary of 36th Division.
14 TNA WO95/2285, War Diary of 29th Division, Report on Operations, Period 14 October 1918-22 October 1918.
15 Falls, *36th Division*, p. 284.

Regiment was delayed by having to fight its way forward from the Lys and so it fell to British troops to capture the village.[16]

Overnight there was heavy shellfire onto the division's lines from enemy artillery, HE and gas, plus machine gun fire.[17] Within 29th Division, 86 Brigade swung its line to the south-east, pivoting on St Louis, and launched its attack under a covering barrage. For 88 Brigade a creeping barrage had been arranged. Both brigades adopted a one battalion front with supporting battalions moving up and through as the line of each objective was achieved. The village of Staceghem was reported captured at 0730 hours, the Esscher Wood at 1000 hours, and troops continued to press south eastwards. It should be noted that there are contradictions between the division, brigade and battalions' war diaries regarding the actual disposition of the attacking and support battalions: briefly, the 88 Brigade diary has the battalions moving forward in the initial order of 2/Hampshires (lead), 2/Leinsters (support) and 4/Worcesters (reserve); the division's record has a two battalion front attacking with 2/Leinsters (right) and 2/Hampshires (left); the battalion diaries are unclear. I suspect that the division wanted a two battalion front (which was consistent with the view of senior commanders) but 'on the ground' the brigades decided to operate the one battalion and leapfrogging arrangement.[18]

There was a strong emphasis throughout on the front units maintaining contact with their neighbours on the flanks; to ensure that the advance of Second Army was made in concert with a steady and coherent forward manoeuvre across the allied front.[19] 41st Division was checked around Courtrai and touch was lost for a time with 29th Division on its left.[20] II Corps issued orders for the advance to be resumed on 22 October, once its three divisions were in line and contact re-established with 41st Division.

Through such operations the enemy was subject to a constant pressure and opportunities to check the British troops by enfilade fire were prevented. One can now sense an almost irresistible momentum to the forward movement of Second Army and its French and Belgian allies. This is clearly demonstrated by Maps 8 and 8A which denote the lines of advance from 4 to 30 October. One can also detect the hardening of German defence in front of the Schelde – and the corresponding operational fatigue that must have been a growing factor for the advancing allied troops.

20 October also saw 35th Division (XIX Corps) attack in a south-east direction. After assembly east of Courtrai the attack commenced at 0615 hours on a broad frontage, with 104 Brigade on the right, 105 Brigade in the centre (its own left following the line of the Courtrai-Bossuyt Canal), and 88 Brigade of 29th Division to the left. There was no artillery barrage to cover the advance but the troops made good progress, with the exception of 4/North Staffs. The battalion was delayed in front of the small hamlet of Blokken (lying about two miles east of Courtrai) by:

16 Falls, *36th Division*, pp. 285-6.
17 TNA WO95/2502/1, War Diary of 107 Infantry Brigade, Narrative of Operations carried out by the 107th Inf. Bde. 28.9.1918. to 28.10.1918.
18 TNA WO95/2285, War Diary of 29th Division, Report on Operations, Period 14 October 1918-22 October 1918; TNA WO95/2307/4, War Diary of 88 Infantry Brigade.
19 TNA WO95/2299, War Diary of 86 Infantry Brigade.
20 TNA WO95/2285, War Diary of 29th Division, Report on Operations, Period 14 October 1918-22 October 1918.

> [S]everal machine guns and two 15c.m. Howitzers, the latter firing over open sights at our advancing troops who were but three hundred or four hundred yards distance.[21]

Shortly after 0700 hours the hamlet of Beekstraat (one mile south of Blokken) was captured; at 0730 hours there were troops on the outskirts of Sweveghem village. This was a period of intense fighting as the German defenders sought to hold back the attacking forces:

> Up to this point the fighting, along the whole of the [105] Brigade Front, had been very heavy and dangerous owing to the exposed nature of the ground and stout manner in which the enemy contested the approach of every farm. Advantage was taken of ditches and by crawling up these our troops were able to work round the flanks of the enemy's Machine Gun nests and Farms.[Having taken most of Sweveghem village]... shortly before 0900 the enemy, reinforced, worked forward into the village and for some time very heavy fighting ensued in the neighbourhood of the church, during which we suffered heavy casualties. Eventually our troops were forced back to the Western outskirts of Sweveghem where they were heavily fired upon by the enemy's artillery and Machine Guns causing further casualties.[22]

This account of the clashes occurring as the troops of 35th Division fought their way forward from Courtrai (taken from the war diary of 105 Brigade) provides a succinct picture of the warfare in Flanders during this final stretch of the campaign. It does not show a beaten enemy or German defenders whose will to resist has been lost. Nor does it present a British Army lacking in initiative, commitment or drive. These diary records describe a mode of warfare that would have been very familiar to British forces engaged in a later war in Europe – fighting their way up the Italian peninsular, scrambling through the bocage of Normandy, or street fighting in French towns, in 1944. It is also a very different kind of warfare from the popular image of the First World War which sees a picture comprised of lines of trenches, and a barren landscape; featuring 'the big push' which colours modern perceptions. These British soldiers are fighting their way through strong and determined enemy resistance, farm by farm, hamlet by village, to liberate an occupied country. This is the dark side of war – dirty, challenging, confused, dangerous – where nothing is won easily or without pain.

Army operations reports concluded that 'hard fighting has taken place for all high ground, where the enemy has defended himself obstinately... [the] fighting... has been severe'.[23] The forward drive by the troops of 35th Division was not to be stopped however, as this extract from the war diary of 105 Brigade shows:

> Commanders of the Field Batteries were sent forward to get in touch with Battalion Commanders but the situation was so obscure that very little was possible in the way of Artillery Support. On the left, the 4th North Staffordshire Regiment had overcome the enemy resistance at BLOKKEN at about 0900 and resumed the advance but this progressed very slowly and was eventually held up before the North Western outskirts of

21 TNA WO95/2486, War Diary of 105 Infantry Brigade.
22 TNA WO95/2486, War Diary of 105 Infantry Brigade.
23 TNA WO158/218 Summary of Operations, Week ending 25 October 1918.

> SWEVEGHEM ... At about 1100 a heavy artillery barrage was put down on the Ridge South East of the stream KIEBEK and was continued until 1200 but the intensity of the Machine Gun fire, being in no way diminished, the 15th Cheshire Regiment were unable to push forward as ordered. At 1330, when the enemy's resistance was less determined, the 15th Cheshire Regiment pushed patrols across the KEIBEEK, the 15th Sherwood Foresters entered and captured SWEVEGHEM and the 4th North Staffordshire Regiment resumed the advance on the Left, but after a short period of time, our line which ran along the Eastern outskirts of SWEVEGHEM and the South eastern side again became stationary and the left of the 4th North Staffordshire Regiment was much exposed to fire from the Northern side of the CANAL.[24]

After a further pause to take stock of the situation, 35th Division issued new orders for the objectives to be captured. At 2330 hours, a new attack by 105 Brigade supported by an artillery barrage made progress, taking the line of the Kreupel-Pontlevis Bridge (one and a half miles south-east of Sweveghem). Overnight the Germans were still holding the neighbouring Kappelle Milaene Farm, but a sharp action at 0500 hours compelled them to withdraw.[25]

Elsewhere on the 35th Division front, troops were moving towards the village of Hoogstraatje (less than half a mile south of the Courtrai Bossuyt Canal). 106 Brigade moved through 104 Brigade to take up position. Although delayed in part because of the weather conditions, the attack began shortly after the set start time of 1715 hours, supported by a creeping barrage. Progress was steady – and early the following morning the support battalion, 17/Royal Scots, was ordered forward so as to align with the left of 106 Brigade's forward battalions (12/Highland Light Infantry and 18/Highland Light Infantry); and then to make a link with Hoogstraatje. These moves were successful; the battalion sent patrols up from the west of the village to the canal, thereby establishing a direct line on the division's front and securing the objective.[26]

With the advance of Second Army gathering pace as it pursued the withdrawing German forces, it was crucial to maximise the effectiveness of the artillery fire support for the infantry. The need was for clear guidelines and instructions that reflected the new demands of this war of movement – this war of manoeuvre – that faced the British forces. In many respects any new directions would only be confirming what was already happening in practice on the ground – we have already seen various references to different methods of partnering infantry and artillery when on the attack; for example, attaching a field gun and crew to a company of infantry, or placing an artillery liaison officer at the forward HQ of a battalion.

Senior officers were obviously anxious to ensure that there was the closest possible co-operation between the two arms, not least to minimise the potential number of casualties amongst the infantry when an attack was launched on enemy positions. The following examples are taken from the updated instructions issued by 34th Division in October 1918:

24 TNA WO95/2486, War Diary of 105 Infantry Brigade.
25 TNA WO95/2486, War Diary of 105 Infantry Brigade.
26 TNA WO95/2489, War Diary of 106 Infantry Brigade.

34th Division: General Staff Instructions No. 14 21-10-1918

- During the present open warfare a Brigade of Field Artillery is included in each Infantry Brigade Group. The object of this distribution is to provide close and immediate Artillery Support to our advancing infantry and to prevent checks.
- These Artillery Brigades will be under the command of [the] Brigades to whose group they are attached and the Artillery Brigade Commander will invariably accompany the G.O.C. Infantry Brigade and act as his Artillery Adviser.
- ... further Artillery support... will be provided from the Artillery of the Brigade Groups in support or reserve. The Artillery sent up in support and the Artillery of the Brigade Group in action will then come under Divisional control.
- The normal method of action for the Artillery of a Brigade Group [includes]:
  Sections can be pushed forward with Battalions; batteries put into action to cover the advance against any particular locality or to take on any fleeting opportunity.
  - The guns in action will, of course, engage any hostile guns which can be seen but locations of any such hostile guns should be sent in to Divisional Headquarters at once to enable Heavy Artillery to engage them also.
  - Application to Divisional Headquarters for Artillery support should not be made until the full power of the Artillery of a Brigade Group has been employed.
  - It should be pointed out to all Battalion and Company Commanders that this Artillery is under the immediate command of their own Brigadier and demands for Artillery support should be made to Infantry Brigade Headquarters. The message should when possible, be supplemented by sending an Officer or good N.C.O. to the nearest guns in action who will probably be able to deal with the situation at once.
  - Attention is drawn to Training Leaflet No.5, 'The Action of Artillery in CLOSE Support of Assaulting Battalions'. The present form of warfare gives splendid opportunities for practising the very excellent methods laid down in this pamphlet.
- The principal role of Heavy Artillery will be Counter-Battery work; the assistance of Heavy Artillery for bombardment will only be available if a very strong and obstinate centre of resistance is encountered.[27]

These orders can be seen to have consolidated the existing good practice, and provided clear rules for the exercise of command and control between infantry and artillery commanders.

There was a also a growing recognition that an even greater flexibility during operations was called for if the Army was to take full advantage of the momentum of the recent advances. This was seen to place particular responsibilities on officers and section leaders. The pace of the advance created the need for far greater initiative to be demonstrated as an attack developed and different challenges arose – which had to be confronted and overcome by those soldiers on the ground, in order to maintain the forward thrust of the infantry. These factors are reflected in the following examples from a further set of instructions from 34th Division, issued two days after the new rules regarding artillery co-operation:

27 TNA WO95/2437, War Diary of 34th Division, General Staff Instructions No. 14, 21-10-1918.

<u>34th Division: General Staff Instructions No. 15 23-10-1918</u>

- The fighting of the last few days has become more mobile than has hitherto been the case and is now practically open warfare.
  This fact necessitates a certain re-arrangement of ideas on the part of all commanders and the following paragraphs are written as a guide to such re-arrangements.
- Field Service Regulations Part I is still the true guide for all troop leading, and it is essential that all commanders down to Section and fire-unit commanders should study it.
- Headquarters of Infantry and Artillery Brigades and of Battalion Commanders must be further forward than is the case in trench warfare. This does not mean that every Battalion and Bde. Commander should be in a position whence he can control the movements of every unit under his command, but he should be so located with reference to the troops engaged and the positions of reserves, that he can influence the progress and action of the fight by the use of his reserves and auxiliary weapons. To do this effectively, two things are necessary: observation of the greater part of the area in which the action is taking place, and close proximity to reserve troops. Of the two, the latter is the more important provided that communications with troops engaged are in good order.

The instructions then proceed to specify in detail the responsibility of the unit commander for taking control of the situation when an advance stalls because of enemy resistance. While the rules are quite prescriptive in outline, they have the effect of empowering the commander to assess the immediate problems and take decisions as he interprets the prevailing circumstances. These decisions included the deployment of fire support, auxiliary weapon teams, and unit reserve troops:

- The moment these communications fail or the advance is checked, the Commander must go forward, taking his reserve and auxiliary arm commanders with him, at the same time maintaining communication with his reserves, and get into touch with the situation, making if necessary a personal reconnaissance: he should then interview his subordinate commanders and issue the necessary orders on the spot, including instructions for the employment of reserves and auxiliary arms: Only by this means can a Commander ensure the effective co-operation of the different arms at his disposal, retain control of the fight and impress his own personality upon the course of events.

Finally, the instructions sought to take account of particular issues presented by the defensive methods applied by the Germans:

- The enemy is now fighting rearguard actions. The object of every rearguard action is to make advancing troops deploy. It follows therefore that premature deployment should be guarded against. No more troops than are actually necessary should be employed until the enemy has been located in some definite position. When this has been done the position must be attacked without delay with sufficient troops, Artillery and M.G. support to make its capture a certainty.

- Troops should not be dispersed on too wide a front. They are more easily controlled in depth and disposition in depth facilitates disposition for an attack as indicated in para.4. To cover a Brigade front of 2000 yards and over, if opposition is expected, with one Battalion is unsound.
- The practice of delegating responsibility for the co-operation of Artillery and Machine Guns to subordinate commanders should not be overdone.

  No more than a Battery of Artillery or Section of a M.G.Coy. should ever be attached to one Infantry Battalion. Battalion Commanders must keep control of the Artillery and Machine Guns attached to them in their own hands, and should employ them on certain definite tasks which may if necessary include the pushing forward of sections of Artillery (never single guns) or ½ sections of M.Gs.[28]

These points reflect a number of apparent concerns in the minds of senior commanders and staff. There is the desire to conserve troop numbers and not to take risks that will result in unnecessary casualties. To this end there is a heavy emphasis on maximising the fire support available to the infantry when assaulting occupied and defended enemy positions. There have been many previous references in the descriptions of Second Army operations where attacking brigades have deployed on a one battalion front. While this in itself was probably the result of concerns to not risk too many troops in the firing line at any one time, a new problem could be created in that the attack would not prove to be sufficiently strong for the size of the front. Hence the guidance that a front of 2000 yards should be treated as a maximum for one battalion to assault. In addition, these orders make it clear that commanders are expected to take full responsibility for the combined arms nature of the forces they lead. In other words, they have the benefit of being supplied with a broad range of resources (in terms of the quality and quantity and variety of the available weaponry) and they are expected to make full use of these.

20 October also saw 1/6 Cheshires of 21 Brigade (30th Division) carry out an 'advanced guard action' in pursuit of the retreating Germans. The latter made a final stand on the ridge below the hamlet of Saint Genois. Under the cover of darkness the position was successfully 'stormed and captured'.[29] Meanwhile II Corps had been ordered to 'stand fast until flanks come up into line' at which point 9th Division would move through to drive for the Scheldt.[30]

Map 9 illustrates the progress of Second Army operations through the period 20-27 October 1918.

Over the next few days the troops of II Corps continued to push the enemy back. On 21 October, 36th Division launched an attack with units from 107 and 108 Brigades, operating in conjunction with the 133rd French Infantry Regiment; there was no artillery barrage. Touch was temporarily lost with the 133rd Regiment – 'As the French on our left were unable to advance it was found necessary for a Coy. of the 12th Royal Irish Rifles to take up a position to guard our left flank which was exposed'.[31] That day also brought a brigade of French cavalry as an attachment to the division in order to assist with liaison, as well as for reconnaissance and support. There were reports of the cavalry looking to attempt to break through on the 107

28 TNA WO95/2437, War Diary of 34th Division, General Staff Instructions No. 15, 23-10-1918.
29 TNA WO95/2330, War Diary of 1/6th Battalion, Cheshire Regiment.
30 TNA WO95/1771/5, War Diary of 27 Infantry Brigade.
31 TNA WO95/2504, War Diary of 108 Infantry Brigade.

Brigade front though this did not materialise.[32] On the left of Second Army there were reports of French operations in the area of Spitaals Bosche Wood and the village of Waereghem.[33]

On the following day units from all three divisions in II Corps were involved in operations focused on and around Vichte. Subsequent reports from prisoners stated that orders had been given for it to be held 'at all costs' but if taken then the German defenders should fall back northwards in the direction of Waereghem.[34] The village was successfully captured, together with Hill 50 to the south. However, attempts to then push on towards Ingoyghem met heavy enemy fire from both that village and the village of Ooteghem, such that '… it was obvious that no progress could be made to INGOYGHEM until OOTEGHEM was taken'.[35]

Further south, 41st Division attacked through 35th Division, the latter then withdrawing in order to refresh. The objective was the line of the River L'Escaut from Bossuyt to Autryve. Initial progress was very good but some home-made problems caused subsequent delays as the war diary of 124 Brigade describes:

> The attack … met very little opposition to begin with, and progress was rapid especially on the right where the Durham L.I. [20/Durham Light Infantry] were able to push ahead, and by noon had occupied the villages of BAVEGHEMKNOK… and POELDRIESCH …On the left, progress was slower, the enemy holding the tunnel over the COURTRAI-BUSSUYT Canal … in considerable strength. The 10th Queens R.W.S. Regt. [Royal West Surrey Regiment] had to cross the canal by this passage in order to work down the N.E. bank, but were blocked by troops of the [122] Inf. Bde. who were in front and failed to force this strongly wired and defended enemy position. In the meantime, the 26th Bn. Royal Fusiliers passed through The 'Queens', and against considerable opposition occupied the DUIKINGBERG-ACHTERBERG Road … facing the Canal.[36]

That night, 41st Division consolidated the line Poeldriesch-Baveghemknok, pending a further drive forward in the morning.[37]

Also on 21 October, 30th Division made its arrangements to drive across the Scheldt. During the morning 1/6 Cheshire's captured the hamlet of Helghin (Helchin).[38] Currie's brigade group assumed the lead position for the division, advancing to establish posts along the west bank of the river; all the existing bridges had been destroyed by the enemy. The prospects of a daylight crossing were considered unlikely, given the weight of the fire from the German defenders; the group was ordered to seek for an opportunity to make an assault that night. Initially frustrated, it was dusk on 22 October when Royal Engineers were able to construct a pontoon bridge for the troops. One platoon of 2/South Lancs managed to cross but was then forced to withdraw by heavy artillery and machine gun fire.

32 TNA WO95/2492, War Diary of 36th Division.
33 TNA WO95/1771/5, War Diary of 27 Infantry Brigade.
34 TNA WO95/1771/5, War Diary of 27 Infantry Brigade, 23 October.
35 TNA WO95/1771/4/5, War Diary of 27 Infantry Brigade, Narrative of Operations 28 September-28 October 1918.
36 TNA WO95/2642, War Diary of 124 Infantry Brigade, Report on Operations commencing 20 October 1918.
37 TNA W095/2618, War Diary of 41st Division.
38 TNA WO95/2330, War Diary of 1/6th Battalion, Cheshire Regiment.

The following day saw the bridge partially destroyed by enemy shells and it was again at dusk when engineers were able to put two new bridges in place; one in front of 2/South Lancs, one in front of 2/17 London Regiment. Three South Lancs platoons fought their way across but were again pushed back. Their pontoon bridge was destroyed during the fighting and the surviving troops were forced to crawl along the other bridge in order to get back to the west bank. The Germans were holding the east bank of the river 'in strength… [particularly] enemy snipers and M.Gs.'.[39]

During 22 October, II Corps continued its advance with the aim of seizing the crossings over the Escaut, contact now having been re-established with the neighbouring French forces. The 5th French Division had captured St Hubert. The 4th French Cavalry Brigade was placed under 29th Division with the aim of passing through the advancing infantry to seize crossings over the Scheldt at Avelghem, Rugge and Berchem; should the bridges be destroyed, the cavalry were to drive north east along the river and attempt to impede enemy defensive operations.[40]

At 0900 hours, 36th Division, 107 Brigade leading, attacked towards and through Knock. This advance was subsequently met by a determined counter-attack on the left flank of the brigade in the early afternoon. This opportunity for the enemy had been created through 108 Brigade failing to keep pace with the advance. The attack prompted 107 Brigade to send forward reserve units though in the event the Germans were pushed back without the extra manpower being required. The strength of the enemy assault is shown by the fact that neighbouring units were also being pushed back before the line was re established.[41]

There were subsequent reports from prisoners that suggested this enemy attack had been a determined effort to 'turn the Klijtberg Ridge position from the North' and that it had been 'carried out by a Prussian Assault Battalion sent up for the purpose'. This is evidence of the increasing concern of German commanders to take all possible steps to delay the advancing British forces so that the planned withdrawal could proceed at a manageable pace. Further evidence from prisoners confirmed the decision of the Germans to pull back in an easterly direction.[42]

During the day, 36th Division captured and consolidated the Klijtberg Ridge. The intensity of the fighting taking place and the instances of fierce enemy resistance are reflected in the need for 27 Brigade (9th Division) to be reinforced by 8/Black Watch from 28 Brigade in order to ensure there were no gaps in the British line and that the captured ground could be consolidated effectively.[43] 29th Division also came up against strong opposition and only limited progress was made. French Cavalry patrols encountered very heavy machine gun fire and any outflanking manoeuvre by them was considered impossible.[44]

That same morning, 41st Division, utilising the temporary footbridge erected at Knokke, attacked along the north-east bank of the Courtrai-Bossuyt Canal. This move was checked by

39 TNA WO95/2332, War Diary of 89 Infantry Brigade.
40 TNA WO95/2285, War Diary of 29th Division, Report on Operations, Period 14 October 1918-22 October 1918.
41 TNA WO95/1771/5, War Diary of 27 Infantry Brigade, as recorded at 1716 hours on 22 October.
42 TNA WO95/2502/1, War Diary of 107 Infantry Brigade.
43 TNA WO95/1771/5, War Diary of 27 Infantry Brigade.
44 TNA WO95/2285, War Diary of 29th Division, Report on Operations, Period 14 October 1918-22 October 1918.

heavy machine gun fire, and intense fighting broke out around Keiberg. 12/East Surreys flanked left and right of the canal tunnel (which civilians had reported as mined); Stokes mortars were used to take out the machine guns still firing from within.[45] A fresh attack was made at 1400 hours and after some heavy fighting the north bank of the canal tunnel was cleared. This position was secured and held until relief by 34th Division on the night of 23 October. 41st Division then 'side stepped Northwards' to relieve 29th Division along a line facing Hoogmolen.[46]

Reports to II Corps HQ in the evening spoke of hard fighting right across the front line with a number of references referring to the use by the enemy artillery of gas shells in its defensive barrages. At 0730 hours on the following day, the Germans were reported to be retiring along the front of VII French Corps.[47] By noon, it was reported that 29th Division had taken Ooteghem but this proved to be premature. However the fighting taking place there allowed 9th Division to consider an attack from the south towards Hill 50 where the enemy was still resisting. At 1301 hours, 6/King's Own Scottish Borderers reported the capture of the Hill. Enemy fire from in and around the village of Ingoyghem continued to cause problems for II Corps forces.[48]

On 23 October, 36th Division sent forward advance guards, moving towards the Escaut at Tenhove. Later that morning there was a demonstration of the commitment of the French to co-operate with Second Army:

> [1110 hours]
> Captain DESNOYERS, Commanding 3rd Squadron, 28th Regt. de Dragons [sic], French Army, reported to [107] Brigade Commander. He was instructed to proceed towards TENHOVE, to try to seize KLEINEBERG and BERGWIJK and bridge over L'ESCAUT.[49]

However long range enemy machine gun fire proved sufficient to prevent much progress and the squadron was subsequently withdrawn. Falls describes how 'a squadron of French dragoons… made a spirited dash for the Escaut crossing at Berchen, but came under heavy machine-gun fire from the second line of hills, which it was evident the enemy held in force.[50]

On the left of the division, 108 Brigade was striving to maintain contact with the 41st French Chasseurs, coming up against particular difficulties at the railway halt at Heirweg (Heinweg) due to German machine gun fire. An 'International Post' was subsequently established at the nearby level crossing.[51]

In front of the division the Germans were occupying strong positions, defending a line (north to south) Heinweg – Huisbosch – Scheidhoek – Ingoyghem. 109 Brigade now took over the front line role. In recognition of the hard fighting it had taken part in, 107 Brigade was withdrawn

45 TNA W095/2618, War Diary of 41st Division.
46 TNA WO95/2642, War Diary of 124 Infantry Brigade, Report on Operations commencing 20 October 1918.
47 TNA WO95/2492, War Diary of 36th Division.
48 TNA WO95/1771/5, War Diary of 27 Infantry Brigade.
49 TNA WO95/2502/1, War Diary of 107 Infantry Brigade, Narrative of Operations carried out by the 107th Inf. Bde. 28.9.1918. to 28.10.1918.
50 Falls, *36th Division*, p. 287.
51 TNA WO95/2504, War Diary of 108 Infantry Brigade.

into divisional support and for training. For 14th Division, 42 Brigade spent most of 24 and 25 October making 'endeavours… to find any possible means of crossing River L'ESCAUT'.[52]

16/Manchesters subsequently crossed on 29 October and established advance posts on the eastern side. The attack took the form of three 'assault parties', each with its Lewis gun teams placed so as to provide covering fire. There was also a fire plan for support from trench mortars and artillery.[53] 41Brigade took over the new line on the final night of the month.

On 24 October, 41st Division attacked the Hoogmolen Spur but was beaten back by heavy machine gun fire. The division would now take part in the 'Action of Ooteghem' which was planned to take place the following day.[54]

The Germans had set up intermediate defensive positions to the east of the Lys. Some were heavily wired and carefully sited to maximise the effectiveness of the defence. Their lack of troops led the Germans to maximise the use of the resources available to them, notably field guns deployed well-forward, snipers, and reinforced machine gun posts. These arrangements appear to have been intended to delay the attacking forces while the German Army sought to re-establish itself on the *Hermann Position* beyond the River Schelde. The existence of these defences does not appear to have been detected in advance by Second Army. Supporting artillery was still being transported forward – until 24 October, most heavy guns and howitzers were awaiting the completion of satisfactory bridges across the Lys. The war diary of 36th Division for that day noted that a bridge was to be constructed over the Bossuyt Canal which was robust enough to take horse transport.[55] Infantry found themselves advancing without significant artillery cover other than attached field guns. The marshy ground, made worse through the heavy rainfall, made progress difficult.

One of the more unexpected problems of supply during this period was recorded in the war diary of 43 Brigade. The Medical Officer of 20/Middlesex had approached the ADMS complaining about *[the]* "difficulty of supplying [Battalion] men with dentures."[56] Whether or not the problem was resolved is not stated.

Air support was minimal due to the continuing bad weather and its impact on visibility, although the RAF was now able to move squadrons forward to occupy former German aerodromes.[57] The lack of air reconnaissance caused problems for operational planning, in terms of knowledge of the terrain, enemy movement, and the deployment and targeting of the artillery.

Progress along the line was further hampered by the slow advance of the French Sixth Army to the left of British forces. The enemy was increasing its resistance in front of Second Army because it was essential to hold these positions until its units opposing the French could themselves pull back. The delay in the French advance was also causing II Corps to again have to regulate its own rate of progress in line with that of its ally. The Second Army operations report concluded that 'the flank of the 36th Division was consequently refused'.[58]

52 TNA WO95/1899, War Diary of 42 Infantry Brigade.
53 TNA WO95/1899, War Diary of 42 Infantry Brigade, Brigade Order No.32, 29 October 1918 and Artillery and Stokes Mortar Time Table and Targets.
54 TNA WO95/2642, War Diary of 124 Infantry Brigade, Report on Operations commencing 20 October 1918.
55 TNA WO95/2492, War Diary of 36th Division.
56 TNA WO95/1905, War Diary of 43 Infantry Brigade, 25 October 1918.
57 TNA WO158/218 Summary of Operations, week ending 25 October 1918.
58 TNA WO158/218 Summary of Operations, week ending 25 October 1918 .

Action of Ooteghem: 25 October 1918

The circumstances improved for Second Army's increasingly weary formations from 25 October, although there were exceptions. 7/Seaforth Highlanders recorded that they were prevented from a further advance by the weight of machine gun and shellfire.[59] Orders for 36th Division were to continue the advance with artillery support, with the immediate objectives of Hofdries – Caenkouter – Caster; to be followed by a drive for the Scheldt. 9th Division was set the objective of the village of Tiegham. If these attacks were successful then the 4th Cavalry Brigade was on stand-by to pass through the line after Tiegham, followed by a wheel left in order to capture the neighbouring high ground. This proved to be optimistic given the strong resistance from the German defenders, and the exploitation by the cavalry was deferred. Evidence of the determination of the enemy to hold up the British advance was noted in 36th Division's diary, there being 'very few cases of surrender' and 'in many cases enemy soldiers continued firing M.G.s until bayonetted'.[60]

Notwithstanding these delays, by 25 October heavy artillery was finally in place to support a set-piece attack. Plumer identified the line of the Schelde as the objective. Involved in what has been designated as the 'Action of Ooteghem' were north to south):

II Corps (9th and 36th Divisions)
XIX Corps (41st Division)
X Corps (34th Division)

(With the co-operation of the French 164th Division and a French cavalry brigade).

In addition, 35th Division was put on stand-by to relieve 41st Division on completion of the operation.

Commencing 0940 hours, the infantry moved forward under the cover of a creeping barrage. The artillery support was not wholly successful as the war diary of 124 Brigade (41st Division) explains:

> Our barrage was put down at Zero minus 4, practically on our original front line, in order not to miss any enemy posts which were close thereto, but it appeared fairly certain that the enemy suspected our attack, and withdrew his forward posts about 300 yards. He replied to our barrage in about three to four minutes, putting it down just in front of our original front line, and, in consequence, in moving up to this position, and onto[?] our barrage, the Brigade suffered a fair number of casualties, especially amongst officers, the 26th Roy. Fus. [Royal Fusiliers] losing four and the 20th D.L.I. [Durham Light Infantry] two or three in the first five minutes.[61]

The attack was pressed home to take and consolidate the high ground east of the village of Ooteghem, despite the weight of enemy machine gun fire from the north. 41st Division

59 TNA WO95/1765, War Diary of 7th Battalion, Seaforth Highlanders.
60 TNA WO95/2492, War Diary of 36th Division.
61 TNA WO95/2642, War Diary of 124 Infantry Brigade, Report on Operations commencing 20 October 1918.

captured the high ground around Hoogemolen by 0945 hours then advanced on Kiebermolen. 11/Queens (123 Brigade) was reported to have cleared Heersteert by 1420 hours. There were however further frustrations with units of 9th Division subsequently forced to withdraw from Ooteghem, as the result of a 'mistaken order'. In so doing they also caused the left flank of 124 Brigade to pull back from the forward slopes above the village although this position was subsequently recovered.

By mid-afternoon, 9th Division was being held at Zaveleinde, 34th Division was making limited progress and had lost touch with 41st Division, while the latter ordered 124 Brigade to refuse the left flank (given the check to 9th Division) and ensure it was in touch with 123 Brigade (which was advancing on Avelghem).[62] During the night, advance patrols pushed forward along the road from Driesch to the outskirts of the village.[63]

102 Brigade of 34th Division was located just east of the Courtrai-Bossuyt Canal and it was from these positions that its troops attacked alongside their colleagues from 41st Division. The successful outcome was the clearing of the whole front of the canal, from Knocke southwards, including the capture of Moen. This latter operation by 1/4 The Cheshires, saw the village 'smoked'; following this barrage the troops surrounded the dwellings and then moved in to carry out the mopping up. By the evening, the British forces had secured a stretch of the River Scheldt running southwards from Autryve to Bossuyt. The previous night had seen 1/7 The Cheshires make two attempts to cross the Canal at Locks 3 and 4, but they had been beaten back. On the afternoon of 25 October they made a third successful attack, allowing them to join up with 1/4 The Cheshires, south-east of Moen. The 34th Division also captured Autryve as part of the operation.[64]

The Action of Ooteghem was a partial success, the southern divisions (34th and 41st) achieving their objectives but II Corps had been frustrated in its attempt to capture Ooteghem itself. The war diary of 5/Cameron Highlanders recorded that '... the Enemy's counter Barrage was the heaviest yet experienced since the 28 Sept.'[65] The weekly operations record for Second Army applies classic understatement to its reporting of the fighting which took place, concluding that it 'was of a severe character'.[66] Such commentary is unusual and confirms that there had been intense fighting at close quarters.

Scout patrols sent out on the morning of 26 October reported that the Germans had evacuated large areas of the front, retreating to the east of the Escaut. It was likely that this information originated from local Belgians, as the war diary of 18/King's Royal Rifle Corps recorded:

> [Advance patrols] met civilians who reported that Driesch and Avelghem were clear of the enemy; forward patrols confirmed this position.[67]

62 TNA W095/2618, War Diary of 41st Division.
63 TNA WO95/2642, War Diary of 124 Infantry Brigade, Report on Operations commencing October 20th 1918.
64 TNA WO95/2437, War Diary of 34th Division, Summary of War Diary for October 1918.
65 TNA WO95/1767, War Diary of 5th Battalion, Cameron Highlanders.
66 TNA WO158/218 Operations Reports; TNA WO95/2486, War Diary of 105 Infantry Brigade.
67 TNA WO95/2365, War Diary of 18th Battalion, King's Royal Rifle Corps.

The subsequent move forwards by 41st Division into Avelghem was followed by heavy enemy shelling of the village. (The last enemy patrol seen leaving the village fired 'a white light' as it left, interpreted as the signal for the barrage). The report of 124 Brigade lists the various villages entered by its troops as they advanced: Avelghem, Waffelstraat, Rugge, Kaphoek, Langestraat, Bosch, and Kloosterhoek. That night 41st Division was relieved by 35th Division.[68]

The war diary of 36th Division records information from prisoners suggesting the Germans were now carrying out a further withdrawal to the River Schelde (Scheldt);[69] instilling an urgency into further progress by the British forces. X and XV Corps on the right of the Army's front, were now able to extend the length of the line held on the west bank of the Schelde. The 26th Brigade of 9th Division now occupied Ooteghem, but II Corps was still short of the west bank. Air action on 27 October saw 14 German aircraft and 6 balloons shot down, for the loss of 6 RAF planes.[70]

The 26 October also brought the start of a realignment of the Corps fronts and the deployment of divisions, to allow some rest for those units which had borne the brunt of the fighting. For instance, 34th Division was transferred to II Corps, relieving the 36th Division on the front facing the Anseghem-Langestraat Ridge.[71] 40th Division returned to the line, allowing 31st Division to redeploy north. There were now just seven divisions operating in the line, while the Army continued to retain the four corps command structure.

From 28 October the disposition of Second Army, north-to-south, was as follows:

II Corps	34th Division 35th Division
XIX Corps	31st Division
X Corps	30th Division 29th Division
XV Corps	14th Division 40th Division

On the night of 27-28 October, 42 Brigade (14th Division) relieved units of 40th Division to its right and also took over the line from 30th Division on its left.[72]

Thus the first seven days of action beyond the Lys had produced a limited advance by Second Army of no more than seven miles, which represented poor progress when compared with earlier forward moves. Crucially however the right wing of the Army had now reached the Schelde.

The 40th Division operated under daily orders combining defence arrangements with an emphasis on continuing to advance in the event of enemy withdrawal'.[73] Its advance patrols

68 TNA WO95/2642, War Diary of 124 Infantry Brigade, Report on Operations commencing 20 October 1918.
69 TNA WO95/2492, War Diary of 36th Division.
70 TNA WO158/218 Operations on the Second Army Front: 14 October to 31 October1918
71 TNA WO95/2437, War Diary of 34th Division, Summary of War Diary for October 1918.
72 TNA WO95/1880, War Diary of 14th Division, Administration Section; TNA WO95/2594, War Diary of 40th Division.
73 TNA WO95/2594, War Diary of 40th Division, entries for 26 October-1 November.

experienced various skirmishes with enemy positions across the river in the vicinity of Warcoing and Pecq. On 1 November, the division held a line of outposts along the west bank of the Escaut, from south of Pecq up to the canal at Espierres.

For the other British units and the French and Belgian forces operating further north, the fighting, particularly on the fronts of II Corps and XIX Corps, had been intense at times. It had taken considerable perseverance by the infantry, reinforced whenever possible by artillery support, to keep up sustained pressure upon the retreating German forces. The operations report of 124 Brigade (41st Division) for the period 20-26 October provides an illustrative summary of the offensive and its outcomes:

> As a result of the six days operations described herein, which included two advances to the line of the river L'ESCAUT to a depth of 7,000 and 6,000 yards respectively, involving two big attacks and one minor one, more than twelve villages were liberated from the enemy and very heavy casualties were inflicted, besides the capture of in-numerable machine guns.
>
> During these operations the Brigade had attached to it two companies of the 41st Bn. M.G.C., and one section of the 187th Bde. R.F.A., one gun being placed at the disposal of the O.C. of each front line battalion.[74]

The following table[75] records the casualties of the brigade during the same period.

	Killed		**Wounded**		**Missing**	
	Officers	**Other Ranks**	**Officers**	**Other Ranks**	**Officers**	**Other Ranks**
10/Queens Royal West Surrey	–	4	1	19	–	2
26/Royal Fusiliers	2	19	8	112	–	10
20/ Durham Light Infantry	3	26	6	144	–	8
Totals	5	49	15	275	–	20

There had been consistent and unrelenting pressure upon the main combat units of Second Army since the launch of the original attack by the GAF on 28 September. The 36th Division had been one of its key formations in bearing the brunt of the fighting, with consequences which demonstrated the continuing capacity of the retreating Germans to hurt the British forces. Falls describes the nature of the division's circumstances in stark terms:

> The bolt of the 36th Division was now shot ... The casualties since the beginning of offensive operations numbered over three thousand. Of these, six-sevenths were wounded, and a very

74 TNA WO95/2642, War Diary of 124 Infantry Brigade, Report on Operations commencing 20 October 1918.

75 TNA WO95/2642, War Diary of 124 Infantry Brigade, Report on Operations commencing 20 October 1918.

> large proportion, most fortunately, suffering from light wounds from machine-gun bullets, or a temporary disabling whiff of gas. But not more than a tenth of these casualties… had been replaced by reinforcements. As a consequence battalions in action had seldom more than two hundred or two hundred and fifty bayonets. Other arms had suffered in less, but still in high proportion, while the loss of transport animals was becoming serious. [On 27 October] a wire from the X. Corps [was received] to the effect that the Division would be relieved by the 34th [Division]… Though little they knew it, [36th Division's] part in the war was finished.[76]

As further evidence of the continuing threat to British troops, on 29 October a senior officer was wounded by enemy shellfire. The GOC 120 Brigade, Brigadier-General W.P. Hore-Ruthuen, who had only been in post for just over a week (Hore-Ruthuen took over command of the brigade on 18 October, replacing General C.J. Hobkirk who was transferring to England), was visiting his front line units when: "At dawn enemy heavily shelled the area. The G.O.C. was slightly wounded in the back."[77] Happily, the General was sufficiently recovered to sign off the war diary record for the month

The large amount of civilian traffic being generated as areas were liberated was causing problems for the British artillery, causing its fire to be 'confined to definite targets'. Second Army records that the Germans were using a high proportion of gas shells, causing regular casualties amongst Belgian civilians.[78]

Action of Tiegham: 31 October 1918

Plumer now set in train the arrangements for a major attack by II Corps and XIX Corps, in cooperation with French forces, originally planned for 30 October. The date was finally deferred to 31 October following a request from the French. Map 10 denotes how the 'Action of Tiegham' would have the strategic consequence of bursting open the German defences and provide the opportunity for further exploitation. The operation helped create a springboard for the advance of French Sixth Army; and cleared the way forward for a full advance by Second Army towards and ultimately across the Schelde.

The attack was carried out by II Corps (34th and 35th Divisions) and XIX Corps (31st Division). The orders for 35th Division stated:

> 35th Division to resume advance on 31st. October with 104th. Infantry Brigade attacking, 106th. Infantry Brigade holding line on right, and 105th. Infantry Brigade in reserve and placing one Battalion [15th. Cheshire Regiment] at tactical call of Brigadier-General Commanding 104th Infantry Brigade…

In the event "… 15th. Cheshire Regiment was not called upon to assist in the attack of 104th. Infantry Brigade which was entirely successful."[79]

76 Falls, *36th Division*, pp. 289-90.
77 TNA WO95/2610, War Diary of 120 Infantry Brigade.
78 TNA WO158/218, Operations Reports.
79 TNA WO95/2486, War Diary of 105 Infantry Brigade; including 35th. Division Order No. 207.

Each of the attacking divisions had the support of three or four brigades of field artillery. Every possible means of firepower to support the attack and suppress the German defenders was brought together. All the available corps artillery as well as the guns of resting brigades and the heavy artillery of X Corps were utilised. A key objective was the neutralisation of enemy batteries and machine gun positions, plus the masking by smoke shells of enemy-held high ground on the east bank of the river.

On the British left, French and American Divisions would also be attacking. Two companies of French tanks were deployed with II Corps. For 34th Division, 103 Infantry Brigade would lead, with 5/King's Own Scottish Borderers on the right and 8/Cameronians on the left, each supported by one company of 5/Argyll & Sutherland Highlanders, together with thirty tanks of the 18th French Tank Battalion. Each attacking battalion had ten tanks attached, with the remaining ten held in reserve.[80] During the operation, the tanks and infantry worked well together, with the British troops reporting that the tanks 'were of very great assistance'.[81] Major-General Nicholson, commanding 34th Division, was to note subsequently that these proved to be 'of great value on the right'.[82] At the same time:

> … the Tank crews, on the other hand, were full of praise for the manner in which the infantry co-operated with them.[83]

Nicholson also recorded the importance of the Second Army actions in assisting the French, noting that the commander of 41st French Division was:

> [A]ll over the 34th Division for having held his flank for him the day before. He practically acknowledged that his own men were not taking any [ie capturing any ground] and that our taking the Southern end of the high ground in front of them enabled them to get forward.[84]

At zero hour of 0525 the infantry moved forward under a creeping barrage of artillery and machine guns, moving at a rate of 100 yards in three minutes. This would cease for two hours upon reaching the first objective, to allow guns to be moved forward.

Overall, the attack proved to be an important success with a series of villages liberated during operations. 5/KOSB made good progress south of Anseghem 'with the aid of the tanks':

> Three tanks volunteered to go out in front of [the advance line] to clear enemy M.G. posts. Two of these were destroyed by hostile gun fire and the crews badly wounded.[85]

80 TNA WO95/2437, War Diary of 34th Division, Narrative of Operations From 26 October to 1 November 1918.
81 TNA WO95/2437, War Diary of 34th Division, Summary of War Diary for October 1918.
82 Nicholson, *34th Division*.
83 TNA WO95/2437, War Diary of 34th Division, Summary of War Diary for October 1918.
84 Nicholson, *34th Division*.
85 TNA WO95/2437, War Diary of 34th Division, Narrative of Operations From 26 October to 1 November 1918.

Advancing via Hill 41, 8/Cameronians (Scottish Rifles) had cleared and captured Anseghem by 1100. The aim had been to turn the village on both northern and southern flanks, mopping up the remaining defenders later. However the flanking manoeuvre north of the village by three companies failed – these were forced to abort the operation and instead dig in and set up a defensive flank facing south-east. The battalion therefore had to mount an attack on the village from the south and it was this that proved to be the successful turning point.

The reason for the failure north of the village was that the French advance on the left had been frustrated by fierce enemy resistance; in the evening the Germans still held strong positions on high ground above Boschkant, and the French and American forces were pinned in the valley to the north-west. The French tanks with the left half-company of 8/Cameronians were unable to operate effectively, finding the ground too marshy and the approaches to the enemy positions too exposed:

> The enemy had a sniping field gun [deployed] during the whole day which fired over open sights at any movement N.E. of ANSEGHEM. This gun was eventually silenced by a forward section of 180th Brigade R.F.A. which moved forward with 1/8th Scottish Rifles.[86]

An 'International Liaison Company' had been formed under the command of a British Officer, consisting of half-companies from the 23rd French Regiment and 2/4 Queen's (Royal West Surrey). However the lack of progress by the French delayed this unit near Winteeken. In the afternoon, a company from 2/4 Queen's moved to fill the gap between the liaison company and Anseghem.[87]

To address the problem of the German machine guns and artillery sited above Boschkant, 5/Argyll & Sutherland Highlanders sent forward fighting patrols overnight in order to maintain pressure on the defenders. The end result was that British troops eventually took possession of the positions, without opposition, by 0300 hours on 1 November. This action relieved the pressure on the allied troops who moved forward at dawn. The French and American units then went on to clear all of the high ground west of the Scheldt, as far north as Audenarde.[88] The detonators of explosive charges placed by the enemy on the bridge at Rugge were successfully removed by an NCO from the Tunnelling Company.[89]

By 1 November the Second Army line was secure along the length of the west bank, with a small number of posts established subsequently across the river. II Corps transferred to Army Reserve.[90] The orders of 40th Division summarise the approach of Second Army at this point of the campaign:

> [The] enemy [is] continuing preparations for the destruction of roads and railways east of SCHELDE… therefore should enemy defence weaken then units are to establish advance

86 TNA WO95/2437, War Diary of 34th Division, Narrative of Operations From 26 October to 1 November 1918.
87 TNA WO95/2437, War Diary of 34th Division, Narrative of Operations From 26 October to 1 November 1918.
88 TNA WO95/2437, War Diary of 34th Division, Summary of War Diary for October 1918.
89 TNA WO95/2483, War Diary of 104 Infantry Brigade.
90 TNA WO158/212, Second Army Operations, 1 October 1918-20 January 1919.

> guards east of the Inundations and prepare to carry out further advance to capture high ground to the front.[91]

From 14-31 October, Second Army had captured 7,422 prisoners, 172 guns plus considerable numbers of machine guns and trench mortars. During this same period, 76 German aeroplanes were destroyed and four balloons, for the loss of thirty British planes. 14 October had in fact seen 20 enemy planes and four balloons destroyed, which was a record for one day – nine British planes were lost.[92]

From the beginning of November, Plumer commenced plans for a forced crossing of the Schelde. 41 Brigade noted on 31 October, following a briefing at 14th Division HQ, 'the policy of offence to be adopted… [the] keyword being the SCHELDT must be crossed at all costs'.[93] Artillery, sufficient to protect the west bank and conduct counter-battery work, was maintained in action. All other guns were to be held in preparation for supporting the crossing. Provisional orders were prepared to take advantage of any identified reduction in the German defences. Bridging material was being brought together. Probing patrols were sent forward regularly including two minor bridging operations. The enemy continued to resist in force, employing harassing fire including gas bombardments. 124 Brigade recorded that during four days in line, 1-4 November:

> [T]he enemy showing considerable artillery activity, and considerable machine gun fire was experienced from posts on the East bank of the river [Scheldt].[94]

Despite this, the British succeeded in establishing a number of advance posts on the eastern bank of the river. 20/Durham Light Infantry (124 Brigade, 41st Division – the division had returned to the line from the beginning of November) established a bridgehead across the Schelde, opposite Berchem, on 2 November. There was no immediate enemy opposition but the night brought heavy shelling and regular sniping such that it was decided to withdraw the post.

What happened next is perhaps indicative of the growing sense within the Army that the end of the war was in sight. On the following night 3-4 November, further crossings were made by soldiers from the brigade's other battalions, 10/Queen's and 20/Durham Light Infantry, and posts were set up on the eastern bank. Having confirmed the ability to carry out such operations – 'and since it was just as easy to command the Eastern bank from our side' – the brigade ordered that these posts were withdrawn.[95] This action was no doubt influenced by the prospect of an end to the war, and a desire to ensure that the lives of British soldiers were no longer placed at risk unless there was no other alternative. In this case the priority was for the units of Second Army to have all possible arrangements in place for a strong and successful crossing of the Schelde – and at a time of the Army's choosing.

91 TNA WO95/2610, War Diary of 120 Infantry Brigade, 40th Division Order No. 226.
92 TNA WO158/218 Operations on the Second Army Front: 14 October to 31 October1918.
93 TNA WO95/1894/6, War Diary of 41 Infantry Brigade, 31 October 1918.
94 TNA WO95/2642, War Diary of 124 Infantry Brigade, Report on Operations from 1 November to the commencement of the Armistice at 11.a.m. 11 November 1918.
95 TNA WO95/2642, War Diary of 124 Infantry Brigade, Report on Operations from 1 November to the commencement of the Armistice at 11.a.m. 11 November 1918.

The main activities of 124 Brigade throughout this period were designed to prepare for a crossing:

> During the whole of this period in the line, active patrolling was carried out along the banks of the river, positions being reconnoitred for contemplated foot and pontoon bridges. These positions were subsequently adopted by the bridging parties.[96]

Over the next few days, while in divisional reserve, the brigade concentrated on training for the river crossing.

The 40th Division had been looking to cross at Pecq with a subsidiary crossing east of Warcoing. Enemy resistance was considerable – machine gun, trench mortar and artillery fire – and 1 November brought an enemy counter-attack which was repulsed.[97] A small number of advance posts were set up on the eastern bank during 2-3 November despite enemy mortar and artillery fire. By 5 November, patrols were operating east of Pecq and Warcoing, and enemy withdrawal had allowed troops to push forward towards Herrines.[98]

The night of 4-5 November saw an attack by units of 14th and 29th Division to force a crossing of the Escault, between Helchin and Bossuyt. Previous attempts to cross, through taking advantage of operations by 121 Brigade (40th Division) on the right, had failed despite covering fire from trench mortars and machine guns. During the early hours, engineers threw a number of bridges across the water and parties of infantry crossed in the face of minimal enemy defensive fire. By 0530 the positions were secured, with no fatalities and three men wounded.[99]

Following repeated pressure from Haig, on 4 November Foch had agreed that British Second Army would be removed from the GAF and restored to Haig's command, as part of the BEF. This decision is discussed in more detail later in the following chapter. Second Army would now be responsible for maintaining 'close contact with the enemy and to follow up and press him with advanced guards in the event of his withdrawing';[100] and to force a passage of the River Escaut, the attack being carried out under the command of XV, X and XIX Corps. The operation would be in cooperation with British Fifth Army and its 39th Division, advancing in the Tournai area.[101]

Meanwhile the successes of the campaign were being acknowledged. On 5 November, 9th Division (in Army reserve) was inspected by the King of the Belgians at Hulste Aerodrome. In recognition of this, the GOC declared the following day as a holiday for all troops.[102]

On 6 November, 40th Division held a conference which considered the plans for the forced crossing of the Scheldt, by frontal attack if necessary. Two days later, 119 Brigade (40th Division)

96 TNA WO95/2642, War Diary of 124 Infantry Brigade, Report on Operations from 1 November to the commencement of the Armistice at 11.a.m. 11 November 1918.
97 TNA WO95/2614, War Diary of 121Infantry Brigade.
98 TNA WO95/2594, War Diary of 40th Division, entries for 2-5 November.
99 TNA W095/1894/6, War Diary of 41 Infantry Brigade.
100 TNA WO158/212, Second Army Operations, 1 October 1918-20 January 1919, GHQ_OAD 950: 3 November 1918.
101 Referred to in TNA WO95/1899, War Diary of 42 Infantry Brigade, Instructions No.1, 8 November 1918.
102 TNA WO95/1771/4, War Diary of 27 Infantry Brigade.

crossed the river 'in pursuit' of the enemy.[103] Patrols reported weakening resistance and some troops penetrated through Herrines. The following day the division advanced over seven miles, liberating a series of small villages and hamlets.[104]

For the intended final phase, II and XV Corps were withdrawn into reserve. The number of front line divisions had been reduced over time to the point where, for the purpose of operations beyond 9 November, there would be only five divisions operating in the line, under a two corps structure. The disposition of Second Army, north-to-south, would be as follows:

XIX Corps	41st Division
	35th Division
	31st Division
X Corps	30th Division
	29th Division

By now it was clear that German forces had given up on holding the line of the Schelde and Second Army sent forward advance units, using pontoon bridges and boats, onto the eastern bank. On that day 35th Division was tasked to seize and hold Bercham railway, crossing the Schelde by the use of canvas boats (the RE would then erect floating foot bridges).[105] 20/Durham Light Infantry spent the night on the eastern bank at Meersche.[106] For 30th Division, 89 Brigade forced a passage over the River Escaut, with 21 and 90 Brigades ordered to follow up in support.[107] Following reports from patrols of enemy withdrawals, 43 Brigade (14th Division) moved forward to secure canal locks. 42 Brigade took up 'assault positions' to cross between Pecq and Helchin.[108]

Army orders were issued to include confirmation of the crossing of the Scheldt that morning (XV Corps: 14th and 40th Divisions – who were then withdrawn to Army Reserve) and the securing of the line Cordes-Anseroeul-Renaix-Nukerke. In particular:

- On the left, XIX Corps to maintain touch with the French Army; the French tank detachment to transfer to Army Reserve
- X Corps to seize the ridge above St. Sauveur before pushing east
- 36th Division to transfer to XV Corps
- XIX and X Corps to push on to the River Dendre, with XV and II Corps following.[109]

During the final three days of the war, Second Army advanced 22 miles, reaching the Dendre.

103 TNA WO95/2611/4, War Diary of 11th Battalion, Cameron Highlanders.
104 TNA WO95/2594, War Diary of 40th Division, entries for 7-9 November.
105 TNA WO95/2486, War Diary of 105 Infantry Brigade.
106 TNA WO95/2642, War Diary of 124 Infantry Brigade, Report on Operations from 1 November to the commencement of the Armistice at 11.a.m. 11 November 1918.
107 TNA WO95/2328, War Diary of 21 Infantry Brigade.
108 TNA WO95/1899, War Diary of 42 Infantry Brigade, Instructions No.1, 8 November 1918.
109 TNA WO158/212, Second Army Operations, 1 October 1918-20 January 1919; TNA WO158/218, Second Army Summary of Operations, 24 August 1917-16 November 1919, Report week ending 15 November 1918.

At 1020 hours on 11 November, 124 Brigade HQ was set up at Nederbrakel, four miles east of the Dendre, 'where an enemy machine gun, with one officer and six other ranks were captured'.[110] Its battalions were deployed along the river, having spent the morning advancing to that line.

By way of the Army's final act before the Armistice took effect at 1100 on 11 November, a squadron of the 7th Dragoon Guards, attached to X Corps, advanced towards the bridge over the Dendre at Lessines. At around 1045 the troops charged the village, taking 130 prisoners and a machine gun; more importantly, the bridge, which was wired for demolition, was captured intact. A further 41 prisoners were captured on higher ground overlooking the village; it now being after 1100, these prisoners were released.

During the period 1-11 November, 719 prisoners were captured by Second Army, plus 18 guns, six trench mortars, 142 machine guns, together with two complete trains and ten locomotives.[111] The Army held the final line of East of Lessines – South and West of Ghoy – Ginintreau – La Livarde – Goeffendinge – part of Grammont – due North and West to the French right at Paricke.[112] Thus the British Second Army concluded its war. As a commentary on the Army's achievements, Harris has concluded 'The Flanders operation… was a major success'.[113]

110 TNA WO95/2642, War Diary of 124 Infantry Brigade, Report on Operations from 1 November to the commencement of the Armistice at 11.a.m. 11 November 1918.
111 TNA WO158/218 Operations on the Second Army Front: 1 November to 11 November 1918.
112 TNA WO158/218, Second Army Summary of Operations, 24 August 1917-16 November 1919, Report week ending 15 November 1918.
113 Harris & Barr, *Amiens to the Armistice.*

7

War of Liberation: The Liberation of Occupied Flanders

> The last phase of the war took place in hitherto undamaged country where civilians still lived and were often surprised and killed by the cruel storm of the approaching force of war.[1]

The Belgians refer to this final campaign of the war as the *Liberation Offensive*. This term is crucial to understanding the full import of this period for the people of Belgium. The eastward drive of the fighting in Flanders was liberating areas of the country which had been under German occupation for over four years. As Second Army pursued the retreating enemy its troops were playing their part in releasing Belgians from foreign rule. The resulting consequences of their liberation brought scenes which the British public today most closely associate with the closing stages of the Second World War rather than this earlier conflict in Europe. To appreciate the wider context of Second Army's successes it is necessary to take a step back from the fighting and see, through the words of the British forces, what the advance meant for the Belgian people.

Two days into the Battle of Courtrai, the diary of 41st Division commented on the 'large number of civilians passing through our lines'.[2] 121 Brigade recorded on 17 October: "From this [point] onwards during the advance civilians were found in all villages and houses."[3]

On 18 October, Second Army Intelligence reported that thousands of civilians were being drawn towards the main towns including Tourcoing, Lauwe and Courtrai.[4] Although there had been assurances from the enemy that Courtrai would not be shelled, there had been artillery fire on 16 October with a number of civilian casualties. In general, across the front, private houses were being found intact although many had been looted. Civilians were still being forced to assist the German soldiers in the construction of defensive positions.

Arrangements were now required to manage the consequences of the British forces moving into formerly occupied towns and villages, and the movement of civilians through and behind the moving front line of the advance. It was important for the British troops to remember that

1 B. Stichelbaut and P. Chielens, *The Great War Seen From the Air: In Flanders Fields 1914-1918* (Brussels: Mercatorfonds, 2013), p. 259.
2 TNA W095/2618, War Diary of 41st Division.
3 TNA W095/2614, War Diary of 121 Infantry Brigade.
4 TNA WO157/129, Second Army Intelligence Summary, 18 October 1918 'Civil Population'.

their presence was as liberators and their conduct with regard to the civilian population was expected to reflect this. The British soldiers were also expected to behave in a manner which would distinguish them from the former occupying German soldiers which they were, if only temporarily, replacing.

Towards the end of the Battle of Courtrai, 92 Brigade (31st Division) issued orders regarding those troops withdrawn into rear areas:

> <u>92nd INF. BDE. ORDER NO. 309</u> <u>18.10.18</u>
>
> Troops of Battalions in support will be billeted as closely as possible… No houses except those in which troops are billeted will be entered…
> Men will not leave their billet areas.
>
> The strictest discipline will be maintained in the town. Men will walk about properly dressed, and will present a smart appearance and impress the civilians by their marked contrast to the German troops. Men will not wear garlands or flags in their hats or on their tunics.[5]

The principal concerns appear to have been to ensure that the Belgian population was adequately fed and supplied, with arrangements for evacuation where possible or necessary during the fighting. 88 Brigade (29th Division) encountered this problem during the Battle of Courtrai:

> There are [a] considerable number of civilians going down to the Collecting Station at LEDEGHEM … The forward area is under direct observation from COURTRAI, and is shelled, which puts the civilians in some danger. No arrangements seem to have been made for evacuating them, so we have made our own, which will be put into operation tomorrow.[6]

The success of the Army's logistical arrangements meant that the British assumed much of the initial responsibility for coping with the welfare of the local populations. On 18 October the Deputy Director Supply & Transport recorded that:

> A very considerable quantity of civilians are now being fed by the British. This feeding is limited to 4 days rations in order to give the French and Belgians time to get rations from their own bases. The French will probably do this but it is perfectly certain that the Belgians, who are devoid of any idea of organisation, will never do it.[7]

On the following day he notes that XV Corps have demanded assistance to feed civilians around Tourcoing and Roubaix.

5 TNA WO95/2356/5, War Diary of 92 Infantry Brigade.
6 TNA WO95/2307/4, War Diary of 88 Infantry Brigade, 16 October 1918.
7 TNA WO95/292, Deputy Director Supply & Transport: Daily Visits and Inspections, 18 October 1918.

With the increasing contact between troops and civilians, units were also charged with identifying any possible spies for the enemy. A conference of commanders at 43 Brigade (14th Division) considered the issue of liberated villages:

> C.O.'s or Senior Officers to be Commandants of the villages where they are and to see to questions of lights, supplies and suspects. Suspects to be reported to Brigade.[8]

The concern regarding the actions of suspected spies or saboteurs was a new problem for the British as advancing units encountered fresh numbers of civilians. On 22 October, 93 Brigade (31st Division) recorded that telephone wires between its HQ and the HQ of 13/York & Lancaster had been found to be cut in several places:

> In one case a piece of telephone wire 300 yards long had been cut out of the line. Several civilians were arrested as spies and handed over to the Belgian police attached to the Brigade.[9]

There was concern that the retreating enemy would have made arrangements for the collection of information on British operations. On 20 October, XV Corps issued a set of orders designed to guard against the potential for intelligence to be passed to the Germans, through putting restrictions in place for the monitoring and control of civilian movement. The full text tells us much about the seriousness with which this danger was viewed by high command:

1. It is certain that the enemy will have left behind him the means of obtaining the fullest information about our troops, dispositions, strength, intentions, etc.
2. This will be transmitted to him by means of
    a) Agents, posing as French civilians, passing through our lines.
    b) Pigeons.
    c) Telephone or buzzer.
        i. Conversations by an agent.
        ii. Intercepts.
3. With very few exceptions, all the civilians in the recaptured territory will do their utmost to assist us and the loyal French inhabitants will be the first to recognise that extreme reticence on our part does not amount to mistrust in our Allies, but rather to our desire to spare them and their homes from further suffering and damage.
4. A number, however, of pseudo French civilians, though not perhaps actually concerned with the transmission of information to the enemy, will be well paid by him for any information they may be able to collect and give to those who are charged with its despatch.
5. The means for preventing information reaching the enemy and thus, possibly, saving many casualties are perfectly clear:
    a) Great reticence in conversation either with or within hearing of all civilians.

8 TNA WO95/1905, War Diary of 43 Infantry Brigade.
9 TNA WO95/2360, War Diary of 93 Infantry Brigade.

b) The detention of all civilians proceeding eastwards through our lines.
c) Immediate detention of all suspicious individuals who may show undue interest in our movements and reporting at once any pigeons flying Eastwards or places from which pigeons are observed to have been released; in the latter case immediate investigation should be made by the observer.
d) Avoidance of existing cables and lines until these have been traced out and reported safe for use by the Signal Service. Care in conversation on the telephone and an intelligent recourse to cipher in all signal messages.
e) Enquiries as to the bona fides of civilians in whose houses headquarters are established.[10]

Two days later, the war diary of 41Brigade (14th Division) recorded:

> Belgians names [sic] VAN HOENACKER arrested on the 21st was sent under escort to A.P.M., charged with being a German agent.[11]

Then on 24 October:

> Two women arrested charged with being German agents and were sent under escort to A.P.M.[12]

While there is no evidence to link these incidents with the earlier orders from XV Corps, it is likely that units would be more suspicious of civilian activity following the briefing from senior command. There is no information on what caused the Belgians to be arrested, nor on their subsequent fate.

Where possible, forward areas were to be evacuated, to reduce the risk of civilian casualties and prevent the troops' concern for civilians from impeding military operations. 93 Brigade noted on 22 October that:

> Our artillery was quiet owing to civilians moving about in the enemy's forward areas.[13]

During the Battle of Courtrai the war diary of 7/Seaforth Highlanders recorded that 'During the afternoon and evening a large number of civilians passed through our lines on their way to Winkle-St-Eloi.[14]

At 1100 on 17 October, 90 Brigade recorded that:

10 TNA W095/2610, War Diary of 120 Brigade, XV Corps No. I.G.41a/10, 40th Division.
11 TNA WO95/1894/6, War Diary of 41 Infantry Brigade, 22 October 1918.
12 TNA WO95/1894/6, War Diary of 41 Infantry Brigade, 24 October 1918.
13 TNA WO95/2360, War Diary of 93 Infantry Brigade.
14 TNA WO95/1765, War Diary of 7th Battalion, Seaforth Highlanders.

> Civilians... came into our lines who said that the enemy had evacuated Turcoing and surrounding area ... There were no civilians in [Bousbecque, Menin, Halluin] but 40 or 50 were in Roncq and these greeted our troops with every sign of joy.[15]

The retreat of the German Army in the face of the advance by the Allied forces brought conflicting experiences for the immediate populace. In many cases the enemy's withdrawal brought unexpected but very welcome relief. Towards the end of the Battle of Courtrai, 41 Brigade (14th Division) was marching into reserve at Roncq:

> Civilians were met on the line of march who appeared somewhat dazed but nevertheless delighted.[16]

However the hasty departure of the occupiers could cause short-term problems as noted by 27 Brigade (9th Division) on the second day of that battle:

> The inhabitants of CUERNE told us that not an hour before we arrived there the enemy had streamed through a panic stricken mob of 2,000 soldiers who looted everything they could lay their hands on. Two Uhlan officers were killed at CUERNE trying to escape.[17]

On the morning of 21 October, 1/6 Cheshire's (21 Brigade, 30th Division) had captured the hamlet of Helghin (Helchin):

> Civilians were occupying the farms and houses in the area through which we had advanced and our troops were warmly welcomed everywhere. Belgium flags were flying and bells ringing half an hour after the enemy had been forced to evacuate each place. The casualties amongst the civilians were promptly attended to by our medical staff.[18]

In a report on operations during the second half of October, 124 Brigade noted that on 26 October it liberated seven villages; during the period 20-26 October 'more than twelve villages were liberated from the enemy ...'[19] Troops began to see the battered landscape through the eyes of its besieged civilians:

> A few days ago we marched through a town which was once in German hands; it is a fearful mess now, nothing but one vast heap of bricks and timber and scarcely a wall standing.[20]

15 TNA WO95/2338, War Diary of 90 Infantry Brigade.
16 TNA WO95/1894/6, War Diary of 41 Infantry Brigade, 19 October 1918.
17 TNA WO95/1771/4/5, War Diary of 27 Infantry Brigade, Narrative of Operations 28 September-28 October 1918.
18 TNA WO95/2330, War Diary of 1/6th Battalion, Cheshire Regiment.
19 TNA WO95/2642, War Diary of 124 Infantry Brigade, Report on Operations commencing 20 October 1918.
20 From the letters of D E Griffin, 2/1st East Riding Yeomanry, letter dated Thursday 5 September 1918, IWM collection.

This destructive consequence of the clash of arms was not always the case as the war diary of 2/South Lancs recorded:

> The country through which the battalion marched, and which had been evacuated by the enemy, offered a marked contrast to that in which it had been operating for so long. Villages were more or less intact, the country showed little sign of war in comparison to what we had been accustomed for so long, and a number of civilians were seen… All villages through which the battalion marched were decorated with the Belgian flag and the inhabitants were most enthusiastic. Traces of fighting could be seen here and there and occasional shell holes were noticed on the roads.[21]

The same battalion was received with even greater enthusiasm the following month, on Armistice Day:

> During the march great enthusiasm was shown by the inhabitants and on arrival in Flobecq the people were much excited and gave the troops an extraordinary welcome. The Band of the Battalion performed in the Square of the town much to the satisfaction of the inhabitants.[22]

By this time, given the successful advance of the liberating armies, there are various references within unit diaries to positive contact with welcoming Belgian civilians. Stationed for a time in reserve at Herseaux, the senior command of 41 Brigade attended a banquet given in honour of the brigade by the Burgomaster and local representatives:

> In a short speech the Burgomaster gave a hearty welcome to the B.G.C. and the troops under his command and thanked them as liberators.[23]

A few days later a team from brigade HQ played a team of civilians at football; the war diary recorded the result as 'a walk over'. The winner is not named but presumably it was the British soldiers who secured such an easy victory.

There are other examples of local civilians demonstrating their formal appreciation of the efforts on their behalf by the liberating troops. The following example is taken from the war diary of 121 Brigade for 24 October 1918:

> At 16.30 the Mayor and Council of CROIX attended at Brigade Headquarters for the purpose of presenting the Brigadier-General Commanding with an address of thanks for freeing the inhabitants of ROUBAIX and CROIX from the Germans. They also intimated that they had made the Brigade Commander a free Citizen of CROIX.[24]

21 War Diary, 2nd Battalion, South Lancs Regiment, 19 and 20 October 1918.
22 War Diary, 2nd Battalion, South Lancs Regiment, 11 November 1918.
23 TNA WO95/1894/6, War Diary of 41 Infantry Brigade, 23 and 27 October 1918.
24 TNA WO95/2614, War Diary of 121 Infantry Brigade.

A typeset copy of the presentation is appended to the diary; it is not clear when or how the copy, which is dated 24 October 1018, was produced, having been first (presumably) translated. The address fills a side of A4 paper, with an initial paragraph describing the sufferings of the civilian population under German rule. The list includes forced labour, deportation for work purposes, loss of property, the taking of hostages and other deprivations and restrictions. The document goes on, in terms of most flowery prose, to praise the 'valour and bravery of the... British' for freeing the town and its people from the 'boche'; ending with the bold: "Vive la 121st Brigade! Vive son General!"[25]

On 25 October, bands from the British army, including105 Brigade (35th Division) had performed for the citizens of Courtrai.[26] Two days later, 90 Brigade (30th Division) recorded that:

> At the request of the inhabitants a detachment of one Officer and 25 Other Ranks from each Battalion attended a thanksgiving service in Aelbeke Church, to celebrate their deliverance from the enemy.[27]

On 28 October, troops from 5/Cameron Highlanders had the opportunity to bathe and 'get cleaned up', prior to being paid and proceeding 'to fraternize with the people they had liberated a week before'.[28]

> On the 18th [October, 1918] General Woodcock and the headquarters of the 101st Brigade made a triumphant entry into Lauwe, which was the first Belgian Town we had entered which was still inhabited. The inhabitants gave the general a demonstrative and enthusiastic welcome. The enemy was evidently in full retreat, and a crowd of liberated civilians were met on all sides.[29]

13/East Lancs were involved in the liberation of Tourcoing. On entering the town they found it:

> [F]ull of civilians who received the battalion with the greatest enthusiasm: the streets were thronged with people, many of whom were most anxious to press refreshment of all kinds upon the first British troops they had seen.[30]

The Battalion History of the 10/East Yorkshires (1st Hull Pals) recounts similar events at Wattrelos, a suburb of Roubaix, in the third week of October 1918:

25 TNA WO95/2614, War Diary of 121 Infantry Brigade, AN ADDRESS to Brigadier-General G.C. Stubbs, D.S.O. commanding the 121st Brigade of Infantry, CROIX, 24 October 1918.
26 TNA WO95/2486, War Diary of 105 Infantry Brigade.
27 TNA WO95/2338, War Diary of 90 Infantry Brigade.
28 TNA WO95/1767, War Diary of 5th Battalion, Cameron Highlanders.
29 Wylly, *The Loyal North Lancs Regiment*, p. 151.
30 Major-General Sir L. Nicholson and Major H. McMullen, *History of the East Lancashire Regiment in the Great War 1914-1918* (Liverpool: Littlebury Bros., 1936).

> Ordered marching was impossible, women pressed flags and flowers upon us and when we were free to fraternise we found every house open to us. Food and drink of every kind were pressed upon [the] men … [The inhabitants] could not do enough for us to show their delight and gratitude at their deliverance from the Germans …[31]

However, where it had been necessary for troops to mount an assault and take by force a town or village, then the opportunity of being liberated was potentially a very dangerous experience for civilians, as well as the soldiers. Second Army took steps to emphasise the importance of minimising the risk of casualties amongst the local population resulting from its operations. However the defensive fire from German positions as British forces moved forward did not always make efforts to discriminate between soldiers and civilians:

> [At Wattrelos] there was street fighting before the town was cleared of enemy rear guards, and casualties were inflicted on the advancing troops and civilians from the heavy bombardment of gas and high-explosive shells to which the town was subjected.[32]

There were also instances when war and peace co-existed – daily life rolled on as normal while the war passed it by:

> A curious feature of this period of the operations was the attitude of the Belgian farmers who lived within range of the enemy's fire. Apparently oblivious to the dangers that surrounded them, they continued to occupy their farms, and to till their lands from sunrise to sunset, indifferent (at any rate outwardly) to the efforts of their allies to restore to them the freedom of their native land.[33]

As the advance proceeded, efforts were made to interview civilians in order to obtain information on German troop dispositions, movement and the morale of the enemy troops. The following case examples are taken from a summary report for 14th Division:[34]

> <u>Maurice Courcelles</u>
> Forcibly evacuated from Minove on 1 October 1918; managed to escape… at Audewarde [on the River Scheldt] [he saw] a great movement of heavy artillery drawn by tractors… on 17 October the German commandant left the town… all tugs and barges (about 300 in number) were ordered to proceed at once up the Scheldt to Antwerp… he saw a continuous line of German infantry and artillery proceeding long the west bank [of the Scheldt] proceeding in the direction of Audewarde.

31 Quoted in D. Bilton, *The Trench: The Full Story of the 1st Hull Pals* (London: Leo Cooper, 2002), p. 204.
32 Nicholson et al, East Lancs, p. 558.
33 Nicholson et al, East Lancs, p. 558.
34 TNA WO95/1877, 14th Division General Staff, October-December 1918.

Edmond Delcroix
Forcibly evacuated on 1 October 1918... travelled to Herseaux... no troops noticed on the way... At Ruyen one of the local civil authorities informed [him] that Selles and Escanaffles had been evacuated and that German artillery was in position on the Mont de l'Enclus... The canal bank at Bosschuyt [Bossuyt?] was being converted for defence.

George Declerq
States that all the men forcibly evacuated from Roubaix and Tourcoing are concentrated at Ophasselt and Nederbrakel – and are allowed full liberty of movement in these areas

Evarist Cluyse
Recently escaped from Brussels... where on 9 October he saw a general evacuation of all heavy artillery and other heavy material proceeding in the direction of Liege. Tractors, lorries and tanks were being employed to draw the guns... [From an overheard telephone conversation by German officers billeted at his house]: The German line is to be withdrawn to the frontier – but in order to gain time for the necessary removal of military stores etc. the following position is to be taken up at once: the east bank of the Scheldt to Termonde and then along the east bank of the Dendre river... all then farmhouses along the north bank of the Courtrai – Bossuyt canal had been fortified for machine-gun defence... All roads behind the line are in excellent condition.

Several other civilians were questioned but could give no further information, except that in every case they stated that the Germans intended to withdraw immediately to their frontier.

The Maire of Herseaux, who was only released from prison ten days ago after seven months confinement for an unknown crime, states that the morale of the soldiers is completely broken and that this was more noticeable after their return from leave. On leave the germans stated that they could not obtain sufficient food to exist upon and had they not taken some food with them they would have been starved.

A number of conclusions can be drawn from this summary report, its preparation and contents:

1. As the troops of the GAF advanced, civilians were being liberated through their areas being taken over by Allied forces or by being able to make their way to the Allied lines.
2. Army Intelligence Officers were taking steps to obtain information about the enemy from these civilians.
3. The Germans were attempting to forcibly evacuate civilians from areas in the path of the Allied advance.
4. The German forces were preparing new defensive lines in order to create the time and space for a planned withdrawal in the direction of the German frontier.
5. An Allied advance along the coast could threaten to outflank the withdrawal and threaten the cohesion of the German armies.
6. The morale of German troops was not good; obviously effected by the reverses suffered at the hands of the Allied armies and being made worse by news (and some first-hand

> experience of soldiers on leave) of the conditions being experienced by their families and neighbours back in Germany.

It is interesting to note that the original typed report has been proofed or corrected – the name of each civilian is crossed out and the words 'a civilian' or 'another civilian' written in pencil; was the intention to produce a corrected report which was anonymised to protect the previously named individuals should the report fall into enemy hands?

A report by the CO of 23/Middlesex suggests that there was a residue of ill-feeling from some German troops towards the Belgian people. On 25 October, a report on operations by the battalion records that the German artillery had fired gas shells into a village and, as villagers moved away into the open, they were subject to machine gun fire. There is no further comment on the incident and the village is not named, nor is there a named witness – there is no other information to confirm the incident. One can only speculate on what factors, if the description of the event is correct, could have caused what would now be called a war crime. There may have been some particular circumstances which had led to animosity from the Germans, not that there could have been any just cause for the action.[35] Earlier, on 17 October, following its capture that day by British forces, the Germans had used gas at the village of Cuerne:

> The enemy gassed CUERNE that night. The town was full of civilians who had no masks. The gas had no effect on operations as we had our masks and it is one more instance of the kind of enemy we have to deal with.[36]

Arrangements were required for the Army to be able to direct civilians to sources of support and also to have authorities available to take responsibility for the welfare of civilians overtaken by the fighting. The following orders are taken from instructions issued by 36th Division, which spent part of the campaign operating alongside French and Belgian forces:

> Civilians
> The Divisional Belgian Liaison Officer, Lieut. R.G. KRIEGLINGER, who will be located at Advanced Divisional Headquarters, and the D.A.P.M. [Deputy Assistant Provost Marshal] will be informed at once if any civilians are found. The D.A.P.M. will make the necessary arrangements for escorting civilians.[37]

The risk to local Belgians remained as the location of the fighting continued to move eastwards. On 6 November, 41 Brigade noted that 'DOTTIGNIES shelled during the afternoon, 3 civilians killed and 2 soldiers wounded'.[38]

35 TNA WO95/2639/3, War Diary of 23rd Battalion, Middlesex Regiment, Report On Operation of the 23rd Middlesex Regiment on 22nd., 24th and 25th October, 1918.
36 TNA WO95/1771/4/5, War Diary of 27 Infantry Brigade, Narrative of Operations 28 September-28 October 1918.
37 TNA WO95/2509, War Diary of 109 Infantry Brigade, 36 (Ulster) Div. Administrative Instructions No. 39, 19.10.1918.
38 TNA W095/1894/6, War Diary of 41 Infantry Brigade.

There were associated problems regarding the increased movement of civilians, many of whom were heading back to the area where they had originally lived but without necessarily having a home available to live in. One of the practical consequences for Second Army was that these refugees were taking up, or wanting to occupy, accommodation needed for its troops. These problems had occurred as early as 15 September, with the success of the initial attacks east of Ypres. 14th Division was deployed south east of Ypres:

> [Further Administrative Notes...]
> Difficulty in accommodation will be overcome when Belgian Refugees are moved from Billets allotted to Troops. Tents will be drawn... and returned as billets become available.[39]

Once the Armistice came into force then attention to the movement of civilians, and concern for their welfare, became a priority for the Army; within 41st Division:

> [12 November]
> Posts were established at bridge-heads within [124] Brigade boundaries, and the main roads leading from the North and East, for the examination of civilians and refugees passing through our lines.[40]

There are various references within unit war diaries to the praise paid to Second Army by the Belgians, including King Albert. On 5 November, 9th Division attended a parade at Hulste Aerodrome, where it's troops were inspected by King Albert together with his Queen and the II Corps commander Jacobs. The accompanying music from the division's band included the National Anthem of Belgium and the Scottish pipe march *The Barren Rocks of Aden*. In his address to the assembled soldiers the King paid tribute to the achievements of the division (which had operated for so much of the campaign along the right flank of the Belgian Army); he stated (as recorded in a battalion war diary) that he had prior knowledge of the division:

> ... [having] followed the career of the 9th Scottish Division since the Battle of Loos... during recent operations the 9th Division had worked in closest liaison with his army in recovering a vast stretch of his beloved country... [he] hoped that members of 9th Division would return happily to his country after a victorious peace.[41]

It being Flanders then it is perhaps no surprise that the event took place in wet weather. However '... in spite of rain the inspection was a great success'.[42]

39 TNA WO95/1899, War Diary of 42 Infantry Brigade, S.30/19A, Further Administrative Notes to 42nd Infantry Brigade Order No.17.
40 TNA WO95/2642, War Diary of 124 Infantry Brigade, Report on Operations from 1 November to the commencement of the Armistice at 11.a.m. 11 November 1918.
41 TNA WO95/1765, War Diary of 7th Battalion, Seaforth Highlanders.
42 TNA WO95/1767, War Diary of 5th Battalion, Cameron Highlanders.

8

Fall Out: The Ending of the Groupe d'Armées des Flandres

> Wartime cooperation [is] continually fraught with tension and mutual suspicion. The economic theory of coalitions emphasizes the incentives for each country to hold back and wait for its partners to do the job in hand.[1]

Less than two months previously Douglas Haig had been pleased to see Second Army join the coalition army group under King Albert; however, by the end of October, Haig became demonstrably exasperated with the delay in returning Second Army to the BEF and under his command.[2] While the five British Armies had now advanced to form a coherent forward line 'Haig only controlled four of them'.[3] Foch's desire had been to see King Albert enter Bruges at the head of a joint coalition force, only to be met by Haig's insistence that Second Army had now fulfilled its agreed task.

There have been various reasons put forward for Haig's insistence on bringing Second Army out of the GAF coalition at this time, including from Haig himself; but these have not explained the single-minded determination with which he pursued this goal, even to the point of threatening to resign his command of the BEF unless his demand was complied with. There were a number of factors influencing Haig's thinking at the time, which combined to cause him to engage in brinkmanship with Foch. Undoubtedly the level of stress under which this man was operating was immense. To fully understand his motives it is necessary to consider the argument within the context of the German attempts to secure an armistice, and the discussions around this within the allied military and political leaderships.[4]

1 M. Harrison, 'Industry and the Economy', in D.R. Stone, ed., *The Soviet Union At War 1941-1945* (Barnsley: Pen & Sword Military, 2010), p. 39.
2 Elizabeth Greenhalgh has included valuable descriptions and commentaries on these events in her books *Victory Through Coalition*, pp. 254-261, and *Foch in Command*, pp. 454-457.
3 Sheffield, *The Chief*, p. 332.
4 The sources for a description of these processes include: Terraine, *To Win A War*, pp. 177-184, 193-200, 207-226; Stevenson, *Backs To The Wall*, pp. 509-534; (from the German perspective) R.M. Watt, *The Kings Depart: The Tragedy of Germany: Versailles and the German Revolution* (London: The Literary Guild, 1969), pp. 32-38, 109-110, 170-172; (Douglas Haig's recorded views) Sheffield and Bourne, *Haig Diaries and Letters*, entries for October and November 1918.

Following the ceasefire agreed with Bulgaria on 29 September, the German leadership had begun a process to seek a ceasefire, initially through an approach to President Wilson of the USA. At a meeting of the European leaders on 8 October, Foch provided a note on the essential terms which he believed the ceasefire agreement should contain. These included liberation of the occupied territories including Alsace-Lorraine; allied occupation of the left bank of the Rhine (as security for the demand for reparations) and bridgeheads across the river to prevent any resumption of hostilities by the Germans; plus various requirements regarding the retention and safeguarding of materiel and infrastructure consequent upon the withdrawal of the German Army. Foch showed his paper to Haig on 10 October who recorded his views in his diary:

> I remarked that the only difference between his (Foch's) conditions and a general surrender is that the German Army is allowed to march back with its rifles, and officers with their swords…[5]

Haig's CGS, General Lawrence, was concerned that the Germans still retained the ability to counter-attack; the British Army would have to shoulder the main response and could expect little assistance from the French. On this subject Haig remained optimistic, doubting the enemy's ability to launch a strong attack and confident that the allies were facing a beaten army; no reference is made regarding the French Army. It should also be noted that Haig had wired Foch the previous evening making reference to British Second Army, recommending to the Marshal:

> [M]y advance on the battle front should now be between the Scheldt and Sambre with the object of joining hands with my Second Army and the other troops under King of the Belgians …[6]

While the meaning is somewhat ambiguous regarding whether control of Second Army resides with Haig or King Albert, this choice of words displays no obvious concerns about the command arrangements existing at that time. Four days later, the Battle of Courtrai opened. Haig wrote in his diary:

> [15 October]
> The Second Army did very well today… The French divisions now in Flanders are reported not to be fighting. The Belgians, on the other hand, have done splendidly.
>
> [16 October]
> General Cavendish [attached to King Albert's staff] writes last night that French troops in Flanders are not fighting at all. They take no interest in 'Flanders for the Belgians!' Also the King now seems only anxious to stop his offensive and rest on his laurels.[7]

5 Sheffield and Bourne, *Haig Diaries and Letters*, pp. 471-2.
6 Sheffield and Bourne, *Haig Diaries and Letters*, p. 471.
7 As recorded in Terraine, *To Win A War*, pp. 203-4.

Suddenly it seems that Haig had developed two concerns regarding the deployment and disposition of Second Army. Firstly, Plumer's troops had become the strike force for the fighting undertaken by the GAF, without the expected strength of support from the French. In addition, while Haig acknowledged that the Belgian Army had proved to be an effective force, he had doubts (which were not new) about King Albert's commitment to a sustained offensive. In practical terms, Second Army had achieved the original task for which Haig had agreed its release to the GAF, that of securing the left bank of the Lys, by the close of the second day of the Battle of Courtrai.[8] The progress made by the British, French and Belgian forces during the first two days of fighting – and relative to the objectives set for each – is demonstrated in Map 6A.

On 18 October Haig telephoned Foch to make his request that Second Army should now be returned to his command.[9] This phone call is confirmed in a subsequent letter, 25 October 1918, from Haig to the Secretary of the War Cabinet. That same day he travelled to London for a meeting of the British War Cabinet, having had a further discussion with Lawrence about the terms of an armistice. The latter had given Haig a note which argued that the conditions should not be too demanding because it was in Great Britain's interest to try to bring the war to a conclusion sooner rather than later. Throughout, Haig had been convinced that the war could and should be ended in 1918, and he argued this at the meeting on 19 October when asked by Lloyd George for his views on the armistice terms:

> I replied that they must greatly depend on the answers we give to two questions:
> 1. Is Germany now so beaten that she will accept whatever terms the Allies may offer?
> 2. Can the Allies continue to press the Enemy sufficiently vigorously during the coming winter months as to cause him to withdraw so quickly that he cannot destroy railways, roads, etc.?

The answer to both is in the negative. The German Army is capable of retiring to its own frontier, and holding that line if there should be any attempt to touch the honour of the German people, and make them fight with the courage of despair.[10]

This final opinion was also shared by the members of the German military command – but no one on the allied side at that stage knew of the split over this matter between the German military and the new political leaders in Germany. In due course it was to be the views of the latter group that would lead to the acceptance of armistice terms which in practice were close to an 'unconditional surrender'.[11]

Haig then gave his opinion of the state of the allied armies. While the British Army was more efficient than it had ever been, the hard fighting meant it faced issues around the reinforcements needed for its losses, such that morale could be at risk. He was concerned that the French Army

8 Dewar, *Haig's Command, Vol. II*, pp. 330-3; see also Map 6A (based upon the map in Dewar's book) which shows the relative progress made by the British, French and Belgian forces during the first two days of fighting.
9 TNA WO32/5102, (General, Code 86(A)), Field Marshal Haig requests return of 2nd British Army to his command from the King of the Belgians.
10 Sheffield and Bourne, *Haig Diaries and Letters*, p. 475.
11 Terraine, *To Win A War*, p. 211.

was 'worn out and has not been fighting latterly'.[12] In conclusion he pointed out that the French and American Armies were not capable of taking part in the immediate allied offensive (to take advantage of the fading capabilities of the enemy at that particular time) which would be needed to defeat the German Army in the field. In his subsequent diary entry, Haig summarised the views he presented on the British forces:

> The British alone might bring the enemy to his knees. But why expend more British lives – and for what? … The British Army has done most of the fighting latterly, and everyone wants to have done with the war, provided we get what we want. I therefore advise that we only ask in the armistice for what we intend to hold, and that we set our faces against the French entering Germany to pay off old scores. In my opinion, under the supposed conditions, the British Army would not fight keenly for what is not really its own affair.[13]

It was against this background that Haig returned to France. Foch had now set out his view of the strategic priorities for all the allied forces in a letter 'Directive No. 4925' to Army Commanders dated 19 October.[14] This would presumably have been waiting for Haig's attention when he arrived at GHQ.

The letter required the GAF (including Second Army) to 'march in the general direction of Brussels… forcing the major river lines: ESCAUT – DENDER'. To the south, the four British Armies (with French First Army) were to maintain their current objectives which would also 'assist the advance of the Flanders Army Group' through 'action on the flank'. These orders suggest that Foch saw the ongoing operations of the remaining British Armies aiding the drive through Belgium.[15]

It was with this confirmation of Foch's aims that Haig attended a subsequent meeting with the Generalissimo on 24 October. He was now deeply suspicious of French motives. Furthermore, he believed that the excessive demands of the French regarding armistice terms would mean a continuation of the fighting, the brunt of which would have to be borne by his troops. The British Ambassador in Paris, the 17th Earl of Derby, recorded a summary of the dispute between Haig and Foch in his diary, based upon a conversation with the Secretary of State for War, Viscount Alfred Milner.[16]

The most obvious practical illustration of Haig's nightmare was occurring now in Flanders – with British Second Army fronting an army group in which the French formations appeared to be failing and the Belgian King seemed increasingly reluctant to commit his own forces because

12 Sheffield and Bourne, *Haig Diaries and Letters*, p. 475.
13 Sheffield and Bourne, *Haig Diaries and Letters*, p. 475; Terraine, *To Win A War*, pp. 211-3.
14 TNA WO32/5102, (General, Code 86(A)), Field Marshal Haig requests return of Second British Army to his command from the King of the Belgians; letter from 'F. Foch' to 'Commandement en Chef des Armées Alliées', DIRECTIVE GENERALE No. 4925, 'G.Q.G.A., le 19 Octobre 1918'. The full translated text, which sets out Foch's strategic objectives for the Belgian, British, French and American forces, is included in Appendix III.
15 TNA WO32/5102, (General, Code 86(A)), Field Marshal Haig requests return of 2nd British Army to his command from the King of the Belgians; letter from 'F. Foch' to 'Commandement en Chef des Armées Alliées', DIRECTIVE GENERALE No. 4925, 'G.Q.G.A., le 19 Octobre 1918'.
16 D. Dutton, ed. *Paris 1918: The War Diary of the British Ambassador, the 17th Earl of Derby* (Liverpool: Liverpool University Press, 2001), pp. 293-4.

of the risks of heavy casualties and the impact of the fighting on his people and the fabric of the country. Now, Foch's objectives for the GAF and Second Army went beyond the original line of the Lys. Haig was also bolstered in his opinions on the armistice proposals by a meeting on 23 October with General Pershing, commander of the American forces in France. In Haig's opinion, Pershing agreed with his views on the 'state of Enemy, and state of allied Armies, and as to what our demands should be'.[17] The Army Council in the War Office also shared Haig's opinions.[18]

Having already made an initial request the previous week, the issue was pursued by Haig at a meeting with Foch on 24 October, prior to a conference of the Commanders-in-Chief the following day. The meeting was primarily to discuss the terms of an armistice with the Germans but Haig also used the opportunity to ask for the immediate return of Second Army to his command. On the former matter, Haig perceived Foch's reasoning in support of the occupation of German territory as 'political not military',[19] and he remained concerned that the Allies would demand conditions that they could not enforce. Haig's reservations were not shared by the CIGS, General Sir Henry Wilson, or Viscount Milner, who both supported a tougher line; or by the Earl of Derby.[20]

His request regarding Second Army was met with a refusal by Foch and, after discussion, an agreement between them to refer the matter to the British Government.[21] Haig recorded an outline of the argument and the reasoning for his request in his diary:

> We then dealt with the question of the Second Army which I asked last week should be again placed under my orders. On the 9th September I agreed that it should co-operate under the King of the Belgians for a specific purpose, namely, to cover the right of the Belgian Army on the River Lys, and enable the Belgians, supported by the French, to advance on Bruges and Ghent. That phase of the operation is over, and all the five Armies of which the BEF is composed are either along or approaching the line of the Scheldt and are confronted with the same problem, viz., the passage of that river. The manner in which the line of the Scheldt can most easily be forced is to cross it in its upper course where my Fourth, Third and half of the First Armies have already crossed it. From Oudenaarde downwards the minimum number of troops should be employed as a menace. To force a passage there, in the face of hostile opposition, would be most costly.
>
> Foch declines to return the Second Army to me because he says of the political value of having the King of the Belgians in command of an Allied Army, when he re-enters his capital, Brussels! His real object is to use the British Second Army to open the way for the 'dud' divisions (of which the rest of the King's Army is composed) and ensure that they get to Brussels. France would then get credit for clearing Belgium and putting the King back in his capital. De Goutte is nominally Chief of Staff to King Albert: really he is the Army Commander.

17 Sheffield and Bourne, *Haig Diaries and Letters*, p. 478.
18 Stevenson, *Backs To The Wall*, p. 523.
19 Terraine, *To Win A War*, pp. 215-6.
20 Stevenson, *Backs To The Wall*, p. 523; Dutton, ed., *Paris 1918*, p. 294.
21 Terraine, *To Win A War*, pp. 225-6.

> I explained the military reason why the Second army must now be under my orders. If there were political reasons requiring the Second Army to remain under King Albert, then the British Government must direct me on the subject. Until I was so informed, I must continue to view the situation from a military standpoint, and insist on the return of the Second Army without delay. Foch asked me to submit my request in writing...
>
> I am disgusted at the almost underhand way in which the French are trying to get hold of a part of the British Army – and so ungenerous too, because in the first instance, I handed over all the troops of that Army at once to operate under the French Staff of the King of the Belgians, without raising the smallest difficulty... I told [Foch and Weygand] a few 'home truths'... the British Army has defeated the Germans this year and I [alone] am responsible to the British Government for the handling of the British troops not Foch.[22]

On 25 October Haig wrote two letters setting out his arguments for the return of Second Army to his command.[23] In his short letter to Foch, Haig summarised the terms of his agreement to the deployment of Second Army in Flanders, this being the employment of two divisions 'under the command of His Majesty the King of the Belgians' to cover the flank of the GAF in its eastern advance; and the use of Second Army to exploit any resulting successes. As we have seen, there had been no secondment or similar of any British divisions to the GAF; rather, Second Army had operated as part of a combined Army Group, recognising its responsibilities for the Belgian right flank, and co-operating in the achievement of agreed strategic objectives (although Plumer had reserved for himself the decisions on Army operations consistent with these aims).

Haig pointed out that with the heavy commitment of his other British armies,

> It was well understood that... the Second Army was not to be committed to any other operation than that of clearing the ground up to the LYS River. The whole scope of the operation had as its objective the 'clearing of the Belgian coast and the country between the coast and the River LYS'.

Haig must have known that by this time, Second Army was up to ten miles beyond the Lys and preparing to tackle the Scheldt. His letter concluded:

> This has now been accomplished and I request that the Second Army be forthwith returned to my command. If, as I understand, further operations by the Army of Flanders have as their objective the capture of BRUSSELS, this can be equally attained by the co-operation of all the British Armies including the Second Army operating under my control.

22 G. Sheffield, and J. Bourne, ed., *Douglas Haig: War Diaries and Letters 1914-1918* , Thursday 24 October, pp. 478-9. Haig's position is also summarised by the Earl of Derby following a meeting between the two on 26 October 1918: Dutton, ed., *Paris 1918*, pp. 295-296.

23 TNA WO32/5102, (General, Code 86(A)), Field Marshal Haig requests return of 2nd British Army to his command from the King of the Belgians: letter, 25 October 1918, from Haig to 'The Commander-in-Chief, Allied Forces in France'; letter, 25 October 1918, from Haig to the Secretary of the War Cabinet. The full text of both letters is included in Appendices IV and V.

Reference here to 'Army of Flanders' indicates that Haig was well aware of Second Army's increased role within the Army Group. His comments also demonstrate his concern that if Plumer and his troops continued to remain within the GAF, then the critical British role in the further liberation of Belgium would overlooked, while credit went to King Albert and the French.

This interpretation is confirmed by Haig's second letter, a longer letter to the War Cabinet, enclosing copies of his letter to Foch and the 19 October 'Directive No. 4925' from the latter.[24] Haig proceeds to restate his commitment to co-operation with French forces, giving examples of temporary detachments he has made of British units, 'on the AISNE in May and on the MARNE in July'. Such arrangements were 'of a purely temporary nature' and the units were 'to be returned on the completion of the specific operation in hand'; this agreement had also applied to Second Army and the GAF. In the interests of balance it should be pointed out, as Haig does not, that there were occasions when French forces were placed under British command. A current example was Debeney's formation, deployed under Rawlinson and Fourth Army, as noted by the Earl of Derby at the time.[25]

He then reviews the achievements of Second Army, pointing out that it had 'successfully' provided flank protection and secured the left bank of the River Lys, taking 'the heaviest share of the work in driving the enemy back' and incurring 'some 22,000 casualties'. Haig had again made specific reference to 'two divisions [attacking] in conjunction with the Belgian Army' which, as referred to previously, did not reflect Plumer's orders on the deployment of Second Army at the start of the Battle of Ypres. In his conversation with Lord Derby on 26 October 1918 Haig had actually explained that while he had been requested originally to place two British divisions under Albert, it had been his (Haig's) decision to offer to transfer the full Second Army.[26] However, somewhat peculiarly, most of his references to this action only describe the deployment of two divisions.

Haig also highlights the 'considerable casualties' resulting from the 'series of important attacks [by First, Third and Fourth British Armies] on a wide front against positions of vital importance to the enemy' held by 'a considerable number of his best troops'. Haig then emphasises the main point of his letter to Foch, namely, that the drive of Second Army to force the Rivers Scheldt and Dendre 'can be equally well undertaken under my [Haig's] control'; and so allow him to 'balance the casualties so that their incidence may not fall unduly on the British forces'.

This is Haig's central concern. As his penultimate paragraph describes, he sees that 'the brunt of the offensive operations has fallen on the British troops' and 'Owing to our lack of effectives this cannot be allowed to continue much longer'. Crucially, regarding the position of Second Army:

> It is therefore most necessary that I should exercise the greatest care in engaging the five Armies of which the British Expeditionary Force is composed. The responsibility for this

24 TNA WO32/5102, (General, Code 86(A)), Field Marshal Haig requests return of 2nd British Army to his command from the King of the Belgians; letter from 'F. Foch' to 'Commandement en Chef des Armées Alliées', DIRECTIVE GENERALE No. 4925, 'G.Q.G.A., le 19 Octobre 1918'; see Appendix III.

25 Dutton, ed., *Paris 1918*, p. 293.

26 Dutton, ed., *Paris 1918*, p. 295.

> can alone rest on me, and *ought not in the case of any portion of the British forces to be delegated to any foreign Commander, of no matter how high a rank.* (My emphasis).[27]

Thus Haig sought the support of the War Cabinet in bringing Second Army back under his command – allowing him to manage all the remaining resources of the BEF, particularly its troops, as effectively as possible. Importantly, the letter does state his commitment to carrying out Foch's overall aims and 'instructions' in the latter's 19 October letter. Despite the strength of his disagreement with Foch over the command of Second Army, Haig made clear that he was 'anxious to carry out Marshal Foch's wishes and instructions to the full'. That he has no problem in using such terms shows that he continued to acknowledge and respect the *Generalissimo*'s authority. This evidence that Haig continued to hold respect for Foch's position and still sought to cooperate under the direction of Foch, was crucial to the eventual resolution of this particular disagreement between the two men.

Haig's concerns were taken up by Sir Henry Wilson as CIGS. An internal covering note 28 October 1918, attached to Haig's letters, records that:

> No action on this to be taken at present.
> CIGS has gone to discuss it & has a copy.[28]

Haig was apparently unaware of this action. On 26 October Haig met the Earl of Derby, Britain's Ambassador in Paris, and asked him to try and intercede via the French Prime Minister, Georges Clemenceau. He emphasised his strength of feeling through the threat of resignation. If his government would not support him then Haig intended 'to be asked to be relieved of his command'.[29]

On 27 October Haig wrote formally to Foch in terms which turned the argument into one which was directly linked to his authority – that the refusal to return Second Army directly undermined his position as Commander of the BEF.[30] His letter was no doubt also influenced by the outcomes from the conference of allied commanders on 25 October. There he had been a dissenting voice, as the final armistice proposals were in accord with the views of Foch, supported by the other commanders: 'nothing less than unconditional surrender, but without actually using that phrase'.[31]

Haig's reasoning continued to be heavily influenced by his belief that the British Army was carrying the weight of the fighting and making most progress; that the French forces were not pulling their weight; that the increased casualty rates resulted from the open and offensive warfare being waged, would mean increased complaints from London and exacerbate the problem of reinforcements. Elizabeth Greenhalgh has attributed Haig's strength of feeling to

27 Letter, 25 October 1918, from Haig to the Secretary of the War Cabinet, p. 2.
28 TNA WO32/5102, (General, Code 86(A)), Field Marshal Haig requests return of 2nd British Army to his command from the King of the Belgians; Minute Sheet No. 1, 121/France/3035.
29 As recorded by the Earl of Derby: Dutton, ed., *Paris 1918*, p. 293, diary entry for 26 October 1918. See also E. Greenhalgh, *Victory Through Coalition: Britain and France during the First World War* (Cambridge: Cambridge University press, 2005), p. 258.
30 Haig to Foch, 27 October 1918, referred to in Sheffield and Bourne, *Douglas Haig War Diaries*, p. 479, footnote.
31 Terraine, *To Win A War*, p. 218.

'... resentment [over the British Army carrying the main weight of the fighting], pessimism over casualties, and jealousy [over King Albert making a triumphal entry into Bruges] – together with, perhaps, pique at the memory of having had the French First army removed from his command in August.[32] This assessment is unjustly harsh on Haig in my opinion. He had shown genuine concern at the disproportionate share of the fighting being undertaken by British forces, of which Second Army's changed role within the GAF was a practical example. He was also worried about the consequences of the casualty rate and believed that he could manage this more efficiently if he reassumed command of all the British Armies. This was also why he did not support the submission of ceasefire proposals which the Germans would feel unable to accept, thereby prolonging the war.

The evidence of personal jealousies, or of a desire by Haig for the limelight, influencing his views is limited – Haig's actions and demeanour following his return to Britain after the Armistice do not suggest that these would have been primary factors in his dispute with Foch. He had confirmed in writing his agreement to the overall authority and direction set by Foch. There were also plenty of times during the Hundred Days when Haig could have chosen to lead a triumphal British Army through a liberated major town or city. If his personal feelings were a contributory factor – and this is perfectly possible – then this was more likely linked to his perception that the British Government, and the Prime Minister in particular, attached more weight to Foch's opinions and views than they did to those of Haig. For example, his reaction to the faint praise in the telegram from Lloyd George on 9 October, which was written following Foch's report to the Prime Minister of the British Army's recent victories.[33]

With regard to Haig's pessimism concerning the fighting abilities of the French Army, Greenhalgh acknowledges that while 'relations between Degoutte and Plumer were said to be of the best... the Belgians were critical of the French units who were not fighting well'.[34]

The degree of feeling in the dispute that arose between Haig and Foch over the question of Second Army can seem disproportionate unless the broader context of the proposed terms for the armistice is considered, alongside Haig's assessments of the present fighting capability of the allied armies. Although he makes no mention of the armistice terms in his 25 October letters, they were written on the same day as the conference of allied commanders, at which Haig had appeared isolated in his concerns at setting armistice terms which were close to an unconditional surrender (and which the Germans might therefore feel compelled to reject). What I consider to be the crucial issue is that Second Army's situation in relation to the GAF and the circumstances in Flanders at that point, represented in microcosm Haig's broader concerns about the position on the Western Front and the present allied approach regarding the armistice discussions.

Some blame for the dispute has been directed at the GHQ staff, and CGS Lawrence, given the latter's pessimistic views on continuing the war, the pressures on British forces, and the state of the German Army. 'Lawrence was reported as intending to oppose 'with all his force' the retention of Second Army under Albert's command'.[35] Sheffield refers to Haig 'ascribing to Foch devious political motives for keeping Plumer under the command of the King of the

32 Greenhalgh, *Victory through Coalition*, p. 258.
33 Terraine, *To Win A War*, p. 200-1.
34 Greenhalgh, *Victory through Coalition*, p. 255.
35 Greenhalgh, *Victory through Coalition*, p. 255.

Belgians';[36] he quotes Haig as viewing Foch's refusal to transfer Second Army back to the BEF command as striking 'at the very foundation of my [Haig's] position'.[37]

On 27 October, Lord Derby met at breakfast with CIGS, General Henry Wilson, and Secretary of State for War, Viscount Milner. The latter was able to report that the Cabinet supported the return of Second Army to Haig's command and that the issue was to find a method acceptable to all parties for arranging this. That morning, at his meeting with Clemenceau, Lord Derby pursued Haig's request. Despite confiding that he and Foch 'were not on the best of terms', Clemenceau had expressed his support for Haig and undertook to discuss the issue with Foch at a meeting that afternoon.[38]

Haig was sceptical:

> [Clemenceau] would settle the question if Foch was in a reasonable mood! It seems that Clemenceau and Foch are not on good terms. Foch is suffering from a swelled head and thinks himself another Napoleon! So Clemenceau has great difficulties with him now.[39]

Haig's doubts reflect Derby's conversation that morning with Clemenceau – and the latter duly reported back to Derby that Foch had proved to be 'immovable' on the issue.[40] Foch had also complained that Haig had not supplied his reasons for the return of Second Army. Derby saw this point as a possible way of allowing the Generalissimo to maintain his authority while agreeing to Haig's request – which now had the crucial support of the British government. That evening Derby and Wilson persuaded Haig to write 'a private and conciliatory letter to Foch' setting out his case (though Haig complained that this he had already done).[41]

The responsibility for finally resolving the dispute is claimed by the CIGS, Henry Wilson, who met with Foch on 28 October to deliver Haig's letter. Terraine describes how:

> In the end it fell to Foch's old friend, Sir Henry Wilson, to persuade the Generalissimo. They met… at Foch's headquarters. Wilson recorded: 'I had rather a stormy meeting with Foch, but I think I was able to put my case strongly but quietly'.[42]

Greenhalgh also believes that the 'stormy words' between Wilson and Foch were the turning point.[43] In his biography of Plumer however, Powell credits Milner with bringing 'pressure to bear upon Clemenceau' which then led to Foch conceding.[44] Perhaps unsurprisingly, Haig's subsequent report to Derby suggested that it was Haig's own meeting with Foch which had delivered a 'satisfactory' conclusion.[45]

36 Sheffield, *The Chief*, p. 332.
37 Sheffield, *The Chief*, p. 332, reference Haig's manuscript diary 24 October 1918; Haig to Foch, 27 October 1918, Haig's papers 132.
38 Dutton, ed., *Paris 1918*, p. 297, diary entry for 27 October 1918.
39 Sheffield and Bourne, *Douglas Haig War Diaries*, p. 481-2.
40 Dutton, ed., *Paris 1918*, p. 298, diary entry for 27 October 1918.
41 Dutton, ed., *Paris 1918*, p. 298, diary entry for 27 October 1918.
42 Terraine, *To Win A War*, p. 226.
43 Greenhalgh, *Victory through Coalition*, p. 257.
44 Powell, *Plumer*, p. 277-8.
45 Dutton, ed., *Paris 1918*, p. 300, diary entry for 28 October 1918

Their meeting on 28 October had proved to be a cordial coming together over 'tea and cakes' initiated by Foch (though Haig pointed out that he never 'took tea'!). The agreement was for Second Army to complete its pending operation to advance to the Scheldt, at which point command would transfer back to Haig. Despite the strong feelings displayed by Haig, in the end the issue was perhaps one of a lower priority for Foch.[46]

In a note back to London on 29 October, Wilson, in his own inimical style, summarised the resolution of the dispute:

> The little trouble about 2nd Army is completely removed and we are sailing in a summer sun with steady fair and gentle breezes.[47]

This message was relayed that same day to the War Cabinet.[48]

One person's views are – perhaps crucially – missing from this narrative: what was the opinion, in support of Haig or otherwise, of the Commander of Second Army? None of the texts make any mention of Plumer, or whether his views were sought; no related discussion was recorded. And there are no personal papers to refer to.

No-one, including Haig, seems to have thought to consult Plumer directly. However there is evidence of Plumer's loyalty to Haig on previous occasions,[49] so it is unlikely that Plumer would have done or said anything that would appear to conflict with the Commander-in-Chief of British forces. Given his pragmatic approach to his responsibilities, his commitment to his immediate commander, and the lack of any evidence to the contrary, it would seem that Plumer simply got on with the job in hand.

In practical terms, the Second Army completed its drive to the Scheldt and then continued with preparations to assault the enemy across the river (offset by the retirement by German forces during 8-10 November). Greenhalgh probably has the correct take on it when she concludes: 'It is unlikely that Plumer's Second Army would have done anything differently if it had remained under King Albert's command in the GAF'.[50] It is however worth observing that a subsequent failure to have agreed armistice terms might have led to very different developments – and Haig's concern to have all the British armies under his direct command might have been viewed as a very wise and necessary precaution on his part.

Plumer had not been present at the conference of British Army commanders held on 31 October. It was four days later when Second Army formally resumed its place alongside the other British armies under Haig.

> At 1 p.m. on the 4th November, one hour after the Second Army had reverted to the command of Sir Douglas Haig, General Plumer visited him at G.H.Q. and received his orders to reconnoitre actively, follow the Germans with advanced guards if they withdrew,

46 This point, within a concise exposition of the dispute, its causes and resolution, and the views of the main protagonists, is made in Greenhalgh, *Victory Through Coalition*, pp. 254-61.
47 TNA WO32/5102, (General, Code 86(A)), Field Marshal Haig requests return of 2nd British Army to his command from the King of the Belgians; memo from Sir Henry Wilson to P. S. to C.I.G.S., B.L.662 October 29th H.W. Personal.
48 TNA WO32/5102: Handwritten notes on Henry Wilson's memo.
49 Simkins, 'Herbert Plumer', p. 147
50 Greenhalgh, *Victory through Coalition*, p. 258.

> and be prepared to attack and cross the Schelde on or about the 11th November, by which date the commander of the Second Army said he could be ready.[51]

On 6 November Haig met with Degoutte, who was still operating as Chief of Staff to King Albert. The meeting discussed Haig's proposal to force the passage of the Scheldt, as he recorded in his diary:

> ... by my Fifth and Second Armies on Monday next [11 November]...
> De Goutte quite agreed with me, and said he would co-operate on the same day.[52]

Second Army was back within the BEF and under Haig's command. Situation normal was resumed.

51 Edmonds, *Official History, Vol. V*, p. 451; TNA WO158/212, Second Army Operations, 1 October 1918-20 January 1919, GHQ OAD 950: 3 November 1918.
52 Sheffield and Bourne, *Douglas Haig War Diaries*, p. 484.

9

Conclusion

> The pragmatic Plumer – an apostle of teamwork, who was at the very least endowed with sound tactical instincts and great common sense – did as much as anyone, and more than most, to encourage and develop the type of all-arms attack that proved the key to victory in 1918.[1]

Over the course of the final campaign in Flanders – the Liberation Offensive of 1918 – British Second Army developed and refined its fighting methods. The outcome was that its original task of protecting the right flank of the Belgian Army became subsidiary to its eventual responsibility of being the strike force for the GAF. The successful performance of the Army led it to become the cutting edge of the allied forces in the liberation of Flanders.

The above summary of Plumer as commander by Peter Simkins was demonstrated through Second Army's performance during the Hundred Days. As Simkins goes on to point out, while Plumer may not have been innovative in his methods and tactics, he was a facilitator and a catalyst who played a crucial part in demonstrating the war-winning combined arms approach of the British armies. In so doing he was also helping create a blueprint for the battlefield tactics of a later world war.

The fighting by his troops involved finding the method and the means for the systematic assault of entrenched or prepared positions. These were commonly defended by well-sited machine guns and artillery with planned fields of fire. In part, this application of heavy weaponry reflected the lower number of troops available to the Germans during the latter part of 1918; although the problem of units operating below their theoretical fighting strength also applied to Second Army. Similarly both sides possessed troops of variable experience and quality, which had implications for tactics and organisation.

As the allied advance gathered pace the Germans were increasingly forced to position their defenders well forward. Previously they had enjoyed the advantages of time and space to adopt a series of defensive lines, with the British attackers forced to enter a 'killing ground' beyond a thinly-manned first line of defence. The changed situation certainly helped Second Army. The weight of the artillery support available to the attacking force allowed its infantry, upon breaking through the first and main line of defence, to enter into open ground. It was only when

1 Simkins, 'Herbert Plumer', p. 154.

the Germans were able to execute planned retirements – which were a repeating feature of their operations in Flanders – that the defenders could block the British advance, hence the persistent emphasis in the orders issued by Plumer for the retreating troops to be harassed by every means possible. There are constant references in the British operational reports of the Germans withdrawing and of 'enemy resistance stiffening'. In this the Germans were helped considerably by the terrain they were defending.

The nature of the Flanders' geography was ideally suited to defence. The Germans generally held higher ground with clear sight lines, particularly at the start of the campaign, and made very effective use of available cover and buildings. The clever use of demolitions also proved to be a stumbling block for attacking troops. Initially, the British were attacking over ground destroyed by earlier fighting. This terrain, pock-marked by shell craters and war debris, hindered forward movement and caused delays in transport, supplies and movement of supporting artillery. It provided excellent opportunities for creating defensive positions quickly and successfully, providing ample sites for machine gun nests and snipers.

As the front lines moved forward so British troops entered ground with which they were unfamiliar. Maps varied in their availability and quality; RAF reconnaissance was hindered by variable flying conditions. The terrain was divided by canals and rivers, obstacles which aided the defenders yet had to be crossed by the attackers. There are many examples within unit diaries and histories of river and canal crossings, either via careful pre-planning or hasty improvisation. In either case the actual method of getting troops across the water was complemented by effective tactics and deployment in order to take and secure that vital first bridgehead.

The following example of a battalion operation from the regimental history of the Loyal North Lancs Regiment provides a typical experience:

> At 9.30 on the 17th [October 1918] 'B' Company of the [2nd Battalion, Loyal North Lancs] crossed the river [Lys] near Royal Farm – one man at a time – by means of an improvised raft, and established posts in a semi-circle covering the crossing place. An hour later 'D' Company was ordered to cross and advance on Lauwe, supported by Lewis Gun fire by 'A' [Company]; and by 2pm Lauwe was occupied, and on the arrival of 'C' company a defensive flank was formed facing north-east between the Courtrai and Arbeke roads.[2]

Reliable intelligence on the strength and position of the enemy, and whether the resistance encountered was based upon a hasty rear-guard action or through an established defence line, was also variable. The valuable ability of RAF reconnaissance to assist was regularly undermined by poor weather conditions – particularly significant in Flanders. Here the problems of rain and fog, exacerbating the difficulties of transport and communications, were acute on a number of occasions. What the *Official History* has called 'the usual difficulties of the supply of advancing troops' were exacerbated by the Flanders terrain and climate, creating major challenges for the GAF and British Second Army. The roads in Flanders, already poor in terms of both quality and quantity, became virtually impassable in bad weather. These were totally inadequate for the transport requirements of Second Army, but the supply of forward troops was in general

2 Wylly, *Loyal North Lancs*, p. 151.

maintained throughout the advance. One regimental history makes this very clear, referring to the 'wonderful work' of the transport services:

> The railhead was far behind, the roads were bad, every bridge had been destroyed, and the distances that had to be covered to reach [the battalion] increased almost daily by about ten miles. Yet on no single occasion did the supply of daily rations fail to arrive.[3]

As noted, there was heavy use of gas shells by both sides during the fighting in Flanders, creating a further cause for transport delay:

> During offensive operations, it was often necessary to cross contaminated ground, with all the inherent hazards such activity entailed ...[4]

Falls has referred to '... the section of the [36th] Divisional Train bringing up its wagons through valleys wreathed and stinking with gas...'[5]

Plumer's attention to the problems of logistics led to a strong emphasis on forward planning. Effective use was made of railway lines with these extended forward towards the new front line at the earliest opportunity. Units were encouraged to consider flexible arrangements for ensuring lines of supply, including the use of mules where appropriate. The supply by air of advance units cut off from support was a notable feature of the army's campaign.

Maginniss has summarised the successful logistic support of the British Army during the Hundred Days as 'robust and innovative ... capable of supporting an advance equating to an average of twenty eight miles per month'. He proceeds to point out that 'whilst these distances were exceeded by the 50 miles per month of the fully mechanized allied armies in France in the period June 1944 to February 1945, they were higher than the average monthly advance in Italy between September 1943 and May 1945 [25 miles per month]'.[6] These results are consistent with the best performance of Second Army formations, competing with the geography and climate of Flanders, with Maginness noting that 'between 8-10 November, Second Army advanced an amazing twenty-two miles'.[7] He concludes that such outcomes 'were impressive achievements' for military forces that were at best only semi-mechanized and without the motorised logistical support enjoyed by allied armies in the Second World War.

The scale and pace of the advance brought its own problems. One was the fatigue of the front line units. British Second Army made a number of changes in troop disposition during the advance, in order to try and maintain a degree of freshness in its attacking forces. There was much emphasis upon training and in particular, being aware of and responding to the implications of the changed nature of the fighting taking place. However the fighting did fall disproportionately upon units, demonstrated by the casualty figures in the tables below.

3 Nicholson et al, *East Lancs*, p. 559.
4 Lieutenant-Colonel. C. H. Maginniss, 'Heads of Steel: Logistic Support to the BEF's Mobile All Arms Battle: July-November 1918', *The Royal Logistics Corps Review 2008*, pp. 165-180, p. 172.
5 Falls, *36th Division*, p. 279.
6 Maginniss, *Heads of Steel*, p. 174.
7 Maginniss, *Heads of Steel*, p. 174;

Summary of weekly battle casualties – by Corps
The Final Advance in Flanders

Compiled from weekly operations reports produced by Second Army HQ – Source: WO 158/218

Week commencing	21 Sept		28 Sept		5 Oct		12 Oct	
Formation	O	OR	O	OR	O	OR	O	OR
Army troops	–	1	–	1	1	5	1	13
II Corps	4	145	154	1,874	90	3,190	95	2,271
X Corps	14	183	30	627	19	425	54	868
XV Corps	7	168	72	1,179	19	382	23	249
XIX Corps	29	332	47	711	95	2,807	46	306
Total	54	829	303	4,392	224	6,869	219	3,707

Week commencing	19 Oct		26 Oct		2/9Nov	
Formation	O	OR	O	OR	O	OR
Army troops	–	–	1	3	–	7
II Corps	104	2,423	81	1,314	46	763
X Corps	24	564	20	229	10	102
XV Corps	10	164	14	93	14	232
XIX Corps	64	1632	55	1,133	46	754
Total	212	4,679	172	2,772	116	1,958

Summary of total battle casualties – Second Army
The Final Advance in Flanders

Compiled from weekly operations reports produced by Second Army HQ – Source: WO 158/218

Formation	Total battle casualties 21 Sept – 15 November 1918 The Final Advance in Flanders	
	O	OR
Army Corps	3	30
II Corps	574	11,980
X Corps	171	2,998
XV Corps	159	2,467
XIX Corps	382	7,675
TOTAL	1,289	25,150

The formations of II Corps, operating on the left wing of the Army and alongside Belgian or French forces, bore the heaviest load. The following message was sent to the 36th Division, by Lieutenant-General Jacob of II Corps, following the battles of Ypres and Courtrai. It provides a succinct summary of the challenges faced and overcome:

> The 36th (Ulster) Division has been fighting continuously since the 28th September in the operations in FLANDERS. The spirit, dash and initiative shown by all ranks have been splendid and beyond all praise. The leadership displayed by… Commanders could not have been better. The conditions under which the men have had to fight have been and still are very trying, but nothing seems to stop [the] Division.
>
> When the history is written of what the Division has done in FLANDERS during the past month it will prove to be a record of magnificent fighting and wonderful progress, for during this period an advance has been made of about 25 miles over the worst of the country and under the heaviest machine gun fire ever experienced in this war. This advance has entailed constant fighting but the 36th Division has overcome every obstacle and has proved itself one of the best fighting divisions in the Army, well commanded and well staffed…[8]

This particular role of II Corps was also recognised at an even higher level, reflecting the importance of the contact point during operations between Second Army and the Belgian or French forces to its left:

Marshal FOCH visited the Army Commander today and asked him to send his congratulations to the II Corps and to the 9th, 29th and 36th Divisions for their splendid work in the operations since the 14th October…[9]

The variable strength on paper of the units comprising Second Army, and issues such as the reconstituted divisions and the nature of the replacement troops,[10] has been described in chapter two. However, it is also evident that the three divisions which fought under II Corps for the two principal battles, 9th (Scottish), 36th (Ulster) and 29th (the one Regular Army Division), were of proven ability. Terraine has described them as '…three very good divisions indeed'.[11] It was surely not chance that saw these formations bear the brunt of the fighting at the centre of the coalition force; and demonstrate a military prowess that proved capable of punching through the main centre of German resistance east of Ypres and subsequently beyond Courtrai.

It has been calculated that the ten divisions of Second Army registered an average success rate of 55.7 per cent for opposed attacks during the Final Advance in Flanders. For comparison purposes, the success rates during the Hundred Days for the British divisions in Third (seventeen) divisions and Fourth (nine) divisions Armies were 64.4% and 70.7% respectively. The lower rate for Second Army can be explained by the identified problems for logistics and

8 Written into: TNA WO95/2504, War Diary of 108 Infantry Brigade, *23rd October.*
9 Written into: TNA WO95/2504, War Diary of 108 Infantry Brigade, *23rd October.*
10 Writing a few years after the end of the war, G.A.B. Dewar pointed out that '… the six British divisions which took the main part in the Flanders offensive on the British side had suffered in the period between March 21 and July 15, 1918, an average of 6250 casualties per division': Dewar, *Haig's Command Vol. II*, p. 337, note 1.
11 Terraine, *To Win A War*, p. 203.

artillery support as a consequence of the weather and terrain; together with the strength of enemy resistance associated with the strategic importance of the Channel coast for the German command. Allowance should also be made for the overall weaker composition of Second Army at the start of the campaign. One of the remarkable results was that two of the divisions rebuilt from cadre (30th and 34th) were amongst its most successful. It should also be noted that of the seven British divisions which had an outright failure rate of 25% or more, only one (41st Division) was with Second Army.[12]

Within Second Army, the average success rate was equalled or bettered by the 30th, 34th, 35th and 36th Divisions and, most notably, by the remarkable 9th (Scottish) Division; the latter was shown to have had a success rate of 93% against opposition, making it the third most successful of all the British divisions on the Western Front.[13] It is notable that these five divisions were deployed across the Second Army front and not concentrated in just one or two Corps.

Also of note is the turnaround in the performance of 35th Division, which was one of the more successful Second Army divisions during the final campaign, despite a previous history of problems and failures. It has been identified that the likely key to this was the opportunity afforded to the formation within Second Army's plan of campaign, to prepare and carry out a series of attacks as a complete division.[14]

Second Army also made the best use of the troop resources available to it. Hence what can be summed up as the solid performance of 40th Division, a scratch formation made up from garrison guard battalions, deemed 'semi-mobile', and initially designated as only capable of holding a quiet sector of the line. For most of the campaign it secured the Army's right flank, ensuring that touch was maintained with 59th Division, Fifth Army. While not involved in a major set-piece attack, its patrols and advance guards continually harassed the retreating Germans, and took every opportunity to push forward through weakening defences up to and eventually beyond the Scheldt. As part of XV Corps, it helped deliver the pace of advance that saw Second Army achieve a north-south axis by the close of the Battle of Courtrai; and then act as a pivot for Second Army to deploy along the line of the Schelde, prior to a further advance and then its withdrawal for the final few days of the war.

The issue of the high casualty rates in the Hundred Days campaign, affecting all the British armies involved including Second Army, should be placed in context. The nature of the fighting was that of a modern war, a war of movement with the killing being carried out by a plethora of large and small machines, dwarfing the exposed infantryman. In considering the high troop losses, the common perception potentially re-emerges of this being due to failings by senior

12 For an analysis of the performance of British Divisions during the Hundred Days, and the supporting methodology for the calculation of 'success rates', see P. Simkins, 'Co-Stars or Supporting Cast?: British Divisions in the 'Hundred Days', 1918', in P. Griffith, ed., *British Fighting Methods in the Great War (London: Frank Cass, 1996)*, pp. 50-69.

13 This 93% success rate for 9th Division was greater than the average success rate for the Dominion divisions: 72.5%, (four Canadian Divisions), 70.7% (five Australian Divisions), 64.5% (New Zealand Division). Simkins, 'British Divisions', p.56.

14 P. Simkins, 'Each One A Pocket Hercules: The Bantam Experiment and the Case of the 35th Division', in Sanders Marble, ed., *Scraping The Barrel: The Military Use of Substandard Manpower 1860-1960* (New York: Fordham University Press, 2012), pp. 79-104.

commanders. Adverse comparison has also been made with the lower overall British casualty figures for the Second World War.

On closer examination a different picture emerges. Max Hastings points out that:

> Much-diminished Western allied losses [in 1939-45] reflected not better leadership than that of the earlier conflict [1914-18], but the fact that the second time around, the Russians bore the overwhelming burden of necessary sacrifice. On the only occasion that a large Anglo-American army went head to head with the Wehrmacht on a limited front, in Normandy in 1944, some infantry rates of loss were briefly comparable with those of 1916, until the German line was broken and Eisenhower's armies could exploit their terrific mobile capacity, such as did not exist in World War I.[15]

The different character of the two wars, as experienced by the British Army, is explored by Corrigan:

> From beginning to end of the First war, the bulk of the British army was fighting the main enemy in the main theatre of war (the Western Front)...
>
> In terms of men deployed, and in the intensity of the fighting, the British army was far less involved in the Second War...
>
> Hence British army casualties between 1939 and 1945 were considerably less than those between 1914 and 1918, and miniscule compared to those of the Russian army, which spent most of the Second War fighting the main enemy on land.[16]

Corrigan points out that between the evacuation of the British Army from Europe in 1940 and the Normandy invasion of 1944, British forces were deployed in theatres such as North Africa, Crete and the Far East, where they did not have to face the main body of the German Army.

John Ellis has shown that when allowance is made for the smaller share of British troops in the Second World War who were deployed in combat units, compared with the situation in the First World War, the casualty rates for each war become very similar.[17] He also emphasised a number of key actions and battles during the Second World War which involved very high casualty rates for the British combat units involved – examples include certain actions at the Battle of El Alamein, assaults during the Italian campaign and at the Anzio beachhead. He points out:

> ...Most fighting in World War II [by British and USA forces] was done by a remarkably small proportion of troops whose casualties were very high...
>
> If you were an officer, the outlook was even bleaker...
>
> ... in World War II [officer casualties] tended to be proportionately higher than in World War I.[18]

15 M. Hastings, *Catastrophe: Europe Goes to War in 1914* (London: William Collins, 2013), pp. 551-2.
16 Corrigan, *Mud, Blood*, p.70; In this section of his book, pp. 52-72, he seeks to debunk the common myth of 'the lost generation' resulting from the casualty figures for the First World War.
17 J. Ellis, *The Sharp End of War: The Fighting Man in World War II* (London: David & Charles, 1980), pp. 156-169.
18 Ellis, *The Sharp End*, pp. 162-4.

Another important difference during the Second World War was that casualty rates were significantly reduced through advances in medical science. The key areas of progress were antibiotics (penicillin and sulpha-drugs) and the use of blood transfusions.[19]

The broad conclusion is a pretty blunt one:

> Being issued with a rifle and being told to close with the enemy was about as dangerous during World War II as during World War I.[20]

As Sheffield concludes:

> In 1945, as in 1918, high intensity warfare took a fearful toll of soldiers' lives.[21]

Most Second Army units were not at effective strength. The end of month figures for 12th Battalion Norfolk Regiment (31st Division) are one example:[22]

	Officers	Other Ranks
30 June	36	780
31 July	40	956
31 August	29	786
30 September	36	784
31 October	42	800

This book had drawn regular attention to the issues surrounding the potential quality of the troops making up the formations in Second Army. In the event their performance seems to have surprised and impressed their commanders, given many of them were young conscripts or men re-classified as fit for front line duty from other occupations. Brigadier-General Pereira (GOC, 43 Brigade), in his subsequent report on the opening day of the Battle of Ypres, referred to:

> … the fine fighting spirit of the men. Although looked down on before the fight as 'B' men, of an inferior type to the 'A' men they showed all the energy, keenness and fighting spirit of 'A' men, and though they may not be physically capable of undergoing the same hardships for a long strain, I feel the utmost confidence in them, and that, if some allowance is made for physical disabilities by giving them more rest than the 'A' men they will hold their own with the latter when it comes to fighting.[23]

19 Ellis, *The Sharp End*, pp. 170-2.
20 S. Bungay, *Alamein* (London: Aurum Press, 2003; original hardback edition, 2002), p. 199.
21 Sheffield, *Forgotten Victory*, p. 230.
22 Records of 31st Division, TNA WO95/2366.
23 42 Brigade, *Report on Operations September 28th 1918* (from TNA WO95/1876 War Diary of 14th Division: General Staff).

In 1927 one writer commented:

> In view of the results attained [by Second Army during the final campaign] the spirit, the fitness, and the power of endurance of all ranks had proved to be remarkable. The more remarkable when we remember that the forces had been bled white five months before, and the ranks were filled up with recruits, many being mere boys.[24]

Through his study of a particular draft of conscripts, Tim Lynch has commented on perceptions of British troops during the final period of the war:

> There is a tendency to assume that by this stage of the war the ranks were filled with war-weary volunteers and reluctant conscripts waiting only for the end of the war but, with no end in sight, the men arriving at the front could still show high levels of motivation.[25]

From his research Lynch concludes that:

> … the war-winning army of 1918 was largely made up of teenage conscripts who formed the largest force Britain had ever put into the field and, at that time, the most professional and capable army it had ever known. Despite devastating losses, battalions of soldiers who in 1917 would have been regarded as too young to serve formed and re-formed to keep pressing home the attack and never lost cohesion, never followed the examples of the French, Russian and German armies by mutinying, and never lost their motivation to fight.[26]

Corrigan has concluded that the conscripts 'made a vital contribution to the war'.[27] The successful outcomes from Second Army's final campaign add credibility to such a conclusion.

Although perhaps anticipated, there does not appear to have been any particular conflict between the existing troops and the new arrivals. Perhaps they all accepted that they were here because they were here. So it was that, despite the different origins of their service:

> As men arrived in their units the exigencies of war, shared by all, volunteer and conscript alike, soon welded men together into one battalion family…[28]

The scrutiny of war diaries for this book supports these conclusions on the performance of British troops in 1918. The diaries make little reference to the background of replacement troops and there is no subsequent distinction drawn between soldiers by virtue of their recruitment via a voluntary or conscripted route. The records demonstrate that field commanders had mastered the necessary tactics to harness the potential of the combined

24 Brice, *The Battle Book of Ypres*, p. 49.
25 T. Lynch, *They Did Not Grow Old: Teenage Conscripts on the Western Front, 1918* (Stroud, Gloucestershire: Spellmount The History Press, 2013), p. 202.
26 Lynch, *Teenage Conscripts*, p. 230.
27 Corrigan, *Mud, Blood*, p.74.
28 Corrigan, *Mud, Blood*, p.74.

arms available to them – and that their troops, volunteer or conscript, veteran or teenager, had the training and commitment to make the model work in practice on the battlefield. As noted in many examples in this book, by this stage of the war there was also a level of quality to the leadership provided on the front line, which also assisted drawing out the best from the available troops.

The soldiers of Second Army also had to cope with unfamiliar terrain and adapt to a type of warfare with which even the old hands would have unfamiliar. As the advance proceeded, the increasing number of civilians in the area, liberated and remaining in situ, or taking the opportunity to move to other areas, hindered the operation of artillery (due to the risk of civilian casualties) and exacerbated the problems of movement on the roads. It was also necessary to bring forward additional supplies for the many civilians who faced starvation.[29]

British Second Army had no tanks (though use was made of French tanks from the end of October), and therefore relied heavily upon the effectiveness of its artillery. The use of a creeping and/or rolling barrage, linked to counter-battery neutralisation of enemy artillery sites, and the targeting of key defensive positions and communications links, were all regular features of attacks. For the British forces in the GAF, particularly as the advance progressed, there was often no preliminary bombardment, in order to maximise the potential of surprise. Second Army Artillery Instructions No 1, 20 September 1918, authored by Lt-Col C R Newman, referred to the importance of preserving secrecy, and gave as an example, the successful attack on the Clercken-Paschendaele ridge in September 1918.

Attacks usually took place before dawn, to take advantage of early mist as a means of evading the full impact of enemy machine guns. Plumer frequently insisted upon the use of smoke shells as a means to provide as much screening as possible for his infantry. Gas shells were used to disorientate the defenders. Feint attacks were staged in order to try and identify enemy positions and forecast the likely response to an assault.

The range of the original artillery barrage often limited the length of the initial advance. We regularly see Second Army making contingency plans to bring forward supporting artillery with the initial attack, in order that advance forces can subsequently push onto second and third objectives during the course of a day.

The war diary of 7/Seaforth Highlanders for 25 October includes words of praise for the field artillery of 9th Division, highlighting the:

> accurate and effective shooting… always come as far forward as possible… [enthusing the infantry by] coming into action beside them.[30]

However the German policy of putting the majority of its defenders in the front line did mean that once this was broken through then the attackers could then manoeuvre over more open ground. We then see the application of small unit tactics, with local commanders using their initiative to exploit the initial breakthrough. Increasingly the nature of the fighting became localised to individual farms and villages. British troops became engaged in forms of what can be termed 'street-fighting' more familiar in subsequent conflicts. The British were able to deploy

29 Falls, *36th (Ulster) Division*, p. 279.
30 TNA WO95/1765, War Diary of 7th Battalion, Seaforth Highlanders.

their sections of infantry, equipped with rifles, grenades, Lewis guns and small mortars, to good effect.

The evidence presented in this book has shown various examples of the infantry unit's art of attack. Lynch provides a very clear picture of assault tactics in operation:

> In order to make the best use of the firepower available to them, every section needed to be able to work together to concentrate their fire at the same time. Once in position, the men would open with a fierce volley of all weapons to try to gain fire superiority over the defenders. Usually this would lead to an equally fierce response followed by a slackening of the fire by both sides as the initial shock wore off, then by bursts from one side, then the other. It was up to the platoon commander to judge the level of fire coming from the defenders so that when he felt that their response was slackening (because of casualties or weapons failures, for example), he would order the riflemen into the final assault as the Lewis gunners and rifle bombers kept up covering fire. If the attack was successful, it would be necessary to regroup and make ready to defend against a possible counter-attack, and to be aware of what was happening to the platoons to either side and be prepared to assist them if necessary.[31]

Much of the campaign was of a stop-start nature, with British units pursuing a withdrawing enemy to the point where the latter would turn and attempt to halt the advance, mainly through machine gun fire and artillery barrages. This pattern of manoeuvre can be termed 'staccato',[32] to reflect the stop-start rhythm of the advance as troops met apparently unlinked and unpredictable points of resistance. The result was the frequent pauses made by the advance troops of Second Army, before fire support or flank deployments could be carried out. The following comments are from a summary of the campaign by 107 Brigade (36th Division, II Corps), covering the period 28 September to 28 October 1918:

> The operations were of a trying and exhausting nature. Opposition chiefly met was machine gun fire, against which our Infantry showed courage and fighting qualities of a high order.
>
> The constant movement, entailing 'digging in' in many cases, was a test of endurance of a severe nature, and all ranks 'carried on' in a manner indicative of a high morale and confidence in our superiority over the enemy.[33]

The need for devolved command was crucial in this more fluid type of warfare. Second Army continually emphasised the need to keep close up to the enemy as he retreated:

> [The Army had the] policy of harassing the Germans without intermission, even though the main advance might be temporarily held up owing to the difficulty of getting supplies forward across the devastated regions in the wake of the pursuers, and the desire to avoid needless casualties. These harassing tactics, in the conditions of open warfare now

31 Lynch, *Teenage Conscripts*, pp. 180-1.
32 *Staccato… with each sound or note sharply detached or separated from the others (Concise Oxford Dictionary).*
33 TNA WO95/2502/1, War Diary of 107 Infantry Brigade, *Narrative of Operations carried out by the 107th Inf. Bde. 28.9.1918. to 28.10.1918*, (signed off by the Brigade Commander).

prevailing, gave ample scope for initiative and skill on the part of company and platoon commanders...[34]

Other steps taken to support the infantry included the forward use of field guns, engaging and taking out enemy machine gun nests over open sights. This was only possible due to the effective neutralisation of enemy artillery, and through the exercise of initiative on the ground by battalion and company commanders. Peter Simkins has emphasised the obvious point that:

> The BEF's ability in the 'Hundred Days' to overcome such a wide variety of tactical obstacles and challenges – ranging from set-piece operations to street fighting and canal crossings on improvised rafts – would simply not have been possible without good junior leadership.[35]

These 'obstacles and challenges' had regularly confronted Second Army, requiring initiative and adaptability in the tactics adopted. In his study of Third Army,[36] also made up of British formations (plus the New Zealand Division), Jonathan Boff concludes that it was 'diversity and flexibility, rather... than a set 'formula for success'' which led to that Army's achievements.[37] While there were many common features to the organisation of the successful attacks made by units of Second Army during the Flanders offensive, these also required the effective application of command and control. Front line officers had to be capable of making immediate and practical decisions in response to changing circumstances.[38]

The campaign also saw close co-ordination between the arms of infantry, artillery and RAF. This was not always successful, mainly due to the impact of weather and terrain, and frustrated by the limited technical developments in communications. When this co-operation could take place the results were a successful attack, and fewer casualties. The numerical superiority enjoyed by the RAF was a significant advantage, when the weather allowed. Writing to Plumer after the Battle of Ypres, Gillain emphasised the valuable support provided to the Belgian Army by Second Army artillery and the 'glorious and fruitful exploits' of the RAF.[39]

Advance infantry units were frequently reinforced by sections of support weapons to provide direct fire support when facing strengthened enemy positions. This combined arms approach was a regular feature of operation by Second Army and the other formations within the BEF; it would be commonplace in the Second World War. The exact arrangements and the command

34 Whalley-Kelly, *Ich Dien*, p. 66.
35 Simkins, 'British Divisions', p.65.
36 J. Boff, 'Combined Arms During the Hundred Days Campaign, August-November 1918', *War in History, 2010, 17(4)*, pp. 459-477, online at http://wih.sagepub.com/content/17/4/459.
37 Boff, 'Combined Arms', p. 477.
38 It should be noted that there were some particular differences between the circumstances of Second and Third Armies, requiring of a longer and more considered discussion. Briefly, Third Army (the largest of the British Armies) was twice the size of Second Army; it had regular access to support from the Tank Corps (when Second Army units had support from French tanks this was largely a success); there were some variations over the course of both Armies' campaigns with regard to the terrain features encountered and the consequent organisation of the German defences.
39 Letter from Chief of Staff, Belgian Army to General Plumer, British Second Army, 3 October 1918; a copy is included with the War Diary of 15th Battalion, West Yorkshire Regiment (Prince Of Wales' Own Regiment of Yorkshire Museum). Translated into English from the original French.

and control structures to manage the deployment were varied between different battalions, brigades or divisions. The most radical organisation was that of 'Brigade Groups', implemented by 30th Division during the Battle of Courtrai. Each group comprised the brigade's three infantry battalions together with units drawn from division level support arms; under the overall command of, and named for, the brigade commander. The term *Battlegroup* is a more recognisable term for such a formation of combined arms. This was an approach widely adopted by the German army in the Second World War: a *Kampfgruppe* (plural *Kampfgruppen*) – was a combat group of variable size, often a combined arms task force, typically named after its leader.[40]

A more typical arrangement in Second Army was the deployment of one or more support weapons' teams – field guns, mortars, heavy machine-guns – with an infantry company or battalion for a particular operation or period of time; with orders detailing the respective command and reporting responsibilities of the infantry and support units' commanders. For instance, in the same battle, 120 Brigade had a Stokes mortar team attached to each of its battalions;[41] there are many similar examples quoted throughout this book.

As part of an army group, and officially subordinate to King Albert and Belgian (or, in practice, through Degoutte, French) control, Plumer was not able to operate independently. However, despite its initial role of flank guard, the effective performance of the Second Army was such that it was subsequently designated as the strike force for the GAF. In fulfilling either its initial or subsequent responsibilities Second Army was not assisted by the command arrangements of the GAF – it became clear very quickly that Plumer had no confidence in Degoutte, the French Chief of Staff. Second Army's commander looked to follow his own informed instincts in plotting the deployment and operations of his Army; while ever mindful of securing outcomes that supported the coalition forces operating to his left. During the Battle of Ypres, Powell comments that 'The fatuous orders that emanated from Degoutte's headquarters continued to plague Plumer'.[42] Despite this, the evidence indicates that King Albert developed a strong confidence in his British ally, much of this due to the assistance provided to the Belgian Army at both operational and planning levels. The British forces impressed their allies at both command level and in the field.

Within the war diary of 15/West Yorkshires (31st Division) there is a copy of a letter passed from HQ Second Army through command levels to brigade, for the attention of all troops. Dated 3 October 1918, it is from Major-General Gillain, Chief of Staff of the Belgian Army, to General Plumer, following the cessation of the Battle of Ypres.[43] It is quite long, the type fills an A4 page, and it pays warm tribute to the performance of the British forces during the battle. The cooperation between II Corps (which operated on the Belgian right flank, at the junction between the two armies) and the Belgian forces is recognised, and General Jacob is named. The support of the British artillery and the RAF is also acknowledged.

40 This definition of the German Army *Kampfgruppe is taken from the Glossary in P. Caddick-Adams, Snow & Steel: Battle of the Bulge 1944-45 (London: Preface Publishing, 2014).*
41 TNA W095/2610, War Diary of 120 Infantry Brigade, *Brigade Instructions No. 3, 7th October 1918.*
42 Powell, *Plumer*, p. 275.
43 Letter from Chief of Staff, Belgian Army to General Plumer, British Second Army, 3 October 1918; a copy is included with the War Diary of 15th Battalion, West Yorkshire Regiment (Prince Of Wales' Own Regiment of Yorkshire Museum). Translated into English from the original French.

BELGIAN ARMY
CHIEF OF STAFF, ARMY HEADQUARTERS

3rd October 1918

Dear General,
Since I am unlikely to find the time to come and see you, I hasten to send you my very warmest congratulations for the magnificent success carried out by the troops of the British 2nd Army in the offensive launched on 28th September last.

Your expert leadership and the marvellous momentum of your combatants have not only delivered part of our national territory from enemy oppression, they have also allowed the Belgian Army to successfully work to the same objective; the joint attack victoriously carried out on this occasion by the second corps provided the perfect assistance. For this, I wish to express my greatest gratitude to you as well as to General Sir Jacob.

In addition to this support, the British 2nd Army effectively provided aid to our operations with a section of its artillery and its aircraft.

The latter in particular, despite the most unfavourable weather conditions, demonstrated such outstanding fighting spirit that our Army will forever keep the vivid memory of the glorious and fruitful exploits witnessed in recent days.

I would be truly happy, my dear General, if you would transmit my admiration, my gratitude and my congratulations to the fine 2nd Army under your command and most especially to the Aviation and Artillery which have directly assisted our operations.

Yours very sincerely
(signed) GILLAIN
To Lt. General Plumer
Commander of British 2nd Army

The length and tone of the letter goes well beyond that required for the sake of formality. It suggests genuine feelings of gratitude and respect from the Belgians for their British allies and their leader.

Philpott has praised the success of the coalition:

> Although the Flanders offensive was not without friction in the field and behind the lines, after four years' experience this was easily overcome, and in comparison with what had gone before the offensive must be seen as a model of allied military cooperation.[44]

There can be no doubt that this success in cooperation, at the level of high command, owed much to the demonstrable good sense and commitment of General Plumer.

When considering the relative strength and quality of the opposition confronting Second Army and the GAF, there are conflicting factors to consider. In general, the advantages offered by the weather and terrain to troops on the defensive, allied to the heavy small arms and artillery available, offset to a considerable degree the disadvantages of variable troop quality and lower troop numbers of the German forces in Flanders. It is important

44 W. J. Philpott, *Anglo-French Relations and Strategy on the Western Front 1914-18* (London: Palgrave Macmillan, 1996), p. 159.

to stress that British Second Army was itself beset with the potential problem of troop quality; and the rate of casualties during the campaign meant that obtaining replacements was a continual headache. The logistical issues surrounding transport and supply for the advancing troops were present throughout. In addition the ongoing challenge of attempting to move artillery forward to support infantry attacks further beset the Army. At the strategic level, Second Army had to conform to coalition requirements, and to plan and pace its advance in alignment with its allied neighbours. All this, whilst adjusting to the new demands of a war of manoeuvre. Casualty lists were high but this does not appear in general to result from failures in planning or command. This was a product of the firepower available to the armies of this time, and the lack of technology to counter this. When a soldier has to climb out of his trench then the level of risk increases directly – he becomes a visible and more tangible target.

We know that Haig was firm in his view that the opportunity to agree an armistice should be seized. He believed that German resistance would only stiffen as the Allies approached the borders of Germany, with consequent loss of life for allied troops; not to mention the destruction that warfare leaves in its wake. It is unlikely that Second Army could have sustained its advance, not least because of the high casualty rate and the likelihood of a further escalation of the logistical difficulties as winter weather approached. Further progress would have required the close co-operation of the fresher Belgian Army, as the latter became more familiar with the tactical and operational demands of open warfare in 1918. However, it is extremely unlikely that King Albert would have been prepared to bear the increasing death toll of his soldiers, and Belgian civilians too – alongside the laying waste of much of his country – any longer than was absolutely necessary to see the invader leave his country. The enemy defence would have solidified and resistance become more stubborn, the closer that allied forces came to the borders of Germany. The example of the fierce defence mounted by the German Army in the Second World War would support such conclusions.

However, it is to Second Army's credit that it found various ways of addressing or coping with the majority of the problems which confronted it during the Hundred Days. In early 1918 Plumer is quoted as complaining that his troops 'are untrained, with indifferent officers and although as brave as possible they simply don't know their business'.[45] This was not the case during the final months of the war. Throughout this period the techniques and set-piece operations of Second Army became routinely successful – its advance progressed in an almost irresistible manner. There is no doubt that, as Peter Simkins concludes:

> [The circumstances in Flanders in the autumn of 1918 allowed] a rolling series of limited-objective and all-arms attacks to be conducted on an almost daily basis. As a leading proponent and practitioner of [such tactics], Plumer surely deserves considerable credit for his contribution to the BEF's 'learning curve' and his part in the eventual German defeat.[46]

David Stevenson notes that the success of the 'Flanders offensive', within the series of allied attacks at the end of September, was 'particularly impressing' to the German military command.[47]

45 Wilson, Diary, 17 April 1918, Wilson Papers, IWM.
46 Simkins, *Herbert Plumer*, p. 159.
47 Stevenson, *Backs to the Wall*, p. 512.

Nick Lloyd points out that the breakthrough at Ypres on 28 September, following allied victories to the south, was the final blow for the German Chief of Staff, Ludendorff. He finally came to recognise that the German Army faced defeat and that an armistice must be actively pursued:

> The heavy British attacks around Cambrai and the crossing of the Canal du Nord were bad enough, but now his northern flank had been broken and there seemed little in the way to prevent the Allies from liberating all of Belgium...
>
> The breakthrough in Flanders seems to have been the point at which Ludendorff's will broke.[48]

Terraine has pointed out the strategic importance of the taking of Courtrai and the wheel eastwards of Second Army's right flank, which offered the prospect of taking the key city of Lille (but with the French Government seriously concerned at the prospect of the city suffering the devastation of a fight to take it):

> The good progress of the Second Army now made possible a further advance by... Fifth Army, which linked King Albert's Army Group in Flanders to Haig's in the centre... Plumer's success on the 14th [October] carried the Second Army well past the Lille fortifications, and Prince Rupprecht at once authorized withdrawal...[49]

The Battle of Courtrai, whilst virtually ignored in the historiography of the Hundred Days, delivered a number of strategic gains both for the GAF and the allied armies generally, making a wider contribution towards the winning of the war. On 17 October, Second Army liberated the important industrial towns of Tourcoing and Roubaix (north-east of Lille). On the same day, the Belgian Army cleared the port of Ostend, a place of symbolic importance to its country, which also released an important new route for the delivery of supplies (though the harbour was found to be blocked and port installations damaged). Two days later, Second Army took Courtrai itself, while the Belgians finally secured Bruges. This victory, together with the capture that day of Zeebrugge, meant that the northern coastline was finally liberated.[50] Terraine has written vividly of the scale of the achievement:

> The great goal of the Flanders offensive of 1917 was gained, the U-boat bases were abandoned, and the Allied left could rest upon the Dutch frontier, which was, in fact, reached next day. More than 12,000 prisoners and 550 guns had been taken by King Albert's Group since 14 October – about half of the prisoners and over 200 guns by the British Second Army. Belgium was becoming a country again, and the raptures of the people of Bruges when their king returned revealed the failure of the German attempt to exploit the divisions of Flemings and Walloons...[51]

48 Lloyd, *Hundred Days*, p. 177-8.
49 Terraine, *To Win A War*, p. 204.
50 Terraine, *To Win A War*, p. 204-5.
51 Terraine, *To Win A War*, p. 205.

There is another dimension regarding Plumer's handling of the campaign that is worthy of note. Much has been written regarding the influence of Haig on the planning and management of operations by his Army commanders throughout the war.[52] Bidwell and Graham summarise the position as:

> Haig insisted that the commander at each level was entirely responsible for making tactical plans within the framework of his [Haig's] own general scheme... The channel of communication between GHQ and the Armies that it directed was further impeded by Haig's tendency to be inarticulate in describing his plans and to overawe not only his subordinate commanders by brusqueness but also his own staff.[53]

Chapter two referred to Haig's refusal to support Plumer's initial plan to attack directly towards Wytschaete and Messines. However, once placed within the GAF and subject to a different chain of command, Plumer was able to carry out his planning, strategy and tactics, largely free from the influence of Haig. Such opportunities had not been possible during Messines and the subsequent battles of Autumn 1917; or in the resistance to the German assault in Spring 1918. The evidence is that he welcomed and exploited this freedom, particularly once he felt confident in the abilities of his troops. Given his dissatisfaction with the leadership and staff work within the GAF, these feelings of independence allowed Plumer to direct his part of the campaign along strategic lines that he had determined. He was also in the position of believing himself able to fall back upon the support of Haig, given Haig's suspicion of both the French and Belgian priorities for the campaign in Flanders, should there be any significant challenge to his approach. Thus it can be concluded that the achievements of Second Army, in terms of strategy and tactics, were very much the result of Plumer's leadership.

The advance of the GAF, underpinned and led by the victories of Plumer's troops, had broad strategic significance. Summarising Second Army performance during the October phase of operations, Gary Sheffield acknowledges that while 'Plumer's role was to protect the flank of the Belgians... the French proved sluggish...' whereupon:

> Plumer interpreted his orders liberally and drove on over the Lys, eventually taking Courtrai on the 19th. This helped trigger a German retreat to the south... Orders were given [by Ludendorff] to hold on to the Belgian coast... as bargaining chips in negotiations to end the war...
>
> With that hope dashed, Ludendorff ordered the evacuation of these areas, suddenly no longer militarily tenable. The German decision to abandon the coast meant that Britain had achieved one of the principal aims for which it had gone to war in the first place.[54]

52 There is not the space to open the debate here and it would have to include a very long list of commentators; for initial reference please see the titles by writers such as Bidwell and Graham, Griffith, Millett and Murray, Prior and Wilson, and Travers, in section IV b. Printed Sources: Books – resources, weaponry, organization and tactics, in the appended Bibliography.

53 Bidwell and Graham, *Fire-power*, p. 72; the authors then proceed to look in more detail at Haig's influence on key battles during the war.

54 Sheffield, *The Chief*, p. 329.

As this book has shown, the victories of British Second Army during the Hundred Days represented far, far more than the defeat of the German Army on the battlefields of Flanders. Through the prosecution of a successful military coalition, the conclusion of the war was brought nearer, and a country, and its people, liberated. These were achievements which should rank as some of the finest within the annals of the British Army.

Postscript: The Last Post

> On the Western Front as a whole one in four of the British dead had no known grave. Around Ypres the figure is one in three, a measure of the extent this small area was harrowed again and again by high explosive and the older graves churned up.[1]

> I should like us to acquire the whole of the ruins of Ypres … A more sacred place for the British race does not exist in the world.
>
> Winston Churchill[2]

It was on 20 June 1927 when the Second Army troops killed and missing during the 1918 Liberation Offensive were officially remembered. On that day near the village of Passchendaele, the Tyne Cot Memorial to the Missing was finally unveiled. The ceremony was led by the Australian soldier and veterans' rights activist Sir Gilbert Dyett, National President of the Returned Sailors' Soldiers' and Airmens' Imperial League of Australia.[3]

Tyne Cot Cemetery and Memorial are situated upon ground assigned in perpetuity to the United Kingdom by King Albert. The grant of the land by Belgium acknowledged the depth of gratitude felt by the country to the British and Empire troops who had fought for so hard and so long to defend Ypres and the salient. Many had made the ultimate sacrifice in that fight; stubbornly refusing to concede that last remaining portion of Albert's battered country that was not under German control. By this most visible of acts, Belgium had recognised the role of its allies in the liberation offensive that saw its land once more restored as an independent country.

Anyone who has had the privilege of making a visit to the site can only feel humbled by the experience. Tyne Cot is the largest British war cemetery in the world. The name is said to have been given by soldiers in the Northumberland Fusiliers who saw a resemblance between the German concrete pill boxes (two of which remain in the middle of the cemetery) and the typical Tyneside workers' cottages – 'Tyne Cots'. There is another theory that the term is from

1 G. Powell, *Plumer: the Soldiers' General. A Biography of Field-Marshal Viscount Plumer of Messines* (Barnsley: Pen & Sword, 2004), p. 228.

2 Quoted in P. Chapman, *Menin Gate South* (South Yorkshire: Pen & Sword Military, 2016), p. 1.

3 The information in this summary and the subsequent text regarding the war memorials in Ypres and Flanders is drawn from: T. V. Holt, *Major & Mrs Holt's Battlefield Guide to the Ypres Salient & Passchendaele* (Barnsley: Pen & Sword Military, paperback, 2008 edition; this guide is reprinted regularly); P. Chapman, (*In Memory and in Mourning* series) 3 volumes – *Tyne Cot Cemetery and Memorial – Menin Gate North –Menin Gate South* (Barnsley: Pen & Sword Military, 2015-16).

contemporary trench maps and the names of rivers in the area – including 'Tyne' – and the name 'Tyne Cot' was originally that of a local barn.

The cemetery, designed by Sir Herbert Baker, is set in ground originally captured by the 3rd Australian Division and the New Zealand Division, on 4 October 1917; two days later a cemetery for British and Canadian war dead was established. The area was retaken by German forces on 13 April 1918 before it was finally liberated by the Belgian Army during the opening day's fighting in the Liberation Offensive on 28 September.

At the centre of the cemetery is the Cross of Sacrifice. This is sited on top of a former German pillbox, rumoured to have been at the suggestion of King George V, who had visited the cemetery in 1922. Around the cemetery are the walls that comprise the Tyne Cot Memorial to the Missing. Upon finishing the work on the Menin Gate Memorial to the Missing, it was found that the latter would not have the space to include all the names it was intended to include.[4] As a consequence the cut-off date of 15 August 1917 was chosen, for practical rather than any other reasons; hence the names of the UK soldiers recorded as missing after this date were inscribed on the Tyne Cot memorial. It is to Tyne Cot we must go in order to view the names of the troops who fought and died and whose bodies were lost during the fighting to liberate Belgium in that final campaign.

One week later on 24 July 1927, Field Marshal Plumer, in the presence of King Albert together with the British Ambassador Sir George Grahame, and President of France Albert le Brun, unveiled in Ypres the Menin Gate memorial to commemorate and pay tribute to the British and Empire fallen of Ypres and Flanders. The most direct route for British troops directed to the Ypres salient and the battlefields of Flanders, was along the Menin Road and through the ruins of an old fortified gate built by the French fortifications' expert Vauban. 'The Gap' – as the passing soldiers termed it – had become the chosen site for what would come to be seen as one of the most important of the First World War memorials. Its iconic design was produced by Sir Reginald Blomfield, together with Sir Herbert Baker, Charles Holden and Sir Edward Lutyens, together four of the most respected British architects of the time.

When completed the Menin Gate comprised 20,000 tons of French limestone, some 25 metres high, 40 metres long, and 20 metres wide. There are over 1,200 inscribed panels, in 30 different sizes, made of Portland Stone. To travel to the site is to undertake what feels like a form of pilgrimage. The visitor cannot but be overwhelmed by the sense of loss and also the deep respect for all those soldiers and civilians whose lives were so cataclysmically altered – or ended – through the Great War.

Present that day amongst the audience of around 40,000 people were ex-servicemen and women, and several thousand relatives of those named on its walls. Together with a number of bands including pipers of 1/Scots Guards, there was also a team from the BBC which delivered a live broadcast of the ceremony. The latter was 'quite successful, and, in view of the difficulties, the reception was good'.[5]

At the conclusion of the ceremony, the buglers of the Shropshire Light Infantry sounded the Last Post. The entrance to the southern staircase bears the words:

4 Chapman quotes the official figure of 54,896 names on the Gate, excluding the addenda panels with approximately another 1,000.
5 Holt, *Guide to Ypres*, p. 28.

> Here are recorded names of officers and men who fell in Ypres Salient but to whom the fortunes of war denied the known and honoured burial given to their comrades in death.

Above the opposite staircase is inscribed the response:

> They shall receive a crown of glory that fadeth not away.

We can only guess at the depth of emotion felt by Plumer as he spoke to that assembled crowd. In his speech he managed to capture in a single phrase the true sense of the Menin Gate – and of Tyne Cot – and their responsibility to eternity as memorials for all who fought and fell in the Belgian salient:

> He is not missing. He is here.

Appendix I

Orders of Battle

British Corps 1918

Headquarters
Corps cavalry
Headquarters Corps Heavy Artillery
Heavy Trench Mortar Battery RGA
Cyclist Battalion
Sharpshooters Group
Corps Signal Troops:
    Corps Signal Company
    Air-Line Sections, Motor, 2
    Cable Sections, 2
Corps M T Column:
Corps Troops MT Company
Divisional MT Companies, 4
Heavy Artillery ASC Company
Medium Ordnance Mobile Workshop
Light Ordnance Mobile Workshop
Area Employment Company

Order of Battle: British Division 1918

Headquarters	
Infantry Brigades	3
Each of 3 Battalions	
With 36 Lewis Guns per Battalion	
Trench Mortar Battalion	
3 Batteries	
8 × 3" Stokes Mortars per Battery	
Artillery Brigades	2
Each of 3 × 18-pounder and 1 × 4.5-inch howitzer batteries	
Trench Mortar Batteries, RA	2
6 × 2" Trench Mortars per Battery	

Ammunition Column	
Field Companies, RE	3
Signal Company	
Pioneer Battalion	
With 12 Lewis Guns	
Machine Gun Battalion	
4 Companies	
Each with 16 Vickers Heavy Machine-Guns	
ASC	4
Field Ambulances	3
Mobile Veterinary Section	
Employment Company	

British Battalion Composition 1918

In March 1918 when Plumer returned to the Western Front, the British Army was completing the required reorganisation of Divisions following manpower restrictions; briefly, Divisions would be made up of ten Battalions, one of which would be its Pioneer Battalion; the remainder were deployed as three Brigades of three Battalions (previously, a Division was composed of four Brigades).

Battalion Headquarters

Commanding Officer:	Lieutenant-Colonel
Second-in-Command:	Major
Adjutant:	Lieutenant or Captain
Quartermaster:	Lieutenant or Captain

Officer of Royal Army Medical Corps

Regimental Sergeant-Major

Sergeants:	Quartermaster Orderly Room Clerk Drummer Cook Pioneer Shoemaker Transport Signaller Armourer (Ordnance Corps)
Corporal/Privates:	Royal Army Medical Corps Medical Orderlies Signallers

	Pioneers
	Drivers
	Stretcher-bearers
	Officers' Batmen
4 Companies	(Major or Captain)
of 4 Platoons	(Subaltern: Lieutenant or Second Lieutenant)
of 4 Sections	(each of an NCO plus 12 men)

British Second Army Order of Battle: The Advance in Flanders

Operations 18 August – 6 September 1918

30 June	XIX Corps relieved French XIV Corps
8 July	X Corps relieved French XVI Corps

On the 18 August 1918 the Second Army held a front of 19 miles, from south of Vieux Berquin to north-east of Ypres

18 August	Capture of Outtersteene Ridge 29th Division – 87 Brigade	XV Corps
18 August	Capture of Hoegenacher Ridge 9th Division	XV Corps
1 September	Capture of Neuve Eglise 30th Division – 89 Brigade	X Corps
2 September	Capture of Wulwweughn 30th Division – 21 Brigade	X Corps
4 September	Capture of Ploegsteert and Hill 43 29th Division – 86 and 88 Brigades	XV Corps
GOC	General Sir H C O Plumer	
Major-General General Staff	Major-General J S J Percy	

II Corps

Lieutenant General Sir C W Jacob

14th Division 34th Division*
35th Division** 49th Division***
American 30th Division****

* Transferred to XIX Corps between 28-30 August
**Transferred to II Corps from XIII Corps on 1 September
*** Left the Corps on 27 August
**** Left the Corps on 1 September

X Corps*
Lieutenant General R B Stephens

30th Division | 36th Division

*X Corps had remained in the back area since the conclusion of the battle of Ypres 1917; on 8 July 1918 with 30th, 35th and 36th Divisions, it took over part of the Second Army front, relieving the French XVI Corps

XV Corps
Lieutenant General Sir B deLisle
9th Division | 29th Division
31st Division | 40th Division

XIX Corps*
Lieutenant General Sir H E Watts

6th Division** | 41st Division
American 27th Division*** | 34th Division****

* On 30 June 1918 XIX Corps (6th and 41st Divisions), then with Fourth Army, took over part of the Second Army front, relieving the French XIV Corps
** Left the Corps on 1 September
*** Left the Corps on 4 September
**** Transferred from II Corps between 28-30 August

British Second Army Order of Battle: The Final Advance in Flanders

28 September – 11 November 1918

By September 1918, the British Second Army held a sixteen mile front line in Flanders. This ran from west of Armentières, at a junction with the River Lys, stretching northwards to just above the town of Ypres; there it linked to the right of the Belgian Army

GOC | General Sir H C O Plumer
Major-General General Staff | Major General J S J Percy

II Corps
Lieutenant General Sir C W Jacob
9th Division | 29th Division
36th Division

X Corps
Lieutenant General R B Stephens
30th Division 34th Division

XV Corps
Lieutenant General Sir B deLisle
14th Division 31st Division
40th Division

XIX Corps
Lieutenant General Sir H E Watts

35th Division 41st Division

28 September 2 October 1918	Battle of Ypres	II Corps 9th, 29th, 36th Divisions X Corps 30th, 34th Divisions XV Corps 31st, 40th Divisions XIX Corps 14th, 35th, 41st Divisions
14-19 October 1918	Battle of Courtrai	II Corps 9th, 29th, 36th Divisions X Corps 30th, 34th Divisions XV Corps 14th Division XIX Corps 35th, 41st Divisions
25 October 1918	Action of Ooteghem	II Corps 9th, 36th Divisions X Corps 34th Division XIX Corps 41st Division
31 October 1918	Action of Tiegham	II Corps XIX Corps

During the final stages, there were a number of changes in the order of Divisions under Corps HQ.

From 9 – 11 November, preparations were in hand to assault the Schelde – actions included the seizing of Leuze and Lessines, and of passages across the Dendre – X and XIX Corps with 3rd Cavalry Division

When the Armistice began at 1100 on 11 November, Second Army held a ten mile front from Lessines to Voorde, occupied by the X and XIX Corps

Since the final advance began on 18 August, Second Army had fought two major battles plus supporting actions, and advanced 53 miles into Belgium in 86 days

Order of Battle: Groupe d'Armées des Flandres – Battle of Courtrai

GOC	Albert, King of the Belgians
Chief of Staff	General Degoutte (France)
British Second Army General Plumer 4 Corps / 10 Divisions	French II Cavalry Corps General Robillot 3 Divisions
Belgian Southern Groupement Lieutenant-General Biebuyck 3 Belgian Divisions 1 French Division (164th)	Belgian Northern Groupement Lieutenant-General Michel 3 Belgian Divisions 1 Belgian Cavalry Division
French VII Corps* General Massenet French VII Corps 2 Divisions	French XXXIV Corps* General Mudant French XXXIV Corps 3 Divisions

plus

- 2 Belgian Divisions holding Yser defences from Dixmude
- 4 Belgian Divisions resting behind the Yser

*On 19 October, the new French Sixth Army under General de Boissoudy entered the line. This consisted of VII and XXXIV Corps plus XXX Corps (5th and 132nd Divisions, under General Peney)

British Second Army: Troops (September – November 1918)

Artillery:

Heavy Batteries:	16 (6, 60-pounder guns per battery = 96 guns)		
Brigades RGA:	Mobile, 3	Mixed, 5	8-inch, 3
	9.2-inch, 4	Army, 2	

Siege Batteries:

Guns	Batteries	Total Guns
6-inch howitzer	36	198
6-inch gun	7	28
8-inch howitzer	8	48
9.2-inch howitzer	9	52
9.2-inch gun	1.5	3
12-inch howitzer	9	18
15-inch howitzer	1	1
TOTAL	71.5	348

Total: 87.5 heavy and siege batteries; 444 heavy guns and howitzers

Anti-Aircraft:	18 sections of 13-pounder guns, 6 sections of 3-inch guns = 48 guns
Field Artillery Brigades:	8

Engineers:

Special Projector Companies	6
Mortar Corps	1
Army Troops Companies	10
Siege Company	1
Tunnelling Companies	4
Electrical & Mechanical	1
Boring Section (Water)	1
Army Workshop Company	1
Field Survey Battalion:	
Sound ranging Sections	5
Observation Groups	5
AA Searchlight Sections	10
AA Searchlight Company	1
Pontoon Park	1
Advanced RE Parks	2
Transportation (Works) Company	1
Signal Service:	
Cable Sections	2
Air Line Sections	3
Light Railway Signal Company	1
Signal Construction Company	1
Area Signal Detachments	7
Pigeon Service:	
Mobile Lofts (1 motor)	14
Fixed lofts	12

Infantry:	
Battalions	3
Machine-Gun Battalions	4
Military Police: Traffic Control Units:	
Company	1
Squadron	1
Army Service Corps:	
Pontoon Park (MT)	1
Army Troops MT Company	1
Auxiliary (Petrol) Company	1
Mobile Repair Unit (MT)	1
Workshop for AA guns	1
Water Tank Company	1
Medical:	
Motor Ambulance convoys	4
Casualty Clearing Stations	12
Advanced Medical Stores Depots	3
Mobile Laboratories	4
Mobile X-Ray Units	2
Mobile Dental Unit	1
Stationary Hospital	1
Sanitary Sections	12
Sanitary Squads	5
Veterinary:	
Evacuating Stations	3
Ordnance:	
Mobile Workshops (heavy, medium, light)	3
Gun Park	1
Officers' Clothing Depot	1
Forestry Units:	
Companies	2
Labour Corps:	
Companies	31
Area Employment Companies	12
Area Employment (artisan) Companies	2
Chinese companies	14
Army Printing and Stationery Services:	
Advanced Photographic Section	1

British Second Army 1918: Headquarters

Note: All the entries below for British Second Army and its constituent units describe its composition from 13 March 1918 onwards (when General Plumer resumed as GOC).

GOC	General Sir H C O Plumer
Major-General General Staff	Major General C H Harington* From 29 April 1918 Major-General J S J Percy
Deputy-Adjutant and Quartermaster-General	Major General A A Chichester*
Major-General Royal Artillery	Major General C R Buckle*
Chief Engineer	Major General Sir F M Glubb*
Anti-Aircraft Defence Commander	Lieutenant General H W Hill
Deputy Director Signals	Colonel A B R Hildebrand* From October 1918 Colonel H C Smith
Deputy Director Supply and Transport	Brigadier General F M Wilson**
Deputy Director Ordnance Services	Colonel H S Bush**
Director of Medical Services	Major General R Porter From 8 April 1918 Major General S G Moores
Deputy Director Veterinary Services	Colonel F W Hunt**
Deputy Director Remounts	Colonel W E Matchem**

GHQ:	13 March 1918	Cassel
	14 April 1918	Blendecques (2½ miles S by E of St Omer)
	1 September 1918	Cassel
	23 October 1918	Chateau Ternynck, Roubaix

* Transferred with Plumer to Italy and returned with him to the Western Front.
** From Fourth Army.

Second Army Artillery

(Major General Buckle)
By November 1918 almost all corps artillery had been concentrated at army level.
11 Army Brigade RFA 83 84 85 D Batteries
23 Army Brigade RFA 107 108 C D Batteries
28 Army Brigade RFA A 123 124 65 Batteries
38 Army Brigade RFA A 24 72 D Batteries
64 Army Brigade RFA A B C D Batteries
96 Army Brigade RFA 407 408 409 410 Batteries
113 Army Brigade RFA A B C D Batteries
119 Army Brigade RFA A B C D Batteries
2 Brigade RGA 177 250 352 66 Batteries
3 Brigade RGA 48 112 88 268 152 21 Batteries
4 Brigade RGA 131 2/1N Midland 223 301 261 129 Batteries
6 Brigade RGA 109 114 111 245 227 42 Batteries
10 Brigade RGA 150 159 113 226 Batteries
33 Brigade RGA 31 279 298 221 Batteries
36 Brigade RGA 140 151 155 353 1Aust 2Aust Batteries

43 Brigade RGA 147 190 351 154 Batteries
59 Brigade RGA 37 335 350 30 Batteries
64 Brigade RGA 100 101 102 61 Batteries
65 Brigade RGA 115 202 21 118 Batteries
70 Brigade RGA 282 285 405 151 Batteries
77 Brigade RGA 9 26 116 119 286 191 Batteries
86 Brigade RGA 141 1/1Wx 203 324 Batteries
87 Brigade RGA 154 156 194 219 Batteries
99 Brigade RGA 15 157 217 12 Batteries
HQ 25 Brigade RGA
HQ 72 Brigade RGA
7 Siege Battery RGA (4 × 6"guns)
29 Siege Battery RGA
187 Siege Battery RGA
193 Siege Battery RGA
479 Siege Battery RGA
526 Siege Battery RGA
528 Siege Battery RGA
546 Siege Battery RGA
45 Siege Battery RGA (2 × 9.2" railway guns)
Section 53 Siege Battery RGA (1 × 9.2" railway gun)
85 Siege Battery RGA (2 × 12" howitzers)
375 Siege Battery RGA
2 Battery Royal Marine Artillery
22 Siege Battery RGA (2 × 12" railway howitzers)
63 Siege Battery RGA
82 Siege Battery RGA
104 Siege Battery RGA
359 Siege Battery RGA
381 Siege Battery RGA
4 Siege Battery RGA (1 × 15" howitzer)
The Bermuda RGA
H AA Battery RGA
J AA Battery RGA
R AA Battery RGA
T AA Battery RGA
U AA Battery RGA

Second Army Engineers

(Major General Glubb)
By November 1918 all Corps engineers had been brought under army command.
6 Siege Company R Mon RE
20 Army Troops Company RE
134 Army Troops Company RE

136 Army Troops Company RE
138 Army Troops Company RE
141 Army Troops Company RE
145 Army Troops Company RE
167 Army Troops Company RE
214 Army Troops Company RE
235 Army Troops Company RE
236 Army Troops Company RE
245 Army Troops Company RE
289 Army Troops Company RE
554 Army Troops Company RE
556 Army Troops Company RE
557 Army Troops Company RE
573 Army Troops Company RE
171 Tunnelling Company RE
173 Tunnelling Company RE
184 Tunnelling Company RE
255 Tunnelling Company RE
3 Canadian Tunnelling Company RCE
Section, 196 Land Drainage Company RE
354 Electrical & Mechanical Company RE
2 Advanced RE Park
3 Advanced RE Park
10 Advanced RE Park
2 Army Workshop Company RE
4 Field Survey Battalion RE
7 Pontoon Park
220 Transportation (Works) Company RE
AA Searchlight Sections-1 11 24 28 31 40 64

British Second Army 1918: Corps

II Corps	
Operations:	The Advance in Flanders The Final Advance in Flanders
GOC	Lieutenant General C W Jacob
BGGS	Brigadier General S H Wilson From 27 October 1918 Brigadier General C Bonham-Carter
DA and QMG	Brigadier General R M Foot
BGRA	Brigadier General A D Kirby
CHA	Brigadier General D F H Logan
CE	Brigadier General C Godby
AD Signals	Lieutenant Colonel C V Monier-Williams From 27 August 1918 Lieutenant Colonel

	E de W H Bradley
DDMS	Colonel S G Moores From 1 April 1918 Colonel G St C Thom
ADVS	Lieutenant Colonel J J Griffith

X Corps

Operations:	The Advance in Flanders The Final Advance in Flanders
GOC	Lieutenant General Sir T L N Morland wef 15 April 1918 Lieutenant General Sir W N Congreve (temp) wef 15 April 1918 Lieutenant General Sir W E Peyton wef 15 April 1918 Lieutenant General R B Stephens
BGGS	Brigadier General A R Cameron wef 2 July 1918 Brigadier General W J Maxwell-Scott (temp) wef 13 July 1918 Brigadier General C Evans
DA and QMG	Brigadier General W K Legge
BGRA	Brigadier General G Gillson wef 12 September 1918 Brigadier General W P Monkhouse
CHA	Brigadier General H O Vincent wef 11 July 1918 Brigadier General A H Ollivant
CE	Brigadier General G H Boileau
AD Signals	Lieutenant Colonel F A Iles wef 12 May 1918 Lieutenant Colonel R F B Naylor
DDMS	Colonel R L R MaCloud
ADVS	Lieutenant Colonel G P Knott

XV Corps

Operations:	The Advance in Flanders The Final Advance in Flanders
GOC	wef 12 April 1918 Lieutenant General Sir H de B De Lisle
BGGS	Brigadier General H H S Know wef 12-24 August 1918 Brigadier General G H N Jackson (temp)
DA and QMG	Brigadier General G R Frith
BGRA	Brigadier General B R Kirwan
CHA	Brigadier General C W Collingwood
CE	Brigadier General C W Singer
AD Signals	Lieutenant Colonel N Harrison

DDMS	Colonel G A Moore
ADVS	Lieutenant Colonel E M Percy

XIX Corps

Operations:	The Advance in Flanders The Final Advance in Flanders

On 30 June 1918 XIX Corps (6th and 41st Divisions) took over part of the Second Army front, relieving the French XIV Corps

GOC	Lieutenant General H E Watts
BGGS	Brigadier General C N MacMullen
DA and QMG	Brigadier General A G Moir
BGRA	Brigadier General W B R Sandys
CHA	Brigadier General C G Pritchard wef 15 April August 1918 Brigadier General F A Wynter
CE	Brigadier General A G Bremner (wounded 22 March 1918) wef 24 March 1918 Brigadier General H Biddulph wef 6 June 1918 Brigadier General E N Stockley
AD Signals	
DDMS	Colonel H J Pocock wef 7 June 1918 Colonel J D Alexander
ADVS	Lieutenant Colonel C E Steel

British Second Army Divisions September – November 1918

9th (Scottish) Division
14th (Light) Division
29th Division
30th Division
31st Division
34th Division
35th Division
36th Division
40th Division
41st Division

9th (Scottish) Division
(New Army Division)

From 4-12 March, 16-24(1400 hours) March 1918 (Acting)
Major-General H H Tudor
From 13-15, 24(1400 hours)-27 March 1918
Major-General C A Blacklock
From 28 March 1918
Major-General H H Tudor

The Battle of Messines
The Battle of Bailleul
The First Battle of Kemmel
The Second Battle of Kemmel
The Advance in Flanders
The Final Advance in Flanders
The Battle of Ypres 1918
The Battle of Courtrai

On 26-27 October, the Division was relieved by 31st Division and moved back to reorganise.

26 Brigade	Brigadier-General J Kennedy From 27 July 1918 Brigadier-General Hon. A G A Hore-Ruthven, VC From 5 November 1918 Brigadier-General H G Hyslop
8th (Service) Battalion, the Black Watch	
7th (Service) Battalion, Seaforth Highlanders	
5th (Service) Battalion, Cameron Highlanders	
26th Trench Mortar Company	
27 (Lowland) Brigade	Brigadier-General W D Croft
11th (Service) Battalion, Royal Scots	
12th (Service) Battalion, Royal Scots	
6th (Service) Battalion, King's Own Scottish Borderers	
27th Trench Mortar Battery	
28 Brigade*	Brigadier-General J L Jack

2nd Battalion, Royal Scots Fusiliers (joined September 1918)
9th (Service) Battalion, Cameronians (Scottish Rifles) (returned September 1918)
1st Royal Newfoundland Regiment (joined September 1918)**

South African Brigade***
2nd Battalion, Royal Scots Fusiliers (April-September 1918)
9th (Service) Battalion, Cameronians (Scottish Rifles) (April-September 1918)
1st, 2nd, 3rd, 4th Battalions, South African Infantry

Division troops
9th (Service) (Pioneers) Seaforth Highlanders
No 9 Machine Gun Battalion
No 11 Motor Machine Gun Battery****
L, LI Brigades RFA
X9, Y9 Medium Mortar Batteries
9th Ammunition Column
63rd, 64th, 90th Field Companies
9th Signals Company
27th, 28th, South African (up to 13 September 1918), 2/1st East Lancs (from 20 September 1918) Field Ambulances
9th Divisional Train ASC (104, 105, 106, 107 Companies)
212th Divisional Employment Company
21st Mobile Veterinary Section

* The Brigade was broken up on 6 May 1916 and reformed on 11 September 1918
** The Battalion joined the 28 Brigade on 13 September 1918, having been attached to GHQ since 29 April 1918; this was initially a temporary attachment because as late as 15 September 1918, Brigadier-General Jack was still expecting 10th Battalion, Argyll & Sutherland Highlanders to be placed with the Brigade
*** The Brigade reported to 9th Division from 22 April 1916 to 13 September 1918. On 24 April 1918, due to heavy casualties, 1st, 2nd and 4th Battalions were amalgamated – forming the South African (Composite) Regiment; they were reformed by 1 September 1918. The 9th (Service) Battalion, Cameronians (Scottish Rifles) was transferred to the Brigade in April 1918 to bring it up to strength; it was restored to 28 Brigade in September 1918
**** Joined Division from 7 October to 7 November 1918

14th (Light) Division
(New Army Division)
Major-General V A Couper
From 22 March 1918
Major-General W H Greenly
From 27 March 1918
Major-General Sir V A Couper
From 31 March 1918
Major-General P C B Skinner

In the Battle of St Quentin and the Battle of the Avre, actions forming part of the first Battles of the Somme 1918, the Division suffered very severe casualties, losing almost 6,000 troops. XLVI and XLVII Brigades, RFA, lost all their guns. The Division was withdrawn from the line and placed on the construction of a new defensive line in the rear. On 26 April, the infantry battalions were reduced to a training cadre. Various units were temporarily attached, before the Division was moved to England for re-establishment, on 17 June 1918, before returning to France. The Division joined Second Army 2-6 July 1918. Placed under XIX Corps, it transferred to XV Corps from 2 October 1918.

The Final Advance in Flanders
The Battle of Ypres 1918

41 Brigade	Brigadier-General P C B Skinner From 31 March 1918 Lieutenant-Colonel B J Curling (Acting) From 3 April 1918 Brigadier-General C R P Winser From 3 September 1918 Brigadier-General W F Sweny

18th (Service) Battalion, the York and Lancaster (joined June 1918)
29th (Service) Battalion, Durham Light Infantry (joined June 1918)
33rd (City of London) Battalion, London Regiment (joined June 1918)
41st Trench Mortar Battery

42 Brigade	Brigadier-General G N B Forster (killed 4 April 1918) From 5-7 April 1918 Brigadier-General C R P Winser (41 Brigade, Acting) From 7 April 1918 Brigadier-General H T Dobbin

6th (Royal Wiltshire Yeomanry) Battalion, the Wiltshires (joined as a cadre June 1918)
16th (Service) (1st City) Battalion, the Manchesters (joined as a cadre June 1918)
14th (Service) Battalion, Argyll & Sutherland Highlanders (joined April 1918)
42nd Trench Mortar Battery

43 Brigade	Brigadier-General R S Tempest From 16 September 1918 Brigadier-General G E Pereira

12th (Service) Battalion, the Suffolks (joined May 1918)
20th (Service) (Shoreditch) Battalion, the Middlesex (joined as a cadre June 1918)
10th (Service) Battalion, Highland Light Infantry (joined as a cadre June 1918, became 10th Battalion June 1918)
43rd Trench Mortar Battery

Division troops
15th (Service) Battalion, Loyal North Lancs (joined June 1918)
XLVI, XLVII Brigades RFA
X14, Y14 Trench Mortar Batteries
14th Ammunition Column
61st, 62nd, 89th Field Companies
14th Signals Company
105th, 106th, 107th Field Ambulance
14th Divisional Train ASC (100, 101, 102, 103 Companies)
215th Employment Company

26th Mobile Veterinary Section
41st Divisional Workshops
No 14 Machine Gun Battalion (created March 1918, disbanded 11 April 1918)

29th Division
(Regular Army Division)

From 12 March 1918
Brigadier-General R M Johnson (Acting)
From 10-24 August 1918
Brigadier-General H H S Knox (Acting)
From 19 March 1918
Major-General D Cayley

The Battles of the Lys
(The Battle of Estaires – first phase of the Battles of the Lys – under First Army)
The Battle of Messines, 1918 (88 Brigade, with 25th Division 10 April 1918, 34th Division, 11 April 1918, IX Corps, Second Army)
The Battle of Hazebrouck (less 88 Brigade) including Defence of Nieppe Forest
The Battle of Bailleul (88 Brigade, with 34th Division)
The First Battle of Kemmel (88 Brigade)
The Advance in Flanders
Action of Outtersteene Ridge (87 Brigade)
Capture of Ploegsteert and Hill 63 (86 and 88 Brigades)
The Battle of Ypres 1918
The Battle of Courtrai

The Division was withdrawn to rest on 24 October 1918. On 7 November 1918 it transferred (via XV Corps) from II Corps to X Corps.

86 Brigade — Brigadier-General G R H Cheape
2nd Battalion, Royal Fusiliers
1st Battalion, Lancashire Fusiliers
1st Battalion, Royal Dublin Fusiliers
86th Trench mortar Battery

87 Brigade — Brigadier-General G H N Jackson
2nd Battalion, South Wales Borders
1st Battalion, King's Own Scottish Borderers
1st Battalion, the Border
87th Trench Mortar Battery

88 Brigade — Brigadier-General B C Freyberg VC
4th Battalion, the Worcesters
2nd Battalion, the Hampshire

2nd Battalion, the Leinster*
88th Trench Mortar Battery

Division troops
1/2nd (Pioneer) Battalion, the Monmouthshire
No 29 Machine Gun Battalion
455th, 497th, 510th Field Companies
1st London Signals Company
87th, 88th, 89th Field Ambulance
29th Divisional Train ASC (225, 226, 227, 228 Companies)
226th Divisional Employment Company
18th Mobile Veterinary Section
XV Brigade RHA, XVII Brigade RFA
X29, Y29 Medium Mortar Batteries
29th Ammunition Column

* The Battalion joined the Brigade on 23 April 1918 from 47 Brigade, 16th Division

30th Division
(New Army Division)

Major-General W Williams

The Battles of the Lys
First Battle of Kemmel (89 Brigade)
The Second Battle of Kemmel (89 Brigade)
The Advance in Flanders
The Final Advance in Flanders
The Battle of Ypres 1918
The Battle of Courtrai

21 Brigade — Brigadier-General G D Goodman
7th Battalion, (South Irish Horse) Royal Irish
1/6th Battalion, Cheshire Regiment
2/23rd Battalion, (County of London) London Regiment
21st Trench Mortar Battery

89 Brigade — Brigadier-General Hon. F C Stanley
From 11 April 1918
Lieutenant-Colonel G Rollo (Acting)
From 12 April 1918
Brigadier-General R A M Currie
From 27 August 1918
Lieutenant-Colonel R A Irvine (Acting)
From 15 September 1918
Brigadier-General R A M Currie

7/8th Battalion, (Service) Royal Inniskilling Fusiliers
2nd Battalion, South Lancashire
2/17th Battalion, (County of London) London Regiment
89th Trench Mortar Battery

90 Brigade ('The Grey Brigade')	Lieutenant-Colonel H S Poyntz (Acting) From 26 March 1918 Brigadier-General G A Stevens From 11 August 1918 Lieutenant-Colonel R J L Ogilby (Acting) From 18 August 1918 Brigadier-General G A Stevens

2/14th Battalion, (County of London) (London Scottish) London Regiment
2/15th Battalion, (County of London) (Prince of Wales' Own Civil Service Rifles) London Regiment*
2/16th Battalion, (County of London) (Queen's Westminster Rifles) London Regiment
90th Trench Mortar Battery

Division
6th (Service) (Pioneers) Battalion, South Wales Borderers
No 30 Machine Gun Battalion
201st, 202nd, 203rd (County Palatine) Field Companies
30th Signals Company
96th, 97th, 98th Field Ambulance
30th Divisional Train ASC (186, 187, 188, 189 Companies)
227th Divisional Employment Company
40th Mobile Veterinary Section
30th Divisional Workshops
CXLIX, CXLVIII Brigades RFA
X30, Y30 Medium Mortar Batteries RFA
30th Ammunition Column

*The Battalion travelled from Egypt in June 1918, joining the Division at the start of July.

31st Division
(New Army Division)

Major-General R Wanless O'Gowan
From 21 March 1918
Major-General R J Bridgford
From 6 May 1918
Major-General J Campbell

With XV Corps for the Final Advance in Flanders, the Division transferred to II Corps for The Action of Tiegham (31 October). On 3 November the Division was transferred into Army Reserve. On 5 November it was placed under XIX Corps.

The Battles of the Lys
(The Battle of Estaires – first phase of the Battles of the Lys – First Army)
The Battle of Hazebrouck – including the Defence of Nieppe Forest
The Advance in Flanders
The Final Advance in Flanders
The Battle of Ypres 1918
The Action of Tieghem

92 Brigade* — Brigadier-General O De L Williams
10th (Service) (1st Hull) Battalion, East Yorkshires
11th (Service) (2nd Hull) Battalion, East Yorkshires
11th (Service) (Accrington) Battalion, East Lancashire
92nd Trench Mortar Battery

93 Brigade* — Brigadier-General J D Ingles (sick, 27 March 1918)
From 27 March 1918
Lieutenant-Colonel G H Gurney (Acting)
From 27 March 1918
Lieutenant-Colonel R D Temple (Acting)
From 5 April
Brigadier-General S C Taylor
(wounded 1 October 1918, died 11 October 1918)
From 1 October 1918
Lieutenant-Colonel A V Nutt (Acting)
From 1 October 1918
Lieutenant-Colonel A W Rickman (Acting)
From 4 October 1918
Brigadier-General G B F Smyth

15th (Service) (1st Leeds) Battalion, the West Yorkshires
18th (Service) (1st County) Battalion, Durham Light Infantry
13th (Service) (1st Barnsley) Battalion, York and Lancaster
93rd Trench Mortar Battery

94 (Yeomanry) Brigade** — Brigadier-General A Symons
(sick, 3 November 1918)
From 3 November 1918
Lieutenant-Colonel J Sherwood-Kelly VC (Acting)
From 12 November
Brigadier-General Hon L J P Butler

12th (Norfolk Yeomanry) TF Battalion, the Norfolks
12th (Ayr & Lanark Yeomanry) TF Battalion, Royal Scots Fusiliers
24th (Denbighshire Yeomanry) TF Battalion, Royal Welsh Fusiliers
94th Trench Mortar Battery

Division
12th (Service) (Miners) (Pioneers) Battalion, King's Own Yorkshire Light Infantry
No 31 Machine Gun Battalion
210th, 211th, 212th (Leeds) Field Companies
31st Signals Company
93rd, 94th, 95th Field Ambulance
31st Divisional Train ASC (221, 222, 223, 279 Companies)
228th Divisional Employment Company
41st Mobile Veterinary Section
CLXV, CLXX Brigades RFA
X31, Y31 Medium Mortar Batteries RFA
31st Ammunition Column

* 92 Composite Brigade: On 16 April 1918 it was decided that, due to the heavy casualties recently sustained, the 92 and 93 Brigades would be temporarily amalgamated and called the 92 Composite Brigade. It was broken up two days later, and the 92 and 93 Brigades were reconstituted soon after.

** 94 Brigade (originally 115 Brigade) was broken up between 11-17 February 1918 and replaced by 4 Guards Brigade; on 20 May 1918, this Brigade was transferred to GHQ Reserve. 94 Brigade was reformed on 30 May 1918 and joined 31st Division the following day. The Brigade was reconstituted on 21 June 1918 with three Battalions from 74th (Yeomanry) Division (the *Broken Spur* Division) and designated 94 (Yeomanry) Brigade.

34th Division
(New Army Division)

Major-General C L Nicholson

The Battles of the Lys
The Battle of Estaires
The Battle of Messines, 1918 (102nd Brigade)
The Battle of Bailleul
The First Battle of Kemmel

The Division suffered very severe casualties during its part in the defence of Kemmel, and was withdrawn and reorganised. In mid-May 1918 the Divisional infantry was reduced to a training cadre, and used for training American troops. Many reduced units were attached for short periods at this time. It was reconstituted as a full first-line Division late in June 1918.

(The Battle of the Soissonnais and of the Ourcq, the Capture of Beugneux Ridge – attached to French XXX Corps)

The Advance in Flanders
The Final Advance in Flanders
The Battle of Ypres 1918
The Battle of Courtrai
The Actions of Ooteghem and Tieghem

On 1 November the Division was withdrawn into Corps Reserve.

101 Brigade	Brigadier-General R G Gore (killed, 14 April 1918) From 14 April 1918 Lieutenant-Colonel A Stephenson (Acting) From 23 April Brigadier-General W J Woodstock

15th (Service) Battalion (1st Edinburgh) , the Royal Scots (left May 1918)
16th (Service) Battalion (2nd Edinburgh) , the Royal Scots (left May 1918)
2/4th Battalion (TF), the Queen's (Royal West Surrey Regiment) (joined June 1918)
11th (Service) Battalion, the Suffolks (left May 1918)
2nd Battalion, the Loyal North Lancs (joined June 1918)
4th Battalion, Royal Sussex
101st Trench Mortar Battery (broken up 16 May 1918 and reformed 2 July 1918)

102 Brigade (Tyneside Scottish)	Brigadier-General N A Thomson From 21 May Brigadier-General E Hilliam

22nd (Service) Battalion , the Northumberland Fusiliers (left June 1918)
23rd (Service) Battalion , the Northumberland Fusiliers (left June 1918)
25th (Service) Battalion , the Northumberland Fusiliers (left June 1918)
1/4th Battalion, the Lincolns (joined June 1918, left June 1918)
1/4th Battalion, the Cheshires (joined July 1918)
1/7th Battalion, the Cheshires (joined July 1918)
7/8th (Service) Battalion, the Royal Inniskilling Fusiliers (joined June 1918 as a cadre, left June 1918)
1/1st Battalion, the Herefordshire (joined June 1918)
102nd Trench Mortar Battery (broken up 16 May 1918 and reformed 10 July 1918)

103 Brigade (Tyneside Irish)	Brigadier-General J G Chaplin From 31 August Brigadier-General R I Rawson

10th (Service) Battalion, the Lincolns (left June 1918)

1/5th (Dumfries and Galloway) Battalion, the King's Own Scottish Borderers (joined June 1918)
1/8th Battalion, the Cameronians (Scottish Rifles) (joined June 1918)
6th (Service) Battalion, the Royal Inniskilling Fusiliers (joined and left June 1918)
1st Battalion, the East Lancashire (left May 1918)
1/5th (Renfrewshire) Battalion, the Argyll & Sutherland Highlanders (joined June 1918)
103rd Trench Mortar Battery (broken up 16 May 1918 and reformed 1 July 1918)

Division Troops
18th (Service) Battalion , the Northumberland Fusiliers (left June 1918)
2/4th Battalion, the Somerset Light Infantry (joined June 1918)
13th (Service) Battalion, the Yorkshire (joined and left as a cadre, June1918)
13th (Service) Battalion (Wandsworth), the East Surreys (joined and left as cadre, June 1918)
2/5th Battalion, the Sherwood Foresters (joined and left as a cadre June 1918)
21st (Service) Battalion (Islington), the Middlesex (joined and left as a cadre June 1918)
8th (Service) Battalion, the King's Royal Rifle Corps (joined and left as a cadre June 1918)
9th (Service) Battalion, the King's Royal Rifle Corps (joined and left as a cadre June 1918)
1/5th Bn, the North Staffords(joined and left as a cadre June 1918)
10/11th (Service) Battalion, the Highland Light Infantry(joined and left as a cadre June 1918)
14th (Service) Battalion, the Highland Light Infantry(joined and left as a cadre June 1918)
6th (Service) Battalion, the Connaught Rangers (joined and left as a cadre June 1918)
6th (Service) Battalion, the Leinster (joined and left June 1918)
8th (Service) Battalion, the Rifle Brigade (joined and left June 1918)
No 34 Machine Gun Battalion
207th, 208th, 209th (Norfolk) Field Companies
34th Signals Company
102nd, 103rd, 104th Field Ambulance
34th Divisional Train ASC (229, 230, 231, 232 Companies)
231st Divisional Employment Company
44th Mobile Veterinary Section
34th Divisional Workshops
CLII, CLX Brigades RFA
X34, Y34 Medium Mortar Batteries RFA
34th Ammunition Column

35th Division

(New Army Division – originally a Bantam formation)
Major-General G McK Franks
Temporary from 27 March 1918; permanent from 7 April 1918
Major-General A Marindin

The Final Advance in Flanders
The Battle of Ypres 1918
The Battle of Courtrai
The Action of Tieghem

104 Brigade — Brigadier-General J W Sandilands
17th (Service) Battalion (1st South-East Lancs), Lancashire Fusiliers*
18th (Service) Battalion (2nd South-East Lancs), Lancashire Fusiliers*
19th (Service) Battalion (2nd County), Durham Light Infantry*
9th (Service) Battalion, the Northumberland Fusiliers (left May 1918)
104th Trench Mortar Battery

105 Brigade — Brigadier-General A H Marindin
From 26 March 1918
Lieutenant-Colonel W A W Crellin (Acting)
From 7 April
Brigadier-General A Carton de Wiert
(Wounded 20 April 1918)
From 20 April 1918
Lieutenant-Colonel L M Stevens (Acting)
From 7 April
Brigadier-General A J Turner

15th (Service) Battalion (1st Birkenhead), the Cheshires*
15th (Service) Battalion (Nottingham), Sherwood Foresters*
4th (Extra Reserve) Battalion, North Staffords
105th Trench Mortar Battery

106 Brigade — Brigadier-General J H W Pollard
17th (Rosebery) Battalion, Royal Scots
12th (Service) Battalion, Highland Light Infantry
18th (Service) Battalion, Highland Light Infantry*
106th Trench Mortar Battery

Division Troops
19th (Service) Battalion, Northumberland Fusiliers**
No 35 Machine Gun Battalion
203, 204, 205 Field Companies
35th Signals Company
105th, 106th, 107th Field Ambulance
35th Divisional Train ASC (233, 234, 235 and 236 Companies)
CLVII (Aberdeen), CLVIX (Glasgow) Brigades RFA
X35, Y35 Medium Mortar Batteries
35th Divisional Ammunition Column (British Empire League) RFA

* These were the original Bantam Battalions making up the Brigades and Division since their formation

** Though not a Bantam formation, the 19/Northumberland Fusiliers had been Pioneers for the Division since its formation

36th (Ulster) Division
(New Army Division)

Major-General O Nugent
From 6 April 1918
Major-General C Coffin VC

The Battles of the Lys
The Battle of Messines, 1918 (108 Brigade)
The Battle of Bailleul (108 Brigade)
The First Battle of Kemmel (108 Brigade)
The Advance in Flanders
The Battle of Ypres 1918
The Battle of Courtrai

On 28 October the Division was relieved of frontline duty and transferred from II Corps to X Corps. On 9 November the Division was transferred to XV Corps.

107 Brigade — Brigadier-General W M Withycombe
From 30 April 1918
Brigadier-General E I de S Thorpe
(Wounded 13 September 1918)
From 14 September 1918
Lieutenant-Colonel R H MacKenzie (Acting)
From 28 September 1918
Brigadier-General H J Brock

1st Battalion, Royal Irish Rifles
2nd Battalion, Royal Irish Rifles
15th (Service) Battalion (North Belfast), Royal Irish Rifles
107th Trench Mortar Battery

108 Brigade — Brigadier-General C R J Griffith
From 21 May 1918
Brigadier-General E Vaughn

12th (Service) Battalion (Central Antrim), Royal Irish Rifles
1st Battalion, Royal Irish Fusiliers
9th (Service) Battalion, Royal Irish Fusiliers
108th Trench Mortar Battery

109 Brigade — Brigadier-General W F Hessey
(Injured 16 April 1918)
From 16 April 1918
Lieutenant-Colonel J E Knott (Acting)
From 21 April 1918

Brigadier-General E Vaughn (Temporary)
From 17 May 1918
Brigadier-General W F Hessey

1st Battalion, Royal Inniskilling Fusiliers
2nd Battalion, Royal Inniskilling Fusiliers
9th (Service) Battalion (County Tyrone), Royal Inniskilling Fusiliers
109th Trench Mortar Battery

Division troops
16th (Service) Battalion (2nd County Down) (Pioneers), Royal Irish Rifles
No 36 Machine Gun Battalion
121st, 122nd, 150th Field Companies
36th Signals Company
108th, 109th, 110th Field Ambulance
36th Divisional Train ASC (251, 252, 253 and 254 HT Companies)
223rd Divisional Employment Company
36th Divisional Workshops
CLIII, CLXXIII Brigades RFA
X36, Y36 Medium Mortar (6x6inch) Batteries RFA
36th Ammunition Column

40th Division
(New Army Bantam Division)*

Major General J Ponsonby
From 3 July 1918
Major General Sir W E Peyton

The Battles of the Lys
The Battle of Estaires
The Battle of Hazebrouck

Following losses in this battle the Division was reduced to a training cadre – a major reorganisation took place, with battalions that had been Garrison Guard units joining and being converted to fighting units. Orders on 14 June 1918 stated that the formation would be a 'Garrison Division' (semi-mobile) and 'required to hold a quiet sector of the line', with training focused on that role.

Note: On 13 July, via a Divisional Order, each *Garrison* battalion in the Division had the word deleted from its title with immediate effect.

The Advance in Flanders
The Final Advance in Flanders
The Battle of Ypres 1918

During the night of 10-11 November, 29th Division (II Corps, Second Army) and 59th Division (Fifth Army) linked up in front of XV Corps, assuming responsibility for the line – XV Corps including 40th Division was withdrawn into Reserve.

119 Brigade (Welsh Bantams) Brigadier-General F P Crozier

13th (Service) Battalion (Wandsworth), the East Surreys (left as cadre June 1918)
18th (Service) Battalion (2nd Glamorgan), the Welsh (left as a cadre May 1918)
21st (Service) Battalion (Islington), the Middlesex (left as a cadre May 1918)
12th (Service) Battalion, the North Staffords (joined June 1918 as 12th (Garrison) Battalion)
13th (Service) Battalion, East Lancashire (joined 1918 as 8th Garrison Guard Battalion)
13th (Service) Battalion, Inniskilling
119th Trench Mortar Battery

120 Brigade Brigadier-General Hon. C S Heathcote-Drummond-Willoughby
From 15 March 1918
Lieutenant-Colonel R F Forbes (Acting)
From 23 March 1918
Brigadier-General C J Hobkirk
From 18 October 1918
Brigadier-General Hon. W P Hore-Ruthuen

2nd Battalion, the Royal Scots Fusiliers (joined April 1918, left April 1918)
10/11th (Service) Battalion, the Highland Light Infantry (left as a cadre June 1918)
14th (Service) Battalion, the Highland Light Infantry (left as a cadre June 1918) 14th (Service) Battalion, the Argyll & Sutherland Highlanders (left April 1918)
10th (Service) Battalion, the King's Own Scottish Borderers (joined June 1918)**
15th (Service) Battalion, the KOYLI (joined June 1918)
11th (Service) Battalion, the Cameron Highlanders (joined as 6th Garrison Guard Battalion June 1918)
120th Trench Mortar Battery

121 Brigade Brigadier-General J Campbell
From 27 April 1918
Lieutenant-Colonel L Lloyd (Acting)
From 6 May 1918
Brigadier-General W B Garnett
From 17 September 1918
Brigadier-General G C Stubbs

12th (Service) Battalion, the Suffolks (left May 1918)
13th (Service) Battalion, the Yorkshire (left June1918)***
20th (Service) Battalion (Shoreditch), the Middlesex (left as cadre May 1918)
23rd TF Battalion, the Cheshires (joined as a Garrison Battalion, June 1918)

10th Battalion, the Worcesters (joined as a training cadre June 1918, absorbed July 1918)
23rd Battalion, the Lancashire Fusiliers (joined as 23rd Garrison Battalion, June 1918)
8th (Service) Battalion, the Royal Irish (joined as 2nd Garrison Battalion, June1918)****
121st Trench Mortar Battery

Division troops
12th (Service) Battalion, the Yorkshire (left June 1918)
17th (Service) Battalion, the Worcesters (joined as a Garrison Battalion in June 1918)
No 40 Machine Gun Battalion (created March 1918, disbanded May 1918)
No 104 Machine Gun Battalion (joined 24 August 1918, left 16 September 1918)
No 39 Machine Gun Battalion (joined 11 September 1918)
224th, 229th, 231st Field Companies
40th Signals Company
135th, 136th, 137th Field Ambulance
40th Divisional Train ASC (292, 293, 294, 295 Companies)
237th Divisional Employment Company
51st Mobile Veterinary Section
CLXXVIII (Howitzer) Brigade RFA
CLXXXI Brigade RFA
X40, Y40 Medium Mortar Batteries RFA
40th Ammunition Column

* Although in order to make it ready for deployment to the Western Front in 1916, it included four 'non-Bantam' Battalions

** The Battalion was formed as 9th Garrison Battalion, the King's Own Scottish Borderers; it was designated as the 10th Battalion on 15 June 1918

*** The 8th (Service) Battalion, the Sherwood Foresters merged with 13th Yorkshire in April 1916

**** The Battalion was designated as 8th Battalion, the Royal Irish on 15 July 1918

41st Division
(New Army Division)

Major-General S T B Lawford

The Advance in Flanders
The Final Advance in Flanders
The Battle of Ypres 1918
The Battle of Courtrai
The Action of Ooteghem.

On 26-27 October the Division was relieved from front line duty and moved to rest around Courtrai. On 1 November the Division reoccupied part of the front line under XIX Corps;

on 9 November the Division carried out a passage of the Schelde, establishing outposts on the eastern bank.

122 Brigade	Brigadier-General F W Towsey From 8 June 1918 Brigadier-General S V P Weston

12th (Service) Battalion, (Bermondsey) East Surreys
15th (Service) Battalion, (2nd Portsmouth) Hampshire
18th (Service) Battalion (Arts and Crafts), King's Royal Rifle Corps
122nd Trench Mortar Battery

123 Brigade	Brigadier-General E Pearce Serocold From 23 June 1918 Brigadier-General M Kemp-Welch

11th (Service) Battalion, the Queen's (Royal West Surrey Regiment)
10th (Service) Battalion (Kent County), Royal West Kents
23rd (Service) (2nd Football) Battalion, Middlesex
123rd Trench Mortar Battery

124 Brigade	Brigadier-General W F Clemson From 21 June 1918 Brigadier-General R L Aldercron

10th (Service) Battalion, Queen's
26th (Service) Battalion, Royal Fusiliers
20th (Service) Battalion (Wearside), Durham Light Infantry
124th Trench Mortar Battery

Division
19th (Service) (Pioneers) (2nd Public Works) (Pioneers) Battalion, the Middlesex
No 41 Machine Gun Battalion
228th (Barnsley), 233rd (Ripon), 237th (Reading) Field Companies
41st Signals Company
138th, 139th, 140th Field Ambulance
41st Divisional Train ASC (296, 297, 298, 299 Companies)
52nd Mobile Veterinary Section
41st Divisional Workshops
CLXXXIII, CLXXXVII Brigades RFA
X41, Y41 Trench Mortar Batteries
41st Ammunition Column

Second Army: Supporting and Attached Units

3rd Cavalry Division
Major General Harmon
(Joined Second Army on 9th November 1918)

The Final Advance in Flanders
6 Cavalry Brigade [Brigadier General E Paterson]
3rd Dragoon Guards
Royal Dragoons
10th Hussars
C Battery RHA
6 Cavalry Brigade Machine Gun Squadron
6 Signal Troop

7 Cavalry Brigade [Brigadier General Burt]
6th Inniskilling Dragoons
7th Dragoon Guards
17th Lancers
K Battery RHA
7 Cavalry Brigade Machine Gun Sqn
7 Signal Troop

Canadian Cavalry Brigade [Brigadier General R Paterson]
Royal Canadian Dragoons
Lord Strathcona's Horse
Fort Garry Horse
Royal Canadian Horse Artillery Brigade
Canadian Cavalry Brigade Machine Gun Sqn

IV Brigade RHA and Ammunition Column
3 Field Squadron RE
3 Signal Troop
6th, 7th, 8th Canadian Field Ambulances
13th, 14th 'A' Canadian Mobile Vetinary Sections
773 Divisional Employment Company
81 (Horse Transport) Divisional ASC
73 (Mechanical Transport) Supply Column
576 Divisional Auxiliary Company

French Army: Flanders, October 1918

Detachement d'Armee du Nord (French Army)
CinC General de Mitry

French 164th Division (deployed as reserve to Belgian Army Southern Groupement)

French II Cavalry Corps General Robillot
2nd Cavalry Division
3rd Cavalry Division
6th Cavalry Division

French VII Corps General Massenet
5th Division
41st Division

French XXXIV Corps General Mudant
70th Division
77th Division
128th Division (Reserve)

On 19 October, the new French Sixth Army under General de Boissoudy entered the line. This consisted of VII and XXXIV Corps plus XXX Corps (5th and 132nd Divisions), under General Peney)

Belgian Army

By the end of 1914, the Belgian army was exhausted and decimated: only 85,000 of the original 117,000 soldiers of the field army and the 80,000 Troupes de Forteresse reached the river Yser. Regiments that had been split on mobilisation to form a second unit had to be merged to maintain their strength. The army was desperately in need of new recruits. In a first appeal (26 October 1914) King Albert asked every Belgian male between the age of 18 and 30 to volunteer. The government in exile decided on March 1 1915, that every male between the age of 18 and 25 and living in Belgium, France or England was obliged to enlist (although there were also volunteers from Belgians living abroad); on 21 July 1916 this was extended up to the age of 40.

In addition many Belgians living in occupied territory, made the risky journey across the Belgian – Dutch border to enlist. This journey was extremely dangerous and many were shot by German patrols. Eventually the Germans erected electrified fences on the entire length of the border, although many Belgians still made the attempt. From Holland they went to England and to training camps in France.

In January 1918 the Belgian Army was reorganised: the initial brigades were abolished and each of the 6 'divisions d'armée' was to be composed of 2 'divisions d'infanterie' (each comprising 3 regiments). The cavalry division had 3 brigades with each 2 regiments, 1 group 'd'auto-canons mitrailleuses' , 2 battalions of cyclists, 3 batteries of 7.5 cm canons, 1 company of engineers and a platoon of 'télégraphistes sur cycles'.

In 1918, the Belgian army had
170000 soldiers
5700 officers
38000 horses
850 artillery pieces (not including trench mortars)
(A further 30000 troops were employed in factories, hospitals etc)

On 28 September 1918 each 'division d'armée' was composed of :
Quartier Général
2 divisions d'infanterie
1 groupement léger
1 régiment d'artillerie
1 régiment du génie (2 bataillons)
1 compagnie de télégraphistes
1 peloton de projecteurs
1 peloton de T.S.F.
1 peloton de fontainiers
1 corps de transport

The Belgian Army 28 September 1918

Commander	H.R.H. King Albert I
Ministre de la Guerre	Lieutenant Général Baron de Ceuninck
Chef d'Etat-major	Lieutenant Général C. Gillain
Sous-Chef d'Etat-major	Général Maglinse
Inspecteur de l'Artillerie	Lieutenant Général Arnould
Inspecteur du Génie	Lieutenant Général Baron Greindl
Inspecteur du Service de Santé	Lieutenant Général Mélis
1' Division d'Armée	Lieutenant Général Bernheim
2' Division d'Armée	Lieutenant Général Drubbel
3' Division d'Armée	Lieutenant Général Jacques
4' Division d'Armée	Lieutenant Général Michel
5' Division d'Armée	Lieutenant Général L Rucquoy
6' Division d'Armée	Lieutenant Général Biebuyck
Division de Cavalerie	Lieutenant General Lemercier

Note: For the attack on 28 September, the Army was deployed in two 'groupements' or corps:

North Groupement	Lieutenant Général Bernheim
South Groupement	Lieutenant Général Biebuyck

Troupes auxiliaires
Corps de troupes auxiliaires du Génie, (3 groupes, 46 compagnies)
Troupes d’étapes
Section de camouflage
Groupe de batteries de parc

Troupes non endivisionnées
Brigade d›Artillerie Lourde (2 régiments)
Bataillon Chemin de fer
Aviation militaire (11 escadrilles)
Aérostations militaire (3 compagnies)
Bataillon des Pontonniers
Compagnie des Projecteurs
Equipage de ponts (hipo et auto)
Groupement des colonnes automobiles auxiliaires
Service des routes

Brigade d’Artillerie Lourde
1’ Régiment d’artillerie Lourde
2’ Régiment d’artillerie Lourde

1 Division d’Armée

Lieutenant Général Bernheim	
1’ Division d’Infanterie	Général Lambert
4’ Régiment de Ligne	Colonel Ouwerx
23’ Régiment de Ligne	
24’ Régiment de Ligne	Colonel Vanniesbecq
1 Bataillon de renfort et d›instruction	
1’ Régiment d›artillerie (3 groupes)	
7’ Division d’Infanterie	Général Van Acker
2’ Régiment de Ligne	
3’ Régiment de Ligne	
22’ Régiment de Ligne	
1 Bataillon de renfort et d›instruction	
7’ Régiment d›artillerie (3 groupes)	

Groupement léger
1 groupe du 3’ Régiment de Lanciers (2 escadrons)
1 compagnie de cycliste
3 autos-mitrailleuses
    13’ régiment d’artillerie
    1’ régiment du génie (2 bataillons)
    1 compagnie de télégraphistes

1 peloton de projecteurs
1 peloton de T.S.F.
1 peloton de fontainiers
1 corps de transport

2' Division d'Armée
Lieutenant Général Drubbel

2' Division d'Infanterie Général Cabra
5' Régiment de Ligne
6' Régiment de Ligne
15' Régiment de Ligne
1 Bataillon de renfort et d›instruction
2' Régiment d›artillerie (3 groupes)

8' Division d'Infanterie Général Detail
7' Régiment de Ligne
16' Régiment de Ligne
17' Régiment de Ligne
1 Bataillon de renfort et d›instruction
8' Régiment d›artillerie (3 groupes)

Groupement léger
1 groupe du 3' Régiment de Lanciers (2 escadrons)
1 compagnie de cycliste
3 autos-mitrailleuses
14' régiment d›artillerie
2' régiment du génie (2 bataillons)
1 compagnie de télégraphistes
1 peloton de projecteurs
1 peloton de T.S.F.
1 peloton de fontainiers
1 corps de transport

3' Division d'Armée
Lieutenant Général Jacques

3' Division d'Infanterie Général Joostens
9' Régiment de Ligne
11' Régiment de Ligne
12' Régiment de Ligne
1 Bataillon de renfort et d›instruction
3' Régiment d›artillerie (3 groupes)

9' Division d'Infanterie — Général Baltia
14' Régiment de Ligne
1' Régiment de Ligne
4' Régiment de Ligne
1 Bataillon de renfort et d›instruction
9' Régiment d›artillerie (3 groupes)

Groupement léger
1 groupe du 2' Régiment de Lanciers (2 escadrons)
1 compagnie de cycliste
3 autos-mitrailleuses
  15' régiment d›artillerie
  3' régiment du génie (2 bataillons)
  1 compagnie de télégraphistes
  1 peloton de projecteurs
  1 peloton de T.S.F.
  1 peloton de fontainiers
  1 corps de transport

4' Division d'Armée
Lieutenant Général Michel

4' Division d'Infanterie — Général Dechesne
8' Régiment de Ligne
10' Régiment de Ligne — Colonel Deisser
18' Régiment de Ligne
1 Bataillon de renfort et d›instruction
4' Régiment d›artillerie (3 groupes)

10' Division d'Infanterie — Général Flebus
13' Régiment de Ligne
19' Régiment de Ligne
20' Régiment de Ligne
1 Bataillon de renfort et d›instruction
10' Régiment d›artillerie (3 groupes)

Groupement léger
1 groupe cavalerie du 1' Régiment de Lanciers (2 escadrons)
1 compagnie de cycliste
3 autos-mitrailleuses
  16' régiment d›artillerie
  4' régiment du génie (2 bataillons)
  1 compagnie de télégraphistes
  1 peloton de projecteurs
  1 peloton de T.S.F.

1 peloton de fontainiers
1 corps de transport

5' Division d'Armée
Lieutenant Général L Rucquoy

5' Division d'Infanterie	Général Collyns
1' Régiment de Ligne	
21' Régiment de Ligne	
2' Régiment de Chasseurs a pied	
1 Bataillon de renfort et d›instruction	
5' Régiment d›artillerie (3 groupes)	

11' Division d'Infanterie	Général Coppejans
3' Régiment de Ligne	
5' Régiment de Ligne	
6' Régiment de Ligne	Colonel Hoonaert
1 Bataillon de renfort et d›instruction	
11' Régiment d›artillerie (3 groupes)	

Groupement léger
1 groupe cavalerie du 1' Régiment de Lanciers (2 escadrons)
1 compagnie de cycliste
3 autos-mitrailleuses
17' régiment d›artillerie
5' régiment du génie (2 bataillons)
1 compagnie de télégraphistes
1 peloton de projecteurs
1 peloton de T.S.F.
1 peloton de fontainiers
1 corps de transport

6' Division d'Armée
Lieutenant Général Biebuyck

6' Division d'Infanterie	Général J Collyns
1' Régiment de Carabiniers	Colonel B E M Brenrer
2' Régiment de Carabiniers	
3' Régiment de Carabiniers	
1 Bataillon de renfort et d'instruction	
6' Régiment d'artillerie (3 groupes)	

12' Division d'Infanterie	Général Lotz
4' Régiment de Carabiniers	
1' Régiment de Grenadiers	

2' Régiment de Grenadiers
1 Bataillon de renfort et d'instruction
12' Régiment d'artillerie (3 groupes)

Groupement léger
1 groupe cavalerie du 2' Régiment de Lanciers (2 escadrons)
1 compagnie de cycliste
3 autos-mitrailleuses
18' régiment d›artillerie
6' régiment du génie (2 bataillons)
1 compagnie de télégraphistes
1 peloton de projecteurs
1 peloton de T.S.F.
1 peloton de fontainiers
1 corps de transport

Division de Cavalerie
Lieutenant General Lemercier

1' Brigade de Cavalerie	Général Baron Buffin
1' Régiment de Guides	
2' Régiment de Guides	Colonel du Roy de Blicquy

2' Brigade de Cavalerie
4' Régiment de Lanciers
5' Régiment de Lanciers

3' Brigade de Cavalerie
1' Régiment de Chasseurs à cheval
2' Régiment de Chasseurs à cheval
1' Bataillon Carabiniers cycliste
2' Bataillon Carabiniers cycliste
Groupe Artillerie a cheval
1 Compagnie du Génie
1 peloton de télégraphistes sur cycles
Corps de Transport

German Army

FAR	Field Artillery Regiment	Co	Company
IR	Infantry Regiment	RGR	Reserve Grenadier Regiment
RIR	Reserve Infantry Regiment	MW	Trench Mortar (Minen Werfer)
RP	Reserve Pioneers/Engineers	Ldw	Landwehr

The GAF was opposed principally by German Fourth Army (General Friedrich Bertram von Armin), which was part of Crown Prince Rupprecht's Army Group (together with Seventeenth and Sixth Armies). As of 26 September 1918, Fourth Army was deployed from north of Armentières to the coast, comprising ten front line divisions and five reserve divisions.

German Divisions facing British Second Army: Battle of Ypres
28 September 1918

Division	**Units**	**Location**	**Comments**
12th Bavarian	26th Bavarian I R 27th Bavarian I R 28th Bavarian I R	East of Ypres	(Mainly opposite the Belgians) Largely rested
6th Bavarian Reserve	25th Bavarian I R 20th Bavarian RI R 16th Bavarian RI R	West of Wytschaete-Messines	Fought near Bapaume in August
40th Bavarian Reserve	181st IR 134th IR	South of Ypres-Comines canal	Involved in 18 July offensive
11th Reserve (Fourth Army)	22nd IR 156th IR 10th RIR	Ploegsteert	Largely rested
56th	118th IR 186th IR 88th IR		Largely rested
4th			Largely rested Believed to be a good division

Additional Divisions brought forward after 28 September

Division	**Units**	**Location**	**Comments**
52nd Reserve Division	238th RIR 239th RIR 240th RIR 52nd FAR	Molenhock Becelaere Moorslede	Moved into line on 28 September
13th Reserve Division	100th Res. Grenadier R		Moved into line on or after 29 September
23rd Reserve Division			
39th Division	132nd IR 126th IR 172nd IR	East of Gheluvelt	

Division	Units	Location	Comments
6th Dismounted Cavalry Division	13th Hussars 7th Reserve Dragoons 9th Uhlans 2nd Cuirassiers	Ledeghem	Moved into line on or after 29 September
40th Division	243rd RIR	Ypres-Menin Road	Reported in line 30 September
1st Bavarian Reserve Division	1st Bavarian RIR 2nd Bavarian RIR	Ledeghem	Moved into line 2 October

German Divisions facing British Second Army: Battle of Courtrai

Division	Units	Location	Comments
1st Bavarian Reserve Division	1st Bavarian RIR 2nd Bavarian RIR 3rd Bavarian RIR 201st MW Co 1st Bavarian RP Co	Ledeghem	
	15th RIR 100th RGR	Dadizeele	
39th Division	132nd IR 126th IR 172nd IR 38th Bearer Co 80th FAR	Gheluwe	
40th Division	181st IR 104th IR 134th IR	Gulleghem & Wevelghem	Reported as reinforcements from 14 October
6th Bavarian Reserve Division	25th Bavarian IR 20th Bavarian RIR 16th Bavarian RIR	Wervicq	
6th Cavalry Division	12th Hussars 2nd Dragoons 3rd Uhlans 9th Uhlans 170th Ldw Brigade	Heule & Gulleghem	Reported as reinforcements from 14 October
11th Reserve Division	22nd IR 156th IR 10th RIR	Deulemont	
7th Cavalry Division	25th Dragoons		Reported as reinforcements from 16 October

Appendix II

British Army Medical Categories[1]

Category A – fit for general service

A1	Men for despatch overseas in all respects, as regards training, physical and mental qualifications
A2	Recruits who should be A1 on completion of their training
A3	Returned Expeditionary Force men who should be A1 once 'hardened'
A4	Men under 19 years of age who should become A1 or A2 once they reach that age

Category B – fit for service abroad, but not general service

B1	In Garrison or Provisional units
B2	In Labour units or on garrison or regimental outdoor employment
B3	On sedentary work as clerks or store men only

Category C – fit for home service only

C1	In Garrison or Provisional units
C2	In Labour units or on command, garrison or regimental outdoor employment
C3	On sedentary work as clerks, storemen, batmen, cooks, orderlies, sanitary duties, etc.

Category D – temporarily unfit for service, but likely to become so within six months

D1	In command depots
D2	In regimental depots
D3	In any unit or depot under or awaiting medical or dental treatment, on completion of which will re-join their original medical category

Category E – unfit for service, and not likely to become fit within six months

1 The information in the table is taken from C. Messenger, *Call to Arms: The British Army 1914-18* (London: Cassell, 2006), Appendix II, pp. 521-2; the sources are War Office, *Statistics of the Military Effort of the British Empire During the Great War 1914-1920* (Uckfield, Naval & Military Press reprint of 1922 edition); TNA WO32/5093, Lawson Report, *The Number and Physical Categories of Men Employed out of the Fighting Area in France.*

Notes:

- In October 1917, following recommendations made in the report of Lieutenant General H. M. Lawson at the start of the year, under ACI 1606/17, Category C was abolished; men listed within this category were recategorised in the corresponding Category B subdivision
- In addition, the following categories were applied in France and Flanders:
  Class A – fit for general service
  Class TB (Temporary Base) – temporarily unfit for general service
  Class PB (Permanent Base) – unfit for general service at the Front, but fit for service on the lines of communication and in army corps areas and capable of being regraded Class A
  Class PU (Permanently Unfit) – those in class PB who are never likely to become Class A, but employed in the same way as Class PB

Appendix III

Letter from Foch to Allied Commanders 19 October 1918

PERSONAL and SECRET

Commander in Chief of Allied Armies G.Q.G.A., 19th October 1918.
General Staff HQ.

1st Section.
3rd Office.

GENERAL DIRECTIVE

No. 4925.

In order to press the advantages we have made, the Allied Armies must take action as follows:

1. The Flanders Army Group will march in the general direction of Brussels; its right side towards HAL, approaching l'ESCAUT at PECQ, – la DENDER at LESSINES.
   On this march, forcing the major river lines: ESCAUT – DENDER… must be combined, when necessary, with action on the flank to turn back these lines, to be carried out by the British Armies.

2. The British Armies (5th, 1st, 3rd, 4th) will advance to the South of the PECQ – LESSINES – HAL line, their right side advancing through FROIDCHAPPELLE PHILLIPEVILLE onto AGIMONT (North of GIVET).
   The British Armies' main objective remains to turn back enemy forces on the ARDENNES massif which is difficult to penetrate, and to cut their main supply lines; – and at the same time, to assist the advance of the Flanders Army Group, enabling them to cross the major river lines: ESCAUT, DENDER … This would otherwise prevent their advance.
   They themselves will be supported by the 1st French Army.

3. The French Armies (1st, 10th, 5th, 4th) and the 1st American Army will operate to the South of the afore-mentioned line.

   Their role consists in:

   For the 1st French Army: to support the British Armies' attack by marching towards la CAPELLE, CHIMAY – GIVET, and manoeuvring to the right, to turn back enemy resistance on the SERRE – SISSONNE line;

   For the 5th, 4th French Armies and the 1st American Army: to reach the MEZIERES – SEDAN region and the upper reaches of the MEUSE, moving down the AISNE line in a two-sided manoeuvre: – on the left wing (5th French Army) in the direction of CHAUMONT – PORCIEN; – on the right wing (4th French Army & 1st American Army) in the direction of BUZANCY – LE CHESNE.

(Sd). F. FOCH

Appendix IV

Letter from Haig to Foch 25 October 1918

SECRET.

O.A.D. 946.

25th October, 1918.

From:-
The Commander-in-Chief,
British Armies in France.

TO:-
The Commander-in-Chief,
Allied Forces in France.

My dear Marshal,
I would point out that at the meeting at CASSEL on the 9th September, it was agreed by me that two divisions of the Second Army should be employed under the command of His Majesty the King of the Belgians for the purpose of covering the flank of the Army of Flanders operating in an easterly direction. It was further agreed that the whole of the Second Army should be used in the event of the enemy retiring from the MESSINESS Ridge, to exploit any success which might be obtained by following and pressing the German forces. It was well understood that in view of the fact that my other Armies were committed to large offensive operations further south, the Second Army was not to be committed to any other operation than that of clearing the ground up to the LYS River. The whole scope of the operation had as its objective the "clearing [of] the Belgian coast and the country between the coast and the River LYS".

This has not been accomplished and I request that the Second Army be forthwith returned to my command. If, as I understand, further operations by the Army of Flanders have as their objective the capture of BRUSSELS, this can be equally attained by the co-operation of all the British Armies including the Second Army operating under my command.

Yours very truly,
(Sd) D. HAIG
Field-Marshal

Appendix V

Letter from Haig to War Cabinet 25 October 1918

SECRET

No. O.A.D. 947.
[Stamped: 'War Office Received 27 OCT 1918']

GENERAL HEADQUARTERS,
BRITISH ARMIES IN THE FIELD,
25th October, 1918

Sir,

I have the honour to forward for the information of the War Cabinet a copy of a letter, No. O.A.D. 946, dated 25th October, 1918, which I have addressed to Marshal Foch, requesting that the Second British Army should revert forthwith to my command.

This request was made by me by telephone on the 18th instant and again verbally to the Marshal on the 24th instant for the reasons given below, but he was not willing to accede to my demand and insisted that the Second Army should remain under the command of the King of the Belgians and continue to operate in Belgium under the latter's orders in accordance with the Directive No. 4925, of the 19th October, of which a copy is attached.

I have always recognised the necessity of making temporary detachments from the British Armies to operate with the French, and I have invariably complied with the demands of the Marshal in this respect, provided the military reasons were sufficient to justify this action. For example, during the fighting on the AISNE in May and on the MARNE in July, I detached four or five divisions on each occasion to operate with the French, and, in order to carry out a combined operation in FLANDERS, I acquiesced on the 9th September in the temporary detachment of the Second Army under the King of the Belgians. On each occasion the detachment was regarded as of a purely temporary nature, and was to be returned on the completion of the specific operation in hand.

In the case of the Second Army, this detachment was made on the 11th September, and, in accordance with Marshal Foch's instructions, two divisions were to make the initial attack in conjunction with the Belgian Army, while the whole of the Second British Army, in combination with the Belgians and a detachment of French Troops, was to exploit any success gained, and subsequently protect the flank of the Franco-Belgian forces by securing positions along the left bank of the River LYS. The Second British Army carried out these operations successfully, and in fact took the heaviest share of the work in driving the enemy back. I have not hitherto pressed for the return of this Army to my command while the operations to secure BRUGES and the line of the River LYS were in progress. This phase, however, is now completed, and the operations naturally are entering a new phase, that of forcing the passage of the River SCHELDT. The Second Army during the course of these operations has already incurred some 22,000 casualties.

The Secretary
War Office
London, S.W.1

In/

In the meantime the First, Third and Fourth British Armies have been carrying out a series of important attacks on a wide front against positions of vital importance to the enemy and to hold which he is utilising a considerable number of his best troops. These operations, though highly successful and productive of far-reaching effects, must necessarily involve considerable casualties.

The operations of the Second Army are now entering on the phase of forcing the passage of the Rivers SCHELDT and DENDRE to enable the allied troops in FLANDERS to cross those rivers in the lower reaches and facilitate an advance on BRUSSELS. I maintain that these operations can be equally well undertaken under my control and that I can thus balance the casualties so that their incidence may not fall unduly on the British forces. In this connection I would draw your attention to Directive No.4925, dated 19th October, 1918, by Marshal Foch, which shews that there is an expectation of the British attacks on the LE CATEAU front producing results which will facilitate the operations of the allies both on the south in CHAMPAGNE and on the north in FLANDERS.

While I am anxious to carry out Marshal Foch's wishes and instructions to the full, at the same time I feel compelled to consider the condition of the British Armies as a whole and generally to control the operations of those Armies in respect of the casualties incurred. So far the brunt of the offensive operations has fallen on the British troops. Owing to our lack of effectives this cannot be allowed to continue much longer. It is therefore most necessary that I should exercise the greatest care in engaging the five Armies of which the British Expeditionary Force is composed. The responsibility for this can alone rest on me and ought not in the case of any portion of the British forces [to] be delegated to any foreign Commander, of no matter how high a rank.

I wish to refer this matter to the War Cabinet as I do not consider that Marshal Foch's action is in accordance with the spirit of the instructions issued to me by the Secretary of State in his letter No.121/France/2357, dated 21st June, and I am of [the] opinion that such action is prejudicial to the welfare of the British Armies in France.

I have the honour to be,
Sir,
Your obedient Servant

[signed 'D. Haig']
Field-Marshal,
Commanding-in-Chief,
British Armies in France.

Bibliography

1 ARCHIVAL

1.1 War Office papers, The National Archives (TNA)

a. War Office and Successors: Registered Files (General Series)

WO32/5102 (General, Code 86(A)), Field Marshal Haig requests return of 2nd British Army to his command from the King of the Belgians

b. War Diaries

WO95/246	11 Motor Machine Gun Battery
WO95/284	Second Army Headquarters Branches and Services: Adjutant and Quarter-Master General 01/08/1918- 31/12/1919
WO95/287	Second Army Headquarters Branches and Services: Director of Medical Services 01/05/1918-31/03/1919
WO95/292	Second Army Headquarters Branches and Services: Deputy Director Supply and Transport 1917-1918
WO95/1757	9th (Pioneers) Seaforth Highlanders
WO95/1765	7th Seaforth Highlanders
WO95/1766	8th Black Watch (Royal Highlanders)
WO95/1767	5th Cameron Highlanders
WO95/1771	9th (Scottish) Division
WO95/1771/4	27 Infantry Brigade
WO95/1771/5	27 Infantry Brigade
WO95/1775	28 Infantry Brigade
	9th Cameronians (Scottish Rifles)
	1st Royal Newfoundland Regiment
WO95/1876	14th Division: General Staff – August/September 1918
WO95/1877	14th Division: General Staff – October-December 1918
WO95/1880	14th Division: Administration Section
WO95/1890	15th (Pioneers) Loyal North Lancs
WO95/1894/6	41 Infantry Brigade
WO95/1899/2	42 Infantry Brigade
WO95/1900	16th The Manchesters (1st City)
	14th Argyll & Sutherland Highlanders

WO95/1902	6th The Wiltshires (Royal Wiltshire Yeomanry)
WO95/1905	43 Infantry Brigade
WO95/2285	29th Division
WO95/2295/5	1/2nd (Pioneers) Monmouthshire
WO95/2299	86 Infantry Brigade
WO95/2300	1st Lancashire Fusiliers
WO95/2301	2nd Royal Fusiliers
WO95/2303	87 Infantry Brigade
WO95/2307/4	88 Infantry Brigade
WO95/2323	30th Division
	6th (Pioneers) South Wales Borderers
	30 Machine Gun Corps
	202 Field Company Royal Engineers
WO95/2328	21 Infantry Brigade
WO95/2330	7th Royal Irish (South Irish Horse)
	2/23rd London (County of London)
	1/6th Cheshire Regiment
WO95/2332	89 Infantry Brigade
WO95/2336	7/8th Royal Inniskilling Fusiliers
	2/17th London (County of London)
	2nd South Lancashire
WO95/2338	90 Infantry Brigade
WO95/2340	2/16th London (Queen's Westminster Rifles)
	2/15th London (Prince of Wales' Own Civil Service Rifles)
	2/14th London (London Scottish)
WO95/2353/1	12th (Pioneers) King's Own Yorkshire Light Infantry
WO95/2356/5	92 Infantry Brigade
WO95/2360	93 Infantry Brigade
WO95/2361	31st Division
WO95/2364	94 Infantry Brigade Headquarters
WO95/2361	13th York & Lancaster
	1/18th Durham Light Infantry
WO95/2365	18th Kings Royal Rifle Corps
WO95/2366	12th Norfolk Regiment
	12th Royal Scots Fusiliers
	24th Royal Welsh Fusiliers
WO95/2437	34th Division
WO95/2451/2	2/4th (Pioneers) Somerset Light Infantry
WO95/2456	101 Brigade
WO95/2461	102 Brigade
WO95/2465	103 Brigade
WO95/2470/1	35th Division: General Staff
WO95/2477/8	19th (Pioneers) Northumberland Fusiliers
WO95/2483	104 Infantry Brigade
WO95/2486	105 Infantry Brigade

WO95/2489	106 Infantry Brigade
WO95/2498/2	16th (Pioneers) Royal Irish Rifles
WO95/2492	36th Division
WO95/2502/1	107 Infantry Brigade
WO95/2502/3	1st Royal Irish Rifles
WO95/2502/4	2nd Royal Irish Rifles
WO95/2504	108 Infantry Brigade
WO95/2509	109 Infantry Brigade
WO95/2510	1st Royal Inniskilling Fusiliers
	2nd Royal Inniskilling Fusiliers
	9th Royal Inniskilling Fusiliers
WO95/2594	40th Division
WO95/2601/4	17th (Pioneers) The Worcesters
WO95/2605	119 Brigade
WO95/2610	120 Infantry Brigade
WO95/2611/2	11th Cameron Highlanders
WO95/2611/4	10th Kings Own Scottish Borderers
WO95/2614	121 Infantry Brigade
WO95/2618	41st Division
WO95/2627/4	19th (Pioneers) The Middlesex
WO95/2634	94 Infantry Brigade
	12th East Surreys
WO95/2638	10th Royal West Kents
WO95/2639/3	23rd Middlesex
WO95/2642	124 Infantry Brigade
WO95/2643	10th Queens
WO95/2644	26th Royal Fusiliers

c. Maps & Plans

WO153/472	Second Army Dispositions (2): 07/07/1918 – 03/11/1918
WO153/508	Second Army: Enemy Organisation: 1918
WO153/986	German Defences in Belgium: 1918

d. Operations & Intelligence files

WO157/128	Second Army Intelligence Summaries: September 1918
WO157/129	Second Army Intelligence Summaries: October 1918
WO157/130	Second Army Intelligence Summaries: 01/11/1918 – 31/03/1919
WO158/211	Second Army Operations: 27/07/1918 – 30/09/1918
WO158/212	Second Army Operations: 01/10/1918 – 20/01/1919
WO158/218	Second Army Operations: Summaries: 24/08/1918 – 16/11/1918
WO158/294	Second Army Headquarters: Effects of Our Gas and Gas Shells 11/10/1915-17/10/1918

1.2 Regimental Archives

The Cheshire Regiment, Cheshire Military Museum, Chester
War Diary: 1/4th Cheshires
War Diary: 15th (Service) Cheshires (1st Birkenhead)
War Diary: 23rd Cheshires
King's Own Royal Border Regiment Museum, Carlisle
War Diary: 1st Border
King's Own Yorkshire Light Infantry (KOYLI) Archive, Pontefract
War Diary: 12th KOYLI
Prince Of Wales' Own Regiment of Yorkshire Museum, York
War Diary: 10th East Yorkshires
War Diary: 11th East Yorkshires
War Diary: 15th West Yorkshires
Queen's Lancashire Regiment Museum, Preston
War Diary: 2nd Loyal North Lancashire
War Diary: 15th Loyal North Lancashire (Pioneers)
War Diary: 2nd South Lancashire
York & Lancaster Regiment Museum, Rotherham
War Diary: 13th York & Lancaster

2 OFFICIAL PUBLICATIONS

General Staff *The German Army Handbook of 1918* (London: Frontline Books, 2008) (Introduction by Dr. J Beach)
Originally issued by the General Staff as *Handbook of the German Army in War, April, 1918*; it was republished in 1977 by Arms and Armour Press as *German Army Handbook, April 1918*
—— SS119 *Preliminary Notes on the Tactical Lessons of Recent Operations* (July 1916)
—— SS135 *Instructions for the Training of Divisions for Offensive Action* (December 1916)
revised and reprinted:
Instructions for the Training of Divisions for Offensive Action (August 1917)
republished:
The Training and Employment of Divisions (January 1918)
republished:
The Division in Attack (November 1918)
—— SS148 *Forward Inter-Communication in Battle* (March 1917)
—— SS143 *Instructions for the Training of Platoons for Offensive Action, 1917* (February 1917) (revised a number of times: 1918-1919)
—— SS152 *Notes for the Training of the British Armies in France* (provisionally published: June 1917) (reissued as instructions: January 1918)
—— SS195 *Scouting and Patrolling* (December 1917) Ministere de la Guerre *Les Armées Françaises dans la Grande Guerre* (Imprimerie Nationale, Paris, 1937) (French Official History)
The War Office *Statistics of the Military Effort of the British Empire during the Great War 1914-1920* (HMSO, 1922)

3 PRIVATE PAPERS, DIARIES & DOCUMENTS

a. Imperial War Museum (IWM), London

3554 J S Blandford, Second Lieutenant, 206 Squadron, typed manuscript, *Sans Escort*
6873 W N Hendry, 2/14th (London Scottish) London Regiment
6877 H T Pope, 2/15th London Regiment
01/14/1 Major-General Sir (Cecil) Lothian Nicholson KCB CMG East Lancashire Regiment, 34th Division
83/6/1 E Miles MSM, 15th Battalion, KOYLI, 40th Division

b. Others

Brown, M., intro. *The Wipers Times: The Complete Series of the Famous Wartime Trench Newspaper* (London: Little Books Ltd., 2006)
Dutton, D. ed. *Paris 1918: The War Diary of the British Ambassador, the 17th Earl of Derby* (Liverpool: Liverpool University Press, 2001)
Terraine, J., ed. *General Jack's Diary: War on the Western Front 1914-1918 – The Trench Diary of Brigadier-General J. L. Jack, D.S.O.* (London, Cassell & Co., 2000 edition; first published, London, Eyre & Spottiswoode, 1964 edition)
Van Overstraeten, R. *The War Diaries of Albert 1, King of the Belgians*
(London: William Kimber, 1954)

4 PRINTED SOURCES

a. Books – Strategy, Military History and General Information (with particular reference to Flanders, French and Belgian forces, and/or the war in 1918)

Baker, C. *The Battle for Flanders: German Defeat on the Lys 1918* (Barnsley: Pen & Sword, 2011)
Banks, A. *A Military Atlas of the First World War* (London: Heinemann, 1975)
Barton, P. *The Battlefields of the First World War* (London: Constable & Robinson, 2005)
Barton, P., Doyle, P. & Vanderwalle, J. *Beneath Flanders Fields: The Tunnellers' War 1914-18* (Stroud, Gloucestershire: Spellmount, 2004)
Beach, J. *Haig's Intelligence: GHQ and the German Army, 1916-1918* (Cambridge: Cambridge University Press, 2013)
Becke, A. F. *Order of Battle Part 4: The Army Council, GHQs, Armies and Corps 1914-18* (HMSO, 1945)
Beckett, I. F. W. *Ypres: The First Battle 1914* (Pearson Education Ltd, 2004)
Beckett, I. F. W. & Corvi, S. J. ed. *Haig's Generals* (Barnsley: Pen & Sword Military, 2006)
Bet-El, I. R. *Conscripts: Forgotten Men of the Great War* (Stroud, Gloucestershire: The History Press, 2009; first published under the title *Conscripts: Lost Legions of the Great War* by Stroud, Gloucestershire: Sutton Publishing, 1999)
Boff, J. *Winning and Losing on the Western Front: The British Third Army and the Defeat of Germany in 1918* (Cambridge: Cambridge University Press, 2012)
Bourne, J., Liddle, P., & Whitehead, I. ed. *The Great World War1914-45: Volume 1: Lightning Strikes Twice* (London: Harper Collins, 2000)
Brice, B. *The Battle Book of Ypres: A Reference to Military Operations in the Ypres Salient 1914-18* (Steven age: Spa Books in association with Tom Donovan Military Books, 1987; first published 1927)

Brown, I. M. *British Logistics on the Western Front 1914-1919* (Praeger, Westport, 1998)
Brown, M. *1918 Year of Victory* (London: Sidgwick & Jackson, 1998)
Cambers, E. *Albert of Belgium: Defender of the Right* (London: Ivor Nicholson and Watson, 1935)
Chapman, P. *In Memory and In Mourning* series: *Menin Gate North; Menin Gate South; Tyne Cot Cemetery and Memorial* (Barnsley: Pen & Sword Military, 2015-6)
Clayton, A. *Paths of Glory: The French Army 1914-18* (London: Cassell, 2003)
Dennis, P. & Grey, J., ed. *1918: Defining Victory – Proceedings of the Chief of Army's History Conference held at the National Convention Centre, Canberra, 29 September 1998* (Army History Unit, Department of Defense, 1999)
Dewar, A.B.D. assisted by Lieutenant-Colonel J. H. Boraston *Sir Douglas Haig's Command: December 19, 1915, to November 11, 1918* (London: Constable and Company Ltd, 1922) (two volumes)
Dixon, J. *Magnificent But Not War – The Second Battle of Ypres 1915* (Barnsley: Leo Cooper, 2003)
Doughty, R. A. *Pyrrhic Victory: French Strategy and Operations in the Great War* (Cambridge, Massachusetts, USA: Belknap Press / Harvard University Press, 2005)
Edmonds, J. *Military Operations France and Belgium 1918: The German March Offensive and its Preliminaries (Official History)* (HMSO, 1935)
—— *Military Operations France and Belgium 1918: March-April Continuation of the German Offensives (Official History)* (HMSO, 1937)
—— *Military Operations France and Belgium 1918 Vol. III (Official History)* (HMSO, 1945)
—— *Military Operations France and Belgium 1918 Vol. IV 8th August-26th September (Official History)* (HMSO, 1947)
Edmonds, J. with Maxwell-Hyslop, R. *Military Operations France and Belgium 1918 Vol. V 26th September-11th November (Official History)* (HMSO, 1947)
Evans, M. M. *1918, The Year of Victories* (London: Arcturus, 2002)
Farrar-Hockley, A. *Ypres: Death of an Army* (Cerberus Publishing, 1967)
Galet, E. *Albert, King of the Belgians in the Great War: His Military Activities and Experiences Set Down with His Approval* (United States: Kessinger Publishing, 2007; first published, Houghton Miflin, 1931)
Gilbert, M. *The Routledge Atlas of the First World War* (London: Routledge, reprint 2002)
Giles, J. *The Ypres Salient: Flanders Then and Now* (London: Picardy Publishing Ltd, 1979; first published by London: Leo Cooper Ltd, 1970)
Greenhalgh, E. *Foch in Command: The Forging of a First World War General* (Cambridge: Cambridge University Press, 2011)
—— *The French Army and the First World War* (Cambridge, Cambridge University Press, 2014)
—— *Victory through Coalition: Britain and France during the First World War* (Cambridge: Cambridge University Press, 2005)
Groom, W. *A Storm in Flanders: The Ypres Salient 1914-1918: Tragedy and Triumph on the Western Front* (London: Cassell, 2003)
Gudmundsson, B. I. *Stormtroop Tactics: Innovation in the German Army 1914-1918* (New York: Praeger, 1989)
Harris, J. P. with Barr, N. *Amiens to the Armistice: The BEF in the Hundred Days Campaign 8 August-11 November 1918* (London: Brassey's, 1998)
Hart, P. *Aces Falling: War Above the Trenches 1918* (London: Weidenfeld & Nicolson, 2007)
—— *1918: A Very British Victory* (London: Wiedenfeld & Nicolson, 2008)

Haythornthwaite, P. *The World War One Source Book* (London: Arms & Armour Press, 1992)
Henniker, Colonel A. M. *Official History of the Great War: Transportation on the Western Front 1914-18* (East Sussex: The Naval & Military Press Ltd, 2013; first published, London: HMSO, 1937)
Hitchcock, Captain F. C. *'Stand To': A Diary of the Trenches* (East Sussex: The Naval & Military Press Ltd, 2009; first published London: Hurst & Blackett Ltd, 1936)
James, Captain E. A. *A Record of the Battles and Engagements of the British Armies in France and Flanders 1914-18* (East Sussex: The Naval & Military Press Ltd, 1998; reprint of original 1924 edition)
James, Brigadier E. A. *British Regiments 1914-18* (London: Samson Books, 1978)
Johnson, J. H. *1918: The Unexpected Victory* (London: Cassell & Co, 2000 edition)
Kitchen, M. *The German Offensives of 1918* (Stroud, Gloucester: Tempus 2005)
Lloyd, N. *Hundred Days: The End of the Great War* (London: Viking, 2013)
Louagie, J. *A Touch of Paradise in Hell: Talbot House, Poperinge – Every-Man's Sanctuary from the Trenches* (Solihull, Helion & Co, 2015)
Lynch, T. *They Did Not Grow Old: Teenage Conscripts on the Western Front, 1918* (Stroud, Gloucestershire: Spellmount (The History Press), 2013)
Messenger, C. *The Day We Won The War: Turning Point at Amiens 8 August 1918* (London: Wiedenfeld & Nicolson, 2008)
Middlebrook, M. *The Kaiser's Battle* (London: Allen Lane, 1978)
Millard, O. E. *Uncensored: The True Story of the Clandestine Newspaper 'La Libre Belgique' Published in Brussels During the German Occupation* (London: Robert Hale and Company, 1937)
Neillands, R. *The Great War Generals on the Western Front 1914-1918* (London: Robinson Publishing Ltd, 1999)
Palmer, A.R. *Victory 1918* (London: Weidenfeld & Nicolson, 1998)
Paschall, R. *The Defeat of Imperial Germany, 1917-1918* (USA: Algonquin Books, 1989)
Passingham, I. *All the Kaiser's Men: The Life and Death of the German Army on the Western Front 1914-1918* (Stroud: Sutton, 2003)
—— *The German Offensives of 1918: The Last Desperate Gamble* (Barnsley: Pen & Sword Military, 2008)
Persico, J. E. *11th Month, 11th Day, 11th Hour: Armistice day, 1918 – World War I and its Violent Climax* (London: Hutchinson, 2004)
Philpott, W. *Anglo-French Relations and Strategy on the Western Front 1914-18* (London: Palgrave Macmillan, 1996)
Philpott, W. *Bloody Victory: The Sacrifice on the Somme* (London: Little, Brown, 2009)
Robbins, S. *British Generalship on the Western Front, 1914-18: Defeat into Victory* (London: Frank Cass, 2005)
Sheffield, G. D. and Bourne, J. ed. *Douglas Haig: War Diaries and Letters 1914-1918* (London: Wiedenfeld & Nicolson, 2005)
Sheffield, G. D. and Gray, P. ed. *Changing War: The British Army, the Hundred Days Campaign and the Birth of the Royal Air Force, 1918* (London: Bloomsbury Academic, Birmingham War Studies, 2013)
Smith, T. and Spagnoly, T. *Salient Points Volume 3: Ypres Sector 1914-18* (Barnsley: Pen & Sword, 2001)

Steel, N. and Hart, P. *Passchendaele: The Sacrificial Ground* (London: Cassell Military Paperbacks, 2007; first published 2000)

Stevenson, D. *With Our Backs To The Wall: Victory and Defeat in 1918* (London: Penguin Books, 2012)

Stichelbaut, B. and Chielens, P. *The Great War Seen From the Air: In Flanders Fields 1914-1918* (Brussels: Mercatorfonds, 2013)

Terraine, J. *The Western Front 1914-1918* (Hutchinson, 1964) (Barnsley: Pen & Sword, 2003)

—— *To Win A War: 1918, The Year of Victory* (London: Cassell, 2008; first published by London: Sidgwick & Jackson, 1978)

Toland, J. *No Man's Land: The story of 1918* (London: Eyre Methuen, 1980)

Van Pul, P. *In Flanders' Flooded Fields: Before Ypres there was Yser* (Barnsley: Pen & Sword Military, 2006)

Wilkes, R. and Wilkes, E. *The British Army in Italy 1917-1918* (Barnsley: Leo Cooper, 1998)

b. Books – Arms and Military Resources, Organisation and Tactics

Bidwell, S. and Graham, D. *Firepower: British Army Weapons and Theories of War 1904-1945* (London: Allen & Unwin, 1982)

Bond, B. et al *'Look to your Front' Studies in the First World War by The British Commission for Military History* (Staplehurst: Spellmount, 1999)

Bull, S. *World War One German Army* (London: Brassey's, 2000)

Clarke, D. & Dennis, P. *World War I Battlefield Artillery Tactics* (Oxford: Osprey Publishing, 2014)

Cron, H. *Imperial German Army 1914-18: Organisation, Structure, Orders of Battle* (Solihull: Helion, 2002)

Freemantle, M. *Gas! Gas! Quick Boys! How Chemistry Changed the First World War* (Gloucestershire: The History Press, Spellmount, 2012)

Griffith, P. *Battle Tactics of the Western Front: The British Army's art of attack 1916-18* (London: Yale University Press, 1994)

—— ed. *British Fighting Methods in the Great War* (London: Frank Cass, 1996)

—— *Forward into Battle: Fighting Tactics from Waterloo to Vietnam* (Chichester: Antony Bird Publications Ltd., 1981)

Grotelueschen, M. E. *The AEF Way of War: The American Army and Combat in World War 1* (New York: Cambridge University Press, 2007)

Hogg, I. V. *Allied Artillery of World War One* (Marlborough, Wiltshire: The Crowood Press, 1998)

Holmes, R. *Tommy – The British Soldier on the Western Front 1914-1918* (London: Harper Collins, 2004)

Johnson, H. C. *Breakthrough! Tactics, Technology and the Search for Victory on the Western Front in World War I* (Navato, California: Presidio, 1994)

Jones, S. *World War I Gas Warfare Tactics and Equipment* (Oxford: Osprey Publishing, 2007)

Messenger, C. *Call to Arms: The British Army 1914-18* (London: Cassell, 2006)

Millett, A. R. and Murray, W. ed. *Military effectiveness: Volume 1: The First World War* (Boston: Allen & Unwin, 1988)

Mirouze, L. *World War I Infantry in Colour Photographs* (Marlborough, Wiltshire: The Crowood Press, 1999)

Mitchinson, K. W. *Pioneer Battalions in the Great War: Organized and Intelligent Labour* (Barnsley: Pen & Sword Military, 2014; first published by Barnsley: Leo Cooper, 1997)
Palazzo, A. *Seeking Victory on the Western Front: The British Army and Chemical Warfare in World War I* (Lincoln, USA: University of Nebraska Press, 2000)
Pawley, R. & Lierneux, P. *The Belgian Army in World War I* (Oxford: Osprey Publishing, 2009)
Pegler, M. *The Vickers-Maxim Machine Gun* (Oxford: Osprey Publishing, 2013)
Pegler, M. & Chappell, M. *British Tommy 1914-18* (Oxford: Osprey Publishing, 1996)
Prior, R. and Wilson, T. *Command on the Western Front: The Military Career of Sir Henry Rawlinson 1914-18* (Oxford: Blackwell, 1992)
Rawling, W. *Surviving Trench Warfare: Technology and the Canadian Corps 1914-1918* (Toronto, Canada: University of Toronto Press, 1992)
Richter, D. *Chemical Soldiers: British Gas Warfare in World War One* (Barnsley: Pen & Sword Military, 2014; first published by Kansas, USA: University Press of Kansas, 1992)
Samuels, M. *Command or Control? Command, Training and Tactics in the British and German Armies 1888-1918* (London: Frank Cass, 1995)
Sumner, I. & Embleton, G. *The French Army 1914-18* (Oxford: Osprey Publishing, 1995)
Travers, T. *How the War was Won: Command and Technology in the British Army on the Western Front 1917-1918* (London: Routledge, 1992)
Travers, T. *The Killing Ground: The British Army, the Western Front and the Emergence of Modern Warfare 1900-1918* (London: Allen & Unwin, 1987)
Young, M. *Army Service Corps 1902-1918* (Barnsley: Pen & Sword, 2000)

c. Books – British Second Army

Bilton, D. *Hull Pals: 10th, 11th, 12th & 13th (Service) Battalions of the East Yorkshire Regiment: A History of 92 Infantry Brigade, 31st Division* (Barnsley: Pen & Sword, 1999)
Bilton, D. *The Trench: The Full Story of the 1st Hull Pals* (Barnsley: Leo Cooper, 2002)
Bond, Lieutenant-Colonel R. C. DSO *History of the King's Own Yorkshire Light Infantry in the Great War 1914-1918* (London: Percy, Lund, Humphries & Co Ltd, 1929)
Cooksey, J. *Barnsley Pals: The 13th and 14th (Service) Battalions (Barnsley), The York & Lancaster Regiment* (Barnsley: Leo Cooper, 1996)
Crookenden, A. *The History of the Cheshire Regiment in the Great War* (Chester: W H Evans Sons and Co., 1938)
Davson, Lieutenant-Colonel H. M. *The History of the 35th Division in the Great War* (East Sussex: The Naval & Military Press Ltd, 2003; first published London: Sifton Praed, 1926)
Ewing, J. *The History of the 9th (Scottish) Division 1914-1919* (East Sussex: The Naval & Military Press, reprint; first published London: John Murray, 1921)
Falls, C. *A History of the 36th (Ulster) Division* (London: Constable, 1996; first published Belfast: McCraw, Stevenson, 1922)
Garwood, J. M. *Chorley Pals – Y Company, 11th (Service) Battalion, The East Lancashire Regiment: a short history of the company in the Great War* (Manchester: Neil Richardson, 1989)
Gillon, Captain S. *The Story of the 29th Division – A Record of Gallant Deeds* (East Sussex: The Naval & Military Press, reprint; first published London, Edinburgh, New York: Thomas Nelson & Sons Ltd, 1925)
Harington, Sir C. *Plumer of Messines* (John Murray, 1935)

McGreal, S. *Cheshire Bantams: 15th, 16th and 17th Battalions of the Cheshire Regiment* (Barnsley: Pen & Sword, 2006)
Nicholson, Major-General Sir L. & McMullen, Major H. *History of the East Lancashire Regiment in the Great War 1914-1918* (Liverpool: Littlebury Bros., 1936)
Parsons, W. D. *Pilgramage: AGuide to the Royal Newfoundland Regiment in World War One* (St John's, Newfoundland: Creative Publishers, 1994)
Stacey, J. E. *Memoirs of a Blue Puttee: The Newfoundland Regiment in World War One* (St John's, Newfoundland: DRC Publishers, 2002)
Powell, G. *Plumer: the Soldiers' General: a biography of Field-Marshal Viscount Plumer of Messines* (South Yorkshire: Pen Sword Military Classics, 2004; first published London: Leo Cooper, 1990)
Shakespear, Lieutenant-Colonel J. *The Thirty-Fourth Division, 1915-1919* (London, 1921)
Stanley, Brigadier-General F. C. *The History of the 89th Brigade, 1914-1918* (Gwent, South Wales: Ray Westlake – Military Books, c. 2002; first published Liverpool: Liverpool Daily Post, 1919)
Turner, W. *Accrington Pals – The 11th (Service) Battalion (Accrington) East Lancashire Regiment* (Barnsley: Pen & Sword, 1998)
Wauchope, Major-General A. J. *A History of the Black Watch [Royal Highlanders] in the Great War, 1914-1918; Volume Three: New Army – 8th, 9th, 10th, 11th, 12th, 13th and 14th Battalions* (East Sussex: The Naval & Military Press Ltd., 2002; first published London: The Medici Society Limited, 1926)
Whalley-Kelly, Captain H. *Ich Dien – the Prince of Wales's Volunteers (South Lancashire), 1914-1934* (Aldershot: Gale and Polden, 1935)
Wylly, Colonel H. C. *The Loyal North Lancs, Volume II, 1914-1919* (Royal United Service Institution, 1933)
Wyrall, E. *The East Yorkshire Regiment in the Great War* (London: Harrison & Sons Ltd, 1928)
—— *The West Yorkshire Regiment in the War 1914-1918: A History of the 14th, the Prince of Wales' Own (West Yorkshire Regiment) and its Special Reserve, Territorial and Service Battalions in the Great War of 1914-1918 – Volume II 1917-1918* (London: John Lane, The Bodley Head Ltd, c1926)

d. Books – Background and Historiography on the First World War

Ashworth, T. *Trench Warfare, 1914-18: The Live and Let Live System* (London: Palgrave MacMillan, 1980)
Barnett, C. *Britain and her Army* (London: Allen Lane, 1970)
Bond, B. ed. *The First World War and British Military History* (Oxford University Press, 1991)
—— *The Unquiet Western Front: Britain's role in literature and history* (Cambridge University Press, 2002)
Bond, B. and Cave, N. ed. *Haig: A Reappraisal 70 years on* (London: Leo Cooper, 1999)
Bourne, J. *Britain and the Great War* (London: Hodder Arnold, 1989)
Braybon, G. ed. *Evidence, History and the Great War: Historians and the Impact of 1914-18* (New York: Berghan Books, 2005)
Cecil, H. and Liddle, P. ed. *Facing Armageddon: The First World War Experienced* (London: Leo Cooper, 1996)
Cooksley, P. *The RFC/RNAS Handbook 1914-1918* (Stroud: Sutton Publishing, 2000)

Corrigan, G. *Mud, Blood and Poppycock: Britain and the First World War* (London: Cassell, 2003)
Cox, M. and Ellis, J. *The World War 1 Data book: The Essential Facts and Figures for all the Combatants* (London: Aurun Press, 2001)
Cruttwell, C. R. M. F. *A History of the Great War 1914-1918* (Oxford: Oxford Publishing Co., 1934, and reprints)
DeGroot, G. *Douglas Haig 1861-1928* (London: Unwin Hyman, 1988)
Falls, C. *The First World War* (London: Longman, 1960)
Ferguson, N. *The Pity of War* (London: Allen Lane, 1998)
Fussell, P. *The Great War and Modern Memory* (London: Oxford University Press, 1975)
Gilbert, M. *First World War* (London: Wiedenfeld & Nicolson, 1994)
Hayward, J. *Myths and legends of the First World War* (Stroud: Sutton Publishing, 2002)
Holmes, R. *The Western Front* (London: BBC Worldwide, 1999)
Holt, T. and V. *Major & Mrs Holt's Battlefield Guide to the Ypres Salient & Passchendaele* (Barnsley, South Yorkshire: Pen & Sword Military, paperback, 2008 edition; this guide is reprinted regularly)
Korte, B. ed. *The Penguin Book of First World War Stories* (London: Penguin Books, 2007)
Lewis-Stempel, J. *Where Poppies Blow: The British Soldier, Nature, The Great War* (London: Weidenfeld & Nicolson, 2016)
Liddell Hart, B. *The Real War 1914-1918* (London: Faber & Faber, 1930, and subsequent reprints)
Livesey, A. *Great Battles of World War I* (London: Marshall, 1989)
MacMillan, M. *The War That Ended Peace: How Europe Abandoned Peace for the First World War* (London: Profile Books Ltd., 2013)
Mead, G. *The Doughboys: America and the First World War* (London: Allen Lane, 2000)
Palmer, A. *The Salient: Ypres, 1914-18* (London: Constable, 2016; first published, London: Constable, 2007)
Philpott, W. *Attrition: Fighting the First World War* (London: Little, Brown, 2014)
Prior, R. and Wilson, T. *Passchendaele: The Untold Story* (Yale University Press, 1996)
Prior, R. and Wilson, T. *The Somme* (Yale University Press, 2005)
Purseigle, P. *Warfare and belligerence: Perspectives in First World War studies* (Leiden, Boston: Brill, 2005)
Reynolds, D. *The Long Shadow: The Great War and the Twentieth Century* (London: Simon & Schuster, 2013)
Roucoux, M. ed. *English Literature of the Great War Revisited* (University of Picardy, 1988)
Sheffield, G. *The Chief: Douglas Haig and the British Army* (London: Aurum Press Limited, 2011)
—— *Command and Morale: The British Army on the Western Front 1914-18* (Barnsley, South Yorkshire: Praetorian Press, Pen & Sword Books, 2014)
—— *Forgotten Victory – The First World War: Myths and Realities* (London: Headline Book Publishing, 2001)
Sheffield, G. and Todman, D. ed. *Command and Control on the Western Front: The British Army's Experience 1914-18* (London: Spellmount Ltd, 2004)
Strachan, H. *European Armies and the Conduct of War* (London: Allen and Unwin, 1983)
—— *The First World War: Volume 1: To Arms* (Oxford University Press, 2001)
Terraine, J. *Douglas Haig, The Educated Soldier* (London: Hutchinson, 1963)
—— *The First World War 1914-18* (London: Leo Cooper, softback reprint)

—— *White Heat: The NewWarfare 1914-18* (London: Sidgwick & Jackson, 1982)
Todman, D. *The Great War: Myth and Memory* (Hambledon and London, 2005)
Tuchman, B. *The Guns of August* (London: Penguin Books, 2014; first published MacMillan, 1962)
Winter, D. *Haig's Command: A Reassessment* (London: Viking, 1991)
Winter, J. *The Great War and the British People* (London: Macmillan, 1986)

e. Books – Selected Chapters from Edited Books on the First World War

Philpott, W. J. 'Britain, France and the Belgian Army', in Bond, B.et al, *'Look to your Front' Studies in the First World War by The British Commission for Military History* (Staplehurst: Spellmount, 1999), pp. 121-135
Sheffield, G. D. 'Blitzkrieg and Attrition: Land Operations in Europe 1914-1945' in C. MacInnes and G. D. Sheffield, ed., *Warfare in the Twentieth Century* (London: Unwin Hyman, 1988)
Simkins, P. 'Co-Stars or Supporting Cast?: British Divisions in the 'Hundred Days', 1918', in P. Griffith, ed., *British Fighting Methods in the Great War* (London: Frank Cass, 1996), pp. 50-69
—— 'Each One A Pocket Hercules: The Bantam Experiment and the Case of the 35th Division', in Sanders Marble, ed., *Scraping The Barrel: The Military Use of Substandard Manpower 1860-1960* (New York: Fordham University Press, 2012), pp. 79-104
—— 'Herbert Plumer', in I. F. W. Beckett, and S. J. Corvi, ed., *Haig's Generals* (Barnsley: Pen & Sword Military, 2006), pp. 141-163

5 JOURNALS & PERIODICALS

Howard, M. 'World War One: The Crisis in European History: The Role of the Military Historian', *The Journal of Military History* 57 (Oct 1993), pp. 127-138
Lynch, T. 'Unknown Soldiers – A 1918 Draft', *Stand To! The Journal of the Western Front Association*, No. 98, September 2013, pp. 3-8
Maginniss, Lieutenant-Colonel C. H. 'Heads of Steel: Logistic Support to the BEF's Mobile All Arms Battle: July-November 1918', *The Royal Logistics Corps Review 2008*, pp. 165-180
Ray, C. 'Britain and the Origins of the First World War', *History Review* (March 1998), pp. 45-49
Travers, T. 'The Evolution of British strategy and tactics on the Western Front in 1918: GHQ, manpower and technology', *The Journal of Military History* vol. 54 issue 2 (Apr 1990), pp. 173-200

6 BIBLIOGRAPHIES

Holding, N. H. *The Location of British Army Records: A National Directory of World War 1 Sources* (Solihull: Federation of Family History Societies, 1987)
White, A. S. *A Bibliography of Regimental Histories of the British Army* (London Stamp Exchange, 1988)
White, T. & S. *A Guide to Military Museums and Other Places of Interest* (Knighton, 1994)

7 ELECTRONIC SOURCES

a. First World War – History and General Information

University of Birmingham Centre for First World War Studies <www.firstworldwar.bham.ac.uk>
First World War – Unofficial website <www.firstworldwar.com>
Imperial War Museum <www.iwm.org.uk>
The Long, Long Trail <www.1914-1918.net>
National Archives <www.nationalarchives.gov.uk>
The Trench <www.worldwar1.com>

b. British Army

Army Museums Ogilby Trust <www.armymuseums.co.uk>
Western Front Association <www.westernfrontassociation.com>

c. Belgium and the Belgian Army

Belgian Fronts – Data on various aspects of WW1 and WW2 in Belgium <http://users.skynet.be/fonck/index.html>

Belgium: history, information, background plus military links and primary sources <http://www.zum.de/whkmla/region/lowcountries/bel191418.html>

Belgium ROOTS project – Army repositories and a range of links inclusive <http://Belgium.rootsweb.com/rep/bel/army>

Brave Little Belgium – Website of summary information on the Belgian Army 1914-18 <http://www.belgianarmy.freeservers.com/>

Cemeteries in Flanders <http://ww1cemetries.com/>

Discovering Family Histories – Belgian Military and links <http://Belgium.rootsweb.com//bel/rr_be_military.html>

Flanders: History – Brief background and information summaries <http://noosphere.cc/flandersHistory.html>

Flanders: In Flanders Fields Museum site <http://www.inflandersfields.be/default2.htm>

8 MISCELLANEOUS

Boff, J. 'Combined Arms During the Hundred Days Campaign, August-November 1918', *War in History*, 2010, 17(4) pp. 459-477, <http://wih.sagepub.com/content/17/4/459>

Index

INDEX OF PEOPLE

INDEX OF PLACES

INDEX OF MILITARY FORMATIONS & UNITS

GENERAL TERMS